WITHDRAWN
07 MAY 2022

The Pronunciation of English

109911
College of Ripon & York St. John

For Carol

The Pronunciation of English

A Course Book in Phonology

Charles W. Kreidler

BLACKWELL
Oxford UK & Cambridge USA

COLLEGE OF RIPON
AND YORK ST. JOHN
YORK CAMPUS
LIBRARY

Copyright © Charles W. Kreidler, 1989

First published 1989
Reprinted 1990, 1992, 1993 (twice), 1995 (twice), 1997

Blackwell Publishers Ltd
108 Cowley Road
Oxford OX4 1JF, UK

Blackwell Publishers Inc
Commerce Place, 350 Main Street,
Malden, Massachusetts 02148, USA

All rights reserved. Except for the quotation of short passages for the purposes of criticism and review, no part of this publication may be reproduced, stored in a retrieval system, or transmitted, in any form or by any means, electronic, mechanical, photocopying, recording or otherwise, without the prior permission of the publisher.

Except in the United States of America, this book is sold subject to the condition that it shall not, by way of trade or otherwise, be lent, re-sold, hired out, or otherwise circulated without the publisher's prior consent in any form of binding or cover other than that in which it is published and without a similar condition including this condition being imposed on the subsequent purchaser.

British Library Cataloguing in Publication Data
A CIP catalogue record for this book is available from the British Library

Library of Congress Cataloging in Publication Data
Kreidler, Charles, W., 1924–
The pronunciation of English: a course book in phonology /
Charles W. Kreidler
p. cm.
Bibliography: p.
Includes index.
ISBN 0–631–16219–4 (pbk)
1. English language – Pronunciation. 2. English language –
Pronunciation by foreign speakers. I. Title.
PE1137.K84 1989
421'.52—dc19

Typeset in 10 on 11.5pt Times
by Joshua Associates Limited, Oxford
Printed and bound in Great Britain
by Athenæum Press Ltd, Gateshead, Tyne & Wear

This book is printed on acid-free paper

Contents

PREFACE xv

1 LANGUAGE AND SPEECH 1

1.1 Language variation 1
1.2 Speech and language 5
1.3 Phonological analysis 10
1.4 Summary 13

2 SOUND . . . AND VOICE 15

2.1 Hearing 15
2.2 Energy, vibration, and medium 15
2.3 The measurement of vibrations 17
2A *Exercises* 17
2.4 Resonance 19
2.5 Air in motion 19
2.6 The human voice 20
2.7 The vocal cords 21
2.8 The vocal tract 23
2.9 Kinds of speech sounds 24
2B *Exercises* 28
2.10 Summary 29
2.11 Addendum: A note on redundancy 30
2C *Exercise* 31
2A *Feedback* 31
2B *Feedback* 31
2C *Feedback* 32

3 CONSONANTS 33

3A *Preliminary exercise: Identifying consonants by matching* 33

3.1 The feature [consonantal] 34
3.2 Lip consonants 37
3.3 Tongue-tip consonants 38
3B *Exercise* 38
3.4 Tongue-front consonants 39
3.5 Tongue-back consonants 39
3.6 Summary chart 39
3C *Exercises* 40
3.7 Articulators or points of articulation? 41
3.8 The feature [lateral] 42
3.9 Summary 43
3D *Exercise: Practice with symbols* 44
3A *Feedback* 45
3B *Feedback* 46
3C *Feedback* 46
3D *Feedback* 46

4 VOWELS AND GLIDES 47

4A *Preliminary exercise* 47
4.1 Analyses of vowels 48
4.2 Dialect differences 49
4.3 A general inventory and particular inventories 50
4.4 The phonetic descriptions 56
4.5 The incidence of vowels 61
4.6 Adding to the general inventory 62
4B *Exercises* 63
4.7 Binary features for vowels 65
4.8 The glides 68
4C *Exercise with phoneme classes* 68
4D *Exercise on vowel incidence* 69
4.9 Summary 69
4A *Feedback* 70
4B *Feedback* 71
4C *Feedback* 72
4D *Feedback* 73

5 SYLLABLES AND STRESS 74

5.1 Syllables 74
5.2 Syllable structure 77
5A *Exercise* 78
5A *Feedback and comment* 78
5B *Exercise* 79
5B *Feedback and comment* 79

5.3 Strong and weak syllables 80
5C *Exercise* 82
5.4 Syllable division 84
5.5 Suffixes and stress 86
5D *Exercise* 87
5.6 Compounds and some other words 87
5E *Exercise* 88
5.7 Identifying weak-syllable vowels 89
5F *Exercise and comment* 91
5G *Exercise and comment* 91
5H *Exercise and comment* 92
5.8 Syllabic consonants 93
5.9 Exercise with syllabic consonants 93
5.10 Summary 95
5C *Feedback* 96
5D *Feedback* 96
5E *Feedback* 96

6 CONSONANT AND VOWEL VARIATION 98

6.1 Variation in point of articulation 99
6A *Exercises* 100
6B *Exercises* 101
6C *Exercises* 101
6.2 An example of mutual assimilation 102
6.3 Variation in lip shape 103
6.4 Variation in nasality 103
6D *Exercise* 104
6.5 Variations in onset and release 104
6E *Exercise* 104
6F *Exercise* 105
6G *Exercise* 105
6H *Exercise* 105
6I *Exercise* 106
6.6 Variation in length 107
6J *Exercise* 107
6K *Exercise* 108
6.7 Multiple variation for /t/ 108
6.8 Some questions of perception 112
6.9 Summary 113
6A *Feedback* 114
6B *Feedback* 114
6C *Feedback* 114
6D *Feedback* 114
6E *Feedback* 115

6F *Feedback* 115
6G *Feedback* 115
6H *Feedback* 115
6I *Feedback* 116
6J *Feedback* 116
6K *Feedback* 116

7 PHONOTACTICS 117

7.1 Word-initial position 117
7A *Exercise* 118
7A *Feedback and discussion* 119
7.2 A note regarding /j/ 121
7.3 Contrast and variation 121
7.4 Word-final position 122
7B *Exercise* 122
7B *Feedback and discussion* 124
7C *Clusters of three consonants* 125
7.5 Word-medial position 125
7D *Exercise* 129
7E *Exercise* 129
7F *Exercise* 129
7.6 Borrowed words 130
7.7 Omission and insertion of a consonant 130
7.8 Limits on vowel occurrences 132
7.9 Free vowels and checked vowels 134
7G *Exercise* 134
7.10 Functional loads 136
7.11 Summary 136
7C *Feedback* 137
7D *Feedback* 137
7E *Feedback* 137
7F *Feedback* 138
7G *Feedback* 138

8 SOME CONSEQUENCES OF PHONOTACTICS 139

8.1 Consonant clusters and some grammatical suffixes 139
8A *Exercise* 139
8B *Exercise* 140
8C *Exercise* 141
8D *Exercise* 141
8E *Exercise* 141
8E *Feedback and discussion* 141
8F *Exercise* 143
8G *Exercise* 144

8.2 Morpheme variation 144
8H *Exercise* 146
8I *Exercise* 147
8J *Exercises* 148
8.3 Differences in morpheme division 149
8.4 Summary 153
8A *Feedback* 154
8B *Feedback* 154
8C *Feedback* 154
8D *Feedback* 154
8F *Feedback* 154
8G *Feedback* 155
8H *Feedback* 155
8I *Feedback* 155
8J *Feedback* 155

9 THE RHYTHM OF ENGLISH SPEECH 156

9.1 Prosody 156
9.2 Tone units 159
9A *Exercise* 159
9.3 Stress timing 160
9.4 Marked accent: Paradigmatic focus 162
9B *Exercise* 164
9.5 Marked accent: Syntagmatic focus 164
9C *Exercise* 165
9C *Feedback and discussion* 166
9.6 A note on 'too' and 'either' 167
9.7 De-accenting: Anaphoric words 168
9.8 Lexical anaphora 170
9.9 De-accenting to embed an additional message 172
9D *Exercise* 172
9E *Exercise* 173
9.10 Accent on operators 173
9.11 Summary 175
9A *Feedback* 177
9B *Feedback* 177
9D *Feedback* 178
9E *Feedback* 178

10 INTONATION 180

10.1 Intonation and perception 180
10.2 The falling tunes 183
10.3 The rising tunes 184

10.4 Comparisons 185
10.5 Compound tunes 189
10A *Exercise* 191
10.6 Summary 192
10B *Additional exercise* 193
10A *Feedback* 195

11 PREDICTING WORD STRESS 197

11.1 Is stress predictable? 197
11.2 Stress rules 198
11.3 Neutral suffixes 200
11.4 Tonic endings 200
11.5 The basic stress rule for verbs 200
11A *Exercise* 202
11.6 The basic stress rule for nouns 202
11B *Exercise* 203
11.7 Rules for adjectives 204
11C *Exercise* 204
11D *Exercise* 205
11.8 Extending the basic stress rules 206
11E *Discovery exercise* 206
11F *Exercise* 207
11.9 Some variations in stress 207
11G *Exercise* 207
11H *Exercise* 208
11.10 Mixed endings 208
11.11 Some 'special' endings 209
11I *Exercise* 210
11J *Exercise* 211
11K *Exercise* 212
11L *Exercise* 213
11.12 Summary 214
11A *Feedback* 215
11B *Feedback* 215
11C *Feedback* 215
11D *Feedback* 216
11E *Feedback* 216
11F *Feedback* 216
11G *Feedback* 216
11H *Feedback* 216
11I *Feedback* 217
11J *Feedback* 217
11K *Feedback* 217
11L *Feedback* 218

12 PREFIXES, COMPOUND WORDS, AND PHRASES 219

12.1 Compounds 219
12A *Exercise* 219
12B *Exercise* 220
12.2 Compounds and phrases 221
12C *Exercise* 222
12D *Exercise* 222
12.3 Compound verbs 224
12.4 Prefixes 227
12E *Exercises* 230
12F *Exercises* 232
12.5 Greek-type compounds 233
12G *Exercise* 235
12.6 A rhythm rule 236
12.7 Summary 238
12A *Feedback* 238
12B *Feedback* 239
12C *Feedback* 239
12D *Feedback* 239
12E *Feedback* 240
12F *Feedback* 240
12G *Feedback* 241

13 PHONOLOGICAL PROCESSES IN SPEECH 242

13.1 Different ways of speaking 242
13.2 Full forms and reduced forms 242
13A *Exercise* 247
13B *Exercises* 248
13C *Exercises* 252
13.3 More about phonological processes 253
13D *Exercise* 254
13E *Exercise* 258
13.4 Summary 258
13A *Feedback* 259
13B *Feedback* 259
13C *Feedback* 259
13D *Feedback* 260
13E *Feedback* 261

14 PHONOLOGICAL PROCESSES AND THE LEXICON 262

14.1 Words and morphemes that change 262
14.2 Underlying forms and lexical processes 264
14.3 Checked vowel reduction 265

14.4 Palatalization 266
14A *Exercises* 268
14.5 Alternation with zero 269
14B *Exercise* 271
14.6 Spirantization 271
14C *Exercises* 273
14.7 Velar softening 273
14D *Exercises* 273
14.8 The sequence of rules 274
14E *Exercises* 275
14.9 Change in voicing 276
14F *Exercises* 276
14.10 The vowel shift rule 278
14G *Exercise* 280
14.11 Free and checked vowels 281
14H *Exercise* 282
14.12 More about augments 284
14I *Exercise* 285
14.13 Applications 286
14.14 Summary 287
14A *Feedback* 288
14B *Feedback* 288
14C *Feedback* 289
14D *Feedback* 289
14E *Feedback* 290
14F *Feedback* 290
14G *Feedback* 292
14I *Feedback* 292

APPENDIX I Some Different Analyses of English Vowels 293

I.1 Why are there different analyses? 293
I.2 Daniel Jones 294
I.3 Two adaptations of Jones's system 296
I.4 Kenyon and Knott 298
I.5 Variations of the Kenyon–Knott system 300
I.6 The Trager–Smith 'overall analysis' 300

APPENDIX II A List of Word-Endings and their Effects on Stress 305

II.1 Neutral suffixes 305
II.2 Tonic endings 307
II.3 Strong endings 307
II.4 Weak endings 309
II.5 Post-tonic suffixes 311
II.6 Some special suffixes 312

NOTES 317

BIBLIOGRAPHY 322

INDEX 329

Preface

Scholarly interest in English is especially strong in two areas today: the varieties of the language which are spoken around the world, and the advances which linguists have made in providing a greater understanding of the nature of language, generally, and of this specific language. I hope that both areas of research are reflected in this book, which began as a series of exercises for a course in English phonology. It is intended as a text for students being introduced to linguistics and to the sound system of English.

One part of studying linguistics is the acquisition of a conscious knowledge of one's native language. All of us know how to use our language in everyday life, but our knowledge is largely intuitive. In speaking we produce utterances which are amazingly complex in the manipulations of vocal organs, the patterns of melody and emphasis, the selection and arrangement of meaningful items, and in listening we grasp meanings from the utterances of others. Yet speakers of the language do all this with very little ability to describe what they do.

I believe that learning linguistics requires a heavy involvement with data. The student needs to *do* analysis, going from observed facts to general statements and then testing these with more observations. While it is obviously inadequate only to know facts and not see how they are interrelated, it is equally wrong – and more common in my experience – to accept a generalization, along with an example or two, and take it as an article of faith.

I have not included discussion of certain recent theoretical developments which, though interesting in themselves, seem to me to do little to illuminate the facts of the language.

I am grateful to colleagues and students at Georgetown University who commented on earlier drafts of this work, especially William Cressey, Robert Hemmer, Arlene Puryear, Shaligram Shukla, and Thomas Walsh. I have a special debt of gratitude to Max Wheeler, who struggled through two versions and made numerous valuable suggestions. None of these is to blame for the final result. I am indebted to Ralph Fasold, Carolyn Nocella, and Tom Sison for other kinds of assistance and, for constant encouragement, to my wife, son, and daughter.

C. W. K.

1

Language and Speech

This book is an attempt to answer a question: How is English pronounced? The question is deceptively simple, of course, and it cannot have a simple answer. English today is the native language of nearly 400 million people and the second language of many others scattered all over the world. A language so widespread is bound to be different in different places. We are all aware that the Scots and the Australians, Londoners and New Yorkers, Irish, New Zealanders, South Africans, Jamaicans, Welsh, and Canadians do not sound the same when they speak. How can anyone describe the pronunciation of so many different people?

The diversity is real and must be treated in an account of how English is pronounced, but the commonality is greater. There is much more to be said about what is common to all speakers of English than there is regarding what is different. Furthermore, although to describe pronunciation obviously requires us to say what people do with their voices, we will be, in a sense, more concerned with the language they possess in common.

1.1 Language variation

In every language there is variety. A language varies from one place to another, from one era to another, from one occasion to another. The differences may be in the choice of words to express a meaning, as with *petrol* versus *gas(oline)* or *dual carriageway* versus *divided highway*. Differences exist in word formation: for the past tense of the verb *dive* does one say *dived* or *dove*? There are possible differences in the ways that words are put together to form phrases and sentences: would you say, for instance, *They gave it me* or *They gave me it* or *They gave it to me*? In this book we are of course concerned with differences in pronunciation. Some words are spoken differently by different speakers of English, for instance *either*, *garage*, and *tomato*. We are more concerned, however, with SYSTEMATIC differences; for example, some speakers of English pronounce an R is such words as *car* and *horn* and other speakers do not; for the former *spa* and *spar* sound different, for the latter group the two words are homophones. There are interesting differences in the vowel systems of different dialects: how different are *stock* and *stalk* (and *stork*), for instance.

We can discuss language variation under two headings: differences among people, the USERS of language, and differences in the USES of language, the ways in which people employ language on different occasions.

First, we are all aware of the differences of the kind mentioned in the first paragraph, above. People who live in different areas speak different REGIONAL, or GEOGRAPHIC, DIALECTS. The geographic differences in English reflect the different times in which speakers of English settled in an area, how diverse they were in their origins, how much contact they have had with other speakers of the language and what influence there has been from speakers of other languages.

Geographic dialects are not the only kind of difference among speakers of a language. In any locality different people grow up with different advantages and opportunities for education; the forms of language used by the more educated are generally considered more prestigious than the forms used by the less educated (but that doesn't mean that the less educated want to speak differently). Such differences are social dialects. We may also speak of age dialects – nobody expects teenagers to talk like their grandparents, or vice versa – and sex dialects – men and women use language differently. Differences of these kinds are mostly in vocabulary, however, and are not of great concern in a book on pronunciation. The geographic differences are important for this book. The next paragraphs briefly trace the expansion of the English language to account for the major varieties of the language in our times. Chapter 4 contains a more technical account of what these differences are.

When Angles, Saxons, and Jutes migrated from the continent of Europe to the island of Britain in the fifth century AD, they spoke a language which was to become English. Within two centuries they had subjugated, intermarried with, or pushed back the people who were there before them, until varieties of English were being spoken in most of what is now England and in the Lowlands of Scotland (though some have maintained that Scots is a language related to English rather than a dialect of it). The Celtic languages of the original inhabitants were confined to Cornwall, Wales, and the highlands of Scotland. In the centuries that followed regional varieties of English developed in a feudal society that had no ruling class nor dominant center.

With the Norman Conquest French became the language of the ruling class, the language of government, just as Latin was the language of religion. Varieties of English developed a grammar quite different from pre-Norman English and a double-barreled vocabulary with numerous synonyms of the type *deep/profound*, *ring/circle*, *last/endure*. When London grew in importance as the political capital and later as the commercial capital, English displaced French in official functions and the variety spoken in

London began to be a standard form, helped by William Caxton and others in the late fifteenth century who made the London dialect the norm for written English. With the establishment of a strong, centralized kingdom under the Tudors in the sixteenth century the importance of London continued to grow, but until the Industrial Revolution, at the beginning of the nineteenth century, most Englishmen spoke some regional variety of English.

The Industrial Revolution brought rural populations into the cities. During the nineteenth century a larger middle class came into existence, and the idea of belonging to the middle classes became associated with speaking a particular form of English. The particular way of speaking it came to be called Received Pronunciation (RP). In the twentieth century the British Broadcasting Corporation selected and trained announcers to speak with an RP 'accent', and RP has been the variety that most foreigners have chosen to learn. But to this day only a small portion of the English population speak RP. Regional and urban dialects remain.

The Tudors, and after them the Stuarts, began the process of annexing their Celtic-speaking neighbors to the English crown. In Wales, English was established by law as the official language of trade, law, and education in the middle of the sixteenth century, but it did not spread widely as the language of daily life until the nineteenth century.

When James VI of Scotland became James I of England he united the Crowns and sought to promote throughout Scotland the reading of the English Bible and the establishment of English schools to make this possible.

Though there were settlements of English-speakers in Ireland from the Norman era on, the Anglicization of Ireland is something that began in the sixteenth and seventeenth centuries, with annexation of Irish estates and settlement of English and Scottish loyalists there.

The English languages of Wales, Scotland, and Ireland are essentially the forms of English adopted centuries ago by people speaking Welsh, Scots Gaelic, and Irish Gaelic, with the inevitable changes that have occurred in the succeeding period of time, and with the constant influence of RP as a prestige model.

If Welsh, Scottish, and Irish English had their origins in the sixteenth and seventeenth centuries, the establishment of English in North America came very shortly after. Newfoundland, Britain's first overseas colony, was claimed for the English Crown in 1588; Jamestown was founded in Virginia in 1607 and Plymouth in Massachusetts in 1620. In the early eighteenth century England gained control of the maritime provinces of Canada and near the end of the century the claim to the whole country. Unlike Ireland, Wales, and Scotland where English was imposed largely on people of Celtic language background, in North America English was, first, the language of people who came from the British Isles and then the language learned by people who migrated later from other parts of Europe and other parts of the world. The same is largely true of South Africa, Australia, and New Zealand. The

English spoken in the Caribbean has a somewhat different history: it was originally imposed, as the masters' language, on people of West Africa speaking a multitude of different languages who were carried as slaves to the New World.

Settlement of the major English-speaking countries of the southern hemisphere dates from the late eighteenth and early nineteenth centuries. The first colony was planted in Australia in 1788, the first settlement of New Zealand in 1792, though in both countries large-scale immigration did not occur until the middle of the nineteenth century.

Britain took possession of the Cape Colony in South Africa in 1806, and migration from England and Scotland grew rapidly after 1820.

It is well to remember that most people who went to settle Britain's overseas colonies originated from the northern and western parts of England or from the lower class of London and did not speak the variety which was to become Standard British English. RP has been, however, a prestige norm in most parts of the Commonwealth – less perhaps in Canada than in the Southern Hemisphere. Contrariwise, those who take pride in being Australian or South African are likely to hold fast to the pronunciations which are endemic. In those two countries one finds a range of dialect differences from Broad Australian or Broad South African to RP or near-RP.

When we talk about differences in the USES of language, we have in mind that speakers vary their output according to where they are, with whom – or to whom – they are talking. Nobody expects the language used at a football game to sound like that in a lecture, and indeed the way the football game is described later probably does not sound much like a subsequent summary of the lecture. Speech is modulated for use in such different circumstances as telephone calls, the giving and getting of information, and dinner-table conversations. Part of learning a language is learning what usage is appropriate to particular situations. Differences that have to do with situations of language use are known as REGISTERS.

Registers reflect not only difference of function but also the kinds of relationship between the people who take part in a discourse. Whatever the situation in which we use language, we talk differently to strangers on the street than to people we know well and have known for a long time. Very roughly, there is a difference between formal and informal usage, but obviously this is not a simple kind of distinction; there are varying degrees of intimacy, and people differ in their ways of expressing them. Every society has established norms of politeness for addressing people according to their status and – though it may not seem that society has established them – there are ways of showing scorn, dislike, contempt, indifference. By observing norms of politeness or by ignoring these norms people express their attitudes toward one another and toward the situation in which they are involved.

Registers differ in syntax: a prepared lecture contains long, carefully crafted sentences, whereas a conversation in the home or between people at work together is likely to consist of numerous short, elliptical utterances. Registers also differ in vocabulary: the conversations of our routine activities are made up of the words we use all the time, while more formal usage is characterized by a search for appropriateness and variety in word choice. And registers differ in their phonetic nature. Casual and rapid conversation is marked by pronunciations which differ considerably from slow, careful delivery. In chapter 13 we discuss these differences, describing casual speech as the result of certain processes which apply to more formal pronunciations.

1.2 Speech and language

In discussing the pronunciation of English we can focus on one or both of two aspects. On the one hand, we may want to describe what people do when they are speaking English. This is the aspect of speech, an activity carried on by people who use English for communicating. On the other hand, we may address the question 'What are the characteristics of English words and sentences that are realized in speech?' This is the aspect of language, a code which exists, handed down from the past with slight changes made by each generation, something that is known by those who speak and understand English.

Speech is not the same as language. For one thing, the voice has characteristics which may carry extra messages: we can often identify someone we know by his or her voice (over the telephone, for instance), and we can sometimes determine something of the speaker's mood – anger, elation, nervousness, impatience, fatigue – from the way of speaking, as distinct from what is said. More important, speech is an activity which is carried on in numerous events; language is knowledge, a code which is known and shared by people who use their knowledge for transmitting and interpreting messages in these events. When someone is speaking, anyone who is close enough can hear – the sound waves set up in the air by the speaker reach the eardrums of the hearer. But only a person who knows the language can understand what is said.

Because we are interested in pronunciation from both these aspects, we will make use of information and concepts drawn from two disciplines, PHONETICS and PHONOLOGY. Phonetics deals with speech in its purely physical aspects – the way sounds are articulated by the speaker, the acoustic properties of sound waves, and the effects that these have on the ear of the hearer (and on the ear of the speaker, for that matter). Phonology is concerned with the way speech sounds are organized into a system, the sound system of a specific language. Phonology relates the physical facts of speech to other linguistic knowledge which speakers possess, knowledge of vocabulary and grammar.

Phonology is concerned with describing pronunciations but, more than that, with accounting for what is relevant in pronunciations, what makes it possible to communicate, what makes one utterance different from another.

Because we are interested in both speech and language, we need certain terms to use in describing both. We start with terms that have to do with speech:

We use the term DISCOURSE to refer to any act of speech which occurs in a given place and during a given period of time. The word *text* is used by some authors with this meaning, described as '... anything from a single proverb to a whole play, from a momentary cry for help to an all-day discussion of a committee.' Unless otherwise indicated, *discourse* here will mean 'spoken discourse'. A written discourse may be the record of something that has been spoken, or it may originate for the purpose of being performed aloud, like a speech or play, or it may exist without ever having been spoken or intended to be spoken, like most articles and books.

A discourse consists of at least one UTTERANCE, which is defined as a stretch of speech produced by a single speaker, with silence before and after on the part of that speaker. Two utterances in a discourse may be (partly) simultaneous, but only when two people speak at the same time. By definition one person cannot produce two utterances at the same time, though of course a speaker may make several false starts and may not complete what he or she intended to say.

An utterance consists of at least one TONE UNIT, a stretch of speech which has describable melody or intonation, one out of a fairly small inventory of intonation contours that exists in the language. Some authors have used *contour*, *tone group*, or *phonological phrase* with this meaning. The melody results from the physical fact that the speaker's vocal cords vibrate at different frequencies in the articulation of the tone unit, producing parts of it at different pitches. The action of the vocal cords is described further in chapter 2, and the intonations are outlined in chapter 10.

A tone unit consists of at least one SYLLABLE and usually a number of syllables. The syllable is an element which is recognized in all descriptions of speech, and yet one that is hard to define. A syllable consists of some vocalic element (to be defined later), with or without (usually with) non-vocalic elements before and after it. When a tone unit consists of several syllables, which is usually the case, they differ in *prominence*. Relative prominence is due to some combination of factors: greater force with which air is expelled from the lungs, higher pitch or changing pitch, the duration, or timing, of the syllable. These matters are discussed in greater detail in chapter 5.

A syllable consists of at least one SEGMENT and usually of more than one. In the production of speech the speaker's vocal organs are continuously moving from one position to another; speech is a dynamic process. Nevertheless, we perceive a succession of different sounds, a chain of speech made up of different segments linked to one another. In the word *meat*, to take a very short example, we think that we articulate three distinct sounds in sequence. This is not quite true. The vocal organs do not assume one position, then another, and then another; they are in motion as long as we are talking. Nevertheless, our perceptions have a reality of their own, and we adopt the convenient fiction that any syllable can be described as a sequence of segments.

The elements listed so far occur more or less sequentially: the utterances of a discourse occur one after another, tone units follow one another, syllables occur in succession, and within syllables the segments come one after another (though there is more overlap than we might think). The last elements of speech to be mentioned occur simultaneously. In the production, or articulation, of a segment the vocal organs have some particular configuration – the lips are rounded or stretched, the tongue is low in the mouth or not, it has a flat surface or not, air is escaping through the mouth or through the nose or not escaping at all, the vocal cords are vibrating or not, etc. Each such position or movement is an ARTICULATORY FEATURE. These features always occur in simultaneous bundles; no segment can consist of a single feature. The segment [m] which occurs at the beginning of the word *meat*, is produced with the vocal cords vibrating, the lips closed together, and air coming out of the nose. These are three articulatory features combined. Other segments may be voiced (made with vocal cords vibrating), labial (articulated with one or both lips), or nasal (produced with air flowing through the nasal cavity), but only [m] is all three – a voiced labial nasal.

We will also need to refer to units of language from time to time in this book. Some terms for units of language are familiar to the reader and we will not attempt to give definitions. In our use of language we express ourselves much of the time in SENTENCES. We recognize different kinds of sentences, such as STATEMENTS, QUESTIONS, COMMANDS. Sentences consist of PHRASES, and phrases consist of WORDS. Words belong to different classes; major classes are called NOUNS, VERBS, ADJECTIVES, ADVERBS; minor classes are DETERMINERS, PREPOSITIONS, CONJUNCTIONS, and others. But we need to introduce a few terms which are not necessarily part of the layman's usage.

Every word consists of at least one MORPHEME, a minimal unit that contributes in some way to the meaning of the whole word. If we compare the words *honest*, *dishonest*, *honestly*, and *honesty*, we will surely decide that they all share some meaning and that the first word, *honest*, has only this meaning and cannot be divided into smaller meaningful units. On the other hand, *dishonest* is obviously *dis-* + *honest*; *honestly* is *honest* + *-ly*; and *honesty* is the same *honest* + *-y*, or perhaps *honest* + *-ty*, analogous to *certainty* and *loyalty*. Each of these meaningful units is a morpheme: *honest*, *dis-*, *-ly*, *-ty*. The first of these is a BASE morpheme, the last three are

AFFIXES, which only exist in combination with a base. The first of these, *dis-*, is a PREFIX, and *-ly* and *-ty* are SUFFIXES.

Some morphemes are expressed in more than one way. Compare the series *seven*, *seventh*, *seventeen* with the series *five*, *fifth*, *fifteen*. The base *seven* does not change; the other base has two forms, *five* and *fif-*, which have the same meaning or function. *Five* and *fif-* are said to be ALLOMORPHS of the same morpheme. Some morphemes are expressed in a variety of ways, sometimes in quite abstract ways. For example, the meaning of 'past time' is contained in all of these verb forms: *ate*, *drank*, *fought*, *waited*; but only the last of these yields to easy analysis, allowing us to say that the morpheme 'Past' is expressed in the suffix *-ed*. The same morpheme is contained in the forms *ate*, *drank*, *fought*, but it is expressed in the more subtle replacement of the vowels which occur in *eat*, *drink*, *fight*, respectively.

More commonly, a morpheme is expressed in just one way, in some sequence of the PHONEMES of the language. The phoneme is the unit which makes the connection between sound and meaning. A phoneme is a unit of sound in a particular language which is capable of differentiating morphemes, the units of meaning of that language. The morpheme *meat* is a sequence of three phonemes, which we represent as /m/ for the first, /ii/ for the second, and /t/ for the third. The morpheme *beet* has a different initial phoneme, which we represent as /b/, and the morphemes *moot* and *boot* have a different medial phoneme, written /uu/. The morpheme *team* has the same phonemes as *meat*, but in a different order, and *tomb* has the same phonemes as *moot*, in a different arrangement. *Eat*, *tea*, *too*, *me*, *bee*, *beam*, *boom* are other morphemes which contain some selection of these five phonemes: /b/, /m/, /t/, /ii/, /uu/.

Different morphemes must have different meanings, but they may sound the same. English *meat* and *meet* are HOMONYMS (or HOMOPHONES) – they are expressed by the same sequence of the same phonemes. Similarly, *beet* and *beat*, *tee* and *tea*, *team* and *teem*, *be* and *bee*, *too* and *two* are homonyms.

One might be inclined to equate the term 'phoneme' with 'letter', but that equation can be misleading. A language has phonemes whether it is written in an alphabetic system or not – indeed, whether it has ever been written or not. Besides, a phoneme may be represented by different letters or sequences of letters, like the *ee* and *ea* of examples above; two letters may represent the same phoneme, as in *kit* and *cat*; or two different phonemes may be represented in spelling by the same letter or letters, like the *th* in *thy* and *thigh*.

One might also be inclined to equate the term 'phoneme' with 'sound' or 'speech sound' or 'segment'. That is not accurate, as the next paragraphs will show.

If you get ready to pronounce – but don't pronounce – *meet*, *moot*, *beet*, *boot*, you will find that all four words begin with lips closed. You should also find that with *meet* and *beet* the lips are stretched but with *moot* and *boot* they are slightly pursed or rounded. We think of *meet* and *moot* as beginning the same way, and likewise *beet* and *boot*. That is true, but not true. *Meet* and *moot* begin with the same phoneme, /m/, but they begin with different segments; the two segments have some articulatory features in common and they differ in another feature, the shape of the lips. Analogous statements can be made about *beet* and *boot*, of course; they begin with the same phoneme, /b/, but the phoneme is realized as different segments.

Let's try another experiment. Get ready to pronounce the words *geese* and *goose* but don't say anything. Instead, note the position and shape of your tongue and lips. You have the back of your tongue raised, touching the roof of the mouth toward the back – you may be able to recognize that the tongue's contact is in different places on the roof of the mouth. At the same time lips are stretched for *geese* and rounded for *goose* – at the very beginning. Next, get ready to say *glee* and *glue* and compare. Some features, in the sounds that you are ready to make, are the same and some are different. The tongue-back, or dorsum, is in contact with the roof of the mouth for all of these. At the same time there is lip-stretching for *geese* and *glee*, lip-rounding for *goose* and *glue*. In addition, note that the sides of the tongue are curled inward for *glee* and *glue*. Now get ready to say *greet* and *grew* and observe. The back of your tongue is again touching the roof of the mouth, and the lips are stretched for *greet*, rounded for *grew*, and the tip of the tongue is drawn back and bunched up.

The point we want to make is an important one: any speaker of English feels that the six words, *geese*, *goose*, *glee*, *glue*, *greet*, *grew*, all begin with the same sound. They don't; they begin with the same phoneme, which we represent this way, /g/. A phoneme is an abstract unit which is realized in speech as different segments in different positions. These different segments are the ALLOPHONES of the phoneme. All six allophones are alike in being dorsal stops – the breath stream is built up behind the closure made with the tongue-back, or dorsum, against the soft palate, ready to be released when pronunciation occurs. There is another common feature, not so easy to observe: the vocal cords are in a position to begin vibrating. In addition to these shared features, there are other features which are only partly shared, present in some of the six but not all: lip-rounding or stretching, lateral tongue curl, retracted tongue tip. The features which are present in all the allophones are DISTINCTIVE FEATURES; those which are present in one or several but not all the allophones are REDUNDANT FEATURES. It is fairly easy to see that the redundant features, in these cases, are 'borrowed' from other phonemes: lip-rounding is a feature of /uu/ in *goose*, *glue*, *grew* while lip-stretching is characteristic of the vowel /ii/ in the other words; lateral tongue curl, occurring with the /g/ of *glee* and *glue* is properly the feature of /l/; in *greet* and *grew* there is the tongue-retraction which is associated with /r/. But redundant features are not necessarily borrowed from neighboring phonemes. Notice carefully the difference between the beginning sound of *team* and the second sound of *steam*. Both words contain an instance of the phoneme /t/. The initial /t/ is aspirated; it is followed by a puff of air that comes from the throat. When /t/ follows /s/, it has no such aspiration. The aspiration is a redundant feature, but it has nothing to do with neighboring phonemes.

Phonemes, then, vary in pronunciation. They combine with other phonemes in sequence to express morphemes, and because they enter into such sequences they contrast with other phonemes, thus serving to differentiate morphemes. *Glue* is different from *clue* and *grew* from *crew*; *glue* contrasts with *blue*, and *blue* with *brew*; *boot* is distinct from *beet*, and *beet* from *meet*. MINIMAL PAIRS like these establish what every speaker of English knows: that /g/, /k/, /b/, /m/, /l/, /r/, /ii/ and /uu/ are separate phonemes: they are capable of signaling differences of meaning. To describe the sound system of English means to establish the phonemes of the language, to tell in what possible sequence they can occur, and what varying pronunciations each phoneme has in its various positions of occurrence.

1.3 Phonological analysis

A language is a number of things together. It is a collection of meaningful elements called morphemes; the technical name for this collection is the LEXICON. And a language is a collection of rules for putting morphemes together to form words and for putting words together to form sentences. The rules for forming words are the MORPHOLOGY of the language, and the rules for forming sentences make up the SYNTAX. Lexicon, morphology, and syntax are not abstractions; they are knowledge which speakers of the language possess, a knowledge which is largely unconscious for native speakers who acquired the language in the earliest years of life.

Phonology may also be thought of as a collection of phonemes and a collection of rules for putting these units together to express the meanings of morphemes, words, and sentences. Phonology is no more an abstraction than lexicon, morphology, and syntax; it is knowledge, largely unconscious, which speakers have and which enables them to communicate, to express meanings which other speakers of the language will understand.

The native speaker of the language is aware of phonemes; the trained phonetician recognizes the variation of these – that each phoneme is pronounced differently in different contexts – has allophones. Phonological analysis is the grouping of segments into phonemes. The linguist observes that in English an aspirated [t^h] occurs in certain positions, word-initially for one, and an unaspirated [t] occurs in other positions, as for example after /s/. The two are not in contrast; they are similar, sharing most of their articulatory features. The linguist decides that they are allophones of a single phoneme.

On the other hand, the linguist establishes that /k/ and /g/, /b/ and /m/, /ii/ and /uu/ are separate phonemes in English.

The development of phonological analysis – and the creation of such terms as *phoneme*, *allophone*, *minimal pair* – was the work of linguists who belong to the discipline of structural linguistics. Structural phonology – sometimes called autonomous phonology or classical phonology – followed procedures which regarded language as an object for empirical investigation, with scrupulous avoidance of mentalistic terms and careful separation of phonological investigation from considerations of a grammatical or lexical nature.

Since the late 1950s many linguists have become adherents to the theory of generative grammar, which regards language as an inseparable whole. A generative grammar of a language is, supposedly, a description of the competence of a speaker of that language, the knowledge which makes him or her capable of producing and interpreting sentences in the language. Phonology, in a generative framework, cannot be separated from syntax and morphology since they are integrated parts of the speaker–hearer's competence.

Generative phonology seeks to establish an underlying representation of a whole sentence and map it onto a pronunciation through a sequence of rules. The underlying representation consists of knowledge of which the speaker is aware, and the rules are the speaker's unconscious knowledge. For example, an English-speaker has an awareness of a word *team*, consisting of phonemes in sequence /tiim/ and *steam* consisting of /stiim/. The speaker unconsciously applies a rule which makes the /t/ of *team* aspirated but not the /t/ of *steam*.

Some rules are optional. Consider the following pieces of utterances:

I hope this won't disappoint you.
We don't want to leave without you.
But you must remember . . .

In all of these (and many more possible utterances) the word *you* follows a word which ends with *t*. A speaker may pronounce the sequence as *t* plus *y* or as *ch* – what we will represent hereafter as /č/. We can think of this as applying or not applying a rule which converts *t* + *y* into /č/. If a rule is optional for any speaker it naturally is different in its applications for different speakers.

Some rules are variable. There is a rule similar to the one above which changes *t* to *ch* when it is followed by *i* and another vowel; compare *suggest* and *suggestion*, *quest* and *question*. If the vowel following *i* is a stressed vowel, as in *Christianity*, *bestiality*, the rule may vary according to dialects. Some speakers have /t/ after/s/ in these words and others have a phoneme /č/.

One assumption of generative phonology is that all speakers of the language store essentially the same underlying representations for the morphemes that they know, and if they pronounce these morphemes differently the differences result from the application of different rules or the same rules in different orders. The implication of this assumption is troubling because in describing a language as widespread as English certain facts emerge which have to be described and yet which cannot be considered facts known, in any sense, by all speakers of the language. As we will see (chapter 4), different varieties of English have different vowel systems. Rules for placement of stress in English words are based, in part, on recognition of two kinds of vowels but these two kinds of vowels are not truly distinct in any physical way for many speakers of the language.

Part of the speaker's knowledge is specific and part of it is general – rule-governed – but the boundary between the two is not at all clear. Our average speaker, let's say, knows the specific words *cat*, *dog*, *horse*, and *ox*. Knowledge includes, certainly, knowing what reference each has. Knowing each word and what it refers to is specific knowledge. The speaker can generalize, no doubt, that these are all related to a word *animal*. Whether the speaker has ever learned the word *noun* or not, he is aware that the words are used in similar ways in sentences. The speaker knows the fact that these words have a plural (not all languages make a distinction between singular and plural) and knows what the plural forms are for these four nouns. Knowledge of the plural form *oxen* is specific knowledge; no other English noun forms the plural in just this way. Knowledge of the plural forms *cats*, *dogs*, *horses* is general knowledge; it is the application of a rule. In speech *cat* and other nouns form their plural by adding a phoneme /s/, *dogs* is one of the nouns which have a final /z/ phoneme, and *horse* belongs to the group which adds a whole syllable for the plural. We describe the complete rule in chapter 8. It is something which all speakers of English know but without knowing that they know it. When we learn a new noun we form the plural automatically. Studies have shown that small children are able to apply this rule. No doubt about it, the rule is part of the competence of a speaker of English.

Now consider these pairs of words: *wise*, *wisdom*; *derive*, *derivative*; *Palestine*, *Palestinian*. We can recognize a rule here: when a suffix like *-dom*, *-ative*, or *-ian* is added to a word with a 'long I' in it, the 'long I' is converted to a 'short I.' This is a different kind of rule. It applies to words which have been formed in the past. If new words are formed today with comparable elements, they would show the application of a similar rule only if formed by a certain part of the population. Strict adherents of the generative approach would say that this is also a rule of the language, something which forms part of the competence of all speakers. We would say, instead, that it is specific knowledge – knowledge possessed by those who use these vocabulary items, but it is not knowledge that will be applied in the formation of new words. The alternation seen in *wise* and *wisdom* is part of the English lexicon and needs to be described. The description is part of chapter 14. But the word *rule* cannot have the same meaning with regard to this alternation as in the formation of regular plural nouns.

1.4 Summary

In any language there is variety, which can be discussed under two headings, variations among **users** and variations in uses of the language. Variations among users include geographic and social dialects, of which the former are of greater interest in this text. Variations in use include differences of **function**, differences of formality and politeness, and differences of tempo, all of which are intertwined. Language varieties based on such matters of use are called **registers**.

Geographic varieties of English result from a long history of regional differences in England itself; the slow development of a standard which, in its spoken form, is called **Received Pronunciation**; the political domination of Celtic-speaking countries by England from the beginnings of the Modern era; and the establishment of colonies overseas from the late sixteenth to the late nineteenth centuries.

It is useful to recognize the distinction between speech, an activity, and language, the code which makes communication possible through numerous speech acts. Language is the knowledge which speakers have and which makes communication possible; it is also an inheritance from the past. A language consists of a **lexicon**, a **phonology**, and a **grammar**. Phonology is the description of the sound system of a language, the link between speech and meaning. **Phonetics** is the science which studies speech sounds as sounds.

Although speaking is ordinarily a continuous movement of the vocal organs, it is convenient to view speech as a chain composed of individual **segments** one after another. Each such segment is a composite of certain **articulatory features**. Some of these features serve to differentiate meanings in a language; such features are distinctive in that language. Features which are not distinctive are **redundant**. Segments which have the same distinctive features constitute a phoneme of the language. Phonemes combine in certain possible sequences to express **morphemes**, the units of meaning of the language. Phonemes contrast with one another to differentiate morphemes from one another.

Units of speech from smallest to largest are; **articulatory feature**, **segment**, **syllable**, **tone unit**, **utterance** and **discourse**.

A **generative phonology** is part of a **generative grammar**, a view and theory of language which holds that a description of a language is a description of the language competence of a speaker of that language. Generative grammar considers phonology to be one component of a language and the description of phonology inseparable from the **grammar** and **lexicon**. Anything that is said in the language has an abstract **underlying**

representation. Various **rules** apply in a particular order to the underlying representation to produce the actual utterance. The rules supposedly encapsulate unconscious knowledge of the speaker, but there is a problem in distinguishing what parts of a person's knowledge are specific and what parts are general, rule-governed.

2

Sound . . . and Voice

2.1 Hearing

'I hear something.' We speak of hearing as if it were something that we do, an action that we perform. Actually, hearing, like seeing, is not so much something that we do as it is something that happens to us, a stimulus that we receive and to which we react. Whenever we hear something – when a door slams, a book falls to the floor, a plane passes overhead, or somebody calls our name – the air around us is disturbed. Something causes particles of air to move. These particles push against other particles of air, which in turn displace other particles, and so on in a 'domino' effect. Finally the particles of air which are next to our eardrums are subjected to a different pressure. The difference in pressure affects some tiny bones behind the eardrums; these bones cause changes of pressure in a liquid stored in the inner ear; and the different pressures in the liquid produce different nerve sensations, which are telegraphed to the brain. We hear.

Receiving these impressions from the world outside our skin seems to be purely passive, but it is not entirely so. Ordinarily we not only hear, we recognize what we have heard. We can distinguish the shattering of glass, the tearing of paper, the boom of an explosion, the pattering of rain, and many, many more sounds. In the storehouse of our memory we compare each new auditory experience with those we have previously recorded, and usually we find a match. Thus hearing is not entirely passive. Nevertheless, to understand what sound is, how sounds differ from one another, we have to focus on the activity of particles of air, not on the activity of the brain.

2.2 Energy, vibration and medium

In order to produce sound, a physical system must include a source of energy and a vibrating body. When you slam a door, pluck a guitar string, or bounce a ball, you apply energy, or force, to a body which can move. The body does not merely move and stop; it moves back and forth, back and forth; it vibrates. The vibration is obvious in the guitar string and the bouncing ball; the vibration of the door when it closes may or may not be visible to us. There is another vibration which we never see. The movement of particles of matter (door, guitar, ball) is transmitted to the surrounding particles of air. Each air particle moves in response to the force that affects it, repeating the back-and-forth movement of the particle of matter that set it in motion. Each particle of air collides with another particle and sets it in the same vibratory motion. Each particle moves back and forth only a little, but altogether the surrounding particles move outward in the form of a wave. The original force is spread over a large distance.

We have mentioned three elements in the phenomenon of sound: an INITIATOR, or source of energy, which causes the door to slam, the book to fall, and so on; a MEDIUM, the air through which the chainlike displacement happens; and a RECEIVER, the ears and brain of the person who hears. Air is not the only possible medium for the transmission of sound. If you have had the experience of hearing voices while swimming under water, you know that water is a possible medium. You may also have had the experience of hearing through a wall of metal, plaster, or wood. And you may be aware that some 'primitive' peoples can hear animals moving in the distance by putting an ear to the ground. Metal, plaster, wood, earth, and water can be media for the transmission of sound, but generally all the sounds that we hear come to us through the sea of air in which we live.

Figure 2.1-a is a conventional way of representing the movement of a particle of air through space (the vertical dimension) over a period of time (the horizontal dimension). The particle, responding to whatever force has been applied to it, moves from point A to point X, then back to A (actually A_1 on the figure since a moment has passed); it then moves to point Y and returns to point A (here A_2 since another moment has elapsed), completing one CYCLE. Then another cycle begins; any sound wave is made up of a number of such cycles. The number of cycles in a unit of time (usually one second) is called a FREQUENCY of that wave, and the amount of time required for one cycle is the inverse, called the PERIOD of the wave. Thus if a particle makes 100 cycles per second, its frequency is 100 cycles per second (also designated 100 Hertz, abbreviated 100 Hz) and its period is 1/100 of a second.

When a regular vibration continues for some time, the cycles are approximately even and the periods are equal. Such a wave is PERIODIC. In contrast, an irregular vibration has unequal cycles and its wave is APERIODIC. Not only is it irregular but it is also of short duration. The sound associated with a periodic wave is musical, whereas the sound associated with an aperiodic wave is noise. To use a rough analogy, a periodic wave is like the repeated bouncing of a spherical rubber ball, and the aperiodic wave is similar to what happens when you try to bounce a ball which is lopsided and too heavy.

2.3 The measurement of vibrations

Just as there are two dimensions, space and time, so there are two important measurements in the description of a sound wave. The maximum distance that a vibrating particle moves is called the AMPLITUDE of the wave. The line XX′ of figure 2.1-a indicates the amplitude of the sound produced by the movement of the particle of air (and its traveling companions) depicted here. The greater the force which produces the movement of the particle, the greater the amplitude of its displacement, and the louder the sound which results. We should have no difficulty in relating this statement to the world of our experience. We all know the difference between the loud slam caused by giving a forceful shove to a door and the mild click which results when the same door is given a gentle push.

The other measurement is frequency, which has already been mentioned. Different materials vibrate at different speeds; a particle of one kind of matter moves away and back to its starting point a certain number of times per second while a particle of another kind of matter moves a greater or lesser number of times in response to the same force. The greater the frequency of vibration, the higher the pitch of the resulting sound. Again, we know this from our common experience. Compare what happens when you slam a light-weight door in a plywood partition and what happens when you give an equal push to a heavy metal door in a concrete wall. In the first instance the vibration is rapid enough to be obvious; in the second case, so slow that it is imperceptible. Similarly, a guitar string under heavy tension vibrates faster and produces a higher-pitched hum than a string which is under less tension.

2A EXERCISES

(a) Figures 2.1-b and 2.1-c show sound waves with equal frequency but different amplitudes. Which is associated with the greater loudness?
(b) Figures 2.1-d and 2.1-e are waves of equal amplitude but different frequencies. Which is associated with the higher pitch?

Our discussion so far has been unrealistically simple. Any sound results not from a simple wave, such as figures 2.1-a to 2.1-e illustrate, but from a complex group of such waves. Take the example of the guitar string again. When the string is plucked, a certain amount of force is applied to one portion of the string, which is under a certain amount of tension. Other parts of the string are under different degrees of tension and receive smaller amounts of the force which moves the string. Consequently different parts of the string vibrate with different frequencies and different amplitudes, and so do the different bits of air which lie along the string. If you strike a chord on

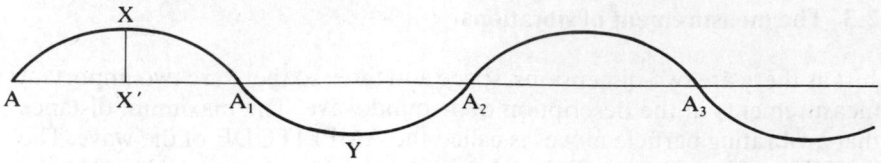

Figure 2.1-a

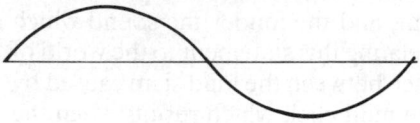

Figure 2.1-b

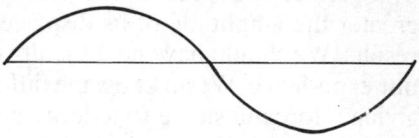

Figure 2.1-d

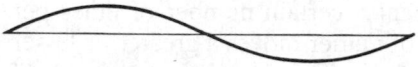

Figure 2.1-c

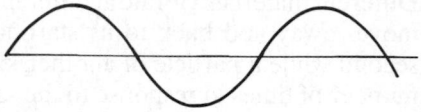

Figure 2.1-e

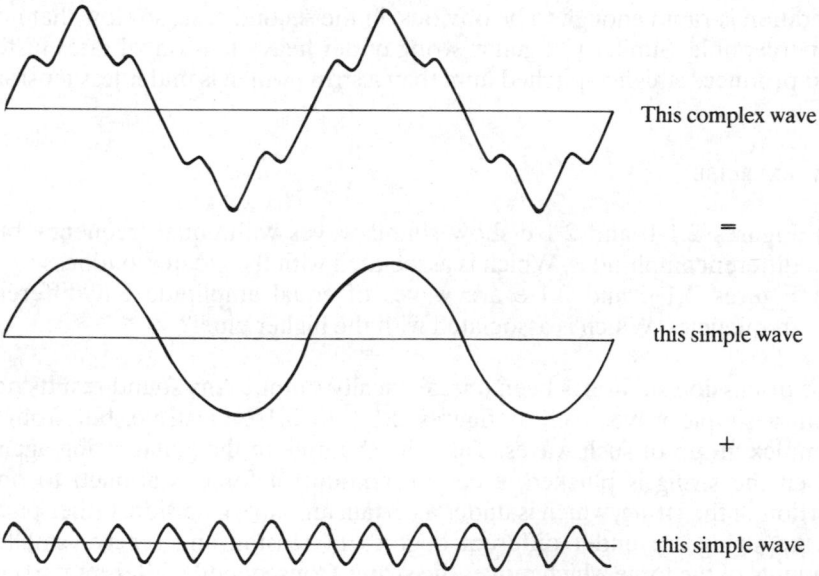

Figure 2.1-f

the guitar – that is, apply force to all the strings one immediately after the other – you produce a complex pattern of amplitudes and frequencies. Differences in complex patterns account for differences of QUALITY in the sounds we hear. A complex wave can be broken down into a number of simple waves. This is illustrated in figure 2.1-f.

2.4 Resonance

An important part of the quality of a sound is due to a kind of secondary vibration called RESONANCE. The classic demonstration of resonance is to strike a tuning fork and listen to its hum-m-m-m, then bring one end of the fork down onto a wooden table and change that metallic hum-m-m-m to a dull buzz-z-z-z. Particles of wood are set into vibration by the tuning fork. They resonate (re-sound) in response to the vibratory force of the particles of metal in the tuning fork, but they vibrate at their own frequencies.

When the strings of a guitar or violin are set in vibration, the box of the instrument picks up the vibration – it resonates. More importantly, the air inside the box also resonates. Different strings on the violin or guitar vibrate at different frequencies. The air in the box vibrates at some of these frequencies but not others, so that it strengthens some of the original frequencies and weakens others. The box of a violin, guitar, or other stringed instrument is a RESONANCE CHAMBER, and so is the area between the skins of a drum, the inside of an accordion or concertina, each pipe of an organ or calliope, and the tube of any wind instrument. If a resonance chamber strengthens certain frequencies, while weakening others, we say that it is resonant to those frequencies. The size and shape of a resonance chamber determine to which frequencies it is resonant.

2.5 Air in motion

Our discussion so far has been mostly concerned with sound created by percussion, force applied to some kind of matter, causing it to move and to displace particles of air. But air can itself be in motion and thus may be displaced by matter in its path, which also creates sound. We are all familiar with the sound of the wind whistling through the trees, or down an empty street between tall buildings, or through the slightly open window of a car speeding along the highway. We are also familiar with wind instruments like the flute, clarinet, saxophone, or organ. Each of these uses air which is blown or pumped into a resonance chamber – or, in the case of the organ, a set of resonance chambers. Some source of energy sends air into the tube(s), a reed furnishes the basic vibration, and differently shaped resonance chambers are created and brought into play by stopping up different holes, as in a flute, piccolo, or harmonica, or by moving a slide in and out, as in a trombone.

When a sound is made by percussion, the length of the sound depends on the force used and the physical nature of the vibrating body. In other words, the DURATION of the sound is not independent of loudness (amplitude) and pitch (frequency). In contrast, when the flow of air produces a sound, that flow can usually be controlled so that duration varies independently. One can, for example, play notes on a flute which are long, loud, and low, or short, soft, and high, or short, loud, and high, and so on.

2.6 The human voice

Human speech is very much like the playing of a wind instrument. Different speech sounds, in any language, are made by moving a column of air through part of the upper body and creating various kinds of vibration and noise as the air moves. It is possible to use air that is drawn into the body from outside (try to say 'Yes' while inhaling). A more familiar way of using ingressive air for sound-production is to produce a click, such as the tongue-tip noise which we represent as *Tsk tsk*, or the clucking sound which is sometimes used in getting a horse to move. To produce such clicks we create a vacuum in the mouth, then open suddenly so that air rushes in. Another way of producing an air stream is to gather a quantity of air in the throat and then eject it all at once. In almost all of our speaking, however, we use a column of air which moves up from the lungs and out the mouth or the nose, or both together, and we modify the air in its passage. Everything that we say about speech sounds from here on will assume the use of egressive lung air.

All of the vocal organs, shown in figure 2.2, have other functions – breathing, sucking, chewing, swallowing. The LUNGS expand and contract to bring in or let out air. The air expelled from the lungs travels up the TRACHEA, or windpipe. At the top of the trachea is a structure of cartilage known as the LARYNX, or voicebox. The primary vibration needed for speech is produced in the larynx by the VOCAL CORDS, which are described in the next section. Above the larynx are three interconnected areas, the PHARYNX, the NASAL CAVITY, and the MOUTH (or ORAL CAVITY) which serve as resonance chambers. The three together are called the VOCAL TRACT.

The functions of these speech organs can be summarized this way: The lungs supply the basic force that is needed (INITIATION). The vocal cords provide the basic vibration (PHONATION). The three resonance chambers are maneuvered in various ways for production of speech sounds (ARTICULATION). In general, variations in the force with which air is expelled from the lungs results in differences of intensity or loudness in speech sounds. Variations in the frequency of vibration of the vocal cords are

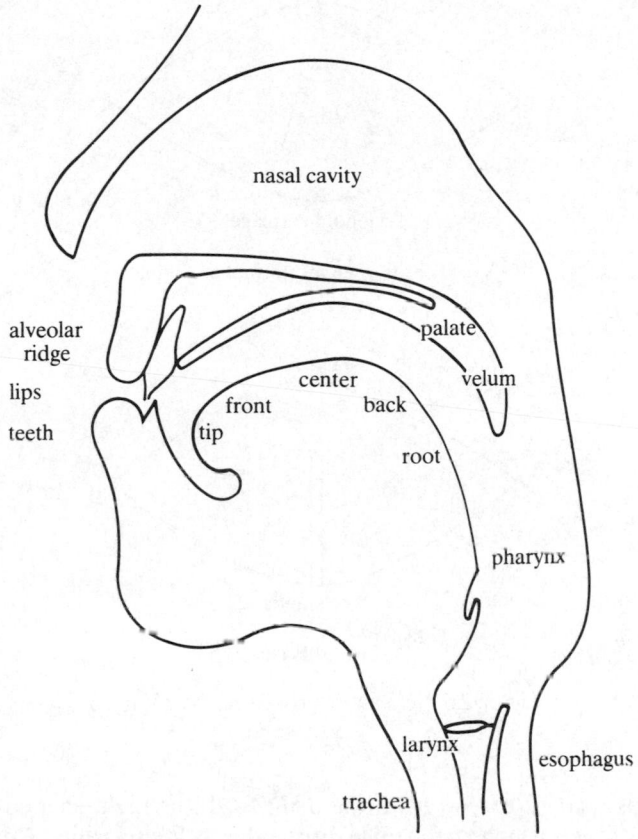

Figure 2.2

responsible for variations of pitch, or tone. Variations in the shape of the vocal tract are related to different speech sounds. In theory, then, loudness, pitch, and articulation are separate from one another. In reality, these things go together. In an English utterance the parts which are more prominent than others are generally louder, higher in pitch, and have certain special articulatory characteristics. Most notably, the prominent parts are longer in duration.

2.7 The vocal cords

The structure of the larynx is shown in a simplified way in figure 2.3. Within the larynx are two elastic bands of tissue, the vocal cords (or vocal bands, or

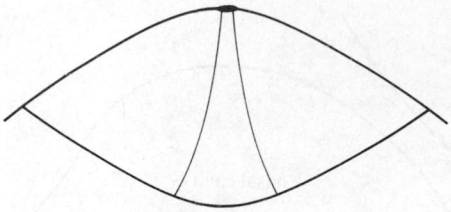

Arytenoid cartilages

Vocal cords open for normal breathing

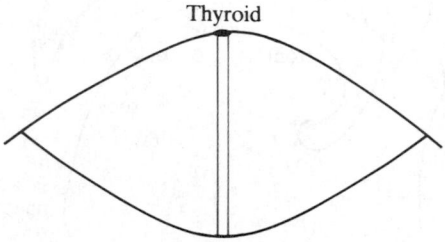

Vocal cords closed

Figure 2.3. Schematic cross-section of larynx

vocal folds). These extend from the THYROID ('shield-shaped') CARTILAGE in front – which, in the male, protrudes as the so-called Adam's apple – to the ARYTENOID ('ladle-shaped') CARTILAGES in the back. The vocal cords are joined together at the thyroid cartilage but are attached separately to the two arytenoid cartilages, which are capable of rotating and thus of moving the vocal cords apart or together. The opening between the cords is called the GLOTTIS. For ordinary breathing the glottis is wide open. For various purposes we can close the glottis, that is, bring the vocal cords together. We do this automatically when we swallow, so that food goes down the esophagus to the stomach and not into the trachea. The glottis also closes in order to lock air into the lungs so that our bodies can exert greater force, as in lifting a heavy object.

When they are neither fully open nor completely closed, the vocal cords are somewhat tense, and then the pressure of the outgoing air causes them to vibrate. The vibration is not audible; speech is produced above the larynx. As we produce a stream of speech, the vocal cords are sometimes vibrating, sometimes not vibrating. Speech sounds produced while the vocal cords are vibrating are VOICED; those made without vibrations are unvoiced, or VOICELESS. If the cords are vibrating, they can be stretched to different degrees of tension, so that they vibrate at different frequencies, producing different pitches in the sounds articulated above the vocal cords. Speech has melody – different melodies or intonation patterns – as a result of different frequencies of vibration of the vocal cords.

How can you tell whether a speech sound is voiced or voiceless? There are three good tests. Take the sound [z] as at the end of the word *buzz* and the sound [s] as at the end of the word *hiss*. Make a long [z-z-z] and a long [s-s-s] as you apply the tests.

(1) Put your thumb and fingers on your throat, on each side of the Adam's apple. You should feel vibration as you say one of these sounds, but not the other. (2) Cover your ears with your hands while pronouncing the two sounds. You should hear greater noise while making the sound which uses vibration in the larynx. (3) Try to sing up and down the scale while making each of these sounds. Singing means changing pitch, which means changing the frequency of vocal cord vibration. If the cords are vibrating, you can sing; if not, you can't.

By this time you should have decided – if you didn't already know – that [z] is voiced and [s] is voiceless. Try the same three tests with the [f] sound of *fife* and the [v] sound of *valve*. This test works well with fricative sounds like [s z f v] and with some other kinds of speech sounds, but it does not work well with stops such as at the beginning and end of *pop* and *bob*.

2.8 The vocal tract

Air which leaves the larynx goes through the pharynx and then out through the nasal cavity or the oral cavity or both at the same time. As noted before, pharynx, nasal cavity, and oral cavity constitute the vocal tract. Some speech sounds result from obstructing the flow of air somewhere in the vocal tract. The obstruction of the air stream may be partial, as in articulating the sounds [f v s z], or it may be complete, as in making the first and last sounds of *pup*, *bob*, *toot*, *dead*. Speech sounds which result from complete or partial obstruction are called OBSTRUENTS; they are essentially noise, the result of aperiodic vibrations. Other, more musical speech sounds are called SONORANTS, or resonants; examples are the vowel sounds of the four words above and the consonant sounds of *mill* and *run*. In the articulation of a sonorant the basic glottal vibration produced in the larynx is modified in the vocal tract. By changing the shape of parts of the vocal tract we create different resonance chambers so that different parts of the basic glottal vibration are strengthened while other parts are weakened.

The shape of the pharynx can be modified only slightly, either by raising the larynx or by retracting the root of the tongue – either of which makes the pharynx smaller. Changes in the shape of the pharynx have only minor importance in the production of English speech sounds.

The nasal cavity cannot be varied at all. It serves as a resonance chamber only if air is allowed to flow through it; speech sounds made with air not going through the nasal cavity have no nasal resonance. At the junction of the pharynx and the mouth there is a sort of trapdoor, the VELIC, the very end of the VELUM (figure 2.2). The velic can be lowered to permit the entry of air into the nasal cavity or raised to prevent it. Pronounce the word *mum* and prolong the final [m] sound. You are making a sound with egressive air, since it can be prolonged, and yet your lips are closed. Where is air escaping? Holding a finger in front of the nostrils will give the answer. And then, is [m] voiced or voiceless?

Of the three resonance chambers the mouth is the one which can be varied most. The jaw and tongue can be lowered and raised. The tongue may touch the roof of the mouth, stopping the flow of air (complete obstruction), or it may be positioned close to the roof of the mouth so that air moves through a narrow opening with friction or turbulence (partial obstruction). In a similar way the lower lip may cause complete or partial obstruction of the air stream at the upper lip or upper teeth. The tongue, but not the lower lip, moves back and forth to cause obstruction, full or partial, in different parts of the mouth. Without any obstruction the tongue, at different heights, can produce resonance chambers of different size and shape. Moreover, the tongue can be curled in at the sides, or back at the tip; it can acquire a groove along the center line or instead maintain a flat surface. The lips can be stretched or rounded. All of these ways of shaping the oral cavity are used in articulating speech sounds. In fact, all the sounds we shall study require some action in the mouth, with or without concomitant use of larynx, pharynx, and nasal cavity.

2.9 Kinds of speech sounds

As we talk, we constantly change the shape of the vocal tract, producing a stream of speech. We are likely to think that this stream of speech consists of one sound after another. In the word *mitt*, to use a very short example, we think that we articulate three distinct sounds in sequence, which can be represented as [m], then [i], and then [t]. This is true enough in terms of what the hearer perceives; it is not so accurate in terms of what the speaker does. The speaker's vocal organs do not assume one position, then another, and then another; they are in motion as long as an utterance lasts. Nevertheless, to describe speech we follow the perceptions of the hearer – we adopt the convenient fiction that any stretch of speech is like a chain with individual sounds, or SEGMENTS, linked together. Each segment is different from any other segment because it is articulated with the vocal tract in one particular configuration: the lips are rounded or not, the tongue is low in the mouth or not, the vocal cords are vibrating or not, and so on. We call these different elements ARTICULATORY FEATURES. Each segment is a unique cluster of articulatory features. The segment [m] has certain features, [i] has a different group of features, and [t] has a different combination of features. For instance, [m] is articulated with the vocal cords vibrating, the lips together, and air coming out of the nose. It is VOICED, LABIAL, and NASAL. There are other speech sounds which are voiced, like [v] and [z], others which are labial, like [b] and [p], and others, like [n] which are nasal, but only [m] is all three of these together. We may say that [m] is the intersection of three sets of articulatory features.

The most fundamental way in which segments differ from one another is in the way the air stream is controlled. Control of the air stream is apparently the first thing that small children learn when they acquire their native language. Up to about the age of eight months an infant BABBLES – produces streams of speech sounds which are not really speech if 'speech' means communication, use of a language code; but they are speech sounds in a physical sense, random products of the human vocal apparatus as the child experiments with the noises it can make while breathing in and out. Babbling prepares the child for the next stage of its linguistic growth, imitating the speech of adults and acquiring a vocabulary of single words.

At this stage of one-word utterances (one word, in the sense that the utterance cannot be broken into smaller parts which are recombined in different ways: something like *where-s-it* may be the child's way of asking the location of any thing or person, any number of things or persons) the child's imitations do not usually sound very close to what older speakers say, but in two respects the child is generally quite accurate. The child recognizes syllables and it has some appreciation of prosody – the melodies of speech. If parents present the youngster with a one-syllable word ('doll', 'milk', 'bath', 'ball', to use English examples), the child's word is also a single syllable; if the adult model is two syllables ('water', 'doggy', 'baby', 'bottle'), the child's rendition is also two syllables long. Apparently the child is equally sensitive to differences of loudness and pitch. It is likely to repeat the final part of Mother's utterances, everything from the last accented syllable to the end. If Mother says 'Where shall we put this?', the child may say, in its own way, 'put this' with a rising pitch. Hearing something like 'Here's a nicer one', the child may produce three syllables with falling pitch which somewhat echo 'nicer one'. So control of the air stream in making syllables and control of vocal cord vibration to produce some intonations seem to be the child's first speech acquisitions.

Each syllable which the child utters is likely to consist of two parts, closure and opening. The air stream is obstructed and then it flows freely; there is a consonant and then a vowel. Later, depending on what the child is imitating, some syllables will consist of closure, opening, and closure; consonant, vowel, consonant. The degree of closure and the amount of opening vary freely at first, and so does the place where closure is made, but eventually the child learns to control these manipulations and begins to sound like other members of the language community. Controlling the manipulations means, first, learning to make different kinds of closure and opening and, then, closure and opening in different parts of the vocal tract.

Different kinds of speech sounds, different manners of articulating, are different ways of manipulating the air stream. We recognize six kinds of speech sounds, VOWELS, GLIDES, NASALS, LIQUIDS, FRICATIVES, and STOPS. The two kinds which are most unlike are vowels and stops (the latter also called *plosives*). Stops are speech sounds made by completely obstructing the flow of air; vowels are produced by allowing the air stream to flow freely. Stops are complete closure; vowels are complete opening. *Bee*, *pa*, *too*, *caw* are examples of stop + vowel; *pet*, *cap*, *book*, *dog* are examples of stop + vowel + stop.

Stops and vowels differ from each other in four ways; there are four characteristics, or FEATURES, in which they differ:

1 Vowels are resonant, the result of periodic waves; when a vowel is articulated, particles of air vibrate in regular, repetitive patterns. Stops are noise; if air particles are vibrating at all during the articulation of a stop, there is no regular pattern. To express this difference we say that vowels are [+ **sonorant**] and stops are [− **sonorant**].
2 A vowel is the center or PEAK of its syllable, more prominent than what precedes or follows in the same syllable. When two or more adjoining syllables differ in loudness or pitch, the difference is in their respective vowels. In a two-syllable word like *baby* the first syllable is more prominent than the second, and that difference is due to the comparative prominence of their vowels. If the voice rises in saying 'Baby?' or instead falls and produces 'Baby!' – that is, whether the vocal cords increase or decrease their frequency of vibration – the change occurs in the vowel. Relative prominence and change of pitch cannot be associated with stops. Thus we say that vowels are [+ **syllabic**] and stops are [− **syllabic**].
3 When a vowel is articulated, air comes continuously out of the mouth. The nature of a stop is that air is stopped – prevented from escaping. We say that vowels are [+ **continuant**] and stops are [− **continuant**].
4 When a stop is articulated, either the lower lip or some part of the tongue is in contact with some other part of the mouth – the upper lip or some part of the roof of the mouth. When a vowel is articulated, there is no such contact. This distinction is captured with a feature [consonantal]. When there is some interruption of the breath stream, as there is for stops, the segment is [+ **consonantal**]. Vowels are [− **consonantal**].

The other four classes of speech sounds, fricatives, nasals, liquids, and glides, are partly like stops and vowels but of course are also different from them and from one another. The four features, [sonorant], [syllabic], [continuant], and [consonantal], describe their similarities and differences.

Fricatives are segments like the [f v s z] of *feel*, *veal*, *seal*, *zeal*, respectively. They are articulated by squeezing the outgoing air stream between an articulator (the lower lip or some part of the tongue) and a point of articulation (the upper lip or some part of the roof of the mouth) so that friction – rubbing – or turbulence results. Fricatives are like stops in three features but different in one. Like stops, they are the result of aperiodic vibration, therefore [– sonorant]; they require some interruption of the air stream, so they are [+ consonantal]; they are not typically the peaks of syllables, and so they are designated [– syllabic]. (There are marginal exceptions to the last statement: a hiss [s-s-s] and the interjection that we write *pst!* have a fricative as the central or only part of a syllable, but there are no English words with such syllables .) Finally, unlike stops, fricatives are [+ continuant] since air is flowing continuously out of the mouth during their articulation. Say *cup* and see if you can prolong the final sound; then say *cuff* and hold the last sound as long as you can.

Nasals are segments like the [m] of *mitt* and the [n] of *knit*, sounds made by stopping the flow of air somewhere in the mouth but letting it exit through the nose. Nasals are musical – [+ sonorant] – as every singer and teacher of singing knows. Since the air stream is interrupted in the mouth, they are [+ consonantal]. Since air does not escape through the mouth, they are [– continuant]. (This is a matter of definition; [+ continuant] is defined to mean 'with air flowing out the mouth'; actually a nasal can be prolonged because air is flowing continuously through another exit. Say *come* and make the last sound continue as long as you have breath.) Last, we classify nasals as both plus and minus syllabic – [± syllabic]. They are usually not the peak of a syllable, but they can be, as in the word *kitten*.

Liquids include the [l] of *lead* and the [r] of *read*. In their articulation the tongue is raised, partly impeding the flow of air, but the tongue is shaped in such a way that air flows around it, creating particular patterns of vibration. Because of the impedance liquids are classed as [+ consonantal]; because of the periodic vibration they are [+ sonorant]; because air flows freely out of the mouth, they are [+ continuant]. Finally, like nasals they are [± syllabic] – usually not the peak of a syllable but sometimes the peak, as in *metal* and *matter*.

Glides include the [j] of *yet* and the [w] of *wet*, for example. Glides are like vowels except in one feature. Slow down the pronunciation of *yet* and *wet* until each word becomes two syllables, the first starting with a vowel like that of *tea*, the second word beginning with a vowel like that of *too*. A glide is like a vowel except that it does not have the prominence in a syllable, does not act as peak of a syllable. Glides, then, are [– syllabic] but in other respects are like vowels: [+ sonorant], [+ continuant], [– consonantal].

Four features have been used to define six classes of speech sounds. The following chart summarizes them, with abbreviations of the feature names that will be used hereafter:

	SYL	CONS	CONT	SON
vowels	+	−	+	+
glides	−	−	+	+
liquids	±	+	+	+
nasals	±	+	−	+
fricatives	−	+	+	−
stops	−	+	−	−

Naturally each class is defined by a different cluster of plusses and minuses.

We have introduced the four features with emphasis on the six manners of articulation that they define. Let's recapitulate, with emphasis on the features themselves.

A speech sound is [+ syllabic] if it is the most prominent segment of a syllable, the principal carrier of stress and pitch. Vowels are [+ syl] always, nasals and liquids may be [+ syl] but are more often [− syl], and other segments are [− syl].

A speech sound is [+ consonantal] if its articulation requires interruption of the breath stream, accomplished with the lower lip or some part of the tongue. Liquids, nasals, fricatives, and stops are [+ cons], vowels and glides are [− cons].

A speech sound is [+ continuant] if it is articulated with air flowing continuously out of the mouth. Vowels, glides, liquids, and fricatives are [+ cont], nasals and stops (which might be called 'nasal stops' and 'oral stops', respectively) are [− cont].

A speech sound is [+ sonorant] if its quality depends on the regular patterns of vibration of air particles within the vocal tract, so that some parts of the vocal tract act as a resonance chamber. Vowels, glides, liquids, and nasals are [+ son], stops and fricatives are [− son].

2B EXERCISES

Referring to the chart above, compare the classes of segments two by two.

(a) Vowels and glides are alike in three features and different in one. In what feature do they differ?
(b) In what feature(s) are liquids and nasals alike? In what do they differ?
(c) How are fricatives and stops alike? How are they different?
(d) How do stops and nasals compare (or differ)?
(e) What difference is there between fricatives and liquids?
(f) How similar, or how different, are vowels and stops?

2.10 Summary

Sound is the result of vibrations strong enough and near enough to affect our eardrums. In almost all of our usual experience the vibrations are transmitted through air (the medium) either because a moving body, the initiator, displaces particles of air or because air is in motion and is displaced by a body in its path or is channeled into some container. Displaced particles of air move back and forth, displacing other particles and causing them to repeat the same vibratory movement in a chain-like effect. The maximum distance that a particle moves in each direction from its starting point is the **amplitude** of the wave that it creates. The total distance, from starting point to farthest distance in one direction to farthest distance in the other direction and back to the starting point, is a **cycle**. The amount of time required for completion of one cycle is a **period**. The number of cycles completed within a given unit of time (usually one second) is the **frequency** of the vibration. Different vibrations have different amplitudes, the auditory correlate of which is difference in the **intensity** or **loudness** of the sounds produced; different vibrations also have different frequencies, and the corresponding sounds differ in **pitch**. Sounds may also differ in **duration**. Vibrating particles which move in regular cycles create **periodic** waves; those which move in irregular cycles, typically of short duration, make **aperiodic** waves.

Ordinarily sounds are associated with complex waves, various particles vibrating at different amplitudes and frequencies. A complex wave can be analyzed as the sum of the component simple waves. Ordinarily, too, there is resonance associated with any vibration. Often particles of air in a **resonance chamber** vibrate in response to some initial vibration outside. A resonance chamber strengthens the initial frequencies to which it is resonant. The size and shape of a resonance chamber determine to which frequencies it is resonant; therefore a resonance chamber determines the **quality** of any sound which has resonance.

Speech is a function of the respiratory system of the human body. Almost always the initiator is air from the **lungs** which moves up the **trachea** and enters the **larynx**. Inside the larynx two bands of tissue, the **vocal cords**, when tense and partly closed, vibrate in response to the flow of air from the lungs and provide **phonation**, the basic vibration for speech sounds. The quality of these speech sounds is determined by the shape of the **vocal tract** above the larynx, where the vibrating air is modified in various ways. Differences in the force with which air is expelled from the lungs are responsible for differences in the intensity of speech sounds, and differences in the frequency of vibration of the vocal cords result in differences of pitch; however, this theoretical distinction between intensity and pitch is not always so clear-cut in actual language performance.

The vocal tract is conventionally divided into three interconnected areas, the **pharynx**, **nasal cavity**, and **oral cavity**, or mouth. Outgoing air must pass through the pharynx and from there through the nasal cavity or the oral cavity or both simultaneously. These areas, especially the mouth, are where specific articulations are accomplished by various modifications of the air stream. While such modifications take place in the vocal tract, the vocal cords vibrate or remain motionless, producing, respectively, **voiced** or **voiceless** sounds.

In our perception a stream of speech consists of **segments**, or individual sounds, one after another, though in the actual articulation there is no such clear segmentation. Although these segments are perceptive units, we describe them in articulatory terms; each segment, or speech sound, is described as a cluster of **articulatory** features. Classification is most efficient if these features are **binary** in nature. Four such binary features express the ways in which the air stream is controlled. A segment is **sonorant**, the result of periodic vibration in the vocal tract, or not. It is **syllabic**, acting as the peak of its syllable, or not. It is **consonantal**, produced with some interruption of the air stream, or not. And it is **continuant**, made with air flowing continuously out of the mouth, or not. These four features, in various plus and minus combinations, serve to define six classes of segments: **stops**, **fricatives**, **nasals**, **liquids**, **glides**, and **vowels**. Stops and vowels are entirely different in their defining clusters of features. Otherwise, any two of the classes share some features and differ in others.

2.11 Addendum: A note on redundancy

It was noted that some articulatory features are distinctive and others are redundant. This chapter has introduced four features for distinguishing classes of speech sounds. The next chapter introduces other features which distinguish segments of the same class from one another. Here, however, we need to recognize that even features which are distinctive in some areas may be used redundantly in other areas.

The way we have used four features – sonorant, syllabic, consonantal, and continuant – to designate six classes is somewhat redundant. Four features, with plus and minus values, would be enough to distinguish 16 classes ($2^4 = 16$), not just six. We can see this not only mathematically but also by direct observation.

The feature [+ syllabic] is sufficient to designate the class of vowels; no other class has this feature. So the other features, [+ son, + cont, − cons], while they indicate true facts about the pronunciation of vowels, have no role in telling how vowels are different from other classes of segments. For classification, one feature is distinctive, the other features are redundant. We can express this fact in a **redundancy statement** like this:

Whatever is [+ syl] is redundantly [+ son, + cont, − cons],

or more briefly like this:

If [+ syl], then [+ son, + cont, − cons].

For glides we need two features together, [− cons] and [− syl], for a distinctive label. The feature [− cons] distinguishes vowels and glides together from other classes, and the feature [− syl] distinguishes glides from vowels. Obviously, then, the feature [+ son] and [+ cont] are redundant. The redundancy statement:

If [− cons,] syl], then [+ son, + cont].

2C EXERCISE

What are the redundancy statements for nasals, liquids, fricatives, and stops?

2A FEEDBACK

(a) Figure 2.1-b
(b) Figure 2.1-e.

2B FEEDBACK

(a) Vowels are [+ syllabic] and glides are [− syllabic]. In the other three features they are alike. This means that glides are the equivalent of certain vowels in their articulation but not in their function within a syllable. A glide is never the peak of a syllable, a vowel always is.
(b) Liquids and nasals are [+ sonorant, + consonantal, ± syllabic]. Liquids are [+ continuant], nasals [− continuant]. In other words, both classes are characterized by some interruption of the air stream, but not so much as to prevent periodic vibration. With liquids air flows out of the mouth, but not so for nasals.
(c) Fricatives and stops both result from aperiodic vibrations, so are [− sonorant]; both require interruption of the air stream – [+ consonantal]; and they are never the peak of a syllable – [− syllabic]. For fricatives air flows continuously out of the mouth ([+ continuant]), while for stops it does not.
(d) Nasals and stops differ only in the feature [sonorant] and in the fact that nasals are sometimes [+ syllabic]. They are alike in being [+ consonantal] and [− continuant].

(e) The difference between fricatives and liquids is exactly parallel to the difference between nasals and stops. Fricatives are [− sonorant] and [− syllabic], liquids [+ sonorant] and sometimes [+ syllabic]. In the other two features they are alike.

(f) Vowels and stops are different in all four features.

2C FEEDBACK

Nasals:	If [+ son, − cont] then [+ cons, ± syl]
Liquids:	If [+ son, + cons, + cont], then [± syl]
Fricatives:	If [− son, + cont], then [+ cons, − syl]
Stops:	If [− son, − cont], then [+ cons, − syl]

3

Consonants

3A PRELIMINARY EXERCISE: IDENTIFYING CONSONANTS BY MATCHING

(a) The words in the left-hand columns below *begin* with 22 different consonants. The words in the right-hand columns begin with the same 22 consonants, but in a different order. Match each word on the left with the word on the right which has the same initial consonant (sound, not letter), and put the appropriate number in front of the word. An example is given.

1	bag	___	tomato	12	pain	___	holy
2	cat	___	Czech	13	ptomaine	___	pest
3	cent	___	yacht	14	room	___	phone
4	check	___	loose	15	shave	___	jest
5	dude	___	there	16	then	___	zest
6	fan	___	guess	17	thick	___	send
7	gas	___	chef	18	vest	___	rhyme
8	gem	___	dare	19	weight	___	main
9	leap	___	vote	20	whole	___	theory
10	meek	___	kneel	21	young	___	boom
11	nail	2	kite	22	zoom	___	wild

(b) The words in the left-hand columns below *end* with 21 different consonants. The words in the right-hand columns have the same final consonants, but in a different order. Match each word on the left with the word on the right which has the same final consonant. An example is given.

1	both	____	love	12	pole	____	fade
2	car	____	rogue	13	rage	____	toll
3	clothe	4	dome	14	rich	____	daze
4	dumb	____	grub	15	rouge	____	lock
5	fate	____	smooth	16	rug	____	loss
6	globe	____	ridge	17	save	____	hope
7	graph	____	sane	18	sign	____	youth
8	lace	____	beige	19	soap	____	care
9	look	____	lung	20	tongue	____	gauche
10	odd	____	gruff	21	wash	____	witch
11	phrase	____	eight				

(c) This time match the *final* consonant of each word in the left-hand columns with the *initial* consonant of a word in the right-hand columns – if there is such a match. An example is given.

1	beige	____	pitch	12	maid	____	vain
2	breathe	____	team	13	meat	____	they
3	chip	____	kill	14	nave	____	zone
4	coach	____	bad	15	nose	____	mode
5	comb	____	dame	16	robe	____	name
6	cough	____	goal	17	rogue	____	lace
7	door	____	choke	18	rung	____	rake
8	face	____	jell	19	rush	____	yell
9	lane	6	fun	20	Ruth	____	wet
10	ledge	____	think	21	sail	____	head
11	lick	____	safe			____	shift

(d) Two of the words in the left-hand columns have final consonants for which there is no match in the initial position. What are the words?

(e) Three words in the right-hand columns have initial consonants for which there is no match in final position. What are they?

3.1 The feature [consonantal]

Stops, fricatives, nasals, and liquids are all [+ consonantal]; in their articulation the lower lip or some part of the tongue impedes the flow of air in some way, in some part of the mouth. The four classes together are called CONSONANTS. Vowels and glides are articulated without such impedance; they are [− consonantal]. For vowels and glides it is the shape of the oral cavity in which air is flowing freely that determines the quality of the sound produced. Glides are like certain vowels in their production, but they are like consonants in the positions they occupy in syllables and larger units. The glides have been included among consonants in the preliminary exercises above, but they are discussed in the next chapter with vowels.

The four classes of consonants differ from one another in their manner of articulation, specifically in whether or not the articulation is characterized by periodic vibration of air particles and in whether or not the air stream is escaping from the mouth during the articulation. In the previous chapter we expressed these differences with the features [sonorant] and [continuant].

liquids	*nasals*	*fricatives*	*stops*
+ sonorant	+ sonorant	− sonorant	− sonorant
+ continuant	− continuant	+ continuant	− continuant

Liquids and nasals are 'musical' like vowels. Although the air stream is obstructed in some way, the vocal tract still acts as a resonance chamber in which air particles flow in periodic waves. Obstruent consonants – fricatives and stops – are articulated with total or near-total obstruction of the air stream so that resonance is minimal or absent. For liquids and fricatives air flows out of the mouth during articulation; thus any of these consonants can be held – continued – as long as the lungs provide air. Nasals can also be prolonged since air escapes during their articulation, but through the nasal cavity alone. (Some phoneticians use the term 'nasal stop'.) A stop, since it involves complete obstruction of the breath stream, is essentially an instant of silence. A stop can be prolonged only in the sense that the silence is maintained for a longer period of time.

Our next task is to investigate the differences within each of these classes. What makes one stop distinct from another stop? How does a fricative, a nasal, a liquid differ from other members of its class?

Here are the symbols for the consonants to be described, with an illustrative word for each consonant:

Liquids	/l/ led /r/ red
Nasals	/m/ rum /n/ run /ŋ/ rung
Fricatives	/f/ fine /θ/ thin /s/ sue /ʃ/ mission /v/ vine /ð/ then /z/ zoo /ʒ/ vision
Stops	/p/ pill /t/ till /č/ chill /k/ kill /b/ bill /d/ dill /ǰ/ Jill /g/gill

To describe the articulation of a consonant is to tell what articulatory features are relevant. In general, three kinds of features are distinctive:

(1) Differences in vocal cord action, or VOICING – The vocal cords vibrate during some articulations and not during other articulations. Articulations with such vibration are voiced, or, in the notation of a binary system,

[+ voice]. Consonants without vocal cord vibration are voiceless, or [− voice]. English stops and fricatives exist in pairs like /t, d/ or /s, z/ such that the two members of the pairs are alike in all respects except that one is [− voice] and the other is [+ voice]. Therefore the feature [voice] is distinctive for stops and fricatives. On the other hand, all liquids and nasals are [+ voice], and voicing is not distinctive in these classes – it is not relevant for telling how one liquid differs from the other or one nasal from the other nasals.

Although we use the feature [voice], with plus and minus values, for both stops like /t, d/ and fricatives like /s, z/, it must also be noted that the feature is not identical in phonetic terms. In the articulation of [s] as in *sue* and *loose* vocal cords do not vibrate, whereas for the articulation of [z] in *zoo* and *lose* they do vibrate. For the articulation of [t] and [d], as in *two* and *do*, the difference is not in vocal cord vibration during the articulation of these stops but rather in VOICE ONSET TIME. In the articulation of stops the air stream is held back, so that no vibration occurs. When the air stream is released at the beginning of *do*, for instance, vocal cord vibration begins almost immediately. When the release is made at the beginning of *two*, vibration does not come immediately. Instead there is first an instant of aspiration – air is released between the closely positioned, but non-vibrating, vocal cords. Then vibration begins. So the 'voicedness' of a voiced stop and the 'voicelessness' of a voiceless stop is not so much in the actual articulation of the stops as in their environment.

(2) Differences in TONGUE SHAPE – The surface of the tongue may be relatively flat, unshaped, or it may be altered so that it has a groove along the center line of the top surface, or it may be drawn in at the sides, or drawn back at the tip. To deal with these differences we recognize two features, [sibilant] and [lateral]. The feature [+ sibilant] indicates the presence of a groove, or slight trough, along the center line, and [− sibilant] means that there is no such groove. The feature [+ lateral] means that the tongue sides are curled inward, and [− lateral] indicates the absence of such curl. The feature [sibilant] is distinctive among fricatives and stops, the feature [lateral] indicates differences in the class of liquids. All nasal consonants are articulated with a flat tongue, so that these features are not distinctive for nasals.

(3) Differences in ARTICULATORS and PLACES OF ARTICULATION – In English the air stream may be obstructed, wholly or partially, by any one of four articulators:

the lower lip
the tip, or apex, of the tongue

the front, or blade, of the tongue (the front third of the upper surface, excluding the tip)
the back, or dorsum, of the tongue (the back third of the upper surface).

These articulators may be said to lie along the lower edge of the oral cavity. Along the upper edge are the areas in which the articulators make contact or near-contact.

the upper lip
the upper front teeth
the alveolar ridge, the 'terraced' hump behind the upper teeth
the (hard) palate, the area which is separated from the nasal cavity by a bony structure
the velum, or soft palate, the posterior area of the roof of the mouth with no bone above it.

The interplay of articulators with places of articulation is shown in the schematic diagram of figure 3.1. Compare figure 2.2. The lines connect articulators and places of articulation. Symbols are placed along the lines to show what articulator and what place of articulation are involved in the articulation of each consonant. Nasals are on the top line, stops on the second line, and fricatives on the third line. The place of articulation is not distinctive for liquids, so /l/ and /r/ are not in the diagram.

The positions of symbols along the lines indicate norms for articulation. As we will see, the place of articulation for any consonant (or any vowel) may vary somewhat according to what precedes and what follows.

3.2 Lip consonants

The nasal and oral stops /m p b/ are typically articulated by stopping the flow of air with the two lips pressed together (bilabial articulation). The

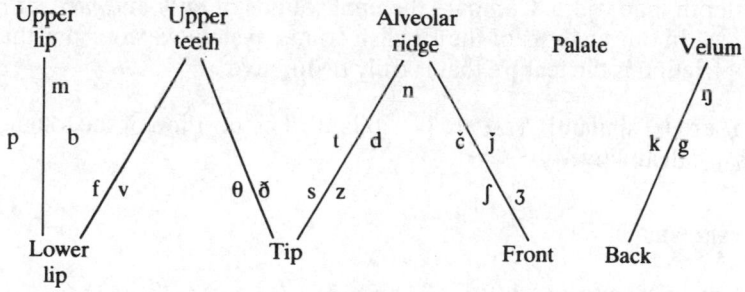

Figure 3.1

fricatives /f v/ are made by resting the lower lip lightly against the upper teeth (labiodental articulation) and letting air flow out between lip and teeth. What makes /f/ and /v/ different from the other labial consonants is the fact that they are fricative, [+ continuant]. The small difference between bilabial and labiodental articulation is not contrastive. Labial fricatives are predictably labiodental, labial stops and nasal are typically bilabial (but see chapter 6, section 6.1a).

As you know, /p/ and /b/ differ in voicing, and the same is true for /f/ and /v/; /p/ and /f/ are [− voice], /b/ and /v/ are [+ voice]. The nasal /m/ is also [+ voice], but that feature is not distinctive for /m/ or other nasals. If English had both voiced and voiceless nasal consonants, as does the Welsh language, voicing would be distinctive for nasals just as it is for obstruents, but this is not the case.

3.3 Tongue-tip consonants

The fricatives /θ ð/ are generally articulated with the tip of the tongue near or lightly touching the upper front teeth – generally at the cutting edge – so that air is squeezed out between tongue and teeth (apicodental articulation). For the nasal and oral stops /n t d/ the apex typically touches the alveolar ridge, stopping the flow of air at that point (apicoalveolar articulation). In the articulation of the fricatives /s z/ air is squeezed between the tip and front of the tongue, on the lower edge, and the alveolar ridge on the upper edge of the oral cavity. (We say that the tongue-tip is the articulator for all the consonants discussed in this section, but for the fricatives /θ ð s z/ the articulator actually includes the area just behind the tip, as well. In fricative articulation the air stream moves over a comparatively long surface.) If we compare the fricatives /θ ð/ and /s z/, we discover another difference between the one set and the other. The apicodental fricatives are articulated with a flat tongue surface, whereas /s z/ are sibilant, produced with a groove or channel along the center line of the tongue surface. Sibilant fricatives are more audible than flat fricatives because the air stream is moving through a channel which has more depth than width. Compare the final sounds of *faith* and *face*, of *bathe* and *bays*. In our analysis of the English sound system we consider that the kind of friction is the feature that is truly distinctive:

/θ ð/ are [− sibilant], /s z/ are [+ sibilant]. The position of the tongue-tip is not distinctive.

3B EXERCISES

(a) How do /t/ and /d/ differ? /θ/ and /ð/? /s/ and /z/?
(b) Is /n/ [+ voice] or [− voice]? Is this feature distinctive for /n/?

3.4 Tongue-front consonants

The consonants /č ǰ/ are called AFFRICATES. An affricate is a combination of stop and fricative. To produce the first and last consonants of *church* and *judge*, for instance, the tongue-front, with a groove along the centerline, makes contact with the alveolar ridge or the area just behind it, stopping the flow of air; then the tongue is lowered and air passes along the groove creating friction. If the tongue-front does not make contact but is positioned near the alveolar ridge, only friction or turbulence occurs. Compare /č/ and /ʃ/, as in *witch* and *wish*; compare /ǰ/ and /ʒ/, as in *pledger* and *pleasure*. All four have the same articulator, the front of the tongue. Fricatives /ʃ ʒ/ are produced with air flowing continuously out of the mouth; they are [+ continuant]. For /č ǰ/ the air stream is first interrupted, then allowed to exit through a narrow channel. Since air does not escape continuously during the articulation, /č ǰ/ are counted as [− continuant]. Though they differ from /p b t d k g/ in being affricates rather than plain stops, they are classified with the plain stops. In classifying consonants we must recognize four articulators, lip, tip, front, back, the stops made with the tongue-front, /č ǰ/, happen to be affricates and there are no plain stops which have this articulator. Stops made with other articulators are plain stops; there are no affricates contrasting with them made by the same articulator.

Like /s z/, /č ǰ ʃ ʒ/ are [+ sibilant]. These six are the only sibilant consonants in English. Of course /č/ and /ʃ/ are [− voice], /ǰ/ and /ʒ/ [+ voice].

3.5 Tongue-back consonants

Back, or dorsal, consonants are articulated by placing the back of the tongue against the velum (soft palate), or a little more forward, against the back part of the hard palate. We make closure between the dorsum and the roof of the mouth for the final consonants of *luck*, /k/, and *lug*, /g/, for instance, so that air is stopped. The same closure is made for the final consonant of *lung*, /ŋ/, but the end of the velum is open so that air escapes through the nasal cavity. Like other stops, /k g/ make a pair which differ only in voice – [− voice] and [+ voice], respectively. Like other nasals, /ŋ/ is [+ voice].

3.6 Summary chart

Altogether we have used a system of seven features to classify 18 English consonants, the stops, fricatives, and nasals. For one feature, the articulator, we recognize a four-way distinction here: *l*(ip), *t*(ip), *f*(ront), and *b*(ack). The other six features are binary, with plus and minus values.

	SYL	CONS	CONT	ART	VOI	SIB
p	−	+	−	l	−	−
b	−	+	−	1	+	−
f	−	+	+	1	−	−
v	−	+	+	1	+	−
m	±	+	−	1	+	−
t	−	+	−	t	−	−
d	−	+	−	t	+	−
θ	−	+	+	t	−	−
ð	−	+	+	t	+	−
s	−	+	+	t	−	+
z	−	+	+	t	+	+
n	±	+	−	t	+	−
č	−	+	−	f	−	+
ǰ	−	+	−	f	+	+
ʃ	−	+	+	f	−	+
ʒ	−	+	+	f	+	+
k	−	+	−	b	−	−
g	−	+	−	b	+	−
ŋ	±	+	−	b	+	−

3C EXERCISES

Referring to the chart above, what is the only difference between

(a) /p/ and /b/?
(b) /d/ and /ð/?
(c) /b/ and /v/?
(d) /ð/ and /z/?
(e) /b/ and /m/?
(f) /n/ and /ŋ/?
(g) /s/ and /ʃ/?
(h) /f/ and /θ/?

In what feature(s) does /d/ differ from

(i) /t/?
(j) /b/?
(k) /ð/?
(l) /n/?
(m) /g/?
(n) /z/?

Finish these statements of proportion:

(o) /p/ is to /b/ as /t/ is to_____.
(p) /č/ is to /ʃ/ as /ǰ/ is to ____.
(q) /b/ is to /m/ as /d/ is to_____ as ____ is to /ŋ/.

(r) ____ is to /s/ as /v/ is to /z/.
(s) Of the four articulators used in English, more consonants are articulated with the _____ than any of the others. Fewest consonants are articulated with the _____.

3.7 Articulators or points of articulation?

The description of consonants used here differs in two ways from what you may find in some other phonology books. For one thing, our description is based on the *articulators* – lower lip or tip, front, and back of tongue. Many phonologists describe the same consonants on the basis of the *point of articulation* – usually the upper lip (*labials*), the upper teeth or alveolar ridge (*dentals* or *alveolars*), the hard palate (*palatals*), and the velum (*velars*). It seems more accurate to classify these consonants with respect to the articulator rather than the point of articulation because the point of articulation can vary quite a bit whereas the articulator does not (see chapter 6, Consonant and Vowel Variation). Furthermore, the term *palatals* is not entirely accurate for the consonants /č ǰ ʃ ʒ/ since these are articulated with the front of the tongue in conjunction with the alveolar ridge, rather than with the palate. Nevertheless, the terms based on place of articulation are traditional and frequently used, so that one needs to be familiar with any classification which has such a basis.

Secondly, some books dealing with the phonology of English, having established four points of articulation (as above), introduce a pair of binary features to produce a more elegant classification. Labial consonants and dental/alveolar consonants are all articulated at the alveolar ridge or more forward, whereas velar and, supposedly, palatal consonants are articulated behind the alveolar ridge. If one takes the alveolar ridge as an arbitrary dividing line in the mouth (comparable to the meridian of Greenwich as an arbitrary dividing line for demarcating east and west longitude on the face of the earth), labial and dental/alveolar consonants are designated [+ anterior] and palatal and velar consonants are [− anterior].

Another binary feature is needed to distinguish labial and velar consonants from those made more toward the center of the mouth, the dental/alveolars and palatals. Notice that there is something in common between articulation at the lip area and articulation at the back of the mouth; the oral cavity has the shape of a long tube, interrupted at one end – the labial end – or the other the velar end. In contrast, for the articulation of a dental/alveolar or a palatal consonant the tip or front of the tongue is raised, dividing the oral cavity into two areas of different size, one in front of and one behind the body of the tongue. The distinguishing feature is named [coronal] after the bone in the skull which lies above this part of the mouth. Dental/alveolar and palatal consonants are [+ coronal], and labial and velar consonants are [− coronal].

Here, then, is the scheme for classifying stops, fricatives, and nasals by point of articulation with binary features:

LABIAL	DENTAL/ALVEOLAR	PALATAL	VELAR
+ ant	+ ant	− ant	− ant
− cor	+ cor	+ cor	− cor
p b	t d	č ǰ	k g
f v	θ ð	ʃ ʒ	
	s z		
m	n		ŋ

Note that the classification is the same four-way division that we have introduced. Only the names are different.

3.8 The feature [lateral]

In chapter 2 liquids, the consonants which begin with words *lead* and *read*, for instance, were shown to be

± syllabic
+ consonantal
+ continuant
+ sonorant

We can now add two other features which the liquids share: they are [+ voice] and [− sibilant].

How do /l/ and /r/ differ from each other? Phonologists who use the features [anterior] and [coronal], as described above, say that /l/ is [+ anterior] and /r/ is [− anterior] since /l/ is sometimes articulated with the tip of the tongue on the alveolar ridge and /r/ is never articulated so far forward. However, both consonants are articulated in different parts of the mouth; neither the articulator nor the place of articulation is truly distinctive for these two consonants. What distinguishes them from each other is the shape of the tongue. One of them, /l/, is articulated with the sides of the tongue curled in and air escaping over the sides. We say that /l/ is [+ lateral].

For /r/ the tongue is also curled but in a different way; the whole body of the tongue is pulled back and bunched up, with a slight groove in the very tip – not a groove along the center line of the surface, which would make it a sibilant. Typically, there is also some rounding of the lips. Instead of pulling the tongue back and humping it up, some speakers turn the tongue-tip backward; hence the term 'retroflex' has been used by some phoneticians, but this name is not appropriate for the most usual articulation. Various appropriate names might be used to describe the physical facts of articulation. To place /r/ in a system of distinctive features it is enough to say that it is [− lateral].

3.9 Summary

Of the six classes of phonemes four of them, stops, nasals, fricatives, and liquids, are alike in being [+ consonantal]. Within each of these classes phonemes are distinguished from one another by three other kinds of features: voice, tongue shape, and articulator. English stops and fricatives exist in pairs such that one member of each pair is [+ voice], articulated with vocal cords vibrating, and the other [− voice], articulated without such vibration. This feature is not distinctive for nasals and liquids, which are all [+ voice].

We recognize two 'special' kinds of tongue shape. For one of these, designated [+ sibilant], there is a groove along the centerline of the tongue through which the air stream travels. Six consonants, /s z ʃ ʒ č ǰ/, are [+ sib], and all other English phonemes are [− sib]. The other special tongue shape is indicated with the feature [+ lateral], an articulation in which the sides of the tongue are drawn inward. In English only the liquid /l/ is [+ lat].

There are four articulators, the lower lip and three parts of the tongue – tip, front, and back – lying along the lower edge of the oral cavity. Each articulates in conjunction with some point of articulation along the upper edge of the cavity. The following list names the articulators and for each gives the general adjective, and then the more precise terms which designate articulator and point of articulation.

lip	labial	bilabial, labiodental
tip	apical	apicodental, apicoalveolar
front	frontal	frontoalveolar, frontopalatal
back	dorsal	dorsopalatal, dorsovelar

(The front of the tongue is also called the *blade*, for which the Latin equivalent is *lamina*. Hence some phoneticians use the adjective *laminal* and the prefix *lamino-* in place of *frontal* and *fronto-*, respectively.)

Rather than describing feature content this way, with the names of four articulators, some phonologists prefer to recognize two features, **[anterior]** and **[coronal]**, based on divisions of the oral cavity. The correspondence in classifying is like this:

labial	[+ anterior, − coronal]
apical	[+ anterior, + coronal]
frontal	[− anterior, + coronal]
dorsal	[− anterior, − coronal]

The consonants /č/ and /ǰ/ are phonetically different from other stops; they are affricates, produced by first stopping the flow of air, then letting it flow out through a slight opening so that friction or turbulence results – a stop with fricative release.

The two sets of obstruents, /p t č k f θ s ʃ/ and /b d ǰ g v ð z ʒ/, differ in that the first are voiceless, [– voice], the second group are voiced, [+ voice]. So far as fricatives are concerned, 'voiceless' means that the vocal cords are not vibrating and 'voiced' means that they are vibrating during the articulation. For stops the difference between voicelessness and voicedness is not necessarily in the articulation but in what follows. For example, after the release of the initial stops in *buy*, *die*, *guy* the vocal cords vibrate immediately; following the release of the initial stops in *pie*, *tie*, *kind* there is a delay in the onset of vibration, a period of aspiration, in which air is squeezed between motionless vocal cords.

3D EXERCISE: PRACTICE WITH SYMBOLS

Each word below has three consonants separated by two vowels. Write the symbols for the three consonants. The first is done as an example.

cherub	č-r-b	thistle	ptomaine
garage		havoc	possess
Philip		jealous	gingham
receipt		package	righteous
machine		Kenneth	sheriff
budget		disease	nothing
behave		cynic	shebang
Janice		sugar	vision
butcher		rhythm	cattle
nickel		button	cousin

3A FEEDBACK

(a)

1	bag	13	tomato	12	pain	20	holy
2	cat	4	Czech	13	ptomaine	12	pest
3	cent	21	yacht	14	room	6	phone
4	check	9	loose	15	shave	8	jest
5	dude	16	there	16	then	22	zest
6	fan	7	guess	17	thick	3	send
7	gas	15	chef	18	vest	14	rhyme
8	gem	5	dare	19	weight	10	main
9	leap	18	vote	20	whole	17	theory
10	meek	11	kneel	21	young	1	boom
11	nail	2	kite	22	zoom	19	wild

(b)

1	both	17	love	12	pole	10	fade
2	car	16	rogue	13	rage	12	toll
3	clothe	4	dome	14	rich	11	daze
4	dumb	6	grub	15	rouge	9	lock
5	fate	3	smooth	16	rug	8	loss
6	globe	13	ridge	17	save	19	hope
7	graph	18	sane	18	sign	1	youth
8	lace	15	beige	19	soap	2	care
9	look	20	lung	20	tongue	21	gauche
10	odd	7	gruff	21	wash	14	witch
11	phrase	5	eight				

(c)

1	beige	3	pitch	12	maid	14	vain
2	breathe	13	team	13	meat	2	they
3	chip	11	kill	14	nave	15	zone
4	coach	16	bad	15	nose	5	mode
5	comb	12	dame	16	robe	9	name
6	cough	17	goal	17	rogue	21	lace
7	door	4	choke	18	rung	7	rake
8	face	10	jell	19	rush		yell
9	lane	6	fun	20	Ruth		wet
10	ledge	20	think	21	sail		head
11	lick	8	safe			19	shift

(d) beige, rung

(e) yell, wet, head

3B FEEDBACK

(a) The first member of each pair is [− voice], the second [+ voice].
(b) /n/ is [+ voice] but the feature is not distinctive since there is no nasal consonant in English which is [− voice].

3C FEEDBACK

(a) −/+ voice
(b) −/+ continuant
(c) −/+ continuant
(d) −/+ sibilant
(e) −/+ sonorant
(f) tip/back
(g) tip/front
(h) lip/tip

(i) −/+ voice
(j) tip/lip
(k) −/+ continuant
(l) −/+ sonorant
(m) tip/back
(n) −/+ continuant, −/+ sibilant

(o) /d/ (p) /ʒ/ (q) /n/ /g/ (r) /f/
(s) tip; back

3D FEEDBACK

cherub	č-r-b	thistle	θ-s-l	ptomaine	t-m-n
garage	g-r-ʒ, g-r-ǰ	havoc	h-v-k	possess	p-z-s
Philip	f-l-p	jealous	ǰ-l-s	gingham	g-ŋ-m
receipt	r-s-t	package	p-k-ǰ	righteous	r-č-s
machine	m-ʃ-n	Kenneth	k-n-θ	sheriff	ʃ-r-f
budget	b-ǰ-t	disease	d-z-z	nothing	n-θ-ŋ
behave	b-h-v	cynic	s-n-k	shebang	ʃ-b-ŋ
Janice	ǰ-n-s	sugar	ʃ-g-r	vision	v-ʒ-n
butcher	b-č-r	rhythm	r-ð-m	cattle	k-t-l
nickel	n-k-l	button	b-t-n	cousin	k-z-n

4

Vowels and Glides

4A PRELIMINARY EXERCISE

(a) In the first column below each word consists of a consonant followed by a vowel. (You may have learned to call some or all of these vowels 'diphthongs'. That is a description based on phonetic features, which we will examine later. Right now we are concerned only with identifying the different vowel-units of English, whether they are to be counted as dipthongs or simple vowels.) In the second column the same eight vowel-units appear again, in a different order, in words which end with one consonant. The third column has words with the same eight vowel-units, re-arranged, followed by two consonants. Identify the vowels of column II and column III by matching with those of column I.

	I		II		III
1	see	____	loaf	____	wild
2	may	____	lake	____	point
3	lie	____	shout	____	boost
4	raw	____	bruise	____	fiend
5	go	____	like	____	pound
6	toy	____	neat	____	range
7	cow	____	hawk	____	bolt
8	shoe	____	coin	____	haunt

(b) The six words in column IV, below, contain vowels which do not ordinarily occur at the end of a word. They may be followed by one consonant, as in Column IV, or two consonants, as in column V, and sometimes by three consonants (e.g. *tempt*, *midst*). Match the words of column V with those of column IV.

	IV		V
a	pit	____	husk
b	pet	____	fox
c	pat	____	rest
d	put	____	wolf
e	putt	____	sift
f	pot	____	fact

4.1 Analyses of vowels

In describing English consonants we needed to see how each consonant is articulated and what features distinguish one consonant from another. As we saw, there are some possible differences in the approach to description: more emphasis may be put on the articulator or on the place of articulation; a description which is best for English alone might well need modification within a general framework for describing more than just one language; consonants like /č/ and /ǰ/ can be viewed as single consonants, as we do, or as each a cluster of two consonants, stop and fricative, symbolized /t ʃ/ and /d ʒ/. But otherwise there is no real question about the inventory of English consonant phonemes; we can identify the consonants and count them, and all analysts agree generally on the number. Furthermore, the differences in description are fairly trivial.

It is different with vowels. There are several different analyses that linguists have made of English vowels. These analyses vary quite a bit from one another, and none of them is entirely satisfactory. The different analyses recognize different numbers of vowels, they use different symbols and combinations of symbols to represent them, and they use different terms to describe them. What is regarded as a simple vowel in one analysis, for example, (and symbolized by a single letter) may be treated as a diphthong in another analysis (and represented by a sequence of two symbols). One unfortunate consequence of these different analyses is that some people assume that the description and symbols which they learned first are the only 'correct' ones.

Why are there such different analyses of English vowels? For two reasons: (1) Different dialects of English have somewhat different systems of vowels (though they have the same system of consonants); these differences are not so large as to prevent English-speakers from different parts of the world from understanding one another but they are enough to be quite noticeable, and the differences make our task of description considerably more difficult than the description of consonants. (2) Different descriptivists give more importance to different features. Because language has redundancy, vowels differ from one another in length, tenseness, tongue movement and in other ways.

Even when describing the same system of vowels, it is possible for two linguists to disagree about which features seem more relevant.

Appendix I gives a comparison of some different analyses of English vowels.

4.2 Dialect differences

Do *lock* and *log* have the same vowel sound? Do *pat* and *bad* have the same vowel? Are *cot* and *caught* homonyms? Do *bomb* and *balm* sound the same? Does *pork* rhyme with *fork*? Does *hurry* rhyme with *furry*?

Any speaker of English has an immediate answer for each of these questions, but in each case there are other speakers who will give the opposite answer. Whereas there is general uniformity in English consonants, there are interesting differences in the vowels. The differences are of three kinds: in the INVENTORY of vowels, in their INCIDENCE, and in their pronunciation, or PHONETIC REALIZATION. What most people think of as differences in pronunciation when they listen to others who come from a different part of the English-speaking world are likely to be a combination of all three of these kinds of difference.

The inventory of vowels is the number of vowel phonemes which contrast with one another – which are capable of differentiating words. Chapter 3 dealt with the inventory of consonants in English. To know the vowel inventory of a language or of a single dialect we have to find out how many distinctive vowels (that is, vowels which are capable of distinguishing one meaning from another) occur in the same or approximately the same phonetic environment. The total number of such distinctive units is the inventory of vowel phonemes in that language or that dialect. Different dialects of English have different vowel inventories. Here are three examples: Most speakers of English pronounce some words with the vowel of FOOT and others with the vowel of BREW; in Scotland, however, all such words are pronounced with the vowel of BREW – there is no FOOT-vowel, and that makes one vowel less in the inventory of Scottish English than in other dialects. In the north of England words like FOOT and words like NUT, which elsewhere have different vowels, are spoken with the vowel of FOOT; we may say that there is no NUT-vowel as there is in other dialects. In most of Canada and much of the United States LAW and LOCK (or *caught* and *cot*) are pronounced with the same vowel, though they represent large groups of words which are differentiated by other speakers. Whenever a group of people have two vowel phonemes corresponding to a single vowel phoneme for another group of people, the two groups have a difference of inventory.

The term *incidence* refers to the occurrence of particular vowels in particular sets of lexical items. Speakers of different dialects may have the same number of vowels available for making distinctions but use them in different sets of words. For example, some speakers of English pronounce *father*, *rather*, and *lather* so that they rhyme, all having the same vowel in the first syllable; other speakers rhyme *father* and *rather* but pronounce *lather* with a different first vowel; still others pronounce *rather* to rhyme with *lather* but have a different first vowel in *father*. To simplify a bit, we have this kind of dialect difference:

Dialect A	*Dialect B*	*Dialect C*
father, rather, lather	father, rather	father
	lather	rather, lather

How these three words are pronounced is a trivial matter in itself, but it illustrates a much bigger matter. There are whole sets of words like *half*, *laugh*, *glass*, *bath* which are pronounced with different vowels by different speakers of English – differences in the incidence of the vowel phonemes they have.

Finally, to understand differences of phonetic realization, it would help if we could all hear a number of people from different parts of the English-speaking world pronounce the word HOUSE. We could say that they all pronounce the 'same' vowel, and they use it in essentially the same large class of words, but their ways of rendering the vowel are quite different, differences in articulatory features – the positions and movements of tongue and lips.

4.3 A general inventory and particular inventories

To describe the most widely spoken dialects of English and to explain how they resemble and differ from one another we need to set up an inventory of vowels which is larger than the inventories of most dialects. Our inventory contains 24 vowels, as described below. (The term 'vowel' is used here as a cover term for what may be a simple vowel, a diphthong, or even a triphthong). These 24 vowels can occur in monosyllabic words or in the stressed syllable of words of more than one syllable. The next chapter deals with vowels in unstressed syllables.

For reasons which will become clear later, we divide these 24 vowels into three groups:

6 checked vowels
9 free vowels
9 R vowels

We use a key word for each of the 24.

The six checked vowels are the ones illustrated in the following key words, with our vowel symbol following

CHICK	/ɪ/	FOOT	/ʊ/
STEP	/ɛ/	NUT	/ʌ/
BAT	/æ/	LOCK	/ɒ/

These vowels are called 'checked' because in one-syllable words such as these they are always followed by one or more consonants. There is no word which begins like CHICK or FOOT, for instance, and ends with a vowel. These are the vowels which formed part (b) of the preliminary exercise 4A.

The pronunciation of each of these vowels differs somewhat from dialect to dialect and depends in part on the total vowel inventory of the dialect. Details of pronunciation are considered later in this chapter, but note the arrangement above: the three vowels illustrated in the left-hand column are articulated in the front of the mouth, those in the right-hand column farther back; and in each column the topmost vowel is articulated with the tongue (front or back) high in the mouth, the second one somewhat lower, and the third one with the tongue low in the mouth.

Here are more examples for each of the six, illustrating their occurrence in monosyllabic words with a variety of consonants following the vowel and as the stressed vowel of some polysyllabic words:

CHICK	bit hip rich sick crib lid ridge dig stiff myth hiss fish give fizz hymn chin sing fill limp lint nymph silk build list ˈticket ˈliver ˈmission ˈcity ˈsilver elˈlipse deˈpict diˈstinct
STEP	bet wretch check ebb led ledge egg clef Beth less flesh gem bell hemp rent friend help melt theft chest next ˈready ˈjelly ˈnever ˈpleasure ˈany diˈrect eˈvent conˈtempt
BAT	map match tack grab lad badge tag math cash ham man gang shall lamp ant bank hand fact tax ˈmatter ˈsalad ˈtravel ˈpacket ˈtraffic colˈlapse atˈtract caˈnal
FOOT	put look good puss bush full wolf ˈbullet ˈpudding ˈcushion ˈsugar ˈwoman
NUT	cup luck rub mud fudge rug muff fuss rush love fuzz rum run rung dull lump hunt funds lunch lunge chunk pulse bulge ˈbutton ˈsudden ˈluscious ˈonion aˈbove inˈduct corˈrupt
LOCK	stop pot crotch rob rod lodge bomb doll fond solve fox prompt ˈbody ˈstocking ˈprofit ˈbother ˈcomet ˈfolly ˈwander aˈdopt conˈcoct

The nine free vowels are illustrated by these key words, with our symbol – always two letters – following:

TREE	/ii/	BREW	/uu/		
DAY	/ei/	TOE	/ou/		
SPA	/aa/	LAW	/ɔɔ/		
TIE	/ai/	TOY	/oi/	NOW	/au/

These are the vowels of part (a) of exercise 4A. They occur in open syllables, as in these key words, and also in syllables closed by one or more consonants; e.g. *treat*, *date*, *tight*, *calm*, *voice*, *brood*, *toast*, *noun*, *lawn*. For some readers of this book SPA and LAW have the same vowel and therefore rhyme. Some readers will find that LOCK has the same vowel as SPA or LAW (or both of them). These facts illustrate the dialect differences which are dealt with below.

Here are more examples of the nine free vowels:

TREE	sleep beat teach week seed siege league beef teeth niece leave tease dream green seal east fiend field ˈevil ˈeasy ˈreason ˈdemon aˈgree beˈlieve proˈceed maˈchine reˈpeal
BREW	loop boot Luke rude fugue proof Ruth truce prove smooth groom prune tool wound boost ˈpupil ˈruby ˈlucid ˈnuisance ˈfusion reˈview aˈmuse apˈprove
DAY	tape bait cake blade rage vague safe faith face save bathe raze beige name lane mail paint change ˈpaper ˈbacon ˈwager ˈfavor ˈancient deˈlay paˈrade deˈbate comˈplain arˈrange
TOE	hope boat coach yoke robe ode vogue loaf rove both dose dome roll bolt fold coast ˈover ˈocean ˈshoulder ˈposter beˈlow eˈrode reˈvoke apˈproach conˈtrol
TIE	type bite like bribe bride life rice drive rise chime fine tile pint find child Christ ˈfiber ˈtiger ˈhyphen ˈsilent deˈny uˈnite colˈlide arˈrive deˈsign
TOY	boy void voice noise coin coil point moist ˈoyster ˈpoison ˈdoily emˈploy exˈploit apˈpoint aˈvoid reˈjoice
NOW	bout couch loud gouge mouth house rouse down owl joust count pound ounce lounge ˈpowder ˈfountain ˈtrousers ˈcouncil alˈlow deˈvout aˈmount surˈround proˈnounce
SPA	palm ˈfather faˈçade
LAW	bought hawk broad sauce cause dawn fall bald salt false flaunt paunch ˈdaughter ˈautumn ˈauthor apˈplaud

The nine R vowels are illustrated by these key words, again with symbols following:

EAR	/ir/	TOUR	/ur/
CHAIR	/er/	DOOR	/or/
		FUR	/ɜr/

STAR	/ar/	WAR	/ɔr/
FIRE	/air/	SOUR	/aur/

Some readers will claim that DOOR and WAR have the same vowel, others will say that WAR rhymes with STAR, and some may claim that EAR and CHAIR rhyme. It is just these dialect matters that lead us to present a general inventory.

More examples of these vowels follow:

EAR	fear beard fierce ˈserum ˈdreary ˈhero sinˈcere apˈpear interˈfere
TOUR	cure ˈtourist ˈmural ˈcurious inˈsurance enˈdure deˈtour maˈture obˈscure seˈcurity
CHAIR	fair scarce stairs ˈarea ˈdairy caˈnary aˈware comˈpare
FUR	chirp shirt church work berg bird urge surf birth nurse curve firm burn curl ˈmurder ˈfurther ˈcircus ˈvirtue ˈperson ˈturtle ˈperfect reˈserve diˈvert conˈfirm reˈhearse
DOOR	bore fort porch pork board forge forth borne ˈportal anˈgora ˈchoral ˈfloral ˈglory ˈstory meˈmorial exˈplore igˈnore reˈport diˈvorce
STAR	harp heart march dark hard large scarf hearth farce marsh carve charm yarn ˈfather ˈarmor ˈtarget ˈpartial ˈsergeant ˈmarvel reˈmark deˈpart diˈscard
WAR	fork short warn horn morning George wart swarm horse form born ˈLawrence ˈorder ˈcorner ˈnormal
FIRE	sire tired iron ˈdiary ˈfiery ˈsiren ˈpirate enˈtire inˈspire
SOUR	ˈflower ˈdowry deˈvour

Dialects of English can be labeled either 'rhotic' or 'non-rhotic' according to whether the words above are pronounced with or without a frictionless continuant [r]. RP and most of England and Wales, Australia, New Zealand, South Africa, and, variably, the southern United States and eastern New England are non-rhotic. South-western England, Scotland, Ireland, Canada, and most of the United States are rhotic, and there are groups of rhotic speakers in areas which are generally non-rhotic, or 'r-less'.

In non-rhotic dialects FUR, STAR, and WAR have long vowels, and EAR, CHAIR, TOUR, and DOOR have vowels in which the tongue moves (from different starting points, of course) to a mid-central position; they are centering diphthongs. FIRE and SOUR have what may be called triphthongs: the tongue moves upward, forward for FIRE, backward for SOUR, then to mid-center. No [r] is pronounced, in any of these, if the vowel is final or followed by a consonant. If any of these vowels is followed by a vowel, [r] is pronounced. This happens within a word (e.g. *serious*, *glory*, *starry*) and when a word with a final R vowel is closely linked to a following word which begins with a vowel, as in *The car is here*, *near a bank*, *war and peace*. This phenomenon is known as 'Linking R'.

The existence of the linking R is due to something that happened in history. In the dialect of south-eastern England during the early modern period the consonant /r/ ceased to be pronounced when final or pre-consonantal (*car*, *cart*) but was retained when intervocalic (*carry*). Intervocalic retention applied not only within words but also to closely linked words in phrases, like those illustrated above. Linking R is usual in most non-rhotic dialects, but not in the American South; speakers there have no [r] in *the car* nor in *The car is here*.

An interesting extension to Linking R is called Intrusive R, from a historical point of view. In non-rhotic dialects WAR rhymes with LAW, STAR with SPA, and *odor* with *soda*. Quite naturally, if *war* and *odor* 'acquire' an [r] in such groups as *war and peace*, *the odor is bad*, the same treatment can result for *law-r-and order* and *the soda-r-is bad*.

To decide if the general vowel inventory is the vowel inventory of a particular English dialect we need to ask (a) if all 24 of these are really different one from another, and (b) if there is any word – or, better, any group of words – which has a stressed vowel different from any of these 24. In other words, is 24 too large a number or too small a number? If 24 is too large a number, that is due to the fact that some of the distinctions indicated above are not maintained in all dialects. If 24 is too small a number for a particular dialect, this means that there are other distinctions made by the speakers of the dialect. There are indeed other distinctions which exist, but we postpone discussion of these to direct attention to the 24 which have been introduced.

Most varieties of English have fewer than 24 vowel phonemes of our general inventory. We now consider vowel inventories of some of the principal dialects of the language. We begin with one which does have the full inventory of 24.

Inventory 1 (rhotic): Ireland

TREE/EAR	CHICK		FOOT	BREW/TOUR
DAY/CHAIR	STEP	FUR	HUT	TOE/DOOR
	BAT	SPA/STAR	LOCK	LAW/WAR
TIE/FIRE		TOY	NOW/SOUR	

All 24 of our vowel distinctions are maintained in Irish English. The R-vowels are pronounced with a sonorant consonant. The R vowels have generally the same quality as free vowels, and the slant line separates each R vowel from the free vowel which is closest to it; the EAR vowel has the same quality as the vowel of TREE, CHAIR the same as DAY, FIRE the same as TIE, and so on.

The English spoken in Scotland is almost identical with that of Ireland, so far as number of vowel contrasts is concerned. The one exception is that words of the FOOT class have the vowel in the BREW class – or, as we put it earlier, there is no FOOT vowel. Making one change in Inventory 1, above, gives us a vowel inventory for Scottish English; the change is: FOOT = BREW/TOUR. For many speakers of Scottish English there are two other changes: the same vowel occurs in the BAT class and the SPA class (BAT = SPA/STAR) and the LOCK class has the same vowel as the LAW class (LOCK = LAW/WAR).

A different change in Inventory 1 will show a vowel system which exists for many people in the north of England. For these speakers there is, as we put it before, no NUT vowel. We make one modification in Inventory 1: NUT = FOOT.

The next inventory indicates the vowel contrasts in a broad variety of dialects: in the south of England, including RP and Cockney, in South Africa, New Zealand, and Australia. Within this range of dialects there are big differences of pronunciation – between Cockney and RP, for instance – but the vowel system is essentially the same.

Inventory 2 (non-rhotic): RP, Australia, New Zealand, South Africa

TREE	EAR	CHICK		FOOT	BREW	TOUR
DAY	CHAIR	STEP	FUR	HUT	TOE	
	BAT	SPA = STAR		LOCK	LAW = DOOR – WAR	
TIE/FIRE			TOY	NOW/SOUR		

The sets represented by EAR, CHAIR, and TOUR have centering diphthongs; FUR and STAR words have long vowels, the latter being identical with SPA. Among older speakers of RP, LAW may have a long vowel and DOOR = WAR a centering diphthong; among younger speakers the three are identical.

Inventory 3 (rhotic): 'General North American'

TREE	CHICK/EAR		FOOT/TOUR	BREW	
DAY	STEP/CHAIR	FUR	HUT	TOE/DOOR	
	BAT	SPA = LOCK/STAR		LAW/WAR	
TIE/FIRE	TOY	NOW/SOUR			

This inventory is the system of vowels in varieties spoken by many Americans and Canadians. The system shown here has DOOR pronounced with approximately the vowel of TOE, followed by /r/, and WAR articulated with the vowel of LAW, plus /r/. An increasing number of North Americans, like speakers of English represented in Inventory 2, have no such distinction, so Inventory 3 can be modified for such speakers with the notation

DOOR = WAR. Unlike most other varieties of English the LOCK vowel is identical with the SPA vowel, as shown here, or with the LAW vowel (so: LOCK = LAW), or all three of these groups of words have the same vowel (SPA = LOCK = LAW). STAR has the same vowel followed by /r/. For most North Americans the EAR vowel is nearer to CHICK than to TREE, CHAIR more like STEP than DAY, TOUR more similar to FOOT than to BREW.

Eastern New England and the American South are variably rhotic. EAR, CHAIR, and TOUR are nearer in quality to the free vowels, TREE, DAY, and BREW, respectively, with a centering off-glide. STAR and WAR may also, especially in the South, have a centering off-glide. Otherwise these dialect areas differ in only minor ways from the above.

4.4 The phonetic descriptions

The features which distinguish stops, fricatives, and nasals do nothing to tell the characteristics of vowels. All vowels are:

[+ syllabic], capable of carrying stress and pitch
[− consonantal], made without impeding the air flow
[+ continuant], articulated with air going continuously out the mouth
[+ sonorant], made with regular patterns of vibration
[+ voice], produced with vocal cords vibrating
[− sibilant], produced with a flat tongue surface.

What are the articulatory features which make vowels differ from one another? Several kinds of features need to be considered:

(1) Vowels differ from one another in QUALITY. Quality is determined by the shape of the resonance chamber, which in turn depends mainly on the position of the tongue. The front, center, or back of the tongue may be positioned at different heights. Following a general convention, we recognize three degrees of height and label them High, Mid, and Low. To a lesser extent the shape of the oral cavity, and therefore the quality of a vowel, depends on the shape of the lips – whether they are more rounded or more spread. It would be impossible to describe vowels without considering their qualitative differences, so we characterize a vowel as front, central, or back, as high, mid, or low, and as rounded or unrounded.

The Phonetic Chart (figure 4.1) contains symbols which we need to refer to later in this section. Each symbol stands for a vowel-like articulation; its place in the chart indicates the tongue height and tongue advancement; and symbols in parentheses are rounded vowels. The diacritics ˆ, ˇ, ‹, › can be added after a symbol to indicate an articulation which is, respectively, higher,

	Front	Central	Back
High	i, ɪ	ɨ	(u), (ʊ)
Mid	e, ɛ	ə, ɚ, ɜ, ɜ̞, ʌ	(o)
Low	æ, a	ɐ, ɑ	(ɔ), (ɒ)

Figure 4.1 Phonetic chart for vowels, showing the quality (tongue height and tongue advancement) associated with each symbol; parentheses indicate lip rounding.

lower, more forward, or more back than the norm represented by the letter symbol.

(2) Vowels can differ in LENGTH. To be sure, any vowel can be stretched out or clipped short; in this sense length depends on the importance of a word in an utterance and on the whims and the habits of the speaker. In describing vowels we are less concerned with this kind of variation and more concerned with determining whether some vowels are typically shorter than others – whether two vowels which are fairly similar in quality also differ in length. The TREE and CHICK vowels, for example, are similar in quality but the first is typically longer than the second; the same is true for BREW and FOOT, and, for some speakers at least, for LAW and LOCK.

In phonetic transcriptions a colon after a symbol indicates a longer vowel sound than the same symbol without the colon.

(3) There may be a difference of COMPLEXITY. This is the familiar distinction between a simple vowel, or monophthong, and a compound vowel, or diphthong. For a simple vowel tongue and lips remain relatively stable throughout the articulation. A diphthong is made with tongue (and lips) moving. For English it is possible to recognize three kinds of diphthong: those made with the front of the tongue moving upward, symbolized in our phonetic descriptions with a raised [ⁱ] after the vowel, those made with back of tongue moving upward, indicated with a raised [ᵘ], and those in which the tongue moves toward a mid-central position, symbolized [ᵊ].

(4) There may be a difference in TENSENESS. Muscles in the lips and, more importantly, in the tongue can be tightened or relaxed. You can feel the muscles in the root of the tongue by putting your fingers where chin and neck come together and thus compare the tension in different vowel articulations. Tenseness alone, however, does not create an audible difference.

As noted in section 4.1, different descriptions of English vowels have treated these features in different ways. Any description of the vowels of English (or of any language) has to recognize differences of *quality*, but with other kinds of features there is redundancy. When we compare our free vowels, as a group, with the checked vowels, as a group, we may describe the former as long, tense, and diphthongal and the checked vowels as short, lax, and monophthongal. And some works on English phonology have used just such labels. However, the facts of articulation for the different vowels in different dialects are much too complex to consider these labels as truly descriptive.

Here are phonetic descriptions of our 24 vowels, with their principal variants:

CHICK – a short, lax high-front unrounded vowel [ɪ]; in South Africa the vowel is high-front only in the environment of a tongue-front or tongue-back consonant (e.g. *chick*, *wish*, *fig*, *bridge*); in other environments it is high-central [ɨ] (*tip*, *build*, *sit*); in New Zealand the high-central vowel is the norm in all positions of occurrence.

STEP – a short, lax, mid-front unrounded vowel [ɛ], without great variation.

BAT – a low-front unrounded vowel, typically longer than the high-front CHICK and mid-front STEP; in North America it is higher and often diphthongal [æˆᵊ], especially before voiced fricatives and sonorant consonants (*jazz*, *jam*, *valve*); the diphthong may be fronting [æⁱ] before /ʃ g ŋ/ (*passion*, *bag*, *anger*); in Britain lower and farther back [æˇ›]

FOOT – a short, lax, high-back vowel with weak rounding [ʊ]; in Scotland and Northern Ireland words which elsewhere have the FOOT vowel have the BREW vowel instead.

NUT – a short, lax unrounded vowel with considerable variation in quality; in northern England those who do not speak RP are likely to have no distinction between the vowels of FOOT and NUT; in Scotland and much of Canada and the United States the vowel is higher mid-central [ʌ], in RP and in the southern hemisphere it is more open, a lower mid-central [ɐˆ].

LOCK – in England, including RP, in Scotland and the southern hemisphere a low-back, weakly rounded short vowel [ɒ]; in Ireland and North America a low-central or low-back unrounded vowel [ɑ˃] which, like the vowel of BAT, tends to be longer than the higher vowels. For many Canadians and Americans the vowels of LOCK and STAR are identical except for the following /r/ in the latter word-type. In New York City and Southern America the STAR vowel is more back, LOCK more forward.

TREE – articulated by all speakers in the high-front area; in some dialects there is length but no movement of the tongue [iː]; for other speakers the front of the tongue moves upward, [iⁱ], though of course there is not a great distance for it to move. In Cockney and in Broad Australian the vowel begins in higher mid-central position and has upward movement of the tongue-front [əⁱ].

BREW – articulated in the high-back area or more forward, between high-back and high-central; just as TREE may be long or have upward movement of the tongue-front, so BREW may be long [uː or u˂ː] or have upward gliding of the tongue-back [uᵘ or u˂ᵘ]. In Cockney and Broad Australian the vowel begins in higher mid-central position and then the back of the tongue moves upward [əᵘ].

DAY – generally articulated with the tongue-front moving upward from the mid-front position [eⁱ]; in northern England, Scotland, Ireland and variably elsewhere the vowel is long but nongliding [eː]; in Cockney and Broad Australian the beginning is lower mid-central [ʌⁱ].

TOE – generally articulated with the tongue-back moving upward; in RP and the southern hemisphere the vowel begins from a mid-central position, [əᵘ], in North America from a mid-back position, [oᵘ]; in Cockney and Broad Australian the beginning is lower mid-central, [ɐᵘ] in Scotland and Ireland and variably elsewhere the vowel may be mid-back long, with no gliding, [oː].

LAW – a long rounded vowel, articulated between low-back and mid-back [ɔː] in RP and the dialects influenced by it; somewhat lower, in the low-back area [ɔ˅] in North America (if a distinction is made between LAW and SPA); some southern Americans have an upward movement of the tongue-back beginning from low-back [ɔᵘ], and metropolitan New York City has a vowel which starts low-back and moves to mid-central [ɔᵊ]; in Cockney the upward-gliding vowel occurs in closed syllables, the centering one in open syllables.

TOY – begins in the low-back area or somewhat higher, with upward movement of the tongue front, [ɔⁱ]; the beginning may be somewhat higher or lower but variation is negligible.

TIE – a variety of articulations, mostly beginning in the low area, low-central or somewhat more forward or somewhat more back, followed by upward movement of the tongue-front – [a^{i}, a$^{‹i}$, a$^{›i}$]; many Londoners, South Africans, Australians, and Americans in the South and South Midland have little or no tongue movement – [a:] – when the vowel is final or followed by a voiced consonant, e.g. *why*, *wide*; other Americans and practically all Canadians have a mid-central beginning point, [ɐ^{i}] before a voiceless consonant, e.g. *white*.

NOW – similarly, a variety of articulations, mostly beginning in the low area, low-front or low-central, with upward movement of the tongue-back – [æ^{u}, a^{u}]; those who have a mid-central beginning point for the vowel of TIE have a similar beginning for NOW, [ɐ^{u}] – that is, whenever this diphthong occurs before a voiceless consonant; in Broad Australian and Cockney the beginning may be mid-front, [ɛ^{u}].

EAR, CHAIR, TOUR – in RP and the southern hemisphere these are diphthongs which begin near the vowels of CHICK, STEP, and FOOT, respectively, with subsequent movement of the tongue toward mid-central position [ɪ^{ə}, ɛ^{ə}, ʊ^{ə}]; in other non-rhotic dialects, most of England and Wales, southern US, eastern New England, they begin nearer the vowels of TREE, DAY, BREW, respectively, with the same mid-central offglide [i^{ə}, e^{ə}, u^{ə}]; in any non-rhotic dialect EAR-words are likely to rhyme with *idea*; in most of the US and Canada EAR is identical with the vowel of CHICK followed by /r/, and similarly CHAIR has the same vowel as STEP, and TOUR the same as FOOT. In other rhotic dialects the EAR, CHAIR, and TOUR vowels are about identical with the vowels of TREE, DAY, BREW, respectively.

FUR – in rhotic dialects this vowel is a mid-central, slightly rounded, comparatively long vowel articulated with the tongue drawn back and with a groove in the very tip; what is viewed as a sequence of vowel + R is actually an r-colored vowel – the groove and tongue retraction are present throughout articulation [ɜ:]. In non-rhotic dialects the vowel is equivalent except that there is no lip-rounding and, more to the point, there is no groove or retraction [ɜ:]. Among some older speakers in the New York City area and in parts of the Southern US the vowel is articulated with upward movement of the tongue front [ɜ^{i}] in checked syllables (e.g. *work*, *bird*, *first*).

DOOR, WAR – the distinction between these is not maintained in all dialects, though it is heavily used in dialects which retain the distinction. Where the distinction holds, the vowel of DOOR can be equated with that of TOE and the vowel of WAR with that of LAW, in both cases followed by a sonorant consonant in rhotic dialects [o^{r}, ɔ^{r}] or a centering offglide in non-rhotic ones [o^{ə}, ɔ^{ə}]. In rhotic dialects which do not have this distinction the articulation may range between [o] and [ɔ] but is likely to be nearer the latter, [ɔ^{r}]. Rhotic dialects are also likely to have the more open vowel, followed by centering offglide [ɔᵊ] or simple length [ɔː], in free variation or with the offglide in open syllables, the long vowel in closed ones. In non-rhotic dialects DOOR, WAR, and LAW may have the same vowel, or the first two may have a centering offglide and LAW a long vowel.

STAR – a long, unrounded low central or low back-central vowel. In non-rhotic dialects it is equivalent to the vowel of SPA; in rhotic dialects it differs from that vowel only in the presence of the sonorant consonant at the end.

FIRE, SOUR – equated with the vowels of TIE and NOW, respectively, plus either a sonorant consonant or the non-syllabic [ə] – [aⁱr, aᵘr or æᵘr] in rhotic dialects, triphthongal [aⁱə, aᵘə] in non-rhotic dialects. The triphthongal pronunciations may be reduced to centering diphthongs [aᵊ, æᵊ].

4.5 The incidence of vowels

As noted in section 4.2 English dialects differ in the occurrence of vowels in certain specific sets of words. What these occurrences are can best be understood by looking at some historical facts.

The following words, all spelled with the letter *a*, were pronounced with the same vowel phoneme until about the seventeenth century. Let us call it 'short A'.

nap hat dance command craft bath class father palm want water fall salt

And all of the following words had the same vowel, a different vowel phoneme that we may call 'short O'.

top hot bomb pond bother log long soft moth loss

The following words were pronounced with a diphthong AU, perhaps close to what is now heard in the word *house*:

law pause dawn laundry sausage

In about the seventeenth century the diphthong AU became a simple low-back vowel. At about the same time the short A vowel and short O vowel 'split', coming to be pronounced in very different ways in different environments – before /l/, after /w/, before voiceless fricatives, before some combinations of nasal + obstruent, and so on. Some of the allophones of short A became identical with some allophones of short O; some allophones of short A and some allophones of short O became identical with the reflex of the diphthong AU, but the details differ from dialect to dialect.

Consider the original short A words, above. The words *nap* and *hat* now have the low-front BAT vowel in all dialects, and *fall* and *salt* have the low-back LAW vowel for all speakers of English. In many dialects *father* and *palm* have the low-central vowel of SPA. The words *dance*, *command*, *craft*, *bath*, *class* represent parts of the vocabulary which may have the vowel of BAT or that of SPA (or *dance* and *command* may have the BAT vowel, while the others have the SPA vowel). *Water* and *want* may have the SPA vowel, the LAW vowel, or the LOCK vowel. The line of words representing the original short O may be pronounced all with the same vowel, or those on the right side with the vowel of LAW and those on the left with the LOCK vowel – and the dividing line may be in different places. Finally, the stressed vowel of polysyllabic words like *sausage* and *laundry* has, in some varieties of the language, become like LOCK and thus different from the LAW vowel of monosyllabic words with the original AU.

All these matters make it somewhat awkward to describe English vowels, but they have little or no effect on communication.

Some historical changes led to a redistribution of phonemes. As noted above, in much of North American English the vowel of EAR is, except for the /r/, identical with that of CHICK, though originally it was the same as the vowel of TREE, the vowel of CHAIR, originally like the vowel of DAY, is now like that of STEP, and so on. There has been a general lowering of vowels before /r/. This means that before an intervocalic /r/ certain contrasts existing in most English dialects have been lost in most Canadian–American varieties. The following list shows the possible contrasts of vowels before intervocalic /r/, and the braces indicate where this opposition may be NEUTRALIZED in North America.

ir	serious			curing	ur
ɪr	Syrian			curate	ʊr
er	Mary	furry	ɜr	story	or
ɛr	merry	hurry	ʌr	sorry	ɔr
ær	marry			starry	ar

4.6 Adding to the general inventory

Twenty-four vowels make quite a large inventory. Even if we consider the nine R vowels to be the equivalents of nine of the other vowels, with an /r/ added (which is possible for some varieties of English), the number 15 is still larger than the vowel inventory of many languages. Some dialects of English, however, have other vowel distinctions.

One kind of distinction is due to morpheme boundaries. For most speakers *praise* and *prays* sound the same, and *pride* and *pried*, *rose* and *rows*, *brood* and *brewed* are likewise homophonous pairs. (In Exercise 4B, below, we treat such pairs as being identical.) Some speakers, however, make a distinction: vowels are shorter when followed by a consonant (*praise*, *pride*, *rose*, *brood*) than when word-final (*pray*, *pry*, *row*, *brew*). The vowel remains long when a neutral suffix, #*z* or #*d*, is added, so that *prays* has a longer vowel than *praise*, and *rowed* may be different from *road*.

Similar differences of length or quality have arisen for one reason or another in certain areas. In the US, along the Atlantic coast from New York City to Baltimore, the vowel of BAT has 'split', into two vowels, a shorter, lower one before certain consonants and in words which are typically unstressed (e.g. *pat*, *back*, *as*, *than*, *cabin*, *can* 'be able') and a longer, higher one elsewhere (*grab*, *grabbing*, *pad*, *can* 'tin container').

4B EXERCISES

(a) The following monosyllabic words are in our transcription. Write each one in the usual orthography.

(i) /fɪt rɪč kɪn gɪft brɪsk ʃɪp
(ii) lɛǰ rɛst θrɛd brɛθ ǰɛm ðɛn
(iii) kæt cæp gæs stæk θæŋks ðæt
(iv) fʊl bʊk gʊd pʊʃ sʊt wʊlf
(v) kʌt sʌm lʌv brʌʃ flʌd θrʌst
(vi) nɒt tɒp flɒk skɒč dɒǰ bɒks
(vii) biik tiim fiist liif kwiin riič
(viii) meik trein beis čeinǰ seif veig
(ix) suup truuθ čuuz muuv fjuum kjuub
(x) roul poust mould ðouz čouk houp
(xi) lɔɔ brɔɔd čɔɔk gɔɔz θɔɔt sɔɔs
(xii) bait daim čaild straid wain θraiv
(xiii) ʃaut paund mauθ gauǰ haus naun
(xiv) point čois soil hoist void ǰoi
(xv) čirz sfir bird pirs klir nir
(xvi) fer skers prer sterz skwer rer
(xvii) hɜrt wɜrk vɜrb čɜrč ɜrθ nɜrs
(xviii) gard marč čarǰ harθ karv harʃ
(xix) kɔrk kwɔrt ʃɔrt nɔrθ wɔrn tɔrč
(xx) wair taird spair airn kwair/

(b) Transcribe the one-syllable words below, in your pronunciation, using our set of consonant and vowel symbols.

(i) plea
please
pleased
lease
least

(ii) list
chip
shift
thin
thing

(iii) wake
vague
rage
grave
space

(iv) wretch
stretch
wedge
jest
dress

(v) track
hatch
gasp
raft
badge

(vi) lock
ox
drop
bomb
romp

(vii) youth
use (noun)
use (verb)
Luke
Ruth

(viii) wood
should
pull
look
bush

(ix) ghost
those
oath
rose
vogue

(x) luck
numb
thus
crutch
judge

(xi) hawk
cause
fault
stalk
broad

(xii) moist
choice
coins
Lloyd
poise

(xiii) rise
grind
chime
knife
jive

(xiv) rouse
ground
crouch
spout
loud

(c) English has fairly numerous sets of homophones, or homonyms, like *pale* and *pail* or *cite*, *site*, and *sight*. Since they are pronounced the same, they are transcribed the same way in a phonological transcription: in our system /peil/ for the first set and /sait/ for the second. Each of the following transcriptions represents a set of homophones – two unless otherwise noted. See if you can write the words that are represented.

/sii/	/sɛl/
/biit/	/miit/ (3)
/breik/	/nait/
/loud/	/jouk/
/streit/	/vein/ (3)
/faul/	/plein/
/hjuu/	/rait/ (3)
/wiik/	/hiil/
/biič/	/seil/
/lɛd/	/piis/
/mein/	/meil/
/sou/ (3)	/piik/ (3)
/swiit/	/ræp/
/greit/	/steik/
/dæm/	/tou/
/dir/	/her/
/fɜr/	/bor/

(d) Another kind of homophonous set is seen in the words *tax* and *tacks*, or *find* and *fined*. In each case the two words are phonologically identical – they sound the same – but are morphologically different – they are different in word formation. We can show the morphological difference in our phonological representation. We write /tæk#s/ for *tacks* and just /tæks/ for *tax*, /fain#d/ for *fined* and /faind/ for *find*. The symbol # indicates that what follows is a suffix, and of course the symbol has no pronunciation.

In the following pairs of homophones, one of the two words has a suffix, which is always one of four consonants, /t d s z/; the other word has the same final consonant, but the consonant is not a suffix. Identify the words.

/deiz, dei#z/	/praid, prai#d/
/čeist, čeis#t/	/rouz, rou#z/
/trækt, træk#t/	/læps, læp#s/
/čuuz, čuu#z/	/toud, tou#d/
/bænd, bæn#d/	/nouz, nou#z/

4.7 Binary features for vowels

As stated previously, traditional categories for describing vowel quality have been high/mid/low for the vertical dimension and front/central/back for the horizontal. There is no physical reason for a three-way distinction in either dimension: vowel sounds can be articulated in any number of possible places or areas from the most front to the most back and from highest to lowest.

Articulated tongue positions make a continuum from front to back and from highest to lowest place of articulation. Categories could be less than three or more than three. For purposes of showing similarities and differences binary classification is most useful.

The most appropriate way of classifying the 24 vowels of our general inventory seems to require some 3-way, or ternary, distinctions as well as certain 2-way, or binary, categories. The classes of vowels are three: checked, free, and R; the degrees of tongue height are three: high, mid, low. On the other hand, it is necessary to recognize only two degrees of tongue-advancement, front vs back, or [+ front] vs [− front]. Checked vowels can be classified almost as we have already described them:

	[+ front]	[− front]
High	CHICK	FOOT
Mid	STEP	NUT
Low	BAT	LOCK

Turning to the free vowels we see that four of them are easily labeled with the same features:

	[+ front]	[− front]
High	TREE	BREW
Mid	DAY	TOE

Depending on dialect, as we have seen, these vowels are either long or up-gliding, front up-gliding in the case of [+ front] vowels, back up-gliding for the [− front] vowels. Further, [+ front] vowels are unrounded, [− front] vowels rounded.

To designate the free vowels which are low requires more features. The vowels of TIE and TOY are, generally, fronting diphthongs, that of NOW is a backing diphthong, and those of SPA and LAW are neither. LAW and TOY begin with lips rounded, the others do not. So we need three more features, [fronting], [backing], and [round]. Then these five are all free and low, and in addition:

[− round, + fronting]	TIE
[− round]	SPA
[− round, + backing]	NOW
[+ round, + fronting]	TOY
[+ round]	LAW

The R vowels can be designated with the feature R and other features already introduced:

High [+ front]	EAR
High [− front]	TOUR
Mid [+ front]	CHAIR
Mid [− front, − round]	FUR
Mid [− front, + round]	DOOR
Low [− round]	STAR
Low [+ round]	WAR
Low [+ fronting]	FIRE
Low [+ backing]	SOUR

Table 4.1 summarizes the vowel features.

Table 4.1 Vowel features

		Height	*Front*	*Class*	*Fronting*	*Backing*	*Round*
CHICK	/ɪ/	H	+	Ch			
STEP	/ɛ/	M	+	Ch			
BAT	/æ/	L	+	Ch			
FOOT	/ʊ/	H	−	Ch			
NUT	/ʌ/	M	−	Ch			
LOCK	/ɒ/	L	−	Ch			
TREE	/ii/	H	+	F			
DAY	/ei/	M	+	F			
BREW	/uu/	H	−	F			
TOE	/ou/	M	−	F			
TIE	/ai/	L		F	+		−
TOY	/oi/	L		F	+		+
NOW	/au/	L		F		+	−
SPA	/aa/	L		F			−
LAW	/ɔɔ/	L		F			+
EAR	/ir/	H	+	R			
CHAIR	/er/	M	+	R			
FUR	/ɜr/	M	−	R			−
DOOR	/or/	M	−	R			+
STAR	/ar/	L		R			−
WAR	/ɔr/	L		R			+
FIRE	/air/	L		R	+		
SOUR	/aur/	L		R		+	

4.8 The glides

The initial phonemes of *yet* and *wet* are classified as glides or semi-consonants. They differ from vowels in being [− syllabic] and are like vowels in these features:

[− consonantal]
[+ continuant]
[+ sonorant]
[− sibilant]

The glides /j/ and /w/ are the non-syllabic equivalents of the vowels /ɪ/ and /ʊ/, respectively. So they are both [+ voice, + high], and /j/ is [+ front, − round], /w/ [− front, + round].

The classification of /h/ is a greater problem. The initial sound of *head* is articulated by bringing the vocal cords close together and forcing air between them while they are, ordinarily, not vibrating. Thus from one point of view /h/ is a voiceless fricative like /f θ s ʃ/. However, it differs from these fricatives in two respects: the friction is produced in the larynx, not in the mouth; and it has no voiced counterpart as the oral fricatives do. Ordinarily voiceless, it may be voiced when it occurs between vowels, as in *ahead*.

From another point of view, if we examine a set of words like *he*, *hay*, *hat*, *hawk*, *hope*, *hoot*, we shall see that /h/ is articulated with the same tongue position and lip shape as the vowel that follows. From this point of view, /h/ is the voiceless equivalent of whatever vowel comes next, and this is one reason for considering it a glide – a vowel-like phoneme which does not function as a vowel. Another reason is that it occurs, like /j/ and /w/, only in syllable-initial position. /h/ is [− syl] like /j/ and /w/. Unlike them it is [− voice]. Otherwise it has no distinctive features; it is neither [+ high] nor [+ low], neither [+ front] nor [− front], neither [+ round] nor [− round].

4C EXERCISE WITH PHONEME CLASSES

Fifteen words are written below. Each word appears twice, first in the conventional spelling and then re-spelled in our phonemic notation. Under each phoneme symbol write the initial letter of the class to which that phoneme belongs – V(owel), G(lide), L(iquid), N(asal), F(ricative), or S(top). Use V for any checked vowel or free vowel; use V for an R vowel if you don't pronounce an /r/ and VL if you do pronounce an /r/. The first three words are done as examples.

shrimp	/ʃrɪmp/ FLVNS	chain	/čein/ SVN	dwarf	/dwɔrf/ SGVLF
quilt	/kwɪlt/	gland	/glænd/	muse	/mjuuz/
breathe	/briið/	junk	/ǰʌŋk/	flesh	/flɛʃ/
stark	/stark/	woods	/wʊdz/	length	/lɛŋθ/
strange	/streinǰ/	clown	/klaʊn/	mirth	/mɜrθ/

4D EXERCISE ON VOWEL INCIDENCE

Sort out the following words according to the vowel phoneme which you have in the stressed or only syllable, putting all the words with one vowel phoneme in one group, those with a different vowel in another group, and so on. The sorting is to be done on the basis of your pronunciation, not what a dictionary says. You may finish with as few as two groups or as many as five.

ham hack wax swamp squad last lost clause psalm
coffee August after example often lot collar caller

4.9 Summary

The description of English vowels is complicated by the fact of dialect difference among speakers of the language. A fairly obvious difference is in pronunciation, or **phonetic realization** of the vowels. More subtle differences exist in the **inventories** of vowel phonemes and their incidence of occurrence. We have used, first, a general inventory of 24 vowel phonemes, divided into six **checked vowels**, nine **free vowels**, and nine **R vowels**. The inventories of specific dialect areas are described in relation to this general inventory; specific inventories are often smaller than the general inventory since a distinction which exists in some parts of the English-speaking world is not maintained by other speakers – and the general inventory includes, essentially, all vowels distinguished in any dialect area. However, we have noted that there are additional phonemes which must be recognized for some dialects. We have recognized **rhotic** and **non-rhotic dialects**; in the former the R vowels are pronounced with constriction – the phoneme /r/ – following the vowel; in the latter there is no /r/ unless a vowel follows immediately.

Differences of incidence reflect historical facts. The most complex difference of incidence concerns the low vowels, which at an earlier time underwent various changes. An original 'short A' came to have quite different pronunciations in different positions of occurrence, and an original 'short O' likewise acquired different positional variants. Some allophones of short A became identical with some allophones of short O and with the reflex of the diphthong AU, but the results were different in different dialects.

Vowels differ from one another in several kinds of features, the most important of which is **quality**, determined by the size and shape of the oral chamber in which particles of air are vibrating. Traditionally, vowel quality has been described through a matrix of two dimensions, **tongue height** (high, mid, low) and **tongue advancement** (front, central, back), with the additional feature of **lip shape** (rounded, unrounded). Vowels also differ in **length** (long, short), **complexity** (monophthong, diphthong), and **tenseness** (tense, lax). Comparing the checked vowels, as a group, with the free vowels, as a group, we can say that checked vowels are short, monophthongal, and lax, while free vowels are long or diphthongal and tense, but the details differ so greatly from dialect to dialect that these categories are not used in this book.

The feature distinctions which are most relevant are seen to be binary in some cases, ternary in others. In addition to the three classes names previously mentioned – checked, free, R – and the three degrees of tongue height, high, mid, low, there are four binary features: ± front, ± round, ± fronting, ± backing.

The glides /j/ and /w/ are the [– syllabic] counterparts of [+ high] vowels; /j/ is [+ front], /w/ [– front].

The phoneme /h/ is not like any other English phoneme. It is a sort of voiceless vowel occurring only at the beginning of syllables, and we classify it as a glide.

4A FEEDBACK

(a)	II	III	(b)	V
5	loaf	3 wild	e	husk
2	lake	6 point	f	fox
7	shout	8 boost	b	rest
8	bruise	1 fiend	d	wolf
3	like	7 pound	a	sift
1	neat	2 range	c	fact
4	hawk	5 bolt		
6	coin	4 haunt		

4B FEEDBACK

(a)

(i) fit rich kin gift brisk ship
(ii) ledge rest thread breath gem then
(iii) cat chap gas stack thanks that
(iv) full book good push soot wolf
(v) cut sum/some love brush flood thrust
(vi) not top flock Scotch dodge box
(vii) beak team feast leaf queen reach
(viii) make train base change safe vague
(ix) soup truth choose move fume cube
(x) roll/role post mold those choke hope
(xi) law broad chalk gauze thought sauce
(xii) bite dime child stride wine thrive
(xiii) shout pound mouth gouge house noun
(xiv) point choice soil hoist void joy
(xv) cheers sphere beard pierce clear near
(xvi) fare/fair scarce prayer stairs square rare
(xvii) hurt work verb church earth nurse
(xviii) guard march charge hearth carve harsh
(xix) cork quart short north warn torch
(xx) wire tired spire iron choir/quire

(b)

(i) /plii	(ii) lɪst	(iii) weik	(iv) rɛč
pliiz	čɪp	veig	strɛč
pliizd	ʃɪft	reiǰ	wɛǰ
liis	θɪn	greiv	ǰɛst
list	θɪŋ	speis	drɛs
(v) træk	(vi) lɒk	(vii) juuθ	(viii) wʊd
hæë	ɒks	juus	ʃʊd
gæsp	drɒp	juuz	pʊl
ræft	bɒm	luuk	lʊk
bæǰ	rɒmp	ruuθ	bʊʃ
(ix) goust	(x) lʌk	(xi) hɔɔk	(xii) moist
ðouz	nʌm	kɔɔz	čois
ouθ	ðʌs	fɔɔlt	koinz
rouz	krʌč	stɔɔk	loid
voug	ǰʌǰ	brɔɔd	poiz

(xiii)	raiz	(xiv)	rauz
	graind		graund
	čaim		krauč
	naif		spaut
	ǰaiv		laud/

(c)

see, sea	sell, cell
beat, beet	meet, meat, mete
brake, break	night, knight
load, lode	yolk, yoke
strait, straight	vain, vein, vane
foul, fowl	plane, plain
hue, hew (Hugh)	right, rite, write (wright)
week, weak	heal, heel
beach, beech	sail, sale
lead, led	peace, piece
main, mane	mail, male
so, sew, sow	peak, peek, pique
sweet, suite	rap, wrap
grate, great	stake, steak
dam, damn	toe, tow
deer, dear	hair, hare
fir, fur	boar, bore

(d)

daze, days	pride, pried
chaste, chased	rose, rows
tract, tracked	lapse, laps
choose, chews	toad, towed
band, banned	nose, knows

4C FEEDBACK

shrimp	/ʃrɪmp/ FL V NS	chain	/čein/ S V N	dwarf	/dwɔrf/ SGV L F
quilt	/kwɪlt/ SGV LS	gland	/glænd/ SLVN S	muse	/mjuuz/ NG VF
breathe	/briið/ SLV F	junk	/ǰʌŋk/ S VN S	flesh	/flɛʃ/ FL VF

stark	/stark/ FSV L S	woods	/wʊdz/ G VSF	length	/lɛŋθ/ L VN F
strange	/streinǰ/ FSLV NS	clown	/klaʊn/ SLV F	mirth	/mɜrθ/ NV L F

4D FEEDBACK

There is no right answer. One way of describing the possible distribution of these words into vowel categories is to say that:

ham, hack, wax have /æ/, the vowel of BAT:
after, example, last may have the same vowel;
and the other words may not have that vowel.

If the other words fall into three groups, a possible distribution is:

psalm	collar	caller
	lot	clause

with the remaining words in the *collar* group or the *caller* group or divided among the two.

5

Syllables and Stress

5.1 Syllables

Every English word consists of at least one syllable, and many words have two, three, four, or more syllables. The syllable is a unit that is hard to define with scientific rigor but fairly easy to recognize. Anyone can tell the number of syllables in, for example, *cat*, *delay*, *wonderful*, *geography*, and *metamorphosis* (though we may not agree on the number of syllables in *girl*, *file*, *sour*, and certain other words), but no one knows just what physical action of the speaker creates a syllable.

In discussing syllables we are concerned with two kinds of facts, the STRUCTURE of a syllable and the RELATIVE PROMINENCE of syllables when two or more occur in sequence.

Every syllable has a structure, a sequence of some of the phonemes of the language. The syllable *cat* consists of the phonemes /k/, /æ/, and /t/ in that order; the syllables *act* and *tack* have the same three phonemes but in different sequences. In discussing syllable structure we want to tell not merely the structures of specific syllables; we want to describe what general structures are possible for English syllables and what structures are impossible. For example, can there be syllables like /ktæ/ or /tkæ/ or /ætk/? Different languages have different kinds of syllable structure. Describing the possible syllable structures is part of describing the sound system of a language.

Every English syllable has a center or PEAK, an element which is [+ syllabic]. As we have seen, all vowels are [+ syllabic] by definition. In addition, the sonorant consonants /m, n, ŋ, l, r/ become syllabic in certain positions, as described in section 5.9. Thus every word, phrase, or sentence has as many syllables as it has syllabic elements, and vice versa.

The peak may be preceded by one or more non-syllabic elements, which constitute the ONSET of the syllable, and it may be followed by one or more non-syllabic elements which constitute the CODA. In *cat* the onset is /k/, the peak is /æ/, and the coda is /t/; in *tree* the onset is /tr/, the peak is /ii/, and there is no coda – or the coda is zero; the word *ox* has a zero onset, the peak is

/ɒ/, and the coda is /ks/. These three syllable structures can be shown as follows:

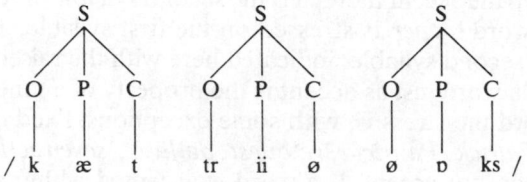

More will be said about syllable structure in the next section of this chapter. First, however, we need to take up the matter of relative prominence of syllables in sequence, in a word or in a tone unit.

Every utterance consists of at least one tone unit, and every tone unit consists of at least one syllable. If there are two or more syllables, one of them is more prominent than the other(s). In a brief utterance of one tone unit such as

Pat took ten **books**

The syllable *books* is likely to be most prominent, indicated here in bold face. We call this prominence the ACCENT of the tone unit. The syllable *books* has the accent, or is the accented syllable. However, a speaker can create certain effects – transmit certain subtle meanings – by accenting a different word:

Pat took **ten** books
Pat **took** ten books
Pat took ten books

What these different meanings are is discussed in chapter 9.

Accent is primarily a change of pitch. In a statement *Pat took ten* **books**, the pitch falls – the frequency of vibration of the vocal cords decreases – as the vowel of the accented syllable is articulated. In a question, *Pat took ten* **books**?, at least in one possible rendition, the pitch rises in the same place – the vocal cords increase their frequency of vibration. Along with the change of pitch there is typically a greater INTENSITY, more force with which air is expelled from the lungs, and greater LENGTH, or duration, in the vowel and other sonorant elements of the accented syllable. Using a binary system we say that the accented syllable is [+ accent] and an unaccented syllable is [− accent].

If an accented word is polysyllabic, the accent is associated with one particular syllable of the word, the syllable which is stressed, or has STRESS.

If we replace *books* in our example with *papers* and keep the accent on the last word, the first syllable of the word bears the accent; if we replace it with *reviews* and keep the accent there, it is the second syllable of *reviews* which is accented. The word ˈ*paper* is stressed on the first syllable, and *reˈviews* is stressed on the second syllable, indicated here with the raised tick. Stress is the property of a word just as accent is the property of a tone unit. In every polysyllabic word the stress is, with some exceptions, fixed on a particular syllable; thus, ˈ*Patrick*, *Paˈtricia*, *reˈquest*, *deˈliver*, ˈ*seven*, *eˈleven*. Stress is, then, the potential for accent. If a word is accented within a tone unit, its stressed (or only) syllable is the accented syllable of the tone unit. Of course, a word pronounced alone constitutes a tone unit by itself, and its stressed or only syllable is accented.

Operating with a binary system we say that some syllables are [+ stress] and others [− stress]; a syllable which is [+ stress] may be [+ accent] or [− accent].

In a tone unit every major word (roughly, every noun, verb, adjective, and adverb) has a stress, indicated below with a raised tick before the stressed syllable, and one word has accent as well as its own stress.

ˈPat ˈtook ˈten ˈ**books**
Paˈtricia reˈquested ˈseven reˈ**views**
ˈPatrick deˈlivered eˈ**le**ven ˈpapers

When a syllable is stressed but not accented, it does not have a change of pitch. It may be spoken at a slightly higher pitch than an unstressed syllable, and it has greater length and intensity; stressed syllables are relatively stronger and longer, unstressed syllables weaker and shorter. The greater strength of a stressed syllable is evidenced in, among other things, the aspiration of voiceless stops. Compare the aspirated /p/ [pʰ] of ˈ*Pat*, ˈ*Patrick*, and the first consonant of ˈ*paper* with the unaspirated /p/ of *Paˈtricia* and the second consonant of ˈ*paper*. The weakness of an unaccented syllable is observed in, among other things, its vowel. The first and last syllables of *Paˈtricia* have a schwa, /ə/, a vowel which does not occur in stressed syllables. The same vowel occurs in the unstressed syllables of ˈ*paper* and ˈ*seven* and, variably, in the first and last syllables of *reˈquested*. The succession of strong stressed syllables and weak unstressed syllables in English utterances is responsible for a kind of rhythm which is called STRESS TIMING (chapter 9).

The two kinds of facts, syllable structure and syllable prominence, are thus interrelated. The structures of stressed and unstressed syllables differ in certain small ways. Some elements can occur only as the peaks of unstressed syllables, not as the peaks of stressed syllables, and some phonemes have different pronunciations in stressed and unstressed syllables. Syllable structure and syllable prominence are interrelated in another way: the onset of an unstressed syllable is generally less precise than the onset of a stressed one. Consider the words *de'pend* and *'deepen*. In *de'pend*, with a stressed second syllable, it is easy to recognize where the first syllable ends and the second syllable begins. In the word *'deepen*, on the other hand, in which the first syllable is stressed, the syllable division is not so obvious. The coda of the first syllable and the onset of the second syllable are not clearly separated; the /p/ may belong to the first syllable or to the second. Thus 'fuzziness' or ambiguity in some syllable boundaries is part of the English sound system.

5.2 Syllable structure

Every language has phonemes, and every language has its own common patterns in which phonemes are arranged to form syllables and the syllables are arranged to form larger units. In some languages all syllables consist of one consonant followed by one vowel (CV), so that no word has a cluster of consonants or of vowels; any word has the form CV, or CVCV, or CVCVCV . . . , depending on how many syllables it has. In English there are never more than two vowels in sequence in a single word (as in *neon*, *poet*, *cruel*, *radio*), but clusters of two, three, or more consonants are fairly common: *prescribe*, *district*, *splints*, *tempts*, for example. Still, not just any two, three, or more consonants can cluster. There are definite limitations, or CONSTRAINTS, on co-occurrence. PHONOTACTICS is the part of phonology which studies and describes such constraints. Phonotactics is the topic of chapter 7, in which the structures of polysyllabic words are examined. In this section we want to treat only the possible structure of a single syllable.

In the exercises of chapter 4 you designated certain words in a special way by writing the class name (*V*owel, *G*lide, *L*iquid, *N*asal, *F*ricative, or *S*top) to which each phoneme of a word belongs; thus *shrimp* /ʃrɪmp/ was designated FLVNS, and *quilt* /kwɪlt/ was shown as SGVLS. Designations like these are called CANONICAL FORMS. We can recognize the canonical form of a syllable, a morpheme, or a word; of course, an item like *shrimp* or *quilt* is at the same time a single syllable, a single morpheme, and a single word. Canonical forms enable us to describe the possible shapes of syllables, morphemes, and words in a language and to compare the shapes of two or more words or syllables. Canonical forms can be indicated with full information about classes (V, G, L, N, F, S) or by just indicating *V*owels and *C*onsonants; *neon* and *poet*, for instance, both have the canonical form CVVC; *plant* and *cramp* are both CCVCC, or, more specifically, SLVNS (stop, liquid, vowel, nasal, stop). For a polysyllabic word the canonical form must include an indication of stress. The words *comic* and *bucket* have the canonical form 'CVCVC, and *arrest* and *event* share the canonical form V'CVCC. In English a canonical form CVC, as in *bed*, *nut*, *sack*, *love*, is obviously more common than CVCV'VCV, as in *tapioca*.

We start by investigating the canonical forms of some one-syllable words. We limit our investigation to words which consist of just one morpheme, without a suffix. Words with non-syllabic suffixes, like *warm-th* /wɔrmθ/, *tempt-s* /tɛmpts/, and *grasp-ed* /græspt/ end with unusual clusters of consonants. No word without a suffix has such clusters of consonants as /-rmθ/ or /-mpts/ or /-spt/. Clusters like these are considered separately, in chapter 8.

A word of one syllable has one vowel, of course. The vowel may be initial in the word (e.g. *and*); it may be preceded by one consonant (e.g *band*), two consonants (e.g. *bland*), or three consonants (e.g. *strand*), but no more. In a word without suffix the vowel may be final (e.g. *go*), or followed by one consonant (e.g. *goat*), two consonants (*toast*), or three consonants (*corpse*), but no more. All the possibilities for a monosyllabic, monomorphemic word can be expressed in this formula:

$$C_0^3 \quad V \quad C_0^3$$

That is, it consists of one vowel preceded by from zero to three consonants and followed by from zero to three consonants.

5A EXERCISE

Here are 25 one-syllable words:

act bald blame chain clay crisp dog drip dwarf edge faith flaw grasp home ice lend ox screw skin snow split spring squaw stretch twin

(a) Which words have a zero onset?
(b) Which have an onset of one consonant (C-)?
(c) Which have an onset of two consonants (CC-)?
(d) Which have an onset of three consonants (CCC-)?
(e) In words with a CCC- onset, what is the first consonant?

5A FEEDBACK AND COMMENT

(a) act, edge, ice, ox
(b) bald, chain, dog, faith, home, lend
(c) blame, clay, crisp, drip, dwarf, flaw, grasp, skin, snow, twin
(d) screw, splint, spray, squaw, stretch
(e) /s/

These words show only a sample of the consonants which can occur in initial position. We can see, however, that initial clusters of two consonants fall into several specific types:

1 certain consonants followed by /l/ (Cl-): blame, clay, flaw
2 certain consonants followed by /r/ (Cr-): crisp, drip, grasp
3 certain consonants followed by /w/ (Cw-): dwarf, twin
4 /s/ followed by certain consonants (sC-): skin, snow

Initial clusters of three consonants are essentially combinations of type 4, above, with types 1, 2, and 3:

sCl-: splint
sCr-: screw, spray, stretch
sCw-: squaw

5B EXERCISE

Here are 25 more words.

bee cast corpse dog false hemp joke lynx nose
opt owe prompt pulse quartz scab silk spark
squirt stand task traipse verb young world zoo

(a) Which words have a zero coda?
(b) Which have a one-consonant coda (-C)?
(c) Which have a -CC coda?
(d) Which have a -CCC coda?

5B FEEDBACK AND COMMENT

(a) bee, owe, zoo
(b) dog, joke, nose, scab, young
(c) cast, false, hemp, opt, pulse, silk, spark, squirt, stand, task, traipse, verb
(d) corpse, lynx, prompt, quartz, world

A variety of single consonants can occur as the coda, only a few of which are illustrated here. Clusters of two consonants in final position are of these types:

1 /l/ followed by certain consonants (-lC): false, silk
2 /r/followed by certain consonants (-rC): spark, squirt, verb

3 a nasal consonant followed by certain other consonants (-NC): hemp, stand
4 less commonly, clusters of stops and of stop and fricative: opt, cast, task, traipse

Clusters of three consonants generally consist of a liquid or a nasal followed by two stops or a stop and a fricative: corpse, lynx, prompt, quartz, world. These different combinations of consonants are dealt with in more detail in chapter 7.

5.3 Strong and weak syllables

The stressed vowel of a polysyllabic word can always be identified with the vowel of some monosyllabic word. For example, the stressed vowel of *aroma* is the same as the vowel of *row*, and the stressed vowel of *cinema* is the same as the vowel of *sin*. To identify unstressed vowels is not always so easy. The most common unstressed vowel is the one which occurs in the first and third syllables of *aroma*; we call it a SCHWA and symbolize it as /ə/. The schwa also occurs in the third syllable of *cinema*. The vowel in the second syllable of *cinema* may be /ə/ or a higher vowel /ɨ/, depending on who is speaking.

Numerous English words contain one stressed vowel and a schwa in every unstressed syllable. Here are some examples:

salad	command	adequate	annoyance
purpose	suppose	bulletin	attainment
talcum	today	elephant	tremendous

Rather than talking about 'the first syllable, the third syllable', etc., we will do better to designate syllables by position in the word – INITIAL, MEDIAL, or FINAL – and by position in relation to stress – PRETONIC, TONIC or POSTTONIC. (Any syllable which is not tonic, whether pretonic or posttonic, is ATONIC.) Thus the words which end the four columns above can be described in this way:

tal	cum	to	day
Initial	Final	Initial	Final
Tonic	Posttonic	Pretonic	Tonic

e	le	phant	tre	men	dous
Initial	Medial	Final	Initial	Medial	Final
Tonic	Posttonic	Posttonic	Pretonic	Tonic	Posttonic

In long words there is often a sequence of 'strong' and 'weak' (or 'heavy' and 'light') syllables alternating with one another, but in a somewhat irregular way. Examples:

```
under'stand     'penetrate     pene'tration
+  -   +         + - +         + -  + -
'architecture   'caterpillar   prestidigi'tation
+   -+  -         +-  + -        +  -+- + -
'modify     modifi'cation
  + -+        + -- + -
```

The strong unstressed syllables are similar to stressed syllables in certain ways:

1 Strong syllables never contain a schwa. (Note that this does not mean that weak syllables always contain a schwa.)
2 The onset of a strong medial syllable is much clearer than the onset of weak medial syllable. The third syllable of *architecture* clearly begins with /t/, that of *caterpillar* with /p/, and that of *prestidigitation* with /d/; on the other hand, the /n/ of *penetrate*, the /t/ of *caterpillar*, and the /d/ of *modify* do not obviously belong to either the first or the second syllable of their respective words. This matter of syllable division is studied at greater length in the next section.
3 Voiceless stops at the onset of strong unstressed syllables are aspirated just as they are at the onset of stressed syllables; compare the aspirated /t/ of '*penetrate* and '*architecture* with the unaspirated /t/ of '*caterpillar*. The variation of phonemes in different environments is the topic of chapter 6.
4 Just as a stressed syllable is potentially an accented syllable, so a strong syllable is potentially a stressed syllable. A phrase like *understand the answer*, with the accent on *answer*, may be

   under'stand the '**an**swer

   but is more likely to be

   'under'stand the '**an**swer

   or

   'understand the '**an**swer.

   The syllable *stand* remains strong even when unstressed, just as *un-* is strong whether stressed or not. This kind of rhythmic variation in stress is dealt with in chapters 9 and 12.

When there are two or more pretonic syllables, the syllable immediately before the tonic syllable is usually weak, the next one (moving to the left) is likely to be strong, the next one weak, and so forth. Similarly, among posttonic syllables the one immediately after the tonic syllable is typically weak, the next one strong, and so on in an alternation of weak and strong.

5C EXERCISE

In the next group of words the vowel letters are italicized. Put a minus sign (−) under each letter which represents the vowel of a weak syllable and a plus (+) under each letter that stands for the vowel of a strong syllable. Underline the + of the stressed syllable.

(a) *comprehensibility* (b) *reconsideration*
(c) *autobiographic* (d) *individuality*

There may be two weak syllables in succession. Mark the syllables of the following words as you did those above.

(e) *justification* (f) *eligibility*
(g) *adequate* (h) *feminine*
(i) *gelatin* (j) *Senegalese*

Before the stressed syllable there are never more than two weak syllables in succession. Thus, if the stressed syllable is the fourth syllable of the word,

S S S 'S...

either the first syllable is strong (as in *justification*)

justifi'cation
+ −− +−

or the second syllable is (as in *hallucination*)

halluci'nation
− + − + −

After the stressed syllable there may be two weak syllables, as in some of the examples above. There may be three weak syllables, but only in words with certain endings:

candidacy gentlemanly hesitancy impenetrable
± − − − ± − − − ± − − − − ± − − −

A tone unit may thus contain four kinds of syllables:

(a) a syllable which is [+ accent] (and also [+ stress] and [+ strong]);
(b) one or more syllables which are [+ stress] (and also [+ strong]) but [− accent];
(c) one or more syllables which are [+ strong] but [− stress] (and therefore [− accent]);
(d) one or more syllables which are [− strong] (and therefore [− stress] and [− accent]).

To put it another way, these four kinds of syllables are related in a hierarchy which can be represented like this:

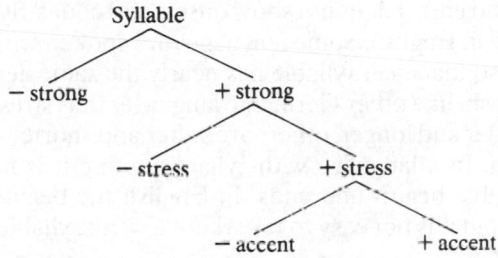

Some phonological analyses of English regard these four kinds of syllables as four degrees of syllable stress and label them as follows:

Primary (corresponding to [+ accent])
Secondary (approximately corresponding to [+ stress, − accent])
Tertiary (generally equivalent to [+ strong, − stress])
Quaternary or weak ([− strong])

(We say 'approximately corresponding' and 'generally equivalent' because there are some differences of interpretation.)

In a four-degree analysis the degrees of 'stress' are indicated by numbers from 1 to 4 or with an acute accent (´) for primary, a circumflex accent (^) for secondary, a grave accent (`) for tertiary, and no mark for quaternary

2 4 3 4 2 4 1 4
Patrick understood Patricia Pâtrick ùnderstood Patrícia.

Most dictionaries mark three kinds of syllables in single words, with a heavier tick before or after the stressed (and therefore accentable) syllable, a weaker tick before or after a strong unstressed syllable, and no mark after a weak syllable. Though there is considerable agreement in recognizing different degrees of syllabic prominence, it is not so certain that these actually refer to different degrees of stress. The last syllable of ˈ*operate* sounds much like the third syllable of *opeˈration* whereas the last syllable of ˈ*opera* does not. Perhaps this similarity has led many people to regard stress as something quantifiable – to think that the third syllable of *operation* has the maximum amount of some substance, the third syllable of *operate* a lesser amount, and the third syllable of *opera* little or none.

5.4 Syllable division

In part of the discussion above vowel letters were underlined to show the peaks of syllables in a word. This form of marking does not indicate where the syllables begin and end; it does not show onsets and codas. Syllable division is not an easy topic in English. Some languages are spoken with syllable timing (see chapter 9), so that each syllable has nearly the same degree of loudness and length. English, like other Germanic languages, has stress timing; certain syllables are louder and longer, others are softer and shorter and usually have a reduced vowel. In a language with syllable timing it is fairly easy to say where each syllable begins and ends. In English the beginning of a strong syllable is clear, but it is not easy to tell where a weak syllable begins unless it is an initial syllable.

A dictionary provides information about how a *written* word should be syllabified – where it can be divided in case one has to put part of it on one line and the remainder on the next line. The dictionary indicates syllable divisions according to certain conventions which have been in use among printers since the eighteenth century. Insofar as the conventions are systematic, they are based on two principles: (1) recognition of certain prefixes and suffixes, which are not divided (*mis.treat*, *un.able*, *free.dom*, *work.ing*); (2) different treatment according to whether the vowel letters A, E, I (or Y), O, and U are 'long' or 'short' – that is, whether they represent free vowels or checked vowels, respectively. If the vowel is 'long', it ends the syllable and the next letter goes in the following syllable, but if the vowel is 'short', the next letter goes with the preceding vowel letter. Thus we have, in writing:

ra.di.al, sa.vor	but	rad.ic.al, sav.age
le.gal, me.di.um	but	leg.a.cy, med.i.cine
fi.nal, ri.val	but	fin.ish, riv.er
co.pi.ous, so.lo	but	op.er.a, sol.id
pu.ny, stu.di.ous	but	pun.ish, stud.y

Note that the first principle takes precedence over the second: we write, for example, *fad.ing* and *writ.er*, not *fa.ding* and *wri.ter*.

Does the second principle, above, also apply to speech? Can we say that a free vowel typically comes at the end of a syllable but a checked vowel 'pulls' the following consonant into its syllable – that, for example, the /p/ of *copious* begins the second syllable but the /p/ of *copy* is at the end of the first syllable? No. Various people, including some linguists, have been misled by the printers' conventions into thinking that there is a similar difference of syllable division in speech. It is more accurate to say that in both these words /p/ is AMBISYLLABIC: in different pronunciations (by the same person) it may end one syllable or begin the next one. There is no clear syllable break. We represent the syllable division this way:

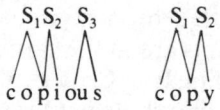

Similarly, when consonant clusters like *pl-*, *dw-*, *gr-*, *st-* (clusters which occur word-initially) are between vowels, the first consonant is ambisyllabic:

In these examples the intervocalic consonant, or the first consonant of an intervocalic cluster, is ambisyllabic because it comes between a stressed vowel and an unstressed one, or between two unstressed vowels. When a consonant, or a cluster like *st-*, *dr-*, etc., comes before the vowel of a strong syllable – whether stressed or not – the consonant or the cluster is clearly in that syllable: *re'peat*, *de'clare*, *de'stroy*, *'pene trate*. Compare *'deepen* and *de'pend*, the noun *'record* and the verb *re'cord*.

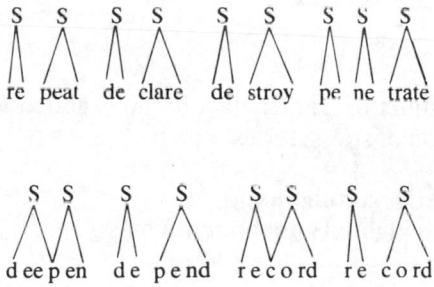

What are the rules for syllabifying spoken English words?

1 If two vowels occur in sequence, the syllable break is between the vowels (V.V): *ne.on*, *cha.os*, *cru.el(ty)*, *bi.o(logy)*, *re.a(lity)*. As we have noted

before, the first of the two vowels is always a free vowel. (Here and in what follows, we indicate the syllable division with a dot.)

2 If one consonant occurs between two vowels and the second is strong, whether stressed or not, the consonant is part of the second syllable: *re.ˈpent*, *va.ˈca(tion)*, *(de)bo.ˈnaire*, *(ˈlon)gi. tude*.

If one consonant occurs between a strong vowel and a weak one, the consonant is ambisyllabic; we represent this with the symbol ˆ before the ambisyllabic consonant: *ˈcoˆpy*, *ˈcoˆpi.ous*, *ˈmoˆdel*, *ˈdeˆvil*, *ˈciˆneˆma*. When a single consonant occurs between two weak vowels, the consonant may be ambisyllabic – *ˈciˆneˆma*, *ˈpoˆsiˆtive* – or it may go in the syllable with the second weak vowel – *ˈciˆne.ma*, *ˈpoˆsi.tive*.

3 If two vowels are separated by a consonant cluster, syllable division depends on what consonants are in the cluster. If the cluster is of the type which can occur word-initially (sC-, Cr-, Cl-, Cw-, sCr-, etc.) and the following vowel is strong, the whole cluster is part of the syllable with the strong vowel: *Pa.ˈtri(cia)*, *de.ˈcline*, *re.ˈquire*, *su.ˈspect* (verb), *di.ˈstress*.

If the second vowel is weak, the first consonant of the cluster is ambisyllabic: *ˈsaˆcred*, *ˈproˆblem*, *ˈproˆbaˆbly*, *ˈmaˆjeˆsty*, *ma.ˈjeˆstic*, *ca.ˈtaˆstroˆphe*.

4 If the consonant cluster is one which cannot occur in initial position, the consonants are divided in such a way that the second syllable begins with a single consonant or a cluster which can occur initially: *can.dy*, *at.las*, *shel.ter*, *em.blem*, *pan.try*, *car.pen.ter*. Note that two consonants which are in the same syllable if they are word-final (e.g. *wind*, *shelve*) go into separate syllables if they occur word-medially: *win.dow*, *sil.ver*, not *wind.ow*, *silv.er*.

In chapter 7 we examine various consonant clusters. In chapter 8 we consider some more variable kinds of syllable division.

5.5 Suffixes and stress

When a prefix or suffix of Old English origin is added to a word, it has no effect on the position of stress; for example:

ˈbrother ˈbrotherly ˈbrotherhood
ˈthoughtful unˈthoughtful unˈthoughtfulness

In contrast, words of Greek, Latin, or Romance origin often show a shift of stress when an affix is added or changed:

ˈorigin oˈriginal origiˈnality
ˈphotograph phoˈtography photoˈgraphic

As a result, the full vowel of one word becomes a reduced vowel in a related word, and vice versa. Compare the first vowel of *origin* and *original*, the second vowel of *photograph* and *photography*.

5D EXERCISE

In the following pairs of words mark the stressed syllable with a superior tick and put a + under each strong syllable whether stressed or unstressed.

(a)	a tom a to mic	(h)	am bi gu ous am bi gu i ty
(b)	Ca na da Ca na di an	(i)	com pose com po si tion
(c)	de fine de fi ni tion	(j)	con ti nent con ti nen tal
(d)	me lo dy me lo dic	(k)	mo di fy mo di fi ca tion
(e)	Ja pan Ja pa nese	(l)	o ri gin o ri gi nal
(f)	pa rent pa ren tal	(m)	in vite in vi ta tion
(g)	ter ri fy ter ri fic	(n)	ca ta stro phe ca ta stro phic

5.6 Compounds and some other words

A compound word consists of two (or possibly more) words, each of which has its own stress as an independent word. Many compound words keep the stress on the first word, and the stressed vowel of the second word is strong but unstressed. Some random examples:

ˈkeyhole	ˈlandlady	ˈmotorcycle	ˈair conditioned
+ +	+ +	+ +	+ +
exˈpressway	ˈtattletale	comˈputer screen	ˈMain Street
+ +	+ +	+ +	+ +

A smaller number of compounds have equal stress in the two parts. If the compound is spoken alone or is the accented part of a larger tone unit, the second word has the accented syllable.

ˈapple ˈpie ˈkitchen ˈsink ˈFifth ˈAvenue

A few compounds are stressed differently by different people:

ˈice cream *or* ˈice ˈcream ˈweek end *or* ˈweek ˈend

In a number of words which were once compounds the vowel of the second part has been reduced (ˈ*breakfast*, ˈ*cupboard*), and many historic compounds are no longer recognizable as such (ˈ*nostril*, ˈ*sheriff*, ˈ*stirrup*, ˈ*window*). In British English this sort of reduction has gone farther than in North American English: *nobody* and *strawberry*, for instance, have a full vowel in the penult in North America; in Britain and the southern hemisphere they are apt to have /ə/ in the penult or to lose the vowel altogether and become two-syllable words. Compare typical British and American pronunciations of such words as the following, which are not compounds:

	British	American
ceremony, difficulty	± – – –	± – + –
necessary territory	± – – –	± – + –
or	± – –	
Lancaster Rochester	± – –	± + –

5E EXERCISE

(a) The words below are all spelled with *-man* as the second element. Some of the words are full compounds; *-man* is strong and has the full vowel /æ/. Other words are reduced compounds; *-man* is weak and has /ə/. Which are the full compounds? (We may not all agree.)

businessman chairman Congressman draftsman fireman foreman freshman gentleman kinsman layman madman mailman marksman midshipman patrolman policeman postman salesman seaman watchman workman woodsman

(b) Similarly, written words in which *-land* is the second element include true compounds, with /æ/ in the second element, and reduced compounds, with /ə/. Which of the following are true compounds?

highland lowland midland woodland hinterland dreamland wonderland England Poland Switzerland Greenland Newfoundland Swaziland Disneyland

(c) English has a few nouns like the words in the first line below and numerous adjectives like those in the second line. Which group are true compounds?

armful bowlful cupful handful spoonful
cheerful graceful hopeful peaceful thoughtful

(d) There are more than a thousand verbs in English with the ending *-ate*. With rare exceptions the stressed syllable is the third syllable from the end, the ANTEPENULT, and the last syllable, the ULT, is strong: *elevate*, *in'timidate*, *re'verberate*. In adjectives and many nouns with the written ending *-ate* that syllable is weak, with /ə/. Compare the verb *graduate* and the noun *graduate*, the verb *moderate* and the adjective *moderate*.

Examine each word in the following list. Tell what part of speech it is by putting V (for verb), N (for noun), A (for adjective), or some combination of these letters after the word. If a verb is *not* pronounced with final /-eit/, make a note of it; if a noun or adjective is *not* pronounced with final /-ət/, note it.

adequate	educate	novitiate
advocate	elaborate	obliterate
affectionate	estimate	obstinate
affiliate	expatriate	passionate
alternate	extricate	penetrate
appropriate	illiterate	percolate
candidate	immediate	predicate
considerate	impersonate	separate
consulate	intimate	stimulate
delegate	marinate	subordinate
duplicate	moderate	temperate

(e) Each of the following written words represents two spoken words, a noun and a verb, pronounced differently by most speakers. How do the pronunciations differ?

complement compliment document experiment implement
ornament regiment supplement

5.7 Identifying weak-syllable vowels

In weak syllables there is often a variation in what vowel is pronounced. For example, the first syllable of *believe* may be pronounced with /ə/ or a high front vowel, /ii/ or /ɪ/, or the high central vowel /ɨ/. Perhaps many speakers vary their pronunciation depending on the tempo of their speech and other factors. Whatever vowel occurs in the first syllable of *believe* is likely to be pronounced also in the first syllable of *deceive*, *pretend*, *review*, and the like.

Examine your pronunciation of the weak syllables designated in the words below. Try to compare your pronunciation with that of others.

	Initial pretonic syllable
/ii/, /ɪ/, /ə/	believe depend enough prefer remain
/ei/ or /ə/	fatality vacation
/uu/, /ʊ/, /ə/	July Louise musician nutritious
/ou/ or /ə/	Korea morale obey opinion protect

	Medial posttonic syllable
/ɪ/ or /ə/	agitate candidate colleges furniture latitude medical relevant telephone
/ʊ/ or /ə/	argument document masculine popular

[If you have a more front vowel in some words and a more central vowel in others, look for a determining factor, such as the kind of consonant which follows the vowel.]

What we observe here is the reduction of contrasts in unstressed syllables. We have seen that there are up to 24 vowel-units in stressed positions. In certain unstressed positions the number of contrasting vowel-units is considerably reduced. Because the contrasts are reduced, there is variation in what vowel is pronounced. Obviously it doesn't matter if *agitate* is pronounced with /ɪ/ or /ə/ in the second syllable; it doesn't matter if *argument* has /jʊ/ or /jə/ in its second syllable; it is irrelevant if the first syllable of *protect* has /ou/ or /ə/.

How should we represent the pronunciation of words which have unstressed syllables when the syllables can be pronounced with one vowel or another? It is not economical to give two (or more) phonemic transcriptions for such a word as *agitate* or *argument* or *protect*. Instead, we shall give one transcription for each such word but use a VARIABLE SYMBOL. We shall use a symbol /ɨ/ for any vowel that ranges from /ii/ or /ɪ/ to /ə/; a symbol /ʉ/ for any vowel that ranges from /uu/ or /ʊ/ to /ə/; and a symbol /ɵ/ for a vowel that ranges from /ou/ to /ə/. Thus we represent the three examples above this way:

agitate	/ˈæǰɨteit/
argument	/ˈargjʉmɨnt/
protect	/prɵˈtɛkt/

5F EXERCISE AND COMMENT

Consider vowels in word-final position.

(a) Is the vowel in the last syllable of these words /ii/ or /ɪ/?

city easy happy silly studies studied

(b) Do these words end with /uu/ or /ʊ/? (or /ə/?)

continue issue sinew value

(c) All of the following words can be pronounced with final /ou/. Some of them are sometimes pronounced with /ə/ by some speakers, and others never are. Which are which?

arrow auto fellow follow motto photo potato yellow

COMMENT

(a) First of all, there is no possible contrast between /ii/ and /ɪ/ in word-final unstressed position, so that speakers vary. The vowel is short and lax like /ɪ/ but may be higher, like /ii/. Some speakers feel that they pronounce the same two vowels in words like *city* or *silly*; others pronounce the same two vowels in *easy* and *needy*.

Since there is no contrast we use neither /ii/ nor /ɪ/ in our transcription but just the symbol /i/, which is the NEUTRALIZATION of /ii/ and /ɪ/.

(b) Similarly, there is no possible contrast between /uu/ and /ʊ/ in this position, and pronunciations vary. In the last syllable of *continue*, for instance, the vowel may be more like /uu/ or more like /ʊ/. Again there is the question of how we should represent this vowel, and again we choose a symbol /u/, a high-back vowel which is the neutralization of /uu/ and /ʊ/.

(c) As it happens, the words spelled with final *-ow*, plus *potato* (and *tomato*), have final /ɔ/ in the speech of some people. *Auto*, *motto*, *photo* never do.

5G EXERCISE AND COMMENT

What is the second vowel of these words?

(a) radio medium video podium

(b) annual arduous casual graduate

COMMENT

When two unstressed vowels occur in sequence, the first is a high vowel, either high-front as in group (a) or high-back as in group (b). Do the words in group (a) have /ii/ or /ɪ/ in the second syllable? Do the words in group (b) have /uu/ or /ʊ/? Once again, there is no possible contrast, but the pronunciation is closer to the higher vowel in both sets. At any rate, we again have instances of neutralization; whether the penultimate vowel of *radio*, for instance, is closer to /ii/ or /ɪ/ there is no contrast, and we represent the vowel with the single symbol /i/. Similarly, whatever the pronunciation of the second vowel in *annual*, there is no contrast of the two high-back vowels, and our symbol is the neutralization, /u/.

5H EXERCISE AND COMMENT

Some speakers make a contrast between *roses* and *Rosa's*, between *rushes* and *Russia's*. There is a high-central /ɨ/ in *roses* and *rushes* and a mid-central /ə/ in the other two words. (The high-central vowel may or may not be part of the /i/ phoneme). Depending on dialect and what kind of consonant follows, one may have /ə/ or some higher vowel, /i/ or /ɨ/, in the final syllable of the following words. What is your pronunciation?

careless longest bucket atlas chicken human sausage ballot salad sandwich orange polish music stomach gallop Philip native plaintiff building

COMMENT

The first point to consider is whether there are different vowels in analogous positions. *Careless* and *atlas* may have different vowels before the final /s/ – the higher or more fronted vowel in *careless* and the more central vowel in *atlas*. Likewise there may be different vowels before /t/ (for example, /ɨ/ in *bucket*, /ə/ in *ballot*), and similarly before /n/ (*chicken*, *human*), before /k/ (*music*, *stomach*), and possibly before /p/ (*Philip*, *gallop*). In all these pairs the first word has the higher vowel. This historical difference is preserved in most of the British Isles and sporadically in various other parts of the English-speaking world. For many others there is no such difference; *chicken* and *human*, for instance, have the same last vowel. If different vowels are pronounced, the difference is likely to depend on what consonant follows. Generally, a higher vowel occurs before tongue-front and tongue-back consonants: sandwich, orange, polish, music, building.

5.8 Syllabic consonants

In the pronunciation of *button* the tongue tip touches the alveolar ridge for the [t] while the velic is closed to block the passage of air into the nasal cavity; then the velic opens, air flows out through the nose, and the vocal cords vibrate. A syllabic consonant [n̩] is articulated without the tongue moving from the position of [t]. There is no vowel beween [t] and [n̩]. Syllabic [n̩] is fairly frequent in English, mostly after the tongue-tip and tongue-front consonants /t d s z č ǰ ʒ/, as in *button*, *wooden*, *listen*, *cousin*, *kitchen*, *virgin*, *motion*, *vision*. Syllabic [m̩] and [ŋ̩] are less common. The former may be heard in a phrase like *keep 'em*, [kiipm̩], or a rapid pronunciation of *open*, [oupm̩]. The latter may occur, for example, in *lookin' good*, [lʊkŋ̩ gʊd], or a rapid *I can go*, [ai kŋ̩ gou]. All these examples have a nasal consonant which is HOMORGANIC with the preceding obstruent – that is, made with the same articulator – lip, tongue-tip, or tongue-back. The articulator remains in place while the air stream finds a new outlet, through the nasal cavity. Though no vowel is articulated, the duration of the syllabic consonant is the same as that of a vowel; *button* and *listen*, for example, take as long to say as *buddy* and *tissue*.

The liquids /l/ and /r/ may be syllabic, as in *total*, [toutl̩], and *rubber*, [rʌbr̩], respectively, or they may not be; there may be a schwa between the preceding obstruent and the liquid. In such words as *girl*, *file*, *foul*, *fire*, *hour* we may find a problem in telling how many syllables there are because we may not be sure if the final liquid is syllabic or not. Pronunciations may vary with speakers or, for a single speaker, with tempo.

Syllabic consonants occur only in unstressed syllables. What is phonetically a syllabic consonant may vary with a sequence of /ə/ and the corresponding non-syllabic consonant; a syllabic consonant is to be interpreted phonologically as that, /ə/ plus a consonant. Thus *button* is phonetically [ˈbʌtn̩] and phonologically /ˈbʌtən/; *battle* is phonetically [ˈbætl̩] or [ˈbætəl], phonologically /ˈbætəl/. These words have the same canonical form as *bullet* and *gallop*, for instance, ˈCVCVC, or more precisely, ˈCVCəC.

5.9 Exercise with syllabic consonants

You may pronounce a syllabic /n/ ([n̩]) in some or all of the following:

cotton	maiden	Britain	sudden	nation
kitten	beaten	brighten	mutton	patient
lesson	prison	reason	present	caution
didn't	wasn't	wouldn't	doesn't	imagine

botany	monotonous	fascinate	president	erosion
coat 'n' hat	bread 'n' butter			

What is the difference in pronunciation between the noun *lightning* and the verb form *lightening*?

When /t/ or /d/ occurs before [n̩], the obstruent consonant is not ambisyllabic; it ends one consonant and the syllabic nasal begins the next syllable: *button* [bʌt.n̩] *widen* [waˈd.n̩].

In words like the following, in which the consonant before /n/ is labial or dorsal, there is likely to be a vowel separating the /n/ from the preceding consonant.

wagon	common	second	even
bacon	open	toughen	ribbon

The following contain some possible occurrences of syllabic /l/ ([l̩]):

whittle	petal	saddle	candle
muscle	muzzle	little	fondle
catalog	tidal	whistle	fizzle
What'll we do?	Wait'll the boss sees this		

Probably all speakers differentiate /t/ and /d/ before syllabic /n/: *written*, *ridden*. In the United States and Canada not all speakers make the distinction before syllabic /l/. Outside North America *petal* is pronounced differently from *pedal/peddle*, and *title* from *tidal*. In Canada and the USA, if *title* and *tidal* are distinguished, the distinction is likely to be in the stressed vowel-unit rather than in the consonant which follows. (See further, chapter 6.)

In the words above the syllabic /l/ is preceded by an apical consonant. After other consonants there is likely to be an intervening vowel:

double	bushel	pickled	evil

The next group of words to examine may be said to have syllabic /r/. Actually, what is pronounced is a vowel with '*r*-coloring' ([ɚ]). The tongue is in the same position as for the articulation of a schwa, but it is retracted somewhat and there is a slight groove in the tip. Compare the ending of *manner* and *manna*. Our way of spelling these two words suggests that after /n/ there is a vowel and a consonant in the first word and only a vowel in the second, but that is not phonetically accurate. What is pronounced is a single segment. This segment may be considered a syllabic consonant (represented phonetically as [r̩]), or we may call it a vowel with *r*-coloring – that is, a vowel like the schwa but produced with retraction and apical groove (represented phonetically as [ɚ]). Of course, speakers who do not pronounce a final /r/

have a schwa in both *manna* and *manner*, and for them the two words are homophones.

better	ladder	cover	dinner
coward	commerce	lantern	drunkard

5.10 Summary

In a tone unit of more than one syllable one of the syllables is more prominent than the other(s) because it is the place where the melody or intonation changes; it is the **accented syllable**, [+ accent]. The accented syllable and perhaps other syllables are **stressed syllables**, [+ stress], having greater intensity and duration than syllables which are [− stress]. Typically every major word in a tone group has one stressed syllable. Finally, stressed syllables and some unstressed syllables are **strong**, [+ strong], and others are [− strong]. A syllable which is [+ strong] is potentially [+ stress] and therefore potentially [+ accent]. Long English words generally have an irregular alternation of strong and weak syllables.

In describing syllables by their position in a word (or longer form) we speak of **initial**, **medial**, and **final** syllables. To describe position with respect to the tonic syllable we use the labels **pretonic** and **posttonic**.

Every syllable has a **peak**, which must be an element with the feature [+ syllabic]. Consonants which precede the peak constitute the **onset** of the syllable, those which follow the peak form the **coda**. The consonants and vowels of a language occur in certain kinds of sequences and not in others. Statements of what sequences may or may not occur are called **constraints**. The full description of such constraints is called **phonotactics**. A notable characteristic of English is that a consonant which occurs between a stressed vowel and an unstressed one or two unstressed vowels may be part of either the preceding or the following syllable – it is **ambisyllabic**.

Compound words have two stress patterns: either the first word of the compound has the stressed syllable (and therefore potentially the accent) or both words have a stress (and the second word may be the bearer of the accent). These are **full compounds**. Some lexical items which were once full compounds are now **reduced compounds**, with a reduced vowel in the second part. In certain sets of words, for which a single spelling is used (*-man*, *-land*, *-ful*, *-ate*, or *-ment*), the final syllable may be strong or not. In the last three of these the difference between strong and weak correlates with a grammatical difference.

5C FEEDBACK

(a) comprehensibility
+ − + − ± − −

(b) reconsideration
+ − + − ± −

(c) autobiographic
+ − +− ± −

(d) individuality
+ − + −± − −

(e) justification
+ − − ± −

(f) eligibility
+ − − ± − −

(g) adequate
± − −

(h) feminine
+ − −

(i) gelatin
± − −

(j) Senegalese
+ − − ±

(If you marked the final syllable of *comprehensibility*, *individuality* and *eligibility* strong, you are not wrong. There are reasons for considering it strong and reasons for counting it weak. We shall take up the matter again at a later point.)

5D FEEDBACK

(a) ˈatom aˈtomic
+ +

(b) ˈCanada Caˈnadian
+ +

(c) deˈfine defiˈnition
+ + +

(d) ˈmelody meˈlodic
+ +

(e) Jaˈpan Japaˈnese
+ + +

(f) ˈparent paˈrental
+ +

(g) ˈterrify terˈrific
+ + +

(h) amˈbiguous ambiˈguity
+ + + +

(i) comˈpose compoˈsition
+ + +

(j) ˈcontinent contiˈnental
+ + +

(k) ˈmodify modifiˈcation
+ + + +

(l) ˈorigin oˈriginal
+ +

(m) inˈvite inviˈtation
+ + + +

(n) caˈtastrophe cataˈstrophic
+ + +

5E FEEDBACK

(a) Answers may vary. The words *businessman* and *mailman* are pronounced with a full vowel /æ/ in the final syllable, and *madman* may have /æ/; the other words are more likely to have /ə/.

(b) The words *hinterland*, *dreamland*, *wonderland*, *Swaziland*, and *Disneyland* have /æ/; *highland*, *midland*, *England*, *Poland*, *Switzerland*, and *Greenland* have /ə/; *lowland* and *woodland* vary; so does *Newfoundland*, which has three different pronunciations.

(c) The nouns with *-ful* are true compounds and have a strong last syllable, with /ʊ/. The adjectives have a weak final syllable with /ə/.

(d)

adequate A	educate V	novitiate N*
advocate V,N	elaborate V,A	obliterate V
affectionate A	estimate V,N	obstinate A
affiliate V,N	expatriate V,N,A	passionate A
alternate V,N,A	extricate V	penetrate V
appropriate V,A	illiterate A	percolate V
candidate N*	immediate A	predicate V,N
considerate A	impersonate V	separate V,A
consulate N	intimate V,A	stimulate V
delegate V,N*	marinate V	subordinate V,N,A
duplicate V,N,A	moderate V,A	temperate A

The nouns marked N* may have /ei/ or /ə/ in the final syllable. Other nouns and all adjectives have /ə/; all verbs have /ei/.

(e) Verbs ending in *-ment* have a strong syllable with the full vowel /ɛ/; the corresponding nouns have a weak syllable, with /ə/. For some speakers, however, noun and verb are homophonous, both having /ə/ in the last syllable.

6

Consonant and Vowel Variation

As pointed out in chapter 1, speech is a dynamic process. It is a constant flowing out of sound as the vocal organs keep changing positions. Air from the lungs is under constant modifications, patterns of vibrating particles keep changing between the speaker and listener(s). But for speaker and hearer this dynamic speech represents elements of language – words and combinations of words – which are expressed as sequences of discrete phonemes. Phonemes are abstract: they are realized as specific articulations, momentary gestures or positions of the vocal organs in the stream of speech. Since any phoneme occurs in different environments within the stream of speech, it has different pronunciations depending on what precedes or follows it. The actual pronunciations of a phoneme are called its ALLOPHONES. All allophones of a phoneme have the same distinctive features but different non-distinctive features. Speakers of the language are aware of phonemes but generally have no awareness of the allophonic variants.

We are interested in two kinds of phenomena: the positions in which variations occur, and the kinds of variations that occur.

Positions of occurrence can be stated in terms of:

1 phonemes that precede or follow – a given phoneme may take on some feature of a neighboring phoneme;
2 position in a word;
3 position in a syllable;
4 whether the syllable is stressed or unstressed.

We examine six kinds of variation here (sections 6.1 to 6.6), and then we consider the numerous variants of the most frequent consonant, /t/.

6.1 Variation in point of articulation

6.1a

The consonants /p b m f v/ are classed together as LABIALS. More specificially, the fricatives /f v/ are labiodental: there is light contact between the lower lip and the upper front teeth, and air is squeezed out between lip and teeth. The stops and nasal /p b m/ are usually bilabial – the lower lip is the articulator and the upper lip is the point of articulation – but these consonants are likely to be labiodental when they precede /f/ or /v/. Compare:

co*m*fort sy*m*phony o*b*vious cu*p*ful

with:

co*m*pass sy*m*pathy o*b*noxious ru*p*ture

Consonants which are typically bilabial become labiodental when they are followed immediately by a labiodental consonant. We can express this in a formula:

labial → labiodental / ____ labiodental

The formula has three parts. Something of some class of things, denoted by the term on the left side of the arrow, has a more specific designation or additional characteristic, indicated by the term on the right side of the arrow, when it is in a certain environment. The environment is indicated by the blank following the slant line and whatever goes with the blank. That may be a term following the blank, as here, or a term before the blank, or both.

When two phonemes occurring in succession have the same place of articulation, as in *comfort*, *cupful*, and *obvious*, they are said to be COARTICULATED.

(Instead of making /m/ labiodental before /f/, as in *comfort* and *symphony*, we may insert a transitional /p/ between the two consonants: /ˈkʌmpfərt, ˈsɪmpfəni/. This kind of insertion is discussed in section 7.8.)

6.1b

The consonants /t d θ ð s z n/ are APICALS. More specifically, the flat fricatives /θ ð/ are apicodental, articulated with tongue-tip near or lightly touching the edge of the upper teeth. The other apical consonants are typically apicoalveolar; the tongue-tip touches or comes close to the alveolar ridge. However, this is not always the case.

6A EXERCISES

(a) Examine your pronunciation of the words and phrases below to determine when you have apicodental articulation for the consonants indicated in italics.

a*t* bat	bi*d*	e*s*teem	i*s* it	te*n*
a*t* that	wi*d*th	e*s*thetic	i*s* this	te*n*th

(b) When there is apicodental articulation, what phoneme follows?
(c) How would you complete this formula?

apical → apicodental / ____

6.1c

The same apical consonants may be articulated with tongue retracted, in a post-alveolar position, when they follow /r/ – in the speech of those who pronounce /r/ as a post-alveolar consonant. Compare the post-alveolar pronunciation of these consonants in

hur*t* car*d* hor*s*e tur*n*

with the apicoalveolar pronunciation in

hu*t* co*d* mo*ss* to*n*

apical → postalveolar / r ____

6.1d

The nasal consonant /n/ is not apical but laminal when it precedes the laminoalveolar affricates /č/ and /ǰ/

branch lunch flange lunge

whereas it is apical in other positions, such as

tent lend noon

6.1e

The dorsal consonants /k g ŋ/ vary in articulation from a more fronted (palatal or prevelar) to a more back (velar) position.

6B EXERCISES

(a) In which of the following words is the more fronted articulation found?

li*ck*	*c*ool	di*g*	*g*eese	si*ng*
look	*k*ill	do*g*	*g*oose	so*ng*

(b) What kind of vowel precedes or follows the more fronted articulation of these three consonants?

6.1f

The lateral consonant /l/ has various articulations, all with lateral curl so that air escapes over the sides of the tongue; there is usually contact between the centerline of the tongue and the roof of the mouth, but not necessarily. A so-called 'clear *l*' is produced with the front of the tongue high in the mouth and the back of the tongue low. A 'dark *l*' is made with the back of the tongue raised; the center is low; the front may be raised, so that the whole tongue has more or less the shape of a spoon, or the tongue-front may be down. However, the variation depends mostly on what position /l/ has in a syllable and only partly on what kind of phonemes follow.

6C EXERCISES

(a) In the following words where do you pronounce a clear(er) /l/ and where a dark(er) /l/?

*l*eaf	*l*et	p*l*ease	c*l*ean	a *l*ittle
fee*l*	te*ll*	he*l*p	mi*l*k	a *l*ot
fee*l*ing	te*ll*ing	me*l*on	ho*ll*ow	Pau*l*a
simp*l*e	simp*l*y	probab*l*e	probab*l*y	

(b) In what environments does each kind of /l/ occur? Consider two sorts of factors, position in syllable and the kind of phoneme that follows.

The first of the paragraphs above, 6.1a to 6.1e, deal with assimilation in place of articulation; consonants are articulated in the position of phonemes which precede or which follow: labial becomes labiodental, apical becomes apicodental, apical becomes postalveolar, dorsal becomes dorsopalatal. On the other hand, the alternation between clear and dark /l/, treated in 6.1f, depends more on position in syllable than on what kind of vowel (front or back) precedes or follows.

6.1g

Looking back at the material in paragraphs 6.1a to 6.1f, we see that two consonants in sequence within a word are likely to be coarticulated. Consider the homorganic sequences of nasal + obstruent:

Bilabial:	temper timber compose combine
Labiodental:	comfort symphony
Apicodental:	month tenth
Apicoalveolar:	Santa sandal contain condemn
Laminoalveolar:	pinch sponge
Dorsopalatal:	tinker finger
Dorsovelar:	bunker hunger

There are exceptions to these homorganic clusters. Sequences of apico-alveolar /n/ and labiodental /f v/ occur in *confident*, *infirm*, *convex*, *invent*, and the like. Words such as *concrete*, *concur*, *income*, *inclose* may be pronounced with /-nk-/ or /-ŋk-/.

6.2 An example of mutual assimilation

The liquids /l/ and /r/ are usually frictionless; for their articulation the tongue is not ordinarily close enough to the roof of the mouth for friction to occur. After certain consonants, however, /r/ may be pronounced with friction between tongue and alveolar ridge, at least by some speakers, when it follows /t/ or /d/, as in

train strain drain

Compare the articulation of /r/ in these words with that in, for example,

rain brain praise crane grain

There is a groove in the tongue-tip for the articulation of /r/, and the tongue-tip touches the alveolar ridge for /t d/. As the tongue is released, air moves through the groove and friction results. Contact is generally farther back for /t d/ than when these consonants precede vowels (e.g. *tame*, *dame*); their place of articulation is modified by the following /r/. We may say that /t/ and /d/ are assimilated to /r/ by moving backward along the horizontal axis of the oral chamber. The change from frictionless to fricative is also a kind of assimilation. To be sure, the stops /t, d/ are not fricative – do not have a feature [+ fricative] that can be 'borrowed' by /r/. But if we look at these manners of articulation on the vertical scale

stops
fricatives
frictionless consonants
vowels and glides

we see that the change from frictionless /r/ to fricative /r/ is an approximation toward the kind of articulation of /t, d/. The change from frictionless to fricative is a movement towards the complete closure of /t d/.

The acoustic effect of /tr dr/ is close to that of /č ǰ/, as in *chain*, *Jane*. The essential difference between /tr dr/ and /č ǰ/ is that the groove is in the tip of the tongue for /tr dr/ and in the front of the tongue for /č ǰ/. Young children who are just beginning to learn to write – who have formed some idea of how English phonemes are represented in writing but have not had much experience with the representation of numerous words – may write, for instance, CHREE for 'tree'.

6.3 Variation in lip shape

A consonant preceding a rounded vowel or /w/ is most likely articulated with anticipatory lip-rounding. Compare

noose goose twin too doom

with

niece geese tin tea deem

consonant → [+ round] / ____ [+ round]

6.4 Variation in nasality

Vowels may be nasalized or not nasalized.

6D EXERCISE

Easy questions: In which of the following words is the vowel most likely to be nasalized? Why?

boot boom sick sing sink camp cap late lane laid

6.5 Variations in onset and release

6.5a

In a very precise description of how a consonant is articulated it is usual to refer to the beginning, the middle, and the end of the articulation with the technical terms ONSET, HOLD, and RELEASE, respectively. When a consonant occurs between vowels, as in *habit*, *ready*, *eager*, it is easy to recognize its onset and its release, but when another consonant precedes or follows, the onset or release may be modified.

6E EXERCISE

The following words and phrases show two stops (or a stop and an affricate) in sequence. Does each stop have a separate onset and release in such sequences?

captain	uptown	rubdown	jump down
actor	Magda	necktie	big turn
hot pad	what kind	nightgown	bad guy
hatcheck	meatball	red balloon	bad joke

6.5b

If an apical or dorsal stop is followed by /l/, the stop usually has lateral release. This is especially true for the apical stops: the tongue-tip touches the alveolar ridge shutting off the flow of air, then the sides of the tongue curl in while the tip remains in place. The same stops sometimes have nasal release: the velic opens to let air through the nasal cavity while the tongue-tip is still in contact with the alveolar ridge.

6F EXERCISE

Find examples of both lateral and nasal release in the following words and phrases

widely fiddler hydrant handy kidney buddy
butter butler catnip atlas nightly mattress
Whitney good time good night good evening

6.5c

The onset of a voiced consonant may be voiceless when preceded by a voiceless consonant or when word-initial (preceded by zero in the word). Similarly, a voiced consonant may have a voiceless release when followed by a voiceless consonant or zero.

6G EXERCISE

In which of the following words are /l r w/ most likely to have voiceless onset – that is, to begin with the vocal cords not yet vibrating?

blade play slow glass class
shrill crazy gravy dry try
twin dwindle Gwen queen swell

6H EXERCISE

The voiced obstruents /b d ǰ g v ð z ʒ/ may be voiced throughout their articulation, or they may have voiceless onset, or they may have voiceless release. They are illustrated below in four positions of occurrence. Which variants are most likely to occur in which positions?

Initial:	buy die jade gate vast that zoom
Intervocalic:	rubber ready magic buggy liver bother easy measure
Final:	rob rod budge bug love smooth fizz rouge
Before voiceless consonants:	obtain bedtime is cold big smile

6.5d

It is quite 'natural' and therefore something of a universal trait that a voiced segment should be partly devoiced in contact with a voiceless segment or when it occurs in word-initial or word-final position. Similar phenomena can be found in many languages. Voiceless stops in English have a kind of release called ASPIRATION which is less common in the languages of the world. In some articulations of English /p t k/ the vocal cords are close together and not vibrating; as the lip, tongue-tip, or tongue-back is released, air is squeezed between vocal folds, producing a sort of *h*-sound, [p^h t^h k^h]. This happens in some positions but not all.

6I EXERCISE

Hold a small strip of paper loosely in front of your mouth as you say the words below; if the stop is aspirated, the paper should flutter as air is expelled; an unaspirated stop does not cause such movement. (The fluttering is especially noticeable with an aspirated labial stop, [p^h].) In one of the seven positions of occurrence illustrated there is likely to be free variation.

Initially in a tonic syllable:

pill present pleasure till treasure kill quiver clever

Initially in an atonic syllable:

potato platoon today tremendous canoe Quebec

After initial /s/ in a tonic or atonic syllable:

spill splint still street skill squint stiletto

Word-medially at the beginning of a tonic syllable:

appoint apply attend attract account acquire

Word-medially in an atonic syllable:

happy temper whisper octopus
water shelter mister sanity
lucky anchor whiskers medical

Word-finally after /s/:

lisp list risk

Word-finally after a vowel or other consonant:

cup camp hat heart look milk

Aspiration of a voiceless stop means that as the release of the lower lip, tongue-tip, or tongue-back is effected, the non-vibrating vocal cords are close enough together that air is squeezed between them. Another variation that affects the voiceless stops /p t k/ and /č/ as well is due to a different action of the vocal cords. These consonants may be GLOTTALIZED: the vocal cords come together just before, or simultaneously with, the closure that occurs in the oral cavity. Glottalization is most frequent when stops are syllable-final before a following stop, fricative, or nasal.

Sleep [ʔp] tight quite [ʔt] nice take [ʔk] sides

6.6 Variation in length

6.6a

When two instances of the same consonant come together, there is only one onset and one release; the hold lasts as long as two consonants. In English two instances of the same consonant can only happen at a morpheme boundary, when the first morpheme ends in a consonant and the second morpheme begins with the same consonant. Compare *bookcase* and *bookish*, *home-made* and *domain*.

misspent ten nights love Vickie

bad day ripe peach unknown

6J EXERCISE

What happens when two consonants which differ only in voice come together?

soup bowl red tie leg cramp five fingers

6.6b

Sonorants (sonorant consonants and all vowels) vary in length according to what, if anything, follows.

6K EXERCISE

Each set of three words below has one phoneme in three different positions of occurrence. Decide where the phoneme is short, where longer, where longest.

s*ee*d, s*eat*, s*ee*	l*u*te, l*ew*d, L*ou*
be*n*t, be*n*d, Be*n*	be*l*t, be*ll*, we*l*d
fie*r*ce, fea*r*s, fea*r*	unke*m*pt, he*mm*ed, he*m*

6.7 Multiple variation for /t/

So far we have been dealing with kinds of variation that apply to groups of phonemes – voiceless stops, apical consonants, all vowels, etc. In this section we take a look at a single consonant and note: (1) its various pronunciations, especially as they are determined by occurrence in tonic and atonic syllables; (2) how these variations affect its contrast with /d/ and other consonants. We have already seen, in section 6.5b, that /t/ and /d/ have nasal release before /n/ and lateral release before /l/. In 6.5d we noted that /t/, like /p/ and /k/, has aspirated release in some positions and not in others. We repeat some of these observations below and then consider two other variants, /t/ as a weak tap and as a glottal stop.

(a) /t/ is aspirated, [t^h] before a stressed vowel.

tie retire absentee guitar contain

In such minimal pairs as *time* and *dime*, *train* and *drain*, the difference is between a consonant which is voiceless and aspirated versus a consonant which is voiced and unaspirated. Phonologically we say that the distinctive difference is in voice – voiceless versus voiced – but the aspiration on /t/ and the lack of aspiration in /d/ may be the more helpful cue in determining what sounds we, as hearers, actually perceive.

(b) /t/ is typically aspirated in initial position before an unstressed vowel, though the aspiration is weaker here.

today Tibet tenacious tuberculosis

Note that there are no minimal pairs with /d/ in this position.

(c) In final position /t/ may or may not be released, as with other stop consonants. If there is release, there may or may not be aspiration. The more emphatic and energetic the speech, the greater likelihood of aspiration. Without aspiration the most obvious perceptual difference in such pairs as the following is not in the consonants themselves but in the length of the vowel preceding.

coat,	code	wet,	wed	seat,	seed
[ko^{u}t,	ko:^{u}d	wɛt,	wɛ:d	si^{i}t,	si:^{i}d]

In such a pair as *tight*, *tide* the difference in vowel nuclei may be more than a matter of length; see the next paragraph.

(d) In North America especially, and to a lesser extent in other parts of the English-speaking world, speakers produce a voiced tap of the tongue-tip, [ɾ], for /t/ and /d/ when these consonants occur between a stressed vowel and an unstressed vowel. The tongue-tip brushes quickly against the alveolar ridge rather than being held there long enough for air pressure to build up behind the tongue as in the usual articulation of a stop.

matter	city	water	ladder	wedding	medical
[ˈmæɾɚ	ˈsiɾi	ˈwɔɾɚ	ˈlæɾɚ	ˈweɾiŋ	ˈmɛɾɨkɨl]

The tapped consonant may be preceded by /r/; the articulation of /-rt-/ is a forward flap of the tongue-tip against the alveolar ridge, [ɾ].

party	mortar	artist	turtle	accordion
[ˈp^{h}aɾi	ˈmɔɾɚ	ˈaɾɨst	ˈt^{h}ɜɾəl	aˈk^{h}ɔɾiən]

Thus Canadians and Americans may not distinguish such pairs of words as the following:

atom	shutter	petal	coated	conceited
Adam	shudder	pedal/peddle	coded	conceded

In Canada and the United States, if a distinction is made in the medial consonant, a clear difference between a voiceless and a voiced stop, the distinction is probably due to social factors. The speaker is likely to have the feeling that non-tapped consonants are 'right' or 'better' and so produces distinct consonants in circumstances where the social motivation is sufficiently strong. If a distinction is made but not socially motivated, the difference is not in the medial consonants themselves but in the vowels which precede. Generally this means that the vowel is longer before the tap which represents /d/ and shorter before the flap that stands for /t/.

For many speakers the difference is more certain when the vowel nucleus is /ai/, as in the following pairs.

writer rider title tidal

Canadians and natives of upstate New York, eastern Virginia, and elsewhere have [ʌⁱ] before a voiceless consonant and [aⁱ] elsewhere: [ˈrʌⁱɾɚ ˈraⁱɾɚ ˈtʌⁱɾl ˈtaⁱɾl]. People in the South and South Midland generally have [aⁱ] before voiceless consonants and [aː] or [aᵊ] elsewhere: [ˈraⁱɾɚ ˈraːɾɚ ˈtaⁱɾəl ˈtaːɾəl].

(e) Some North Americans have a nasalized tap, [ɾ̃], as the articulation of the sequence /nt/ in the same position, between a stressed vowel and an unstressed vowel.

Atlantic county dainty twenty winter
[æˈtlæɾ̃ik ˈkaᵘɾ̃i ˈdeⁱɾ̃i ˈtwɛɾ̃i ˈwɪɾ̃ɚ]

For such speakers the phonetic realizations of /nt/ in *count* and *counter* are quite different: [kʰaᵘnt ˈkʰaᵘɾ̃ɚ]. On the other hand, the phonetic difference between, say, *winter* and *winner* is very small: [ˈwɪɾ̃ɚ ˈwɪnɚ]. Not surprisingly, many speakers make no such distinction and pronounce [n] alone in words like *Atlantic*, *county*, *inventor*, *painted*, making no distinction between *winter* and *winner*.

Note that there is no tap, but a full stop, when /t/ and /d/ are preceded by any consonant other than /r/ or /n/ – and for /d/ when it is preceded by /n/,

actor shelter optical master building fender

And /t/ and /d/ are full stops when followed by /r/,

citrus hatred mattress patron Audrey

(f) In words like the following, where /t/ occurs between unstressed vowels, the consonants may be a tap or a stop.

cavity charity property
negative positive relative
diameter heritage janitor senator

Perhaps the more common the word and the more frequently it is used, the more likely that /t/ will be articulated as a tap, and, on the other hand, the more formal the speech the less likely is the tap pronunciation. There is another difference: the tap is ambisyllabic while the stop articulation begins a new syllable.

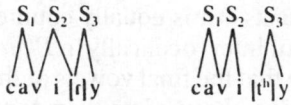

(g) The next words are different from those in group (f). In the words that follow, /t/ is always pronounced with aspiration in Canada and the United States, as in the rest of the English-speaking world.

agitate meditate appetite comatose
longitude gratitude vicissitude
hereditary secretary dormitory territory

In group (f) and group (g) the main stress of each word is on the vowel of the antepenult or preantepenult, and /t/ occurs after the following vowel. In the words of group (f), as we have seen, /t/ may be tapped or aspirated; in the words of group (g) /t/ is aspirated, not a tap. One way of explaining the difference is to say that /t/ occurs in a weak syllable in the words of group (f) but in group (g) it occurs in a syllable which is strong – or which has some degree of stress. However, there may be some circularity in all this. Does /t/ have aspiration *because* the syllable in which it occurs is strong (or stressed), or does the syllable seem to have prominence because of the aspiration of /t/?

The question becomes more difficult to answer when the tap and the stop occur in what appears to be the same environment. American linguists have found a particularly troublesome problem of phonological analysis in words like the following:

auto grotto Hittite motto Otto Plato potato tomato

For dialects in which all these words have consistently either a tap or a stop there is no phonological problem; the intervocalic consonant is /t/. But for most North Americans some of the words – generally *auto*, *motto*, *potato*, and *tomato* – have a tap and the others are pronounced with an intervocalic apical stop. How is this to be explained? Are there two different consonant phonemes which, though never found in contrast, occur in phonetic contexts which cannot be predicted? Or are there some phonetic facts which account for the occurrence of a tap in *potato*, for instance, but a stop in *Plato*? One possible answer is that the final syllable of *potato* is weaker or less stressed than the ult of *Plato*: *potato* ends with a simple vowel /o/ while *Plato* ends with a diphthong /ou/, a difference also found in *window* – with final /o/ – and *elbow* – with /ou/ –, for example. Support for this way of accounting is perhaps found in the fact that *potato* and *window* may be pronounced with /ə/ instead of /o(u)/, but *Plato* and *elbow* never are. However, to most speakers – including linguists – it is equally counterintuitive to suggest that the consonants which occur intervocalically in *Plato* and *potato* are different phonemes and to propose that the final vowels of the two words are different phonemes. A better solution, though less than completely satisfactory, is to propose that a phoneme can have socially determined variants: one speech sound, say [t], is preferred in some social situations and in some parts of the lexicon while another speech sound, [ɾ], is usual in other situations and in other lexical items.

(h) The realization of /t/ may be a glottal stop [ʔ] or a simultaneous – or nearly simultaneous – double closure, the vocal cords coming together while the apex makes contact with the alveolar ridge, [ʔt] or [tʔ]. It would take some space to tell the phonetic environments and the geographic dialects in which these realizations occur. It was noted in section 6.5 that /p t č k/ may be glottalized in syllable-final position before a following stop, fricative, or nasal. In Cockney this glottalization goes further: /p t k/ are likely to be glottalized in absolute final position: *Stop*, *Wait*, *Look*; and in rapid speech they may be replaced by a glottal stop. In Cockney an intervocalic /t/ is realized as a glottal stop alone: *water* [ˈwɒʔə], *city* [ˈsɪʔi]. In other parts of England, in Scotland, in North America, and in the Southern Hemisphere the glottalized /t/ or the glottal stop alone is found, variably, in these environments:

before syllabic /n/ [n̩] – button beaten curtain shirt 'n' tie
especially when /t/ is preceded by non-syllabic /n/ as well as followed by syllabic /n/ – mountain maintenance sentence
before syllabic /l/ [l̩] – bottle total startle that'll do
syllable-final before any consonant – treatment Scotland brightness

6.8 Some questions of perception

pill till kill bill dill gill

In the first three words the initial consonant is voiceless and aspirated, which means that the vocal cords are not vibrating when the consonant articulator is released and they do not begin to vibrate for several centiseconds after the release. The initial consonants of the second three words are voiced, probably with voiceless onset, and unaspirated; the vocal cords begin to vibrate when the release takes place. Considering these stops as part of the whole sound system of the language we have viewed the voiceless/voiced contrast as the distinctive difference. But which feature is actually most important in enabling us to distinguish one stop from its counterpart? Probably the difference in voice onset time, aspirated versus unaspirated.

cap	cat	luck	rich	safe	ice
cab	cad	lug	ridge	save	eyes

In the words of the first line the final consonant is voiceless and follows a vowel which is phonetically short. In the words of the second line the final consonant is voiced, probably with voiceless release, and follows a vowel which is longer in articulation. What is the real cue in our hearing the words of each pair, the voicing of the final consonant or the duration of the vowel which precedes it?

6.9 Summary

Every language has a limited inventory of phonemes, the units of its sound system. Each phoneme is manifested, or articulated, in various ways in the stream of speech. The variations may be seen as ways in which the phoneme is adjusted to its environment: a phoneme may acquire features which are like those of a preceding or following phoneme; it may vary according to whether it comes at the beginning or end of a word, at the beginning or end of a syllable, and it may differ depending on whether its syllable is stressed or unstressed. The principal kinds of variation have been discussed under five headings: variation in place of articulation, in nasality, in lip-rounding, in onset and release, and in duration. The frequently occurring phoneme /t/ is highly variable in its actual articulations, with respect to dialect as well as positions of occurrence in the stream of speech.

A system or structure is made up of elements, units, which have analogous relationships with one another. The contrast between two of the units is the same as the contrast between two other units. Among English consonant phonemes the analogous relations are fairly easy to recognize: /p/ is to /b/ as /t/ is to /d/ as /k/ is to /g/; /b/ is to /m/ as /d/ is to /n/ as /g/ is to /ŋ/, and so on. The distinctive features of a phoneme are the characteristics in which it differs from other phonemes of the system. When we say that /t/ is a voiceless apical stop, we are telling how it differs from /d/, from /p/ and /k/, and from /n/. In its different occurrences, its different allophones, /t/ or any phoneme has various non-distinctive features. From the point of view of a system these 'extra' features do nothing. In terms of human perception, however, the non-distinctive features may be all-important.

6A FEEDBACK

(a) at that, width, esthetic, is this, tenth
(b) /θ/ or /ð/
(c) apical → apicodental / ____ apicodental

6B FEEDBACK

(a) lick, kill, dig, geese, sing
(b) The more forward articulation occurs when a dorsal consonant precedes or follows a front vowel.

dorsal → dorsopalatal / front vowel

(When there is no blank to the right of the slant line, as in the rule above, the context is understood to mean either before or after the determining factor; here, the rule says that a dorsal consonant is dorsopalatal when it occurs either before or after a front vowel.)

6C FEEDBACK

Answers may vary, but in general the darker /l/ occurs in post-vowel position (feel, tell, help, milk) and when syllabic (simple, probable). A clearer /l/ is heard in pre-vowel position (leaf, let, please, clean, simply). Between vowels the articulation may vary somewhat, the clearer phone occurring in the neighborhood of front vowels (feeling, telling, melon, a little) and the darker one near back vowels (hollow, Paula, a lot). There is a rapid pronunciation of *probably* ('probly') with a dark /l/, used by many speakers. (In Ireland and Scotland clear articulation is the rule in all positions.)

6D FEEDBACK

boom, sing, sink, camp, lane

A vowel is nasalized before a nasal consonant.

vowel → [+ nasal] / ____ [+ nasal]

Note that it is possible to pronounce *camp*, *plant*, *tank*, for example, without the nasal consonants, /m n n/, and still be understood so long as the vowels are nasalized. Exactly this sort of articulation seems to be common in rapid speech.

6E FEEDBACK

The first stop does not have a release separate from the following stop. In *actor*, for instance, the tongue-tip is in place for the /t/ before the tongue-back is released from the position of /k/ articulation. This is, in a way, another instance of fuzzy transition between syllables. Compare French *acteur*, in which [k] is clearly released before the onset of [t].

Note that when an affricate precedes another consonant the affricate is clearly released – that is, the stop has clear fricative release: *each boy*, *page ten*, *which card.*

6F FEEDBACK

Lateral release: widely, fiddler, butler, atlas
Nasal release: kidney, Whitney, good night

t, d (k, g) → lateral release / ____ l
t, d → nasal release / ____ n

6G FEEDBACK

play slow class; shrill crazy try; twin queen swell
l, r, w → voiceless onset / voiceless consonant ____

6H FEEDBACK

Voiceless onset is usual in initial position; voiceless release in final position and before a voiceless consonant; voiced throughout between voiced segments.

$$\text{voiced obstruent} \rightarrow \left\{ \begin{array}{l} \text{voiced onset / \# ____} \\ \text{voiceless release / ____ \#} \\ \text{voiceless release / ____ vl. C} \end{array} \right\}$$

6I FEEDBACK

Aspirated word-initially in a stressed syllable
word-initially in an unstressed syllable
(though the aspiration is weaker)
word-medially in a stressed syllable
word-finally after /s/
Aspirated or unaspirated (free variation)
word-finally except after /s/
Unaspirated in other positions

$$\text{p, t, k} \rightarrow \text{aspiration} / \begin{cases} \#\ ___\ (C)\ V \\ \cdots\ ___\ (C)\ \text{stressed V} \\ s\ ___\ \# \\ V\ (C)\ ___\ \#\ \text{[optional]} \end{cases}$$

6J FEEDBACK

There is one onset, one release, and the duration of two consonants, with voice changing during the hold.

6K FEEDBACK

short	*longer*	*longest*
seat	seed	see
lute	lewd	Lou
bent	bend	Ben
fierce	fears	fear
belt	weld	bell
unkempt	hemmed	hem

Sonorants are shortest before a voiceless consonant, longer before a voiced consonant, and longest in final position. The comparison could be carried farther; sonorants are typically shorter before fricatives than before stops, for instance.

7

Phonotactics

In chapter 5 we examined the structure of a one-syllable, one-morpheme word, observing that such a word may begin with zero, one, two, or three consonants and may end with zero, one, two, or three consonants. In this chapter we explore and describe the clusters of consonants which occur initially and finally in all sorts of words, whether monosyllabic or polysyllabic, and the clusters that occur between vowels in polysyllabic words. The next chapter will deal with the occurrence of vowels with respect to the consonants and with respect to stressed and unstressed syllables.

The description which follows deals with the CONSTRAINTS on the occurrence of consonants: certain sequences of consonants are possible in English words and other sequences do not occur. To a large extent the patterns which occur and the constraints on what does not occur are obvious and easily stated. Near the end of the chapter, however, we take note of some facts which do not fit the patterns or which can be interpreted in different ways.

7.1 Word-initial position

The first (or only) vowel of a word may be preceded by:

(0) Zero (that is, the vowel may be initial)

apple, elephant, eager, oblige . . .

(1) Any single consonant except /ʒ/ or /ŋ/*

bell, package, mellow, wild, vest, fat . . .

*Neither /ʒ/ nor /ŋ/ occurs initially in native English words, but /ʒ/ does occur in words borrowed from other languages. Various names, especially, are known to speakers of English, such as *Giselle*, *Zhivago*, *Gitane*. There are no such words with initial /ŋ/.

(2) Certain clusters of two consonants – but we need to classify these clusters further. There are strong constraints on what kinds of consonants can occur together. The next exercise begins with an exhibit of the types of consonant clusters, with examples. Then there are questions to be answered about the words in the exhibit.

7A EXERCISE

First, here is the exhibit:

(i) Cr- (consonant + /r/)
pray brave train drain craze graze
frill thrill shrill
(ii) Cl- (consonant + /l/)
play blade clay glaze
flay slay
(iii) Cw- (consonant + /w/)
twin dwindle quit Gwen
thwart swim
whistle
(iv) sC- (/s/ + consonant)
spy sty sky
sphere
smile snow

And here are the questions. Assume that the exhibit contains all the examples needed for answering the questions.

(a) In the sequence designated Cr-, do both voiced and voiceless stops occur before /r/?
(b) Do both voiced and voiceless stops occur before /l/?
(c) Do the sibilant stops (affricates), /č/ and /ǰ/, occur initially before the liquids /r/ and /l/?
(d) Do voiced and voiceless fricatives occur before /r/? before /l/?
(e) In the sequences Cw- which stops and fricatives occur before /w/?
(f) When two glides occur together initially, the first is /h/ and the second is /w/, as in *whistle*, *wheel*, *white*, *which*, but not all speakers pronounce an /h/ in these words; for them the words begin with /w/. The matter is dealt with further in the section 'Feedback and discussion', below.

All other initial clusters of two consonants have the fricative /s/ followed by a stop, a fricative, or a nasal.

(g) The only stops which can follow initial / ____ / must be voiceless and non-sibilant, specifically, ____, ____, and ____.
(h) The only fricative which is found in second position in an initial

consonant cluster is ____, occurring only in a few words of Greek origin (and always spelled 'ph').

(i) Which nasal consonants can follow initial /s/?

7A FEEDBACK AND DISCUSSION

(a) Both voiceless and voiced stops occur initially before /r/.
(b) Both voiceless and voiced stops occur initially before /l/.
(c) /č/ and /ǰ/ do not occur in that position.
(d) Only voiceless fricatives occur initially before /r/ and before /l/.
(e) /t d k g θ s/

Summarizing a little, we see that only these stops and fricatives occur initially before /r l w/:

/p b f t d θ s ʃ k g/

but /s/ does not occur before /r/, /t d θ ʃ/ do not occur before /l/, and /p b f ʃ/ do not occur before /w/. The occurring clusters can be plotted like this:

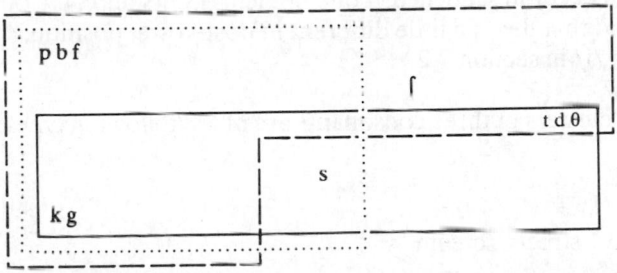

The solid line encloses the obstruents which occur initially before /w/, the dotted line encloses those which occur initially before /l/, and the dashed line those which occur initially before /r/.

(f) Those who pronounce /h/ in *wheel* and other 'wh' words have a contrast between *which* /hwič/ and *witch* /wič/, *whine* /hwain/ and *wine* /wain/. Those who don't pronounce /h/ before /w/ (quite possibly the majority of the world's English-speaking population) have no such distinction. Even those who have /hw/ in *when*, *where*, etc. are likely to 'drop' the /h/ in certain contexts. Consider the two sets below. In which set would /h/ more likely be lost?

When did they leave?	. . . the day when they left
What does he want?	. . . don't know what he wants
Where is it?	. . . find out where it is

The /h/ is more likely to be 'kept' when such words are at the beginning of an utterance, as in the examples on the left and to be omitted when the words are in the interior of an utterance, as on the right.

(g) /p t k/
(h) /f/
(i) /m n/

To summarize some more, we see from these statements that if an obstruent (S or F) and a sonorant (N or L or G) occur together at the beginning of a word, the obstruent precedes the sonorant; in other words, the sonorant is on the 'inside' position, next to the first vowel (or only vowel) of the word. Using the symbol # at the left to represent word-beginning, we have:

$$\# \text{ obstruent} \left\{ \begin{array}{l} \text{nasal} \\ \text{liquid} \\ \text{glide} \end{array} \right\} \text{vowel}$$

This is a SCALE OF SONORITY: a vowel is the most sonorant of all speech sounds, and sonorant consonants are more sonorant than obstruents. In English, nasal, liquid and glide are mutually exclusive in pre-vowel position; they do not occur in sequence; if one of them occurs here, the others do not. We will find that this is a little different in post-vowel position. (And see the note about /j/ in section 7.2.)

(3) Initial clusters of three consonants are of the following types:

(i) sCr-

spry street scream

(ii) sCl-

splendid sclerosis

(iii) sCw-

squint

Here the initial fricative is always /s/; the second consonant is a voiceless stop, /p t or k/; the third consonant is /r l or w/. We can see that the 3-consonant clusters originate, so to speak, by putting together the type sC-, where C has to be /p/, /t/, or /k/, with types Cr-, Cl-, and Cw-, in which /p/, /t/, or /k/ has to be compatible with /r/, /l/, or /w/. Since there is no initial */pw-/ or */tl-/, there is no initial */spw-/ or */stl-/.

7.2 A note regarding /j/

Consider the following words:

puny beauty fuse muse view cue hue spew skew
tube duty new suit student

Words like these begin with one or two consonants followed by the glide /j/. In the preceding section we dealt with the glide /w/ in initial clusters like *twin* and *swim*. Why not treat the glide /j/ at the same time and list the initial clusters in which /j/ occurs? The answer is that there is a difference between /w/ and /j/. When /w/ occurs in an initial cluster, it may be followed by various vowels, as in *sweet*, *twin*, *dwarf*, *quote*, etc., just as /r/ and /l/ in initial clusters can be followed by various vowels. However, when /j/ occurs in an initial cluster, as in the examples above, it is always followed by the vowel /uu/. We notice also that, unlike /w/, /r/ and /l/, /j/ occurs after the nasal /m/ (*music*) and the voiced fricative /v/ (*view*). For these reasons some linguists prefer to consider the whole sequence /juu/ a single vowel unit.

The words in the second line above bring us to a dialect difference. These words have an apical consonant or consonants in initial position. For some speakers such words as *stew*, *student*, *tube*, *Tuesday*, *tune*, *due/dew*, *duty*, *new*, *nude* begin with /stjuu-, tjuu-, djuu-, njuu-/. Others – the great majority of Irish, Canadians, and Americans – pronounce such words without /j/: /stuu-, tuu-, duu-, nuu-/. Some – but very few – of those who have a /j/ after /t d n/ may also pronounce a /j/ after initial /s/ as in *suit* and *super*.

Does /j/ occur after /č/ and /ǰ/, as for example in *chew* and *juke*? In most parts of the English-speaking world the question is irrelevant. In Britain some regional dialects make a distinction between *choose* and *chews*. The former is /čuuz/ and the latter is /čjuuz/, [tʃʲu:z] or /čiwz/ [tʃiʷz]. For other dialects of English, which have no such distinction, the question of whether or not there is a /j/ after initial /č/ (and /ǰ/) is a moot one.

7.3 Contrast and variation

A phoneme is a unit of sound which has different pronunciations (is manifested by different segments) in different positions of occurrence. In some cases the variability is due to what comes before or after a particular phoneme. For example, the vowel of *home* is nasalized (because /m/ follows) while the vowel of *hope* is not nasalized; the first consonant of *too* is likely to be pronounced with rounded lips and the first consonant of *tee* with stretched lips because the speaker anticipates the articulation of the vowel which follows. This kind of variability is treated in chapter 6. But variability is also due to another factor, the amount of 'room' there is for the phoneme. The sketch below is supposed to represent in a crude way the inside of the mouth and the approximate distance of the initial consonants from one another in the mouth.

FRONT			BACK
pay, bait	take, date	chase, jade	Kate, gate
pray, brave	train, drain		craze, grave
play, blame		claim, glaze	

Before a vowel, as shown in the first line, there are four pairs of stops. Each pair has its own 'territory'. A stop can be articulated at different points within that territory but it cannot 'intrude' into the territory of a neighbor. (Actually, of course, the labial stops cannot be articulated anywhere except at the lips.) Before /r/, as the second line shows, there are only three of these pairs of stops. Consequently, the non-labial ones have more room in which to be articulated. Note your pronunciation of the initial stops of *take*, *date* and *train*, *drain*. You may find that your pronunciation of /t/ and /d/ are farther back, [t›] and [d›] respectively, before /r/. The third line indicates that there are only two pairs of stops which occur initially before /l/ – only one non-labial pair. Many speakers have a more forward /k/ and /g/, [k‹] and [g‹] respectively, before /l/ than in the other types of initial position.

7.4 Word-final position

The last (or only) vowel of a word may be followed by:
(0) Zero (that is, the vowel may be word-final)

no, day, agree, supply, soda . . .

(1) Any single consonant except /h/

nap, cub, room, leaf, believe . . .

(2) Certain clusters of two consonants; the exhibit below sorts these clusters by type and gives relevant examples. Questions follow.

7B EXERCISE

Here is the exhibit for final clusters:

(i) -rC

harp verb hurt word arch urge work berg
wharf carve birth force harsh
harm barn
curl

(ii) -lC

help bulb belt weld belch bulge milk
shelf delve filth pulse Welsh
film (kiln)

(iii) -NC (nasal + consonant)

lamp ant hand lunch sponge bank
nymph month rinse lens

(iv) -FS (fricative + stop)

lisp list risk

(v) -SF (stop + fricative)

lapse spitz fox adze

(vi) -SS (stop + stop)

apt act

EXERCISES

(a) If a final consonant cluster consists of an obstruent (S or F) and a sonorant (L or N), the _____ precedes the _____; that is, the _____ is in the 'inside' position, next to the (last) vowel.

(b) If the sonorant consonant is a nasal, it is HOMORGANIC with the following obstruent; that is, it is produced with the same articulator as the obstruent. This means that before the labials /p/ and /f/ only ____ occurs; before dorsal /k/ only ____ occurs; and before other consonants the nasal is ____.
If the sonorant is a nasal, the only voiced obstruents which follow are /d/ and /ǰ/, as in *land*, and *lunge*. Other voiced obstruents do not occur in

this position. Words like *climb* and *thumb* were once pronounced with a final /b/; compare the words *clamber* and *thimble*, originally related words, where the /b/ is not final and still survives. Similarly, words like *fang* and *long* once had a final /g/; compare *finger* and *linger*, where the /g/ survives in medial position. In words like *sing* and *long* the final /g/ is still present in the speech of some people, but it has disappeared in most dialects of English.

If the sonorant is a liquid, either /l/ or /r/, it may be followed by other voiced obstruents – see -rC and -lC, above – but these are relatively rare.

(c) If two sonorants occur together in final position, can both be nasals?

(d) Can both be liquids? If so, in what order do they occur?

(e) When two obstruents occur together in final position, they may be fricative + stop (FS), stop + fricative (SF), or two stops (SS), but two fricatives do not occur finally unless one of them is a suffix (e.g. *cuff-s*, *breath-s*). The word *adze* (homophonous with *add-s*) is exceptional: it ends with the voiced consonants /dz/. All other final clusters of two obstruents are _____.

7B FEEDBACK AND DISCUSSION

(a) The sonorant precedes the obstruent; that is, the sonorant is in the inside position.

(b) Only /m/ occurs before /p/ and /f/; only /ŋ/ occurs before /k/; before other consonants the nasal is /n/.

(c) If a word ends with two sonorants, the two sonorants will not both be nasal; there is no final cluster of the type -NN. The spelling of *damn*, *solemn*, etc. shows that a cluster of /m/ and /n/ once occurred in final position, but no longer; compare *damnation* and *solemnity*, where the cluster is not final.

(d) Two liquids can occur word-finally; /r/ must precede /l/.

(e) Except for *adze* all final clusters of two obstruents are voiceless. Note also that every such cluster contains /s/ or /t/, and perhaps both of them.

From the sequences described above we can establish another scale of sonority. Moving away from the vowel, which is the most sonorous of speech sounds, there is a general sequence like this (where #, at the right end, marks the end of a word):

vowel r l nasal obstruent #

/r/ may precede /l/; either of them can come before a nasal; and any of these three occurs before an obstruent – but of course not all four occur together since there is a constraint against more than three final consonants. Indeed, there are further constraints on what the three final consonants may be, which we examine in the next section.

(3) Three consonants in a cluster; the types and examples are shown in the next exhibit.

7C CLUSTERS OF THREE CONSONANTS

Here is the exhibit:

(i) three obstruents – stop, fricative, stop (SFS)

text, midst

(ii) nasal + two obstruents

NSS: prompt, distinct
NSF: glimpse, jinx
NFS: against, amongst

(iii) liquid + stop + fricative (LSF)

corpse, quartz

(iv) Two liquids + stop (LLS), with only one example: world

(The words *(a)midst*, *amongst*, and *whilst* are very rare in the United States.)

EXERCISE

The word *world* is the only example of a 3-consonant cluster in which all three consonants are voiced. In all other such clusters the last two consonants are ____ obstruents. Furthermore, either /____ / or /____ / occurs in every such cluster, and perhaps both of them.

7.5 Word-medial position

Between two vowels in a word there may be from zero to four consonants. The number of possible consonants is greater than in word-initial or word-final position, and the number of types of clusters is also larger. Since medial clusters are between two vowels, we also need to consider how they divide between syllables.

What can occur between two vowels in a word?

(0) Zero (no consonant at all). In this case the first vowel must be a 'free' vowel since it ends a syllable.

neon poet coward giant

(1) Any one consonant. Most consonants occur between a stressed vowel and an unstressed vowel (where the consonant is ambisyllabic) and also between an unstressed vowel and a stressed vowel (where the consonant belongs to the same syllable as the stressed vowel).

p	ˈcopy	reˈpel	b	ˈrabid	deˈbate
t	ˈmetal	reˈtain	d	ˈmedal	aˈdore
č	ˈhatchet	aˈchieve	ǰ	ˈrigid	reˈject
k	ˈwicker	deˈcay	g	ˈwagon	beˈgin
f	ˈcoffin	afˈfair	v	ˈcover	aˈvert
θ	ˈauthor	meˈthodical	ð	ˈweather	—
s	ˈmessage	masˈsage	z	ˈrazor	reˈserve
ʃ	ˈmission	maˈchine	ʒ	ˈmeasure	reˈgime
m	ˈcommon	comˈmune	n	ˈdinner	deˈnounce
l	ˈrally	reˈly	r	ˈberry	paˈrade

There seem to be no words with medial /ð/ before a stressed vowel, but this is probably due to the fact that the consonant /ð/ is rather rare in any position.

The nasal /ŋ/ is also rare; it occurs between a stressed vowel and an unstressed one (and only in a few words like *gingham*) but not before a stressed vowel.

The glides /j w h/ are just the opposite. In medial position they occur only before stressed vowels: *beˈyond*, *aˈware*, *proˈhibit*. Such words as *bias* and *coward* might be interpreted as /ˈbajəs ˈkawərd/, with /j/ and /w/ followed by an unstressed vowel but this implies a syllable division /ˈba.jəs, ˈka.wərd/. It seems more accurate to regard these words, and others like them, of course, as having complex vowels /ai/ and /au/ which end their syllables: /ˈbai.əs, ˈkau.ərd/. In other words, the first syllable of *bias* sounds like the word *by* and the first syllable of *coward* sounds like *cow*. Even before a stressed vowel the front glide may be part of the preceding vowel unit, as in *Toyota* /toiˈoutə/. /h/ does not occur medially before an unstressed vowel; the word *vehicle* is either /ˈviiɨkəl/ or /ˈviihɪkəl/ – compare *vehicular* /viiˈhɪkjʉlər/, where /h/ is in the tonic syllable.

(2) There may be two consonants. We divide them into two groups.

(a) clusters of the types which also occur word-initially; when they occur between a stressed vowel and an unstressed one, the first consonant is ambisyllabic; when they occur between an unstressed vowel and a stressed one, the whole cluster is in the same syllable as the stressed vowel.

ˈwhisper ˈmaster ˈwhiskey	deˈspair diˈsturb eˈscape
ˈApril ˈcitrus ˈAudrey ˈsacred	deˈpress proˈtract seˈcrete
ˈproblem ˈnecklace (/ˈnɛklɨs/)	suˈblime seˈclude
ˈawkward ˈEdward	reˈquire

(b) clusters which do not occur word-initially; the syllable division is between the two consonants, no matter which is stressed.

ˈcap.tain ˈtip.sy ˈdoc.tor ˈcan.dy ˈtem.per ˈpan.ther ˈran.cid
ˈcar.pet ˈmur.der ˈsel.dom ˈar.my ˈhar.ness ˈhel.met ˈear.ly
dicˈta(tion) conˈdemn imˈpel inˈsist surˈpass perˈtain

The words above have consonant clusters in medial position which also occur finally in other words: *captain* has the same cluster as *apt*, *candy* has the same cluster as *hand*, *carpet* has the same cluster as *harp*, and so on. But medial clusters are more numerous and more varied than those which occur initially and finally. Consider these different types:

(i) two obstruents of which one or both are voiced

rugby husband obtain subside

(ii) two voiceless obstruents, not including /s/ or /t/ (Remember that one or both of these occur in almost every final cluster of obstruents.)

napkin option fracture

(iii) two fricatives

esthetic asphalt diphtheria (/dɪfˈθiriə/ or /dɪpˈθiriə/)

(iv) an obstruent and a nasal

acme acne arithmetic dogma magnet

(v) a voiced fricative and a liquid

gosling every (/ˈɛvri/)

(vi) /t d θ/ followed by /l/

butler maudlin athlete

(vii) a nasal plus a voiced obstruent other than /d/ and /ǰ/ (Remember that these are the only voiced obstruents after a nasal in final position.)

timber finger Denver clumsy

(viii) a sequence of two nasals, or a nasal and a liquid

enmity amnesia only Henry

(ix) /l/ before /r/ or /w/

already always

(x) any consonant followed by /j/ when /j/ is not followed by /uu/

onion failure

In all these cases syllable division is between two consonants.

(3) Three consonants, which can be divided into groups.

(a) clusters which also occur initially; the first consonant must be /s/

mistress resplendent distress

(b) clusters which do not occur initially, and which can be subdivided:

(i) clusters in which the syllable division is after the first consonant

(C.CC)
an.thra(cite) bel.fry coun.try pil.grim pam.phlet

(ii) clusters in which syllable division is after the second consonant

(CC.C)
ant.ler emp.ty func.tion

(iii) clusters in which the second consonant, always /s/, may be ambisyllabic

cap ˆstan in ˆstant par ˆsley textile /tɛk ˆstail/

7D EXERCISE

The type of cluster illustrated in (i), above, is probably more common than the types in (ii) and (iii). In type (i) what kind of consonant is the middle one of the three? What kind of consonants are the first and third, the ones next to the vowels?

(4) Four consonants; the second consonant is always /s/.

instrument obstruct express /ɛkspres/ exclaim /ɛkskleim/

Here /s/ is ambisyllabic in *instrument*, where the stressed vowel precedes; in the other three words /s/ begins the stressed syllable.

7E EXERCISE

Consider the medial clusters in these pairs of words.

disperse	disburse
mistake	misdate
discussed	disgust

While the requirements of communication never make it necessary to distinguish between *disperse* and *disburse*, *discussed* and *disgust*, since the context tells us which word is intended, it is still a fact that any speaker of English can make the distinction and another speaker will perceive it. What is the difference? Is it just a difference between voiceless stop (/p t k/) and voiced stop (/b d g/)?

7F EXERCISE

Divide the following words into syllables.

pansy	doctor	sulfur
skeptic	ethnic	hatred

magnolia	orchestra	influenza
oxygen (ɒksɨǰɨn)	technique	hypnosis
synthesis	spasmodic	linguistics

7.6 Borrowed words

In this chapter we have examined the patterns in which consonants go together in English words. But we should note that, as language changes over a period of time, word patterns are among the things that change. A thousand years ago English (in the form called Old English) had such words as *hnutu* 'nut', *hrof* 'roof', *cnawan* 'to know', *fneosan* 'to sneeze', with clusters of consonants which no longer occur in English words. At some time in history the first consonant in clusters like *hn-*, *hr-*, *kn-*, became silent, and the cluster *fn-* changed to *sn-*.

A language can acquire new phoneme patterns, mostly by borrowing words from another language or other languages. In the English of today we find words, including names, borrowed from other languages, which have uncommon sequences of consonants, e.g. *schwa*, *shtick*, *Schlitz*, *tsunami*, *pueblo*. Can you think of others?

So we need to observe that, although there are general patterns in which consonants go together, there are also innovations in the patterns. Such patterns do not remain static – certainly not in the English of the twentieth century.

7.7 Omission and insertion of a consonant

In this chapter clusters of consonants have been presented as though they are invariable, but that is not really the case. The word *English*, for instance, may have the medial cluster /-ŋgl-/, but it may also be pronounced with just /-ŋl-/. When two morphemes come together in a word, as in *kindly* or *windmill*, new clusters of consonants are created – in these examples /-ndl-/ and /-ndm-/. Often such clusters are simplified – in these two examples by loss of /d/ in the middle of the clusters. Similarly, a word-final cluster like the /skt/ of *asked* is often reduced to /st/ and a cluster like the /sks/ of *asks* becomes just /ss/, that is, [s:], a prolonged [s]. We deal with more kinds of consonant-dropping like these in the chapter on Phonological Processes. Here we want to deal with some instances of what may be called variable clusters.

Consider the consonant clusters in these words:

dreamt tempt hamster Hampshire warmth Thom(p)son
redemption

Is there a /p/ in these words? It won't do to say that some of the words have a /p/ and others do not. It is more accurate to say that each word may or may not be pronounced with the voiceless stop that is made by bringing the lips together. In each word there is a voiced labial nasal /m/, and there is another consonant which is voiceless, non-labial, and non-nasal. Between the two there may be a transitional /p/ which shares some of the features of the consonants on each side.

m	(transition)	t, s, θ, ʃ
+ voice	(− voice)	− voice
+ nasal	(− nasal)	− nasal
labial	(labial)	non-labial

The Old English word *aemtig* has become Modern English *empty*. Textbooks in the history of the English language sometimes cite this as a case of **epenthesis**, the insertion or addition of a consonant, in this case /p/. But was anything really added? In Old English, as in Modern English, there was no possible contrast between a cluster /-mt-/ and a cluster /-mpt-/. The only change is a matter of interpretation.

In a similar fashion, the following words contain the voiced dorsal nasal /ŋ/ and some voiceless non-dorsal, non-nasal consonant. Is there or isn't there a /k/ between them?

thanks linked defunct puncture function

Again, there is no contrast between such sequences as /ŋks/ and /ŋs/, /ŋkt/ and /ŋt/, /ŋkč/ and /ŋč/, /ŋkʃ/ and /ŋʃ/.

When we consider apical clusters, however, we find a different situation. Is there a contrast between /ns/ and /nts/?

prince prints tense tents sense cents
correspondence correspondents

Some speakers do, and others do not, make a distinction. For those who make such a distinction *prince* ends with /ns/ and *prints* ends with /nts/. Notice that /ns/ occurs within morphemes and /nts/ only across a morpheme boundary: /print # s/, etc.

There is a similar relation between /nz/ and /ndz/; some speakers do, and other speakers do not, make a distinction in such items as these:

lens lends men's mends fines finds

Interestingly, those who pronounce *chance* and *chants* alike, for instance, probably have /t/ in both, whereas if, for instance, *lens* and *lends* are alike, there is probably no /d/ in either.

7.8 Limits on vowel occurrences

However many vowels there are in English, or in any variety of English, they are not used as extensively as they might be. Theoretically, if a common canonical form for words is CVC, as in *cat*, *bed*, *lip*, *seem*, *shake*, etc., one might expect that all consonants would occur in initial position, all consonants would occur in final position, and all vowels in between. We have already seen that there are limitations on the consonants in initial and final position, and we shall now see that there are strong constraints on vowel occurrences. It happens that essentially all vowels can occur after all initial consonants but not all occur before all final consonants. For example, before final /ŋ/ or /ŋk/ there are only four possible vowels in native English words, illustrated by:

sing	sang	song	sung
pink	rank	honk	dunk

Foreign names like *Jung* or *Soong* or an odd interjection like *boing* or *oink* are exceptions to this statement, but they are the only kinds of exceptions. Native English words with final /ŋ/ or /ŋk/ can be preceded by only four vowels.

In itself this constraint is a trivial matter, of course, but such constraints affect the number of possible vowel contrasts which exist, and these constraints have an effect on what people pronounce and, as we will examine in the next chapter, on what people have to perceive. With respect to pronunciation, what is the vowel of *sing*, for example? Is it the same as the vowel of *seat* or the vowel of *sit*? Different speakers will give different answers to the question, and why not? If there is no contrast between these two vowels before /ŋ/ – no possible contrast in meaning between something like /siiŋ/ and something like /sɪŋ/ – then there is obviously more room for variation in what is pronounced.

Before tongue-tip consonants in word-final position it is easy to find examples of a large number of different vowels. We illustrate with final /t d n s l/:

ii	beat	bead	bean	niece	feel
ɪ	bit	bid	bin	miss	fill
ei	bait	wade	bane	mace	fail
ɛ	bet	wed	Ben	mess	fell
æ	bat	bad	ban	mass	pal
ɒ	pot	rod	don	moss	doll
ɔɔ	taut	laud	dawn	sauce	ball
ʌ	putt	mud	dun	muss	dull

ou	boat	mode	bone	dose	bowl
ʊ	put	good	—	puss	full
uu	boot	food	boon	moose	fool
ai	bite	bide	dine	nice	file
au	bout	loud	down	mouse	foul
oi	Hoyt	void	coin	voice	foil

As we have seen, not all of these distinctions are maintained in all dialects.

The pronunciation of vowels before postvocalic /l/, as in *feel*, *field*, *bolt*, requires some special comment here. The checked vowels /ɪ ɛ æ ʊ ʌ ɒ/ sound approximately the same before /l/ as before other consonants, and the same is true of the low back /ɔɔ/. The high and mid free vowels, however, have, for most speakers, a slight centering offglide in this position. Compare the pronunciation of these vowels before /l/ and before /t/:

feel, field	[fi^{ə}l(d)]	feet	[fi^{i}t]
fail, failed	[fe^{ə}l(d)]	fate	[fe^{i}t]
pool, pooled	[pu^{ə}l(d)]	toot	[tu^{u}t]
bowl, bold	[bo^{ə}l(d)]	boat	[bo^{u}t]

For some speakers words like *pool*, *bowl* become two-syllable pronunciations and thus rhyme with *cruel*, *Noel*, and the like.

The vowels designated /ai, au, oi/ vary dialectally before /l/ as elsewhere. For each there is a one-syllable and a two-syllable pronunciation:

file	[fa^{i}l],	[fa^{ə}l]	or [fa^{i}əl]
foul	[fa^{u}l]	or	[fa^{u}əl]
foil	[fɔ^{i}l]	or	[fɔ^{i}əl]

Such pairs as *file* and *dial*, *howl* and *towel*, *oil* and *loyal* are potentially one syllable and two syllables, respectively, but the difference is non-existent in some dialects and probably not consistent in some others.

When /l/ follows a free vowel and is itself followed by a vowel, as in the next group of words, there is no offglide. The /l/ may be more 'clear' or more 'dark', depending on dialect.

feeling failing pooling holy calling silent howling toilet

Since some vowels have quite different allophones before final /l/ and in final position, there are possible audible differences in such examples as these:

sea lion	[..i^{i}la^{i}..]	seal island	[..i^{ə}la^{i}..]
too lofty	[..u^{u}l..]	tool office	[..u^{ə}l..]
Am I late	[..a^{i}le^{i}t]	Aisle Eight	[a^{ə}le^{i}t]

7.9 Free vowels and checked vowels

When we turn to other final consonants and consonant clusters we see that constraints can be best stated with reference to the two groups of vowels, the checked ones which typically occur in closed syllables, /ɪ ɛ æ ʊ ʌ ɒ/, and the free vowels which occur in closed and open syllables, /ii ei ai oi uu ou au aa ɔɔ/.

Free vowels occur before single consonants but only before a limited number of consonant clusters (within a single morpheme). The consonant clusters are /nt nd st ld nǰ/, as in:

paint pint point count
fiend find wound pound
feast chaste Christ moist joust boost boast
field wild bold
change lounge,

and less commonly before other clusters, such as /ps/ in *traipse*, /ks/ in *coax*, and /lt/ in *bolt*.

Just as there are constraints on what vowels may occur before certain consonants and consonant clusters, there are constraints on what consonants may occur after certain vowels, notably /ai, au, oi/. The vowel /oi/ occurs in final position (e.g. *toy*) and it may be followed by a consonant but there are only six consonants which occur: /t/ (*exploit*), /d/ (*void*), /s/ (*voice*), /z/ (*noise*), /n/ (*coin*), and /l/ (*coil*); and two clusters, /st/ (*moist*) and /nt/ (*point*). There is scarcely any word which ends with /-oip/ or /-oič/ or /-oik/, for instance. Consonants which occur after /oi/ are all tongue-tip consonants. The constraint is expressed in this formula:

Given: o i C (C) #
↓ ↓
Then: tip tip

7G EXERCISE

There are similar, but less rigid, constraints on the occurrence of consonants after /ai/ and /au/.

(a) Consider these 36 theoretically possible word-endings (/ai/ and /au/ plus 18 consonants). See if you can think of a word for each of these endings. If you can't think of one fairly quickly, the sequence probably doesn't occur.

-aip	-ail	-aup	-aul
-aib	-aič	-aub	-auč
-aif	-aiǰ	-auf	-auǰ
-aiv	-aiʃ	-auv	-auʃ
-aim	-aik	-aum	-auk
-ait	-aig	-aut	-aug
-aid	-ais	-aud	-aus
-aiθ	-aiz	-auθ	-auz
-aið	-ain	-auð	-aun

(b) What kind(s) of consonants occur after /au/?

Before most clusters of two or more final consonants only the checked vowels occur. The high-back vowel /ʊ/is relatively rare, so that there are not usually more than five vowels occurring before most clusters of consonants. Some examples:

/-mp/	limp hemp camp bump stomp
/-pt/	crypt inept apt corrupt adopt
/-kt/	strict sect act conduct concoct
/-lf/	sylph shelf Ralph gulf golf

There are also five vowels contrasting before the next set of consonant clusters, but here /æ/ is replaced by /aa/ in RP and other dialects.

/-ft/	lift left draft tuft soft
/-sp/	wisp clasp cusp wasp
/-sk/	risk desk mask dusk mosque

Before other clusters it may be hard to find even five vowels contrasting. Consider:

/-mf/	nymph
/-ts/	blitz
/-lǰ/	bilge bulge
/-lč/	filch belch mulch
/-lp/	help scalp pulp
/-lk/	milk elk talc sulk
/-lθ/	filth wealth
/-ls/	else pulse false
/-lʃ/	welsh
/-lb/	bulb

The set of vowels in English is not used to the potential limits.

7.10 Functional loads

One consequence of these limitations is a difference in the FUNCTIONAL LOAD of certain vowel contrasts. If we try to find minimal pairs for the high-back vowels /uu/ and /ʊ/, as in *pool* and *pull*, *suit* and *soot*, or even near-minimal pairs like *food* and *good*, we won't easily succeed. On the other hand, for the high-front vowels /ii/ and /ɪ/ there are numerous minimal pairs: *week/wick*, *team/Tim*, *reap/rip*, *seal/sill*, *beach/bitch*, etc. The contrast of /uu/ and /ʊ/ has a low functional load, and that of /ii/ and /ɪ/ has a high functional load.

Because the contrast of /uu/ and /ʊ/ has a low functional load, there is variation among speakers in the choice of one or the other of these. The words below are pronounced by some people with the vowel of *food*, by others with the vowel of *good* – and they don't necessarily all have the same vowel for a given speaker or group of speakers.

root roof hoof hoop coop room broom

The plural of *roof* is *roofs*, which does not necessarily have the same vowel; the plural of *hoof* is *hoofs* or *hooves*, either of which may have either vowel.

7.11 Summary

Speech is, in a way, a sequence of openings and closings of some part of the vocal tract, so that sequences of consonant, vowel, consonant, vowel (like the word *banana*) are perhaps the most fundamental kind of word pattern. Many languages, English among them, have patterns of consonant co-occurrence which are considerably more complex, but still there are contraints on what may occur. While the listing of such occurrences seem to be a matter of tedious detail, the *types* of occurrence are relatively few. People who know the language have a (largely unconscious) awareness of these patterns, which facilitates their perception and comprehension of what they hear. Students of English who come from different language backgrounds may have different degrees of difficulty in acquiring the pronunciation of different sequences of English phonemes and speakers of English may have similar problems in learning another language.

In part, sequences of consonants follow a **scale of sonority**. Before the first (or only) vowel of a word two consonants are most likely to be obstruent + sonorant (e.g. /pr-, tw-, gl-, sn-/); if two obstruents occur, the first must be /s/; if three consonants occur, the first is /s/, the second /p t or k/, the third /r l or w/. In final position the sequence is sonorant + obstruent (e.g. /-mp, -rk, -ld/); if two sonorants co-occur, /r/ precedes /l/ and either may precede a nasal; if two obstruents co-occur, they are both voiceless and include either /s/ or /t/; sequences of three consonants show the same general kinds of constraints. In medial position more clusters and more kinds of clusters occur, but the same general limitations are seen: two obstruents usually agree in voice; in clusters of three consonants, the middle one is typically an obstruent while the first and third – the ones next to vowels – are sonorants.

As with other language matters, the phonotactics of English consonants is not static. There are variant ways in which certain clusters are actually pronounced, especially where no contrast is involved. And there are some novel clusters in recently borrowed words.

There are likewise constraints on the occurrence of vowels. From a theoretical point of view these constraints mean that potential contrasts are not exploited as much as they might be; certain vowel contrasts have a low **functional load** while other contrasts have a high functional load. The limitations on contrasts also account for certain vowel variations among speakers. One particular constraint among vowels is seen in the distinction between **free vowels** and **checked vowels**. The former occur in word-final position and when followed by single consonants and a very small number of possible consonant clusters. The latter do not occur finally but can be followed by single consonants and consonant clusters.

7C FEEDBACK

Voiceless obstruents /s/ or /t/

7D FEEDBACK

The middle consonant is an obstruent, the first and third are sonorants.

7E FEEDBACK

There is a difference in syllable division as well as a difference of voicing. Thus:

di'sperse	dis'burse
mi'stake	mis'date
di'scussed	dis'gust

7F FEEDBACK

The most likely syllable divisions are these:

ˈpan.sy (/.zi/)	ˈdoc.tor	ˈsul.fur
ˈskep.tic	ˈeth.nic	ˈha ˆtred
magˈnol.ia (.jə/)	ˈor.che ˆstra	ˈin.fluˈen.za
/ˈɒk.si ˆǰɨn/	techˈnique	hypˈno ˆsis
ˈsyn.the ˆsis	spasˈmo ˆdic	linˈgui ˆstics

7G FEEDBACK

(a) Sample words are given for the sequences which do exist; a blank appears beside each non-occurring sequence.

/-aip/	pipe	/-ail/	file	/-aup/		/-aul/	howl
/-aib/	tribe	/-aič/		/-aub/		/-auč/	couch
/-aif/	wife	/-aiǰ/	oblige	/-auf/		/-auǰ/	gouge
/-aiv/	dive	/-aiʃ/		/-auv/		/-auʃ/	
/-aim/	time	/-aik/	like	/-aum/		/-auk/	
/-ait/	kite	/-aig/		/-aut/	shout	/-aug/	
/-aid/	side	/-ais/	rice	/-aud/	crowd	/-aus/	mouse
/-aiθ/		/-aiz/	rise	/-auθ/	south	/-auz/	rouse
/-aið/	blithe	/-ain/	dine	/-auð/	mouth	/-aun/	clown

Some of the words given, such as *oblige*, may be the only examples of the particular sequence.

(b) Only tongue-tip and tongue-front consonants occur after /au/.

8

Some Consequences of Phonotactics

8.1 Consonant clusters and some grammatical suffixes

The suffix which forms the past tense of regular verbs is written -(*e*)*d*, as in *looked* and *baked*. The pronunciation is /t/, /d/, or /ɨd/, depending on the last phoneme of the verb to which the suffix is added; for example, *kicked* /kɪkt/, *begged* /bɛgd/, *petted*/ pɛtɨd/. Though these three are different forms, they express the same meaning, 'past tense'. The unit of meaning which we label Past Tense is a MORPHEME. Some morphemes are always expressed in the same way; other morphemes, such as the one we are discussing now, have two or more forms, called its ALLOMORPHS. /t/, /d/, and /ɨd/ are three allomorphs of the morpheme past tense – and there are other allomorphs seen in irregular verbs.

8A EXERCISE

(1) The verbs listed in the exhibit below illustrate all the consonants and some vowels in word-final position. Write /t/, /d/, or /ɨd/ after each verb according to the pronunciation of the suffix. Then figure out the rule which determines the pronunciation.

step	wait	reach	look
rub	need	budge	hug
laugh	race	finish	hum
love	breathe	raise	massage
fan	play	annoy	gnaw

Rule

(a) The regular past tense is pronounced /ɨd/ after verbs that end with ____ or ____;

(b) it is pronounced /t/ after _____;

(c) it is pronounced /d/ after all other phonemes.

(Note the importance of stating the rule in this order. First, the smallest group is identified, then the next group in size, and finally the largest group can be identified simply as 'all others'.

(2) The suffix which forms the plural number of regular nouns, written -(*e*)*s*, is pronounced /s/ or /z/ or /ɨz/, depending on the last phoneme of the noun to which the suffix is added. Thus *cats* ends with /s/, *dogs* with /z/, and *horses* with /ɨz/. These three forms are allomorphs of the morpheme Plural Number (which also has irregular allomorphs).

8B EXERCISE

The nouns shown below illustrate all consonants and some vowels in word-final position. Write /s/, /z/, or /ɨz/ after each noun according to the pronunciation of the suffix, and then determine the rule which tells which of the three variants occurs in what positions.

rib	bed	bridge	leg
cuff	smith	hive	lathe
kiss	wish	rose	garage
arm	pin	ring	bell
tree	day	law	car

Rule
(a) The regular plural suffix is pronounced /ɨz/ after _____;
(b) it is pronounced /s/ after _____;
(c) it is pronounced /z/ after all other phonemes.

(3) The regular possessive suffix, as in *Tom's* and *Jerry's*, also has three variant pronunciations, /s/, /z/, and /ɨz/. This is a different morpheme, Possessive, which has the same three regular allomorphs as the plural number morpheme. (Possessive has no irregular allomorphs.) Here are some representative nouns, ending with most of the possible consonants and some vowels.

Chris Rose Mr Fish Ms Finch the judge
Hope Robert Dick Ralph Beth
Bob Ted Peg Steve Tom Ann Sue Joe Mary

8C EXERCISE

Is the form of the possessive suffix chosen by the same rule that applies to the regular plural suffix?

(4) Another suffix is the so-called 'third person singular present' of verbs, as in (he) *likes*, (she) *loves*, (it) *hisses*, with the same three variants, /s, z, ɨz/. Examine the verbs in the exhibit of paragraph 1, above, and determine the pronunciation of the suffix after each one.

8D EXERCISE

Is the variation in this suffix determined by the same rule as for plural number?

(5) The verb form *is* is often contracted, as in *The milk's here*, *The coffee's boiling*, *The glass's broken*. The auxiliary verb *has* undergoes the same kind of contraction, as in *Steven's been working*, *Alice's told me*, and so on.

8E EXERCISE

What are the variant pronunciations for the contracted forms of *is* and *has*: What are the determining factors?

8E FEEDBACK AND DISCUSSION

The variants are the same, /s, z, ɨz/. The rule is the same as for the /s, z, ɨz/ suffixes.

Note that the contraction of *has* occurs only when *has* is an auxiliary verb. Most speakers of English don't make such a contraction when *has* is a main verb, as in *Sue has an appointment at two o'clock*, *The violin has a broken string*. Of course, contraction can take place in the equivalent *Sue has got an appointment at two o'clock*, *The violin has got a broken string*.

There is one difference between the suffixes (plural, possessive, third person verb forms) and the verbs *is* and *has*. The latter have the forms /s, z, ɨz/ if contraction occurs, but contraction is optional. There is no such option for the suffixes.

In discussing these variations, /d, t, ɨd/ and /z, s, ɨz/, we have so far only described what the variants are and in what environments they occur. But if we look a bit further, we can observe that the choice is partly determined by phonotactic constraints or, we may say, by what is 'natural' in the English sound system.

The variant /ɨd/ occurs after /t/ and /d/: *waited*, *needed*; /t/ occurs after voiceless obstruents except /t/: *slipped*, *kicked*, *kissed*, etc; /d/ occurs elsewhere – after voiced obstruents except /d/ – *rubbed*, *hugged*, *buzzed*, etc. – and after all sonorants – nasals, liquids, and vowels – for example, *fanned*, *called*, *played*.

Thus /d/ is the basic, or fundamental, or underlying form of this morpheme, the suffix which indicates past tense for regular verbs. It occurs in more environments than the other two variants and, more importantly, the other two are the result of necessary adjustments. English words do not end with two identical consonants like /tt/ or /dd/ or with consonants that differ only in voice like /td/ or /dt/; the past tense of *wait* /weit/ and *need* /niid/ can't be */weitd/ and */niidd/. Such consonant sequences occur in some languages but not in English. English requires the insertion of a vowel between /t/ or /d/ and the suffix /d/.

Likewise, English words do not end with two obstruents which differ in voice: the past tense forms of *skip*, *kick*, *kiss* can't be */skɪpd, kɪkd, kɪsd/. An adjustment is made: /d/ becomes voiceless /t/ to match the preceding phoneme.

Finally, we note that /d/ occurs after voiced obstruents, where we would not expect /t/ to occur, but it also occurs after sonorants – e.g. *fanned*, *called*, *played* – where /t/ and /ɨd/ are theoretically possible: /fænt/ and /fænɨd/ are pronounceable. Clearly /d/ is the basic form of this morpheme.

To treat the matter within the framework of generative phonology we say that the suffix has a single underlying form occurring with all regular verbs. We represent the suffix as //#d//. The surface forms, or actual pronunciations, of the suffix are the result of two adjustments, or RULES, which apply to the underlying form in order to make it pronounceable within the general sound system of English. The rules are:

Vowel insertion: after /t/ or /d/ insert /ɨ/ before //#d//.
Voice assimilation: after a voiceless consonant change //#d// to /t/.

We show these changes as DERIVATIONS of surface forms from underlying forms. In the underlying forms the suffix is identical.

Underlying forms	//#pɛt#d#	#kɪk#d#	#bɛg#d#//
Vowel insertion	ɨ		
Voice assimilation		t	
Surface forms	/pɛtɨd	kɪkt	bɛgd/

8F EXERCISE

Could the order of the two rules be changed so that the voice assimilation rule takes effect before the vowel insertion rule? Would the result be the same with either order for the rules?

The alternation of /s, z, ɨz/ is exactly parallel to the /t, d, ɨd/ alternation. /z/ is the basic form of the different suffixes which have this alternation – regular plural, possessive, third person singular. This /z/ cannot occur immediately after a sibilant, /s z ʃ ʒ č ǰ/, so the insertion of a vowel is necessary. /z/ also cannot occur after a voiceless obstruent, /p t k f θ/, so a different adjustment is required, a voice assimilation.

Vowel insertion: between a final sibilant and the suffix //#z// insert /ɨ/.
Voice assimilation: after a final voiceless obstruent change //#z// to /s/.

Here are three sample derivatives:

Underlying forms	//#hɔrs#z#	#kæt#z#	#dɒg#z#//
Vowel insertion	ɨ		
Voice assimilation		s	
Surface forms	/hɔrɔiz	kæts	dɒgz/

The vowel insertion rules for the two suffixes are very similar, so they can be put together as a single rule:

Between a final apical stop and //#d// and between a final sibilant and //#z// insert /ɨ/.

It is even easier to conflate the two voice assimilation rules:

When two obstruents occur together in word-final position, they must agree in voice; assimilation is progressive.

(We say that the 'basic' or underlying form of the plural suffix is //#z//; this is also the underlying form of the possessive suffix and the third person singular suffix in verbs. But we cannot say that *is* and *has* have this underlying form, even though they have the same possible pronunciations as the suffixes. The underlying forms are the full, uncontracted forms.)

8G EXERCISE

The preceding section has dealt with grammatical suffixes which may be single consonants, /z/, /s/, /d/, /t/, in the surface forms. Each of these may be added to a word which already ends in one or more consonants, producing a cluster of consonants. In some instances the consonant cluster may coincide with a cluster which can occur at the end of a word without a suffix; for example the words *lapse* and *laps* end with the same consonant cluster and in fact are homophonous, and the same is true of *chaste* and *chased*.

Another single-consonant suffix is -/θ/, which is actually two derivational morphemes, the Ordinal Number suffix which occurs in *fourth* and *tenth* and the Abstract Noun suffix of *warmth* and *growth*.

All the following words end with the suffix pronounced /t/, /d/, /s/, /z/, or /θ/. In each case the suffix is added to a word which ends in one or more consonants. After each word write in phonemic notation the resulting cluster of consonants. Then decide if that consonant cluster also occurs at the end of monomorphemic words and, if so, give an example. The first two are done for you.

packs	/ks/	Yes, *lax*	bridged
bags	/gz/	No	coughed
lacked			cuffs
lagged			loves
breathed			fourth
rapped			fifth
clips			sixth
rubs			width
rubbed			depth
beds			length
brushed			warmth
shoved			tenth

8.2 Morpheme variation

Some morphemes – indeed most morphemes – are always pronounced the same way; for example, *dog*, *dimple*, *daffodil*. Other morphemes have two or more forms, allomorphs, occurring in different environments. This is true of grammatical morphemes such as past tense and plural number, and it is also true of some lexical morphemes; for example, *thief* /θiif/ has an alternate form, or allomorph, *thiev-* /θiiv/ before the plural ending: *thieves* /θiivz/; it has another allomorph *thef-* /θɛf/ which occurs in *theft* /θɛft/; the auxiliary verb *have* /hæv/ has an alternate form '*ve* /v/ which occurs in contractions like *I've* and *we've*. Some allomorphic variations are due to phonotactic constraints, and we examine some of them below. Other allomorphic variations depend on style of speaking, like *have* and '*ve*; these are discussed in chapter 13. Other variations, like *thief*, *thiev-*, *thef-*, are due to neither phonotactic constraints nor style of speech, and they are dealt with in chapter 14.

8.2a

Some morphemes end in clusters of consonants which are permitted in word-medial position, with a vowel following, but not in word-final position. The word *entrance*, for example, obviously has a suffix *-ance* added to a base *entr-*, which must be the same morpheme that occurs alone as the word *enter*. We see similar variation in *angry* and *anger*, *cylindrical* and *cylinder*. Each of the three base morphemes has two allomorphs.

Before a vowel	*Independent word*
/ɛntr-	ɛntər/
/æŋgr-	æŋgər/
/sɪlɪndr-	sɪlɪndər/

Instead of *entrance* speakers of English could say *enterance*, a sequence of phonemes that is pronounceable but which happens not to be the standard form. On the other hand, they could not say **entr* instead of *enter*, since that is contrary to phonotactic norms. To describe the facts of alternation we say that the basic or underlying form of the morpheme is //ɛntr// and that there is a rule which adds /ə/ where it must be added – between a consonant and /r/ in word-final position. Analogous statements can be made for the other two base morphemes: their underlying forms are //æŋgr// and //sɪlɪndr//, respectively, and of course the same SCHWA INSERTION RULE applies to them.

The schwa insertion rule can be stated in prose or as a formula, but before stating it in any fashion we need to make another observation. Consider these words:

entering angered cylinders

Here the schwa is present even though /r/ is not final. We must reformulate our statement: a schwa is inserted between a consonant and /r/ in final position or before certain suffixes. Three suffixes are illustrated, *-ing*, *-d*, and *-z*. These are NEUTRAL SUFFIXES, attached to an independent word after any necessary adjustments, such as schwa insertion, are made to that word. If we use the symbol # to represent a word boundary and the symbol +

for a word-internal boundary between a base and a non-neutral suffix, the essential information about the items we have discussed can be shown this way:

#enter#	#anger#	#cylinder#
#enter#ing#	#anger#ed#	#cylinder#s#
#entr+ance#	#angr+y#	#cylindr+ical#

And now we are ready to state the rule, in prose and as a formula: insert schwa between a consonant and //r// when a word boundary follows.

0 → ə / C___r#

We show the effects of this rule as a set of derivations:

Underlying forms	//#ɛntr#	#ɛntr#d#	#ɛntr+əns#//
Schwa insertion	ə	ə	
Surface forms	/ɛntər	ɛntərd	ɛntrəns/

8H EXERCISE

The words below are like *entrance*, with a suffix attached to a base. Strip off the suffix and show the underlying form in ordinary spelling (like *entr-*) and the surface form of the base word (like *enter*).

hungry	disastrous	theatrical
wintry	monstrous	central

8.2b

The words *fiddle*, /fɪdɨl/ or /fɪdəl/, and *fiddler*, /fɪdlər/, must have the same underlying form, except for the suffix in the second word: //#fɪdl#// and //#fɪdl#ər//. The insertion rule that applies to the base word without a suffix is similar to the insertion rule introduced in section 8.2a above. Whether the vowel inserted is /ə/ or /ɨ/ is a matter of dialect or even a matter of free variation for any individual. We use schwa in our formula to keep it similar to the formula introduced in section A.

0 → ə / C___l#

8I EXERCISE

The words below are like *fiddler*. Take away the suffix of each and give the base word, in its surface form, that corresponds to *fiddle*.

muffler	peddler	suckling
juggler	sampler	twinkling

8.2c

The words *rhythmic* and *rhythm* have the same relationship to each other as *entrance* and *enter*, the same relationship as *fiddler* and *fiddle*. There are not many such pairs of words with morpheme-final -Cm; two of them are *cataclysmic*, *cataclysm* and *prismatic*, *prism*. But there are somewhat more words like *chasm*, *plasm*, and those with the suffix *-ism*. The same rule applies to all of them:

$$0 \rightarrow \text{ə} \,/\, \text{C}___\text{m} \,\#$$

8.2d

A rule should be as general as possible. In sections A, B, and C three similar rules have been introduced. They are not three different rules but parts of a single rule, which should be stated as such:

$$0 \rightarrow \text{ə} \,/\, \text{C}___\begin{Bmatrix} \text{r} \\ \text{l} \\ \text{m} \end{Bmatrix} \#$$

or, since /r l m/ are sonorant consonants, in this form:

$$0 \rightarrow \text{ə} \,/\, \text{C}___[+\text{cons}, +\text{son}] \,\#$$

8.2e

Now we turn to a different kind of adjustment rule. Consider these items:

autumn - autumnal	damn - damnable	hymn - hymnal
column - columnist	condemn - condemnation	solemn - solemnize

In each pair of words the first is a simple base and the second word has the same base plus a suffix. The underlying form of each base must be the same with or without the suffix, but the surface pronunciation of each base varies slightly because of English phonotactic constraints. Each morpheme ends with *-mn* but that cluster is not permitted in word-final position. Rather than the insertion of a vowel between the two consonants, we have instead the deletion of the second consonant in word-final position:

n → 0 / m____ #

A sample derivation:

Underlying forms	//#hɪmn#	#hɪmn+əl#//
N-deletion	0	
Surface forms	/hɪm	hɪmnəl/

8J EXERCISES

(a) What is the pronunciation of *damning*, *condemned*, *hymns*? What are the underlying forms of these words?

(b) Instead of a rule which deletes the //n// in final position, why not say instead that there is an insertion rule which operates here? The underlying form for *hymn*, for instance, would be //#hɪm#// and the rule would insert /n/ before a non-neutral suffix which begins with a vowel, such as the *-al* of *hymnal*. However, this would be the wrong analysis. Why?

The alternations we have observed above are PHONOLOGICALLY CONDITIONED, but only in part. The rules for schwa insertion and N-deletion are phonologically conditioned, in part, because /ɛntr/ and /dæmn/, for example, cannot occur as whole words or before suffixes which consist of a single consonant, like #*d* and #*z*. There must be a vowel inserted or a consonant deleted to make them conform to English pronunciation standards. However, there is no *phonological* reason for inserting a vowel or deleting /n/ in *entering* and *damning*. The suffix *-ing* begins with a vowel, just like the suffixes *-ance* and *-ation* of *entrance* and *damnation*. So if a schwa is inserted in *entering* but not in *entrance* and //n// is deleted in *damning* but not in *damnation*, these rules are MORPHOLOGICALLY CONDITIONED in part. It is one particular morpheme that blocks the application of the rules.

Now that we have made this point, we have to admit that the facts are actually more complex. The deletion of //n// is consistent; *damning* and *condemning* are never pronounced with /n/ after the /m/. On the other hand, the insertion of a vowel in *-Cr* and *-Cl* clusters is variable. Such words as *ent(e)ring*, *cent(e)ring*, *whistling*, *fiddling*, *simpler*, *noblest* may be pronounced in three syllables or in two – with a schwa inserted or without.

8.3 Differences in morpheme division

What kind of noise annoys an oyster?
A noisy noise annoys an oyster

In the previous chapter we examined the possible sequences of consonants and possible sequences of vowels and consonants. Obviously, we have looked at minute matters which the ordinary speaker of the language takes for granted. Does it really matter what sequences occur? Does this examination lead us to some better understanding of the English language, and of language in general?

Yes, knowledge of this sort is important for speech therapists whose patients are learning to acquire or re-acquire the ability to produce the kinds of utterances that all speakers of the language produce. The therapist or speech teacher needs to diagnose the patient's difficulties in a general way. To make a list of words which are troublesome for the patient is not a systematic approach. To recognize what sequences are troublesome can lead to questions about, and experimentation with, similar sequences. In a similar way, the teacher of English as a second or foreign language can acquire some sense of what difficulties face the student from a particular native language background. Since languages differ in their phonotactics, the learner of a new language does not merely have to acquire new sounds, new phonemes, but also new kinds of sequences. Again, the teacher is not well informed by knowing simply that this or that word is a source of trouble to the student; the teacher will profit from more general knowledge, from a grasp of the scope of the trouble.

Recognition of what can and what cannot occur in the utterances of English (or whatever language) helps us to appreciate somewhat the process of perception. What sort of information about a language do people have stored in the unconscious part of their brains that makes it possible for them to recognize what they have heard. We do not need to hear everything that is in the stream of speech of someone talking to us, and often we cannot – there are various disturbances in the environment, the speaker makes errors, and our attention may be less than 100 per cent. And yet we usually get the message because language has redundancy – or better, messages have redundancy. Part of the redundancy is in syntactic and semantic cues, but it must also be of use to us that we eliminate some potential sequences of sounds, quite unconsciously, because we have an awareness of what sequences do not occur in English. In much the same way, a skilful reader does not need to perceive every possible visual cue because there is redundancy in the sequences of letters which occur in a written text.

Let's be more specific. The consonants /m/ and /p/ occur in word-initial, word-medial, and word-final position. The cluster /mp/ does not occur word-initially. It occurs finally and medially, as in *lamp* and *temper*, but only after a checked vowel. A free vowel, such as /ei/, occurs in final position (e.g. *play*) and before final /m/ (*tame*) and /p/ (*tape*) – among other possibilities – but not before /mp/. A checked vowel like /ɛ/ occurs before /m/, /p/, and /mp/ (*stem*, *step*, *hemp*) but not word-finally. These observations are true, in general, for all checked vowels like /ɛ/, for free vowels like /ei/, and for consonant clusters like /mp/.

To express these facts in formulas (where V = a checked vowel, V: = a free vowel, and # denotes a word boundary), here are the possible and impossible word endings:

V: #	V # (impossible)
V:m #	Vm #
V:p #	Vp #
V:mp # (impossible)	Vmp #

The possible and impossible sequences have an effect on what may occur when two words come together in an utterance – and therefore on what is involved in our processing and interpreting of what we hear. A sequence of

free vowel - /m/ - /p/ - vowel

must divide between /m/ and /p/, as in *tame panther*, *seem poor*, *home power*. A sequence of

checked vowel - /m/ - /p/ - vowel

may divide after /m/ or after /p/, as in *plum pie* or *plump eye*, *jam pot* or *lamp oil*, *trim parade* or *limp away*. To use formulas again,

. . . V: m p . . . = . . . V:m # # p . . .

but

. . . V m p . . . = . . . V m # # p . . . *or* . . . V m p # # . . .

Some sequences of English phonemes are like the first of these (V: m p); they occur only at the boundary of two morphemes, and there is only one way the sequence can be divided between the morphemes. For example, when two instances of the same consonant occur in sequence, they must belong to different morphemes,

night time homemade half fare

and the same is true for sequences of two consonants which differ only in voice,

bus zone red tie log cabin

Usually when any consonant is followed by /h/, the morpheme division is before /h/,

pinch-hit outhouse childhood

(possible exceptions: *abhor*, *adhesive*).
And usually when /ŋ/ is followed by anything other than /k/ or /g/, the morpheme division is after /ŋ/,

singer ring it kingdom

(exceptions: *dinghy*, *gingham*, *hangar*, and names like *Langham*).

Other sequences are like the second, (V m p); they occur in single morphemes like *temper*, and they occur at morpheme boundaries, with two possible places for the boundary, as in *plum pie* versus *plump eye* and in *a noise* versus *an oyster*. Here are some more examples:

I scream	gray day	we dressed
ice cream	Grade A	we'd rest
a name	Lou skis	been selected
an aim	loose keys	since elected
see Mabel	like you	nitrate
seem able	my cue	night rate
		dye trade

(A pair like *ice cream* and *I scream* may differ in stress as well as in syllable division.)

How do speakers of English recognize such differences in syllable division? The first answer is that we don't – not necessarily and not always. It would be a rare occasion on which we might need to decide whether we had heard, for example, 'While they were waiting, we dressed' or 'While they were waiting, we'd rest'. Whichever of these was intended, we would no doubt interpret correctly through our knowledge of the situation – events, persons, and what had been said previously – without even recognizing the possibility of the other utterance.

But if our attention is directed to such potential distinctions (as your attention is directed by reading this section), can we unfailingly catch the distinctions? Not with 100 per cent accuracy. Experiments have been carried out in which subjects heard one utterance of such a pair, saw both sentences (or phrases) written on their test paper, and then matched what they thought they heard with one member of the written pair. The results indicate that, whatever audible clues there are for distinguishing the two or more utterances, performance in perceiving these clues is less than perfect – but then performance is always less than perfect. If people consistently perform with better than 50 per cent accuracy in such discrimination, we may be sure there is something 'there' which makes discrimination possible.

What makes discrimination possible is the presence of a number of phonetic features which are non-distinctive, redundant, on the level of phonemic contrast but which perform a function in the structuring of syllables. In chapter 6 we dealt with such features as roundness of consonants, aspiration on voiceless stops, nasality in vowels, and the like. These features have no role in distinguishing one consonant from another, one voiceless stop from another, or one vowel from another, but they have a role in telling us to which syllable a vowel or consonant belongs or where it belongs in the syllable.

Note how the linguistic forms above are distinguished by presence or absence, or different position, of phonetic features like the following:

Aspiration: The /k/ of *I scream*, *Lou skis*, and *like you* is unaspirated, the /k/ of *ice cream*, *loose keys*, and *my cue* is aspirated. Similarly, the /t/ of *night rate* is not aspirated while that of *dye trade* is.

Vowel nasality: The /ə/ in *an aim* and in *an oyster* is likely to be nasalized, while the /ə/ of *a name* and *a noise* is not nasalized, or at least less likely to be. There is a corresponding difference of nasality in the first syllable of *seem able* versus that of *see Mabel*.

Sonorant length: When a vowel is syllable-final, as in the first syllable of *see Mabel*, *Lou skis*, *gray day*, *my cue*, *I scream*, *dye trade*, it is longer than when syllable-medial (*seem able*, *loose keys*, *Grade A*, *like you*, *ice cream*, *night rate*), and, as we have seen, the phonetic nature of /ai/ especially may be quite different in final position from what it is before a voiceless consonant. Similarly, the syllable-final /n/ of *been selected* is longer than the non-final /n/ of *since elected* (and there may be a /t/ between /n/ and /s/ in the latter).

Fricative /r/: The /r/ of *nitrate*, *dye trade*, and *we dressed* is apt to be articulated with some friction after /t/ and /d/. In *night rate* and *we'd rest*, on the other hand, the articulation of /r/ is similar to that which is found in initial position.

Note that there is often a clustering of such feature differences. In *night rate* versus *dye trade* (or *Nye trait* if one wants a closer contrast) there is a difference in the length and perhaps the starting-point or ending-point of the first vowel, the /t/ which follows is unaspirated in one item and aspirated in the other, and the /r/ is made without friction or with friction.

8.4 Summary

Constraints on the cluster of consonants are responsible, in part, for the fact that certain **morphemes** have more than one phonological form. The suffix which expresses past tense, when attached to regular verbs, has three forms, or **allomorphs**, /ɨd, d, t/. Three other morphemes have the regular allomorphs /ɨz, z, s/: plural number and possessive, which are attached to nouns, and third person, attached to verbs. We see that /d/ and /z/ are the common expressions of their respective morphemes, whereas the other allomorphs are found only where those two are impossible because of phonotactic constraints. We posit //#d// and //#z// as abstract, or **underlying forms**, and we derive **surface forms** from them through **rules**, specifically **vowel insertion** and **voice assimilation**.

Just as **grammatical morphemes** like past tense and plural number have variation, some **lexical morphemes** also have allomorphs. In this chapter we have examined morphemes that have final consonant clusters which are not permitted word-finally. Morphemes which end in a cluster of obstruent + sonorant consonant (−Cr, −Cl, −Cm) insert /ə/ between the obstruent and the sonorant before the boundary marker # – that is, in word-final position and before a **neutral suffix**, morphemes which end in *-mn* delete the *n* under the same conditions. The respective rules are labeled **schwa insertion** and **N-deletion**. The rules do not apply before **non-neutral** suffixes, which are indicated in the underlying form by the boundary marker +.

When the application of a rule depends entirely on sequences of phonemes (or stress), the rule is said to be **phonologically conditioned**; if a rule applies according to some sequence of morphemes, it is **morphologically conditioned**.

Certain sequences of phonemes can only occur across morpheme boundaries. Other sequences are ambivalent, occurring both within a morpheme and across a morpheme boundary. The phonological information by which speakers of English recognize the boundary differences is provided by such phonetic features as aspiration, sonorant length, vowel nasalization – in short, features which are redundant with respect to the system of segmental phonemes. Of course, syntactic and semantic information also facilitate interpretation.

8A FEEDBACK

(a) The regular past tense suffix is pronounced /ɨd/ after verbs that end with /t/ or /d/;
(b) it is pronounced /t/ after other voiceless consonants – that is, /p č k f s ʃ/;
(c) it is pronounced /d/ after all other phonemes.

8B FEEDBACK

(a) The regular plural suffix is pronounced /ɨz/ after sibilants – /s z ʃ ʒ č ǰ/;
(b) it is pronounced /s/ after other voiceless consonants – that is, /p t k f θ/;
(c) it is pronounced /z/ after all other phonemes.

8C FEEDBACK

Yes.

8D FEEDBACK

Yes.

8F FEEDBACK

No, because the voice assimilation rule would change //#pɛt#d#// to /pɛtt/, and then the vowel insertion rule would make it /pɛtɨt/. Of course, this is not the actual pronunciation.

8G FEEDBACK

packs	/ks/	Yes, *lax*	bridged	/ǰd/	No
bags	/gz/	No	coughed	/ft/	*soft*
lacked	/kt/	*act*	cuffs	/fs/	No
lagged	/gd/	No	loves	/vz/	No
breathed	/ðd/	No	fourth	/rθ/	*north*
rapped	/pt/	*apt*	fifth	/fθ/	No
clips	/ps/	*ellipse*	sixth	/ksθ/	No

rubs	/bz/	No	width	/dθ/ or /tθ/	No
rubbed	/bd/	No	depth	/pθ/	No
beds	/dz/	Only *adze*	length	/ŋ(k)θ/	No
brushed	/ʃt/	No	warmth	/rm(p)θ/	No
shoved	/vd/	No	tenth	/nθ/	*month*

8H FEEDBACK

//#hʌŋgr#// hunger //#dɪzæstr#// disaster //#θiætr#// theater
//#wɪntr#// winter //#mɒnstr#// monster //#sɛntr#// center

8I FEEDBACK

muffle peddle suckle
juggle sample twinkle

8J FEEDBACK

(a) /ˈdæmɪŋ, kənˈdɛmd, hɪmz/ //#dæmn#ɪŋ# #kɒndɛmn#d# #hɪmn#z#//
(b) There are words which have a final /m/ but don't add /n/ before a suffix that begins with a vowel: *drummer*, *Vietnamese*. The /n/ pronounced in *condemnation*, *columnist*, *solemnize*, etc. must be derived from the underlying form.

9

The Rhythm of English Speech

9.1 Prosody

Up to this point we have dealt mostly with 'Segmental phonology', the description of the segmental phonemes – consonants and vowels – and of the sequences in which they occur and the variations they have. We turn now to 'Suprasegmental phonology', or 'Prosody', which is concerned with three matters:

1 The ways in which an utterance is broken into 'chunks'. Compare the utterance 'We don't want any' spoken in a single breath and the same sequence of words said in four separate breaths, as perhaps by somebody who is irritated or insistent:

(1-a) / We don't want any /
(1-b) / We / don't / want / any /.

The technical name which we employ for 'chunk' is TONE UNIT. Sentences 1-a and 1-b obviously have the same verbal content but they differ in what Halliday (1967) calls *tonality*: Sentence 1-a consists of one tone unit; Sentence 1-b consists of four tone units. (Other writers have used the terms 'Tone Group' or 'Macrosegment' where we use 'Tone Unit'.) From here on we will show tone groups by putting a slant line before and after each one.

2 Within a tone unit the POSITION OF ACCENT – the emphasis that makes one syllable more prominent than other syllables, and therefore makes one word more prominent than the other words in the tone unit. Each of the sentences below is one tone unit in length and therefore has one accented syllable, indicated by bold face. Notice how the meaning changes when the accent is moved.

(2-a) / We don't want **those.** /
(2-b) / We don't **want** those. /
(2-c) / **We** don't want those. /
(2-d) / We **don't** want those. /

In a sense each of these four utterances has the same meanings: the meaning of ***we*** (whoever 'we' may be), the meaning of ***those*** (whatever 'those' are), the meaning of *want*, and the meanings of Negative and Present Time. However, they differ in an important kind of meaning, FOCUS, which we will study in greater detail in the following pages. In Halliday's terminology these four sentences differ in TONICITY.

3 The INTONATION or melody – or simply what Halliday calls the TONE – the patterned way in which the pitch of the voice changes in the utterance. Compare the two sentences:

(3-a) / You don't **know**. /
(3-b) / You don't **know**? /

The voice falls or the voice rises, and the hearer knows whether the speaker is telling or asking.

This chapter deals with the first two of these matters. The next chapter deals with intonation. Before we get started, we should recognize a few important points:

1 Prosody (sometimes called utterance phonology or suprasegmental phonology) is more subtle than word phonology (sometimes called segmental phonology). As a consequence, numerous languages have writing systems – alphabets or syllabaries – which represent their consonants and vowels adequately if not perfectly, but no language has an orthography which adequately represents the rhythms and melodies of its utterances. Punctuation marks, italics, underlines, and capital letters are crude and inadequate ways of representing prosodic elements.

2 It follows that one written utterance may correspond to two or more spoken utterances (or, if you prefer, one written utterance may be read aloud two or more ways). To take a simple example, compare the pronunciation of 'When?' in these two short dialogs:

A: We're going to have a picnic next huckaluxx.
B: / W h e n? /

(B understands enough of A's utterance to know that the time of an event was mentioned but doesn't understand completely and is asking for a repetition.)

A: We're going to have a picnic.
B: / W
h
e
n? /

(B is asking about something not yet said – new information.) Or compare these two different utterances:

s J
/ This is my on, / o
h
n./

s
/ This is my o n./
n, / Joh

The first utterance suggests that 'John' is the speaker's son, the second, that John is the person addressed.

3 Thus, although prosody deals with subtle matters, these matters are important. There are personal differences in the ways that people use speech, and there are dialect differences, but there are also ways of talking which are common to all speakers of the language. By using differences in the 'tone of voice' we convey different messages which, by and large, are recognized and reacted to by all speakers of the language.

The examples above and others that will follow show that prosodic elements can perform several kinds of functions:

Focus Prosody can highlight one particular word in an utterance and thus make other words less significant by comparison (e.g. /**We** don't want those/ vs /We don't want **those**/) or highlight different numbers of words in what are otherwise identical utterances (e.g. /**We**/ don't want **those**/).

Role in discourse Prosodic elements can indicate the role of an utterance within a larger discourse (/**When**?/ as a request for repetition vs /**When**?/ as a request for information not yet supplied; /The Blakes have a new **car**/, which conveys entirely new information, vs /The Blakes **have** a new car/, which suggests that 'new car' has previously been mentioned.)

Intention of speaker Prosody can make a difference in the way the elements of an utterance are to be interpreted, in the grammatical nature of the whole utterance (the question /You don't **know**?/ vs the statement /You don't **know**/) or in the way the parts of an utterance are related to one another (/ This is my **son**,/ **John**/ where the name 'John' is in apposition with 'my son' or is an address-form added to the sentence).

Still, it would be wrong to exaggerate the role of prosody in communication. We are all likely to feel that we can judge a person's mood by the 'tone of voice' – that we can tell whether he or she is angry, sad, tired, or elated by the way utterances are delivered. But there is no intonation which consistently indicates anger or elation or boredom or any other emotion. Our judgements are determined, in any instance, by the speaker's choice of vocabulary, gestures, and body language and by our knowledge of him or her and the attendant circumstances – not by tone of voice alone. Furthermore, although some grammatical differences may depend on how an utterance is pronounced – /You don't **know**?/ vs /You don't **know**/, for an obvious sort of example – it would be a mistake to assume that there is a close tie between prosodic forms of utterances and their grammatical nature. It is not the case, for example, that questions always have rising intonation nor that only questions have rising intonation. Finally, we should note that, just as the functions of prosody are not specific, neither are they exclusive. The focus that can be achieved by accent in /We didn't give **Ralph** the tickets/ can also be achieved by other devices with or without accent, for example, /It wasn't Ralph we gave the tickets to/.

9.2 Tone units

An utterance may be spoken as a single tone unit or it may be broken into several tone units, as indicated in sentences 1-a and 1-b. The way the utterance is divided into tone units depends partly on the tempo of the speech. The faster a person speaks, the longer and fewer the tone units; the slower the speech, the shorter and more numerous the tone units. We say it depends *partly* on the tempo of speech because speakers can, to a large degree, control the 'chunking' the way they want to.

9A EXERCISE

(a) Each utterance below can be spoken as a single tone unit or can be divided into two or three, or even more, such chunks. Where do you think the breaks are most likely to occur?

We're going downtown this afternoon.
On the way home we'll stop at the library if we have time.
Cape Ann Lighthouse was erected in 1910.
A lot of ships have reached harbor safely because of it.

(b) Sometimes two sentences may have the same sequence of words but still have different meanings because the words go together in different syntactic groups. For instance, *I'd like bread and butter or cheese* can mean *I'd like* (*bread*) *AND* (*butter or cheese*) or *I'd like* (*bread and butter*) *OR* (*cheese*). The way an utterance is divided into tone units by the speaker does not necessarily remove ambiguity, but it may. Consider the sentences below. Can different ways of dividing the sentences determine two different meanings?

She told everyone that she knew the answer.
The tennis courts are to be used by club members only on Thursdays.

Obviously a tone unit must contain at least one syllable – you can't divide *Help!* or *Yes* into smaller chunks. So ordinarily a tone unit contains at least one word. It is possible to divide a polysyllabic word into tone units (e.g. / ab / so /lute / ly /), but that is not very common.

9.3 Stress timing

Notice the staccato rhythm of these unlikely sentences:

Sue bought nice, fresh, warm, sweet rolls.
Ten big white ducks swam home fast.

In each sentence every syllable has equal prominence – held for the same amount of time and given the same amount of stress – except that the final syllable is just a bit longer and louder. The sentences have staccato rhythm, or SYLLABLE TIMING, for two reasons: (1) each word is a monosyllable, and (2) each word is a 'content' word, a noun, verb, adjective, or adverb, each with a definite meaning of its own. We lose the staccato rhythm if we replace one-syllable words with polysyllabic ones:

Susan purchased fancy, sugared cookies.

or if we insert 'function words' – articles, prepositions, conjunctions, or auxiliary verbs:

A group of black and white ducks were swimming in the pond.

In some languages – French is a good example – syllable timing is usual; every syllable has nearly the same prominence, no matter what function it has. In English STRESS TIMING is customary; the stressed syllable, which may be the only syllable, of each content word stands out, and other syllables are relatively weak – the function words and the unstressed syllables of the content words. We can represent the relative prominence of syllables in the four sentences this way:

/ ˈSue ˈbought ˈnice ˈfresh ˈwarm ˈ**rolls**. /
/ ˈTen ˈbig ˈwhite ˈducks ˈswam ˈhome ˈ**fast**. /
/ ˈSusan ˈpurchased ˈfancy ˈsugared ˈ**cook**ies. /
/ A ˈgroup of ˈblack and ˈwhite ˈ**ducks** / were ˈswimming in the ˈ**pond**. /

In each tone unit the accented syllable is most prominent, other stressed syllables are less prominent, and unstressed syllables are least prominent. The vowel of a stressed syllable is long, the vowel of an unstressed syllable is short and it is often a schwa. Sometimes this pronunciation of unstressed syllables is spoken of as 'slurring'. In everyday usage the verb *slur* may be used with negative connotations, but that is unfortunate. In spoken English unstressed syllables are weak and occupy less time than stressed syllables; consequently unstressed syllables do not have the full vowels of stressed syllables. Variant pronunciations of words in stressed position and unstressed position are described in chapter 13.

In a language with syllable timing the amount of time required to produce an utterance depends on how many syllables it has. In English the time, and the rhythm, of an utterance are determined by the number of stressed syllables. Each of the following sentences has two beats – two tone units, two accents – even though the number of unstressed syllables varies. As you say each sentence, hit a table twice with a pencil, keeping the strokes at the same tempo.

The **box** / is **big**.
The **pa**ckage / is **big**.
The **pa**ckage / is **hea**vy.
The **pa**ckages / are **hea**vy.
The **pa**ckages / are **hea**vier.
The **pa**ckages / are the **hea**viest.

However many unstressed syllables there are, they are more or less 'squeezed' into the same amount of time.

Sentences with the same number of syllables and the same arrangements of accented syllables, stressed syllables, strong syllables, and weak syllables have the same rhythm. Sentences with the same rhythm may have the same grammatical structure, as the first two groups of sentences below illustrate; but identical rhythm does not require identical grammar, as the remaining groups below indicate.

I ˈdidn't underˈ**stand**. . + . + . ±
You ˈshouldn't interˈ**rupt**.

They ˈhaven't misbeˈ**haved**.
He's ˈlooking at the ˈ**file**. . + . + . ±
She's ˈwaiting by the ˈ**door**.
We're ˈsitting on the ˈ**floor**.
ˈWhat's the ˈ**ma**tter? + . ± .
ˈBrown's a ˈ**law**yer.
ˈRaise the ˈ**win**dow.
They ˈleft for the ˈ**sta**tion. . + . . ± .
Your ˈtaxi is ˈ**wai**ting.
I ˈdidn't ex ˈ**pect** it.
ˈHow do you ˈknow ˈ**that**? + . . + ±
ˈThis is a ˈnice ˈ**view.**
ˈWhen do they ˈserve ˈ**lunch**?
ˈMister ˈHarris ˈgave us ˈgood adˈ**vice**. + . + . + . + . ±
ˈReserˈvations ˈshould be ˈsent toˈ**day**.
ˈOur comˈpanions ˈhad to ˈwait an ˈ**hour**.

9.4 Marked accent: Paradigmatic focus

As the example sentences in the last section show, the accented syllable of a tone unit is very often the stressed syllable of the last content word in the tone unit. To repeat one example,

/ A ˈgroup of ˈblack and ˈwhite ˈ**ducks** / were ˈswimming in the ˈ**pond**. /

When the accent falls on the last word of a tone unit, we say that the tone unit has a neutral or UNMARKED accent. When the accent falls on an earlier content word or on any function word, we have a MARKED occurrence of accent.

In the unmarked sentence (with tone unit):

/ ˈMary ˈtold ˈJohn ˈall the ˈ**secrets**. /,

it is hard to determine whether there is some special emphasis on the word *secrets* or not. But if accent is moved to an earlier word, the emphasis is obvious, and so is the purpose of this marked occurrence:

/ ˈMary ˈtold ˈJohn ˈ**all** the ˈsecrets. /
[Not just a few secrets]

/ ˈMary told ˈ**John** ˈall the secrets. /
[She didn't tell Harold or Richard or . . .]

/ ˈMary ˈ**told** ˈJohn ˈall the ˈsecrets. /
[She didn't hint, imply, or write them . . .]

/ ˈ**Ma**ry ˈtold ˈJohn ˈall the ˈsecrets. /
[It wasn't Angela or Beatrice or . . .]

This use of accent is contrastive. It is PARADIGMATIC FOCUS. By emphasizing one word the speaker is excluding any other word or term which might occur in the same position or with the same general function; emphasis on a noun makes that noun stand out in contrast to some other noun or nouns which might have been said, emphasis on a verb excludes other possible verbs, and so on. Just what is excluded depends on the context and what the speaker and hearer know about each other.

Sometimes, however, even a casual passer-by can tell what is excluded. Some words belong to very small sets; choosing one word of the set automatically excludes the other word or words of the set. Such sets include *in* and *out*; *up* and *down*; *on* and *off*; *all*, *some*, and *no* or *none*. Some compound words like *inside* and *outside*, *upstairs* and *downstairs*, and the numbers from *thirteen* to *nineteen* are stressed on the ult when used alone, but stress shifts to the initial syllable when contrast is intended, whether the contrast is obvious from the context or just 'in the back of the speaker's mind'. Thus we say *up*ˈ*stairs* in most contexts, as in 'My bedroom is upˈ**stairs**'. But with the contrast we would say, for instance, 'I've spent the whole morning running **up**stairs / and **down**stairs'. If you overheard somebody say, 'Let's put this one **up**stairs', you wouldn't necessarily know what was being put, but you would surmise that something else had been put downstairs.

In a similar way, neutral prefixes can contrast with their absence – contrast with zero. The verb *re-write* typically is stressed on the second syllable, the base of the verb, but in a phrase like *write and re-write* the most prominent syllable is *re*. The contrast with zero is overt when two terms are used together as in that phrase and in the following examples:

the president and the **ex**-president
occupied or **un**occupied
deeds and **mis**deeds

The contrast may be merely implied, as in the second sentence of this short dialog:

ˌIs your ˈboss ˈsatisˌfied with your ˈ**work**?
ˈWell, he's ˈnot ˈ**un**ˈhappy.

One kind of contrast is conversational turn-about, involving the words *you*, *I*, and *we*. Compare:

A: / Hel'**lo**. / 'How '**are** you? /
B: / '**Fine**, 'thanks. / 'How are '**you**? /

Note that the *you* of B's utterance is in contrast with the *you* of A's question. Though it is obviously identical in form, it is different in its reference, its meaning. (A, speaking first, might pose the question as / 'How are '**you**? / instead of / 'How '**are** you? /. Either would be acceptable as the opener in this stereotypical exchange. The choice seems to depend on dialect or even on idiolect. But B's rejoinder must have the accent on the contrasting item. For B to reply / '**Fine**, 'thanks. / 'How '**are** you? / would be impossible.)

9B EXERCISE

(a) Comment on the differences of meaning of these sentences:

1 Her 'new '**dress** / is 'light '**green**.
2 Her 'new '**dress** / is '**light** 'green.
3 Her '**new** 'dress / is 'light '**green**.
4 Her 'new '**dress** is 'light 'green.

(b) In each of the pairs of sentences below the first sentence of the pair is unmarked and the second has marked focus. Say in what way the second sentence of each pair is 'special' – how it differs from the first sentence.

1 A Does 'this 'bus 'go ˌdown'**town**?
B Does 'this 'bus 'go '**down**'town?
2 A Will 'this 'plant 'grow 'better in'**side**?
B Will 'this 'plant 'grow 'better '**in**'side?
3 A I 'said fif'**teen**.
B I 'said '**fif**'teen.
4 A I 'told you to ˌdiscon'**nect** it.
B I 'told you to '**dis**con'nect it.

9.5 Marked accent: Syntagmatic focus

Marked occurrence of accent is not always for contrast. Sometimes the words which are at the end of a sentence are de-accented because they provide little or no information.

The '**te**lephone's 'ringing.
The '**pa**per's just come.
The '**co**ffee's 'perking.

Each of these sentences has a noun phrase followed by a short verb phrase. The speaker of the first sentence, for instance, is not talking about the telephone as opposed to something else (the doorbell, for instance), that might be ringing, though that is one possible interpretation of the sentence. Just as likely, the speaker calls attention to the telephone because it is doing what one expects telephones to do, and that is the reason for calling attention. The other two sentences are similar. Here we may say that *telephone* and *mail* and *coffee* have SYNTAGMATIC FOCUS: they are not emphasized for contrast with some other words which might stand in their place; they are highlighted because what follows is played down.

Part of a sentence may be played down – de-accented – because it represents something that has been said before; it is old information. Compare these sentences:

We ˈspent our vaˈcation in ˈ**Florida**.
We ˈspent our vaˈ**ca**tion in ˈFlorida.

In the first sentence all the information is 'new'. The second sentence, however, would only be possible if *Florida* had recently been mentioned. The information about spending the vacation is 'new', but the rest essentially repeats something which has already been said. The speaker could just as well have communicated this by saying 'We spent our vacation there.'

9C EXERCISE

In the following dialog each sentence consists of one or two tone units, as marked. Each tone unit should have one accent. In some cases the tone unit consists of a single word so that the position of the accent is obvious. In longer tone units the accent is on the last *informative* word. Read the dialog aloud and mark the accent.

A: / Have you taken your family to the zoo yet, / John? /
B: / No, / but my kids have been asking me to. /
/ I've heard this city has a pretty big one. /
A: / Yes, / it doesn't have a lot of animals, / but it has quite a variety of animals. / I think your kids / would enjoy seeing the pandas. /
B: / I'm sure they would. / I'd like to see them, / too. /
A: / Also, / the tigers are worth looking at. /
B: / Is it okay to feed them? /
A: / No, / they're not used to being fed. /
B: / What bus do you take / to get there? /
A: / Number Twenty-eight. / But don't you have a car? /
B: / We used to have one, / but we had to sell it. /

9C FEEDBACK AND DISCUSSION

There is no guarantee that any two people will place accents as we have marked them below, but some placements are more likely than others, and the following are quite probable.

A: / Have you taken your family to the ˈ**zoo** yet, / ˈ**John**? /

(The word *yet* is almost never accented, perhaps because it adds nothing much to a sentence. Notice that the meaning of the question would be much the same without this word.)

B: / ˈ**No,** / but my kids have been ˈ**ask**ing me to. /

(The word *to* stands for the old information 'take the family to the zoo'; it is not accented. In a two-person conversation the pronouns *I-my-me* and *you-your* can generally be taken for granted, therefore are not accented. *Asking* is the last informative word.)

/ I've heard this city has a pretty **big** one. /

(The word *one* is a substitute here for 'zoo', old information.)

A: / ˈ**Yes,** / it doesn't have a ˈ**lot** of animals, / but it has quite a vaˈ**ri**ety of animals. /

(The words *lot* and *variety* are in contrast, paradigmatic focus.)

/ I think your ˈ**kids** / would enjoy seeing the ˈ**pan**das. /

(In the first tone unit *think* might be accented instead of *kids* since the word *kids* has appeared before. In the second tone unit *pandas* is new.)

B: / I'm ˈ**sure** they would. / ˈ**I'd** like to see them, / ˈ**too.** /

(*They would* is likely to be de-accented because it stands for the old information, 'would enjoy seeing the pandas'. However, accenting *would* – / I'm sure they ˈ**would.** / – is also possible, suggesting strong agreement with A's remark. In the next tone unit *I* is accented for two reasons: it contrasts with *your kids* in the previous remark (paradigmatic focus), and the following words *like to see them* are de-accented because they repeat the meaning of 'enjoy seeing the pandas', so that *I* also has syntagmatic focus. The word *too* usually forms a separate tone unit and is discussed in section 11.6, below.)

A: / ˈ**Al**so, / the ˈ**tig**ers are worth looking at. /

(Focus is on another kind of animal. In this context 'to be worth looking at' is another way of talking about seeing.)

B: / Is it okay to ˈ**feed** them? /

(*Them* represents old information.)

A: / ˈ**No**, / they're not ˈ**used** to being fed. /

(*Being fed* is grammatically different from *to feed them* but semantically equivalent – old information.)

B: / What ˈ**bus** do you take / to ˈ**get** there? /

(The verb *take* has little meaning of its own in such expressions as *take a nap*, *take a bath*, *take a ride*, *take a walk*, *take a bus*, *take pictures*, so that it is not accented even when it follows its object, as it does in questions. In the second tone unit *there* stands for the previously mentioned zoo.)

A: / Number Twenty-ˈ**eight**. / But don't you have a ˈ**car**? /

(New topics)

B: / We ˈ**used** to have one, / but we had to ˈ**sell** it. /

(*To have one* repeats the meaning of 'have a car'. *One* is equivalent, in this context, to 'a car', and *it* in the second tone unit is equivalent to 'the car'.

9.6 A note on 'too' and 'either'

Compare these sentences:

/ Harry studied painting in ˈ**Pa**ris, / ˈ**too.** /
/ Harry studied ˈ**pain**ting in Paris, / ˈ**too.** /
/ Harry ˈ**stu**died painting in Paris, / ˈ**too.** /
/ ˈ**Ha**rry studied painting in Paris, / ˈ**too.** /

What is the meaning of *too* (or *also*)? Its 'meaning' is to indicate that what has been said previously with the use of one word or term applies as well with the use of another word of the same form-class, the accented word in the tone unit which *too* follows. The first sentence, then, emphasizes that Harry studied painting in Paris as well as in some other place; the second sentence says that Harry studied painting as well as some other, previously mentioned subject; the third tells us that Harry studied painting in addition to some other activity connected with painting; and the fourth that Harry, as well as some other person or persons, studied painting in Paris.

The word *either* is exactly analogous to *too*, except that it occurs in negative sentences. Consider the following:

/ The maintenance men didn't wash the windows on ˈ**Tues**day / ˈ**ei**ther. /
/ The maintenance men didn't wash the ˈ**win**dows on Tuesday / ˈ**ei**ther. /
/ The maintenance men didn't ˈ**wash** the windows on Tuesday / ˈ**ei**ther. /
/ The ˈ**main**tenance men didn't wash the windows on Tuesday / ˈ**ei**ther. /

9.7 De-accenting: Anaphoric words

It is possible to say, 'I know Archibald but I don't like Archibald', but it is far more usual to say, 'I know Archibald but I don't like him.' English has certain ANAPHORIC WORDS whose function is to refer to what has previously (and recently) been communicated in a different way. The pronoun *he-his-him* refers to 'Archibald' in one context, to 'Paul' in another context, 'the old man selling newspapers on the corner' in another context. The pronoun *he-his-him* is equivalent to the last masculine singular noun or noun phrase that has been expressed. Since anaphoric words contain no new information – in fact, are intended to repeat old information – they are typically not accented.

Anaphoric words include:

1 the pronouns *he*, *she*, *it*, and *they*, which replace definite nouns and noun phrases

Everybody likes **Ar**chibald.	Everybody **likes** him.
I was sitting behind **Li**sa.	I was sitting be**hind** her.
She ordered the **cake**.	She **or**dered it.
We waited for our **friends**.	We **wai**ted for them.

2 the pronouns *one* and *some*, which replace indefinite noun phrases

She ordered a **cake**.	She **or**dered one.
I'll lend you some **mo**ney.	I'll **lend** you some.

3 the pronoun *one*, *ones*, which replaces nouns after certain modifiers

Are you wearing your **brown** suit / or the **blue** one?
Are you wearing the **brown** shoes / or the **black** ones?

(In these examples note that paradigmatic focus – contrast – and syntagmatic focus – the result of de-accenting old information – create a sort of pull-and-push effect. The color words *brown*, *blue*, *black* are highlighted because they are in contrast as modifiers of a following noun. The following noun is replaced by the anaphoric *one(s)*, which is de-accented.)

4 the words *so* and *not*, which replace clauses after certain verbs and adjectives

Did your horse come in *last* / in the third **race**?
I **hope** not, / but I'm **afraid** so.

5 the adverbs *there* and *then*, which replace place phrases and time phrases, respectively

Ever been in **Wee**hawken? I used to **live** there.
Next Monday's a **ho**liday. I think I'll stay home and **rest** then.

6 the auxiliary *do*, which replaces a whole verb phrase

Who tracked in all this mud and got the whole house so dirty?
I did.

(Here again there is a pull-and-push effect. *I* is accented, highlighted, because it contrasts with all the other possible answers to the question word *who*. At the same time, *did* is de-accented because it stands for the previous verb phrase *tracked in all this mud and got the whole house so dirty*.)

7 Finally, there is an anaphoric 'word' which is not a word – zero, nothing at all. Just as a verb phrase in predicate position is replaced by *do*, as in the example above, so a verb phrase after the infinitive marker *to* or after an auxiliary verb, like *be*, *have*, *can*, *will*, *would*, *may*, *should*, and others, is replaced by 'zero'.

Are you going to finish soon?	I ex**pect** to.
Is the committee **mee**ting today?	It **is**.
Has your horse come **in** yet?	I **hope** it has.
Are you going to get a **raise**?	I **should**.

While it sounds silly to talk of de-accenting 'zero', it is important to notice that an anaphoric sentence with 'zero' shows the same sort of accent advancement as any other anaphoric item.

I expect to **fi**nish soon.	It is **mee**ting today.
I ex**pect** to.	It **is**.

I hope it has come **in**.
I **hope** it has.

I should get a **raise**.
I **should**.

When an anaphoric word is accented, the accent signals contrast or something special.

You won't catch ˈ**him** doing work like that, / not ˈ**him**.
Do you know Mr and Mrs ˈ**Brown**? / I know ˈ**her**.

Accented pronouns can tell us to shift the usual references. Consider this:

Pat and *Lou* are names which can belong to either men or women.

Pat shook hands with ˈ**Lou,** / and then he ˈ**kissed** her.
Pat shook hands with ˈ**Lou,** / and then ˈ**he** / kissed ˈ**her**.

Which is the woman in the first sentence? In the second?

9.8 Lexical anaphora

In addition to the anaphoric words listed above, whose only function is to refer back to something already said, we can recall old information by using words which, in a different context, would present new information. Such lexical items are de-accented, and the de-accenting is what tells us that the lexical items are being used anaphorically. There are several kinds of lexical anaphora:

repetition

I've got a **job** / but I don't **like** the job.

[The same meaning can be conveyed by saying . . . *but I don't* ***like*** *it*. Repetition of the same lexical item, this time de-accented and with the definite article *the*, tells us that the object of *I don't like* is the same as the object of *I've got*.]

synonyms

Maybe this man can give us di**rec**tions.
I'll **ask** the fellow.
[*The fellow = the man*.]

superordinate terms

Did you enjoy *Blue* ***High****ways*?

I haven't **read** the book.
This wrench is no **good**. I need a **big**ger tool.

[These sentences would be incomprehensible unless one knows, or can deduce, that *Blue Highways* is the name of a book and that a wrench is a kind of tool, and that is precisely the purpose of de-accenting – to relate the more general term (*book* and *tool*, in these examples) to the more specific term of the preceding sentence.]

The de-accented word or term does not necessarily refer directly to a previous term.

That's a nice looking **cake**.
Have a piece.

But it must be de-accented. That is usually the meaning of de-accenting: the reference for this term is to be found in the previous discourse.

Of course, a word or term does not necessarily refer to something previously said; it may refer to something that is obviously in the physical environment. Suppose one person picks up an object and asks another person

Is this **your** recorder?

De-accenting the word *recorder* expresses the presupposition, or assumption, that both speaker and hearer use this word to refer to this object. Here the speaker takes the name of the object for granted and asks about the ownership of the object (which might also be expressed 'Is this recorder **yours**?') If the speaker said, 'Is this your **recor**der?', it would be a question about the identity as well as the ownership of the object.

It is also true that de-accenting occurs when a word is repeated, even though it has a different referent the second time. We say, for instance,

between one man and **an**other man
a room with a view or with**out** a view

just as we say *deeds and **mis**deeds*, *written or **un**written*. Note that we do a similar thing even with the sequences of numbers and letters. A telephone number, for instance, is usually accented on the name of the last digit, but not necessarily if the last digit repeats an earlier digit.

369–4578 is three six **nine** / four five seven **eight**
369–4575 may be three six **nine** / four five seven **five** or
three six **nine** / four five **se**ven five.

Likewise with acronyms:

FBI is /εf bii **ai** / USA is /juu εs **ei**/
USIS may be /juu εs ai **εs**/ or /juu **s ai** εs/.

9.9 De-accenting to embed an additional message

De-accenting can be used for a very subtle form of communication:

What did you say to **Ro**ger?
I didn't **speak** to the idiot.

The last sentence actually conveys two messages, one embedded in the other: 'I didn't speak to Roger' and 'I call Roger an idiot.' De-accenting the noun phrase *the idiot* is equivalent to saying: the referent for this phrase is the same as the last noun or noun phrase that fits. Just as, in the example above with the word *recorder*, de-stressing means that the name of the item is taken for granted, so here de-stressing of the phrase *the idiot* means that the appropriateness of the term with reference to 'Roger' can be taken for granted.

A clause is often de-accented because it repeats old information:

I think your kids would enjoy seeing the **pan**das.
I'm **sure** they would.

In this context, *they would* stands for 'the kids would enjoy seeing the pandas.'

9D EXERCISE

It is possible to present a new message (somewhat like 'I call Roger an idiot') while actually saying something else. Imagine that you are in the interior of a room at the end of the afternoon and someone else is standing at the window, looking out. Suppose the person at the window says one of the following. What different meanings would you get from the two utterances?

(a) I thought it would **rain** today.
(b) I **thought** it would rain today.

Compare these two short dialogs:

(a) Does Harry want an adding machine or a **cal**culator?
I don't know **what** he wants.
(b) What does Harry **want**?
I don't **know** what he wants.

The second sentence of dialog (**a**) has both paradigmatic and syntagmatic focus on *what*. It has syntagmatic focus because *he wants* repeats something from the preceding question. More important, it has paradigmatic focus because the word *what* matches inanimate noun phrases like *an adding machine* and *a calculator*. The focus is on part of the preceding question. The second sentence of dialog (b) has only syntagmatic focus on *know*. The part that follows, *what he wants*, is de-accented because it repeats, in an indirect way, the whole question that preceded.

9E EXERCISE

(a) Make up two short dialogs similar to those above. Have the first one begin with a question that will bring the answer

I'm not sure **when** she left.

Have the second dialog begin with a question for which the answer is

I'm not **sure** when she left.

(b) What is a possible question that will get this answer?

I can't remember **where** they met.

What is a possible question that leads to this answer?

I can't re**mem**ber where they met.

9.10 Accent on operators

Consider the short dialogs below as three separate conversations which happen to end with the same sentence:

(1) / John seemed very **busy** this morning. /
/ He **was** busy. /

(2) / Is John **bu**sy now? /
/ I don't **know.** / He **was** busy. /

(3) / John wasn't **bu**sy / this **mor**ning, / **was** he? /
/ Oh yes, / he **was** busy. /

Marked accent always has some special function, but what that function is depends on the total context in which it occurs. In these three rather artificial dialogs the word *was* has paradigmatic focus each time, denoting a contrast, but the contrast is different in each instance. These different contrasts are possible because of the different meanings or functions of the word *be*.

In the first dialog the form *was* shows LEXICAL CONTRAST: forms of *be* may occur in contrast with *seem*, as here, or with other verbs that occur before an adjective phrase, such as *look*, *feel*, *appear*, *taste*, *act*. Some other examples of lexical contrast with *be*:

/ This soup tastes **sal**ty. / – / It **is** salty. /

In the second dialog *was* shows MODALITY CONTRAST. More specifically here, the past tense form is contrasted with the present tense form *is*. We will have more to say about modality contrast as we consider other auxiliary verbs, *have*, *do*, *can*, *will*, *may*, and others.

The ending of the third dialog is intended to illustrate POLARITY CONTRAST, the contrast of AFFIRMATIVE and NEGATIVE. The dialog as written contrasts an affirmative sentence with a previous negative one, but the reverse also occurs:

/ It seems John was very **bu**sy. /
/ Oh **no**, / he **was**n't busy. /

These three kinds of contrast are possible with forms of *be* because of three semantic–syntactic properties that this verb has:

1 It is a verb in its own right, contrasting with a limited number of other verbs like *look*, *appear*, *seem*.
2 Its forms contain the kind of modality we call tense, either present (*am*, *is*, *are*) or past (*was*, *were*), which are of course in contrast with each other.
3 It is the locus of the word *not*, commonly reduced to the clitic *n't*. Whether in the full form or the reduced form, *not* is in contrast with its absence – every statement is either affirmative or negative. The clitic *n't* is never accented; the accent is on the form of *be*, or other verb, to which it is attached.

When we consider the many other lexical verbs of English – *walk*, *swim*, *choose*, *describe*, *imagine*, *elucidate*, etc. etc. – we note these facts:

1 Any lexical verb can be accented for lexical focus, as can any lexeme of English.

/ We don't need the **car**. / We're going to **walk** to the meeting. /
/ Did you hear about the **ac**cident? / – / I **saw** it. /

2 Every lexical verb is either present or past in form (*walk*, *walked*; *choose*, *chose*, etc), but focus on tense is achieved by use of the auxiliary verb DO, either present (*do*, *does*) or past (*did*) attached to the simple form of the verb.

/ Alice works at Commercial **Bank**, / **does**n't she? /
/ I'm not **sure**. / She **did** work there. /

/ Peter used to direct the **glee** club, / I **think**. /
/ He still **does** (direct it). /

(/He 'still does. / is also possible.)

3 Similarly, to make a lexical verb negative we use the word DO with *not* or *n't* following. Accordingly, to emphasize that the sentence is negative we accent DO in the negative form (*doesn't*, *don't*) and to emphasize that the sentence is affirmative we use accented DO without the negative particle following.

/ Why don't you like this **pic**ture. / – / I **do** like it. /

9.11 Summary

An utterance consists of at least one **tone unit**, which has a describable **intonation** and in which one syllable, the **accented** syllable, is more prominent than any other. Two utterances which contain the same words in the same sequence may differ from each other in their intonations; in the number of tone units into which they are divided; and in the position of the accented syllable within a tone unit, which determines the **focus** of what is said. The **rhythm** of an utterance depends on the number of stressed syllables it contains. English has **stress timing**, so that stressed syllables are relatively long and prominent, unstressed syllables are short and 'slurred'. In contrast, languages in which all syllables are nearly equal in intensity and timing have **syllable timing**.

We consider the occurrence of accent on the last content word of a tone unit to be neutral, or an **unmarked** occurrence of accent; accent occurring on an earlier word is a **marked** occurrence, giving a marked focus. Two kinds of focus are recognized, **paradigmatic** and **syntagmatic**. These terms do not refer to a difference in what is said and what is heard, but to a difference in how an utterance is related to its context. In paradigmatic focus the speaker is contrasting, explicitly or implicitly, one word or term with other possible words or terms of the same grammatical and semantic set. The word or term is highlighted with respect to other items of the language that might occupy the same position in the utterance. In syntagmatic focus, on the other hand, one word or term is highlighted with respect to other items of the same utterance. These non-highlighted items are **de-accented** because they contribute little or nothing to the information conveyed in the utterance. Most often, de-accented words are **anaphoric**, referring to some previously used linguistic form and thus carrying information which is already 'given', not 'new'. Like any language, English has certain words whose sole function is anaphoric; in addition, it uses **lexical anaphora**; that is, it exploits semantic relationships such as synonymy to refer to something previously said. De-accenting is also used to embed one message in another one, to present what is actually new as if it could be taken for granted.

Paradigmatic focus is LEXICAL CONTRAST, which ordinarily means the contrast of verbs with other verbs, nouns with other nouns, and so on. In the following dialog the verb *be* is in lexical contrast with the verb *look*.

/ John looked quite *tired*. /
/ He *was* tired. /

Forms of *be* may occur in lexical contrast with *look*, as here, or with other verbs that occur before an adjective phrase, such as *seem*, *appear*, *feel*, *taste*, *act*, and others. But *be* and the auxiliary verbs – the so-called 'operators' or 'anomalous finites' – can be the focus of two other kinds of contrast, POLARITY CONTRAST and MODALITY CONTRAST.

Polarity contrast is the simple binary opposition of affirmative and negative. Consider:

/ Today's not *Tues*day. /
/ It *is* Tuesday. /

Modality contrast is the opposition of any items that express modality in English: present vs past tense, perfective vs non-perfective aspect, and anything which is expressed by a modal verb. The first example shows the contrast of tense.

/ Is *Cyn*thia here? /
/ She *was* here. /

The next examples show various contrasts of modality.

/ You ought to see this new *film*. /
/ I *have* seen it. /

9A FEEDBACK

(a) If the first utterance is spoken as two tone units, the most likely division is:

/ We're going downtown / this afternoon. /

If the number of tone units increases, these are possible ways in which the utterance might be divided:

/ We're going / downtown / this afternoon. /
/ We're going / downtown / this / afternoon. /

The second utterance might be:

/ On the way home / we'll stop at the library / if we have time. /

The third and fourth may be divided this way:

/ Cape Ann Lighthouse / was erected in 1910. /
/ A lot of ships / have reached harbor safely / because of it.

(b) The possible meanings of these ambiguous sentences become more obvious if the 'cuts' are made in different places:

/ She told everyone / that she knew the answer. /
/ She told everyone that she knew / the answer. /

/ The tennis courts are to be used by members only / on Thursdays. /
/ The tennis courts are to be used by members / only on Thursdays. /

9B FEEDBACK

(a) Sentence (1) may be considered neutral, unmarked. Sentence (2) seems to emphasize that the dress is not dark green. Sentence (3) tells the color of a new dress, as contrasted with other dresses which are not new. Sentence (4) suggests that the speaker has felt a need to clarify which new garment is of this particular color; it is the dress, not the hat or the sweater or . . .

(b) 1 B suggests that the conversation may already have included information as to whether or not the bus goes uptown. 2 B might be spoken, for instance, after someone has commented that the plant is outside but not growing well. 3 B is very likely when the speaker has been misinterpreted; the speaker wants to clarify that the number is 15, not 16. (Note, by the way, that if *fifty* is misheard as *fifteen*, the person who wants to clarify would not be likely to say 'I said fif'**ty**', moving the stress to a later syllable, even though it is a different, contrasting syllable. More likely, the speaker would just lengthen the last syllable, *-ty*, while keeping the stress on the original *fif-*. Contrastive focus occurs when an earlier syllable or word is emphasized; stress does not move so readily to a later syllable.) 4 B might suggest that the person to whom the sentence is spoken has mistakenly connected some object, having misheard the word *disconnect* as the opposite word, *connect*.

9D FEEDBACK

Sentence (a) is 'normal' or unmarked. One may assume, since the speaker says 'I thought . . . ,' that it has not rained. Sentence (b), on the other hand, has syntagmatic focus: by de-accenting *it would rain today* the speaker presents the notion of 'rain today' as a fact, just as Roger's being an idiot is presented as a fact in the example at the beginning of this section. The speaker seems to be telling you that rain is falling.

9E FEEDBACK

A sentence such as / I'm not '**sure** when she left / is likely to follow a question such as 'When did Mary leave?' or 'Do you have any idea when Mrs Struthers took off?' or a statement like 'I wonder what time it was when the tattooed lady departed from the tent' – in other words, an utterance which contains the meanings of *when*, *leave*, past tense, and some feminine singular noun phrase. The utterance / I'm not sure '**when** she left /, with a focus on time, would more likely be a response to a question such as 'Did Hilda leave on Wednesday?' or 'Did your sister go at noon, or earlier?'

Similarly, a statement like / I can't re'**mem**ber where they met / contains a sort of repetition question 'Where did . . . meet?' and so must be an answer to such a question. On the other hand, the statement / I can't remember '**where** they met / would most likely be a response to a question or a statement which names one or more places: / Did Herb and Hazel meet in Waikiki or Hilo? /

10

Intonation

10.1 Intonation and perception

English utterances are seldom spoken in a monotone. Speakers produce melodies of different kinds, with the voice rising and falling, and hearers perceive different melodies. Strangely, though, the tunes which the speaker produces are not exactly what the listener hears. Recent research has shown that in English (and probably in other languages, possibly in all languages) a speaker begins an utterance at a high pitch. From this beginning the pitch generally falls until the end, except that the downward trend –the LINE OF DECLINATION – is interrupted by one or more EXCURSUS upward or downward from the basic line.

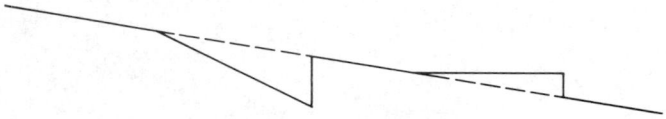

The hearer, however, perceives the excursions more than the basic line. What most listeners would consider a 'rising intonation' seems to be higher at the end than at the beginning of the utterance. In reality, the final pitch may not be as high as the initial one; it is the upward excursion from the line of declination that gives the impression of a high ending. For example, the way a listener perceives the question *Are you going*? (a single tone unit) can be represented as on the left below. On the right below is a way of showing what the actual physical facts are more likely to be.

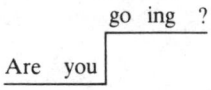

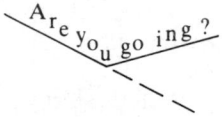

'Pitch' refers, of course, to the relative frequency of vibration of the vocal cords: 'high pitch' is rapid vibration, 'low pitch' is slow vibration; 'rising' and 'falling' indicate increasing and decreasing velocity, respectively. Frequency of vibration depends partly on the force with which air comes up from the lungs and partly on the tension of the vocal cords (due to the positioning of the arytenoid cartilages). Since heavy pressure of air and rapid vibration of the vocal cords often go together, loud stress and high pitch often coincide in English utterances, but not always.

If an utterance consists of a single syllable – for instance, *Yes* or *No* or *Good* – all the change of pitch takes place in the voiced elements of that syllable, and especially in the vowel.

If an utterance, or one tone unit of an utterance, consists of several syllables, the change of pitch (the excursion) may coincide with just one of the syllables

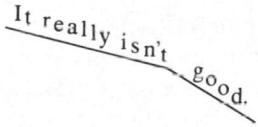

or it may be spread over a sequence of syllables so that part of the change, up or down, occurs with each stressed syllable in the sequence.

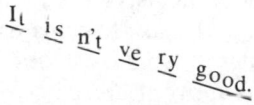

There have been two basic ways of describing melodies of English, the 'levels' approach and the 'contour' approach. The levels approach uses a sort of scale, similar to the scale used in music but simpler. The approach is based on the assumption that English has an inventory of distinctive pitch levels, just as it has an inventory of distinctive vowel and consonant phonemes. Further, just as any utterance is a sequence of vowels and consonants, it is also a sequence of the distinctive pitch phonemes which accompany the segmental phonemes. Some linguists who take this approach have maintained that there are four such levels. The levels may be numbered, say, 1 to 4 from lowest to highest pitch, or given names, such as Low, Mid, High and Extra High. Of course, these levels are relative, not based on any given numbers of vibrations. In absolute terms a child's lowest pitch may be physically identical to an adult's highest pitch. The assumption is that the listener recognizes the *differences* of pitch which the speaker is producing – that the listener recognizes the pitch phonemes even though they are physically different in different speech events, just as segmental phonemes are physically different in different contexts.

For graphic presentation the intonation of an utterance can be shown with lines at four levels with respect to the line of print – just under the line of print, a little below that, just above the print, and a little higher. Less dramatically, the intonation can be shown with letters or numbers interspersed in the line of print. Thus, the utterance *I'm* ˈ*going* ˈ***home*** might appear in one of these forms:

I'm ˈgoing /ˈ**home**

^{2} I'm ˈgoing ^{3} ˈ**home** ^{1}

^{m} I'm ˈgoing ^{hl}**home**^{l}

These alternative exhibits all indicate an utterance which is perceived as beginning at the speaker's middle range, rising to a high note at the beginning of the word *home*, and dropping to low during the pronunciation of that word.

The contour approach to describing intonation assumes that the relevant elements in a tune are not so much levels as *movements*, changes of pitch, rises and falls. This seems to be more in line with the way people actually perceive intonation patterns. As we listen to someone talk, we may recognize a high point or a low point in the utterance, but are probably more aware of the rises and falls of the voice.

If contours are the relevant parts of intonation melodies, how many contours are there? Some phonologists have said that there are basically only two tunes or contours, fall and rise. It seems essential, however, to divide each of these by two, so that we recognize a long fall, short fall, long rise, and short rise. The word 'long' is appropriate, since *long* can refer to distance or to time. The word 'short' may not be so appropriate; perhaps 'abrupt fall' and 'abrupt rise' would be better terms, for it is not the amount of change that is being discussed; it is the time allotted to the change. Though we represent intonation as changes in spatial dimensions, we need to keep in mind that intonation, like other parts of speech, refers to activities, temporal events.

Others have added as a third tune fall-rise and as a fourth tune rise-fall. Whatever the number of contours recognized, there must be some semantic contrasts, or ranges of semantic functions, associated with the different contours.

Contrary to popular belief, all analysts of English intonation have insisted that there is no melody which is exclusively associated with one type of sentence: statements do not necessarily have a falling tune, questions do not necessarily rise. The tunes do not correlate with any specific kinds of grammatical structure, and yet there is an element of truth in the popular belief.

In discussing accent (chapter 9) our procedure was to assume that occurrence of accent on the last lexical item of a tone unit is neutral, unmarked, essentially meaningless, and that other occurrences of accent have meanings which can only be understood in the way they relate to other parts of the discourse and to the expectations of the hearer. In a similar fashion we assume that a falling intonation is 'normal' or neutral because vibration of the vocal cords naturally decreases as the voice moves to the end of an utterance – to silence. With this assumption a long fall is unmarked, and other tunes – long or short rise, short fall, rise-fall, fall-rise – are marked and thus meaningful in special ways.

10.2 The falling tunes

The long fall generally indicates finality: the speaker has delivered a message and that is all. Nothing else is communicated by this tune; the speaker does not indicate an intention to continue speaking and any response expected will fit within a framework of anticipations. Thus the long fall is common in statements; in replies to questions; in Wh-questions, questions that begin with a question word (*who*, *what*, *when*, *where*, *why*) since such questions presuppose the possibility of an answer ('Who told you that?' presupposes that somebody told the hearer something; 'When will the concert be held?' presupposes that a concert will be held at some time). The long fall may be used in commands if the speaker expects that the hearer will carry out the command.

F **Yes.** F **No.** F **Here.** F **Why**?

When the contour consists of a single syllable, as in these examples, the basic falling contour is a 'glide' down: all the change of pitch occurs in the voiced elements of the syllable.

F ˈ**May**be. F ˈ**Sure**ly. F ˈ**Yes** sir. F ˈ**Cer**tainly.

When the contour consists of an accented syllable followed by one or more other syllables, as in these examples, the falling tune is a 'step' down: the accented syllable has a high pitch and the following syllable(s) low pitch.

ˈVery F ˈ**much**. ˈYes, inFˈ**deed.** ˈI underFˈ**stand**.
ˈHow do you F ˈ**do.** ToFˈ**morr**ow. ExFˈ**cuse** me.
ˈWhere are you F ˈ**going**? ˈHow ˈmuch F ˈ**is** it?

Syllables before the tonic syllables are perceived as being on a lower pitch than the tonic syllable, though they are probably not.

F ˈ**Yes**terday.	ˈThis F ˈ**mor**ning.
ˈRight aFˈ**way.**	ˈNot ˈvery F ˈ**oft**en.
They're F ˈ**lea**ving.	I'm ˈrather F ˈ**bu**sy.
ˈStay F ˈ**here**.	ˈPlease ˈclose the F ˈ**win**dow.

ˈWhat ˈtime is your apFˈ**point**ment?
ˈWhere can we ˈget a F ˈ**ta**xi?

The meaning of the short fall can be expressed as 'almost finality'. This tune differs from the long fall in suggesting that more is to follow. Thus, if the speaker says nothing more, the hearer will probably have an impression of abrupt termination. 'Certainly', spoken with a long fall, denotes deliberateness and carefulness on the part of the speaker; the same with a short fall is apt to give the impression of brusqueness, impatience, lack of concern.

The rise-fall adds emphasis to what would be communicated by the long fall alone. What we indicate as a rise at the beginning of a tone unit means simply that the speaker maintains the initial high pitch for a longer time than in the long fall.

ˈI Fˈ**like** it.	ˈShe's Fˈ**won**derful.

It has been suggested that questions which begin 'Why don't you . . . ' are true questions if spoken with a long fall but are meant to be suggestions when uttered with a rise-fall.

ˈWhy ˈdon't you ˈlook for a Fˈ**job**? (a question)
ˈˈWhy ˈdon't you ˈlook for a Fˈ**job**? (a suggestion)

When the rise is not initial in the tone unit, the pitch goes up on one syllable and down on a following syllable. For at least some speakers such a rise is common on words like *actually*, *really*, *very*.

They're ˈˈactually Fˈ**go**ing.
ˈThat's ˈˈawfully Fˈ**kind** of you.

10.3 The rising tunes

The long rise is the opposite of the long fall: it is non-final, not conclusive. In a statement it suggests that the message is uncommon, even absurd, or it contradicts what was said previously. It is used to ask for a repetition of what was said, and it is frequent in yes-no questions, the sort of question that does not begin with a question word, since such questions do not carry the presuppositions of information questions. 'Did Alex tell you that?' and 'Will the concert be held?' for example, presuppose nothing.

If the accented syllable is initial in its tone unit, the 'rise' is simply the maintenance of high pitch. Any unaccented syllables which follow are intoned at approximately the same pitch.

^{R}**Yes**? $^{R\downarrow}$**Ea**dy? $^{R\downarrow}$**May**be.

When the accented syllable is non-initial, that syllable begins an excursion from the line of declination. Any following syllables continue the excursion.

$^{\downarrow}$Are you $^{R\downarrow}$**ea**dy? $^{\downarrow}$Won't you $^{\downarrow}$come a$^{R\downarrow}$**long** with us?

A short rise can be a call for attention or a signal that the speaker is listening and expects the conversation to go on. The word '*Really*?', spoken with a long rise in response to some statement, may suggest doubt or surprise at what was said; the same word with a short rise would be taken only as a show of interest.

The fall-rise can be just a variation on the long rise, another way of asking a yes no question or of signalling that the statement is somehow unusual. If the fall-rise has a meaning of its own, it somewhat combines the meanings of the fall and the rise; it expresses but does not conclude. It states something but implies that more can be said on the subject; what is said is not untrue but it is not necessarily the whole truth or what has been said is open to various interpretations.

(Ellen's rather pretty, don't you think?) $^{\downarrow}$Not $^{F\downarrow}$**bad**^{r}.
(Can you help us out?) I $^{F\downarrow}$**might**^{r}.

Rising tunes are common in various kinds of phatic communion. The circumstances differ dialectally and perhaps idiosyncratically, but it is common to hear a rise or fall-rise in greetings, leavetakings, expressions of thanks and other social formulas.

Good$^{f\downarrow}$**bye**^{r} $^{\downarrow}$See you to$^{f\downarrow}$**morrow**^{r}

10.4 Comparisons

The different tunes contrast with one another semantically. It would be a mistake to assume that each tune has some specific, clearcut meaning, but, for that matter, it would be a mistake to think that lexical items like *table* or *love* or *democracy* have simple, clearcut meanings. The different tunes occurring with the same sequence of words signal differences of meaning, but what the meaning is depends on the context in which the utterance occurs, just as the meanings of words vary with context.

Compare these utterances of the single word *Yes*.

(1) ^{F} ˈYes

An affirmative answer to some question; the speaker leaves no doubt about his or her feelings or beliefs and seems to regard the matter, whatever it may be, as important.

(2) ^{f} ˈYes

Also an affirmative answer, of course, but the speaker seems to indicate diffidence or to regard the matter as obvious or unimportant.

(3) ^{R} ˈYes

A question which, according to the context, may mean 'Did you say "Yes?"' or 'Can we count on this?' or 'Is that the way it's going to be?' – in short, a question for which the speaker expects an affirmative answer.

(4) ^{r} ˈYes

Nothing more than a signal of attention; the speaker's name has been called, perhaps, and he or she is ready to listen.

(5) ^{f} ˈYes^{r}

Expresses partial agreement mixed with doubt or reservations; the message, in effect, is 'Yes, that's true but . . .'.

(6) ^{r} ˈYes^{F}

By maintaining high pitch for an instant longer than in the basic fall, no. (1), the speaker indicates that this message is somehow special – the utterance contains an expression of something extra, which may be enthusiasm or exasperation or some other emotion.

If you replace the word *Yes* with *No* and repeat these six tunes, you will produce utterances with exactly the opposite meaning so far as the lexical meaning is concerned, but the general effects – the meanings of the tune – are practically the same as above.

Here are more examples, first with a name (*Pat*) and then with the sentence *I'm sorry*.

(7)	^{F} ˈPat	Possibly an answer to a question, such as 'Who's playing the piano?'
(8)	^{R} ˈPat	A very brief question, equivalent to, for instance, 'Was it Pat?'
(9)	^{r} ˈPat	A call to Pat, a short distance away
(10)	^{f} ˈPat^{r}	Possibly the same, at a greater distance
(11)	I'm ^{F} ˈ**sorry**	An emotionless, matter-of-fact statement
(12)	I'm ^{R} ˈ**sorry**	Equivalent to 'What did you say?' or 'Would you repeat that?'
(13)	I'm ^{f} ˈ**sorry**^{r}	An apology, quite likely for something foreseen, as when the speaker needs to interrupt
(14)	^{f}I'm ˈ**sorry**^{r}	An apology, perhaps when the speaker has just become aware of his/her mistake

The next utterances have the form of ordinary statements.

(15)	They're ^{F} ˈ**going**	A flat statement
(16)	They're ^{f} ˈ**going**	Incomplete; we have the impression that the speaker has broken off
(17)	They're ^{F} ˈ**going**^{r}	The speaker implies more than he says; this meaning, the implication, has to be derived from the circumstances
(18)	They're ^{R} ˈ**going**	A kind of question – a request for repetition or clarification

The next utterances have the inverted word order which is usually associated with yes-no questions. We describe them all together.

(19) Are they ^{R} ˈ**going**?
(20) ^{f} Are they ^{R} ˈ**going**?
(21) Are they ^{F} ˈ**going**?
(22) Are they ^{R} ˈ**go**^{f}ing?

No. (19) is the most common way of asking a question in North America, fairly flat until near the end, while no. (20) seems the usual way in the rest of the English-speaking world, with a high beginning, a dip down, and then a rise. No. (21) is a different way of asking a yes-no question, used by those whose work requires them to ask numerous such questions, for example, customs inspectors. This falling tune might be used by anyone who has asked a number of similar questions with rising intonation – something like this:

Is it ^{R} ˈ**pink**?
^{r} ˈ**No**? / Is it ^{R} ˈ**or**ange?
^{r} ˈ**No**? / Is it ^{R} ˈ**brown**?
^{r} ˈ**No**? / ˈWell, is it ^{F} ˈ**tan**?

The last of the utterances above, no. (22), is exclamatory: 'How can you ask such a question?!'

Note these melodies in questions which begin with a question word:

(23) ˈWhen are they ^{F} ˈ**go**ing?
(24) ˈWhen are they ^{F} ˈ**go**ing^{r}?
(25) ^{R} ˈ**When** are they going?
(26) ˈWhen are they ^{R} ˈ**go**ing?

No. (23) should be considered unmarked, the usual way of asking a Wh question. With a slight rise at the end, no. (24) asks the same question but is milder, more deferential. No. (25) is a request for clarification; the speaker knows that he/she has been told the time of 'their' going but didn't get it or needs a repetition. No. (26) is quite different; the speaker is repeating someone else's question and asking for verification. It is roughly equivalent to 'Is this what you asked me?'

The difference between the fall, as in no. (23) and the rise, as in no. (26), is especially obvious when the Wh word is used alone. Compare these two short dialogs:

I'll ˈmeet you in ˈfront of the ˈ**Went**worth ˈBuilding.
^{R} ˈ**Where**?

I'll ˈmeet you at ˈhalf ˈpast ˈ**two**.
ˈThat's ^{F} ˈ**fine.** / ^{F} ˈ**Where**?

Consider these sentences which have the form of imperative clauses.

(27) ˈStay ^{F} ˈ**here**
(28) ˈStay ^{F} ˈ**here**^{r}
(29) ˈStay ^{R} ˈ**here**^{f}
(30) ^{f} ˈ**You** / ˈjust ^{f} ˈstay / ˈright ^{F} ˈ**here**

No. (27) is a brusque command; no. (28) softens it, turning it into a plea or entreaty. No. (29) is not a command at all; it might be the answer to a question such as 'Should I go now or stay here?'; the speaker intends to be helpful. No. (30), on the contrary, with its cascade of short falls, can only be said by someone in control of the person to whom this is addressed.

10.5 Compound tunes

A long utterance is almost necessarily a sequence of several tone units, each of which has its own tune. Some combinations of tunes are typical of certain kinds of sentences. In general, it can be said that when two (or more) tone units in sequence have the same kind of tune – both falling or both rising – they fit together; they make a longer unit than either one alone, the whole thing falling or rising. When two tone units in sequence differ in their tunes, rising and then falling, or falling and then rising, they present an antithesis; the message of the tune is special.

Compound statements with two or more clauses may have a short fall on each clause except the last, with a long fall on the last clause.

(31) Mc'Carthy 'plays the 'old bas^{fl}**soon** / and 'Hennesy 'tootles the ^{Fl}**flute**.

A long fall on the first clause here would give an impression of greater deliberation or more seriousness on the part of the speaker.

Of course, a clause is not necessarily a tone unit, nor a tune unit a clause.

(32) We're 'going down^{fl}**town** / 'this after^{Fl}**noon**.

Any long utterance is broken into tone units, as we saw in the previous chapter. The longer the utterance and/or the more slowly and deliberately the style of speaking, the greater the number of 'chunks' in the utterance. Thus, adding to the previous sentence might give us:

(33) We're 'going down^{f}**town** / 'this after^{f}**noon** / to 'do some
^{fl}**sho**pping / 'while the 'big ^{Fl}**sales** are 'on.

A subordinate clause is likely to have a short rise or a fall-rise:

(34) 'While we were (^{f}) '**wai**ting^{r} / ^{Fl}**Jane** 'wandered 'in.
(35) ^{fl}**Jane** 'wandered 'in / 'while we were ^{Fl}**wai**ting^{r}.

Shorter subordinate elements with rise or fall-rise are common:

(36) Ordi^{rl}**na**rily / I 'wouldn't have ^{Fl}**been** 'here.
(37) In ^{fl}**that** 'case^{r}/ I 'wouldn't have ^{Fl}**been** 'here.
(38) I 'wouldn't have ^{fl}**been** 'here / in ^{Fl}**that** 'case^{r}.

The following, though they have the same verbal content, are different questions:

(39) ˈWould you ˈlike ᴿˡ**co**ffee or ˈtea?
(40) ˈWould you ˈlike ᴿˡ**co**ffee / or ᴿˡ**tea**?
(41) ˈWould you ˈlike ᴿˡ**co**ffee or ᴾˡ**tea**?

The first of these is a simple yes-no question. No. (40) is actually two questions. Perhaps while offering coffee to someone, the questioner happens to think of suggesting tea, also. No. (41) is an alternative question, or choice question; the speaker offers two possibilities only and asks the listener to choose between them.

Tag questions are common in English. They consist of an operator – a form of the verb *be* or an auxiliary (*do*, *have*, *can*, *could*, *will*, *would*, *should*, *may*, *might*, *must*) – followed by a personal pronoun (or the form word *there*). A negative tag is common after an affirmative clause (*Robert played goalie, didn't he?*) and an affirmative tag after a negative clause (*There aren't any cookies left, are there?*), but an affirmative tag after an affirmative clause is possible (*You like that kind of music, do you?*). Intonationally, there are two kinds of tag questions:

(42) The ˈCampbells are ˡˡ**co**ming / ᴾˡ**aren't** ˈthey?
(43) The ˈCampbells are ˡˡ**co**ming / ʳˡ**aren't** ˈthey? (or ᴿˡ**aren't** they?)

In the first instance the questioner is not so much seeking information as asking for confirmation of what he/she is asserting. The questioner feels sure of the fact presented and expects agreement. In the second question, no. (43), the speaker is less assured, or not at all sure, and is truly asking for information.

Another kind of tag is an appended name, used as a term of address, a vocative. Attached to a tone unit with a long rise, the tag simply continues the rise – the voice remains relatively high.

(44) ˌAre you ᴿˡ**com**fortable, / Mrs ˈ**Grun**dy?

A similar high continuing tag occurs when a yes-no question is framed within another yes-no question:

(45) ˈWill they be ˈhere ᴿˡ**long** / ˌdo you ˈ**think**?

and even when a yes-no question is framed within a statement:

(46) ˈWill they be ˈhere ᴿˡ**long** / ˌshe ˈ**asked**.
('Will they be here long?,' she asked.)

A low continuation tag occurs after a long fall.

(47) ˌWe ˈwon't be ˈhere ˈvery $^{F\lceil}$**long,** / ˈHarold.
(48) ˈThis is a ˈvery ˈbad $^{F\lceil}$**law,** / it ˈseems to ˈ**me**.
(49) ˈI can ˈhelp with the ar$^{F\lceil}$**rang**ements, / ˈif you ˈ**want** me ˈto.

This low continuation tag may produce, for the hearer, the effect of indifference on the part of the speaker, especially if the tag contains a name, as in no. (47). Any of these utterances can be 'brightened' by the use of a low rise in the tag:

(50) ˈWe ˈwon't be ˈhere ˈvery $^{F\lceil}$**long,** / $^{r\lceil}$**Ha**rold.
(51) ˈThis is a ˈvery ˈbad $^{F\lceil}$**law,** / it ˈseems to $^{r\lceil}$**me**.
(52) ˈI can ˈhelp with the ar$^{F\lceil}$**rang**ements, / ˈif you $^{r\lceil}$**want** me ˈto.

Finally, in our summary of common tunes, consider the serial intonations, those which are used for naming a series of words, phrases, or clauses joined together, often with *and* or *or*. Three familiar patterns are:

(53) $^{F\lceil}$**Jack** / $^{F\lceil}$**J**onathan / $^{F\lceil}$**J**eremy / and Je$^{F\lceil}$**rome**
(54) $^{R\lceil}$**Jack** / $^{R\lceil}$**J**onathan / $^{R\lceil}$**J**eremy / and Je$^{F\lceil}$**rome**
(55) $^{r\lceil}$**Jack** / $^{r\lceil}$**J**onathan / $^{r\lceil}$**J**eremy / and Je$^{F\lceil}$**rome**

The first is a slow, deliberate listing; perhaps the speaker, as each item or individual is named, does not know what will be named next in the list. No. (54) is a highly dramatized enunciation, favored especially by some adults in talking to small children (but children are generally wise enough not to copy it). No. (55) is a normal listing intonation. There is a slight rise on every expression except the last, which has a long fall.

10A EXERCISE

Read the following sets of sentences and decide what tune is appropriate for each sentence. The material in parentheses is intended to explain the meaning of the sentence and/or the context in which it is spoken.

1	a. They're leaving.	(a statement)
	b. They're leaving?	(a request for confirmation)
	c. They're leaving . . .	(. . . but they'll be back.)
2.	a. Are you sure?	(The speaker is questioning.)
	b. Are you sure?	(The speaker is challenging.)
3	a. (I just found something.)	What?
	b. (I said I just found something.)	What?
	(A little gold pin that was lying on the floor.)	
4	a. When are they leaving?	(an ordinary question)

b. 'When are they leaving?'? (a repeated question: 'Is that what you asked me?')

5 a. This is my son, Henry. (Henry is the speaker's son.)
b. This is my son, Henry. (Henry is the person spoken to.)

6 a. Is this your son, Henry? (same difference as above)
b. Is this your son, Henry?

7 a. (Is today Tuesday?) Yes, it is.
b. (Oh, today's not Tuesday.) Yes, it is.

8 a. I'll see you tomorrow. (a statement)
b. (I'll) see you tomorrow. (a way of saying goodbye)

9 a. (Is Pat speaking at the meeting or just attending?)
Speaking.
b. (Voice on telephone: Is Pat there? Pat replies;)
Speaking.

10 a. Good morning, Jack. (brusque, businesslike)
b. Good morning, Jack. (polite, friendly)

11 a. Roses are red, and violets are blue.
b. Although some roses are red, not all of them are.

12 a. Give your ticket to the lady who's sitting by the door.
b. Give your ticket to Ann, who's sitting by the door.

13 a. In 'Winter's End' Lisa Lamarr played the leading role naturally.
b. In 'Winter's End' Lisa Lamarr played the leading role, naturally.

14 a. Do you have a pencil or a pen? (Do you have something to write with?)
b. Do you have a pencil or a pen? (I know you have one of them. Which is it?)

15 a. One. Two. Three. Four. Five. (The speaker is counting slowly, perhaps sighting objects one by one.
b. One. Two. Three. Four. Five. (The speaker is counting dramatically, perhaps handling the objects one by one.)
c. One, two, three, four, five. (normal, fairly rapid counting)

10.6 Summary

There have been two approaches to the description of English intonation, a levels approach and a contour approach. The levels approach is based on the assumption that the tune of any utterance can be described as a sequence of contrasting levels of pitch; almost universally, those who follow this approach consider that there are four such levels. The contour approach is based on the notion that speakers of the language react to the changes of pitch. In this chapter we have used the contour approach and have recognized these contours: **Long Fall**, **Short Fall**, **Long Rise**, **Short Rise**, **Rise-fall**, and **Fall-rise**.

No utterance or type of utterance occurs exclusively with one particular tune. In general, a falling contour often suggests finality; a short fall suggests more abrupt termination than a long fall; a rise-fall is more intense than a simple long fall. A rising contour may indicate the speaker's expectation of some response from the listener, or it may suggest a contradiction of what has been said previously; a short rise is a signal to begin a conversation or a vocal gesture indicating willingness to participate in a conversation. A falling-rising contour is likely to be used to denote that something more will be said, or can be said, or that a larger interpretation is possible. Thus, the fall is likely to occur in statements and often in 'Wh' questions, and a rise in yes-no questions.

Combinations of simple contours produce **compound contours**. These make fairly obvious distinctions between an alternative question and a simple yes-no question; between apposition and attached vocative; between two clauses which are coordinate and two clauses of which the one is modifying or subordinate or introductory with respect to the other; between tag questions that ask for confirmation and those which ask for information; between a common kind of serial enunciation and more dramatic ways of counting.

10B ADDITIONAL EXERCISE

DIALOG ONE

A: /ˈDid you enˈjoy the ᴿˡ**mee**ting ˈlast ˈnight?/
B: /ᶠˡ**Yes**. / ˌIt was an ˈinteresting ᶠˡ**session**./ ˈThere were a ˈlot of ˈdifferent oᶠˡ**pi**nions exᶠˡpressed./
A: /ᶠˡ**Yes**,/ it's ᶠˡ**u**sually ˈthat ˈway./ ˈSometimes we ˈhave some terˈrific ᶠˡ**ar**guments, / but it ˈnever ˈquite ˈcomes to ᶠˡ**blood**ˌshed./
/ˈHow ˈmany ˈpeople were ᶠˡ**there**?/
B: /Aˈbout ᶠˡ**thir**ty, / I'd ˈsay./

VARIATIONS

(a) /ˈDid you enˈjoy the ˈmeeting ˈlast ᴿˡ**night**?/
(b) /ˈDid you enˈjoy the ᴿˡ**mee**ting ˈlast ˈnight?/
(c) /ˈDid you enᴿˡ**joy** the ˈmeeting ˈlast ˈnight?/
(d) /ˈDid ᴿˡ**you** enˈjoy the ˈmeeting ˈlast ˈnight?/
(e) /ᶠˡ**Yes**. / ˌIt was ᶠˡ**in**teresting./
(f) /ᶠˡ**Yes** / ˌit was ᶠˡ**in**teresting./
(g) /ᶠˡ**Yes**ʳ / ˌit was ᶠˡ**in**teresting./

(There is nothing different in what is communicated by these three sentences ((e) to (g)). Some people may find differences in the mood or personality of the speaker, but it is not likely that we could find widespread agreement on what the differences are.)

(h) /ˈHow ˈmany ˈpeople were $^{F\downarrow}$**there**?/
(i) /ˈHow ˈmany ˈpeople $^{F\downarrow}$**were** there?/

(These questions are very different. In (h) *there* means 'in that place'; in (i) *there* is the 'existential there'. A grammatically appropriate answer to (h) would be 'Thirty people were there'; for (i) a grammatically appropriate answer is 'There were thirty people.' Pragmatically, of course, 'Thirty people' is appropriate for either.)

(j) /Aˈbout $^{F\downarrow}$**thir**ty, / I'd ˈ**say**./
(k) /Aˈbout $^{R\downarrow}$**thirty**, / you ˈ**think**?/
(l) /ˌIt was $^{F\downarrow}$**in**teresting./
(m) /ˌWas it $^{R\downarrow}$**in**teresting?/
(n) /It ˈmust have ˈbeen $^{F\downarrow}$**in**teresting^{r}./

DIALOG TWO

A: /ˈHow do you ˈlike ˈthis $^{F\downarrow}$**wea**ther?/
B: /It's $^{r\downarrow}$not $^{F\downarrow}$**bad.** / I en$^{f\downarrow}$**joy** / the $^{F\downarrow}$**snow**^{r}./
/But the $^{f\downarrow}$**wind** / has ˌbeen ˈblowing ˈhard ˈall $^{F\downarrow}$**day** / and ˌI ˈdon't ˈlike $^{F\downarrow}$**that**^{r}./
A: The $^{f\downarrow}$**wea**ther reˈport / ˈsays we'll ˈhave $^{f\downarrow}$**war**mer ˈweather/ to$^{F\downarrow}$**mor**row./
B: /I ˈhope they're $^{F\downarrow}$**right**^{r}./

VARIATIONS

(a) /I ˈhope they're $^{F\downarrow}$**right**^{r}./
(b) /I $^{F\downarrow}$**hope** they're ˈright^{r}./
(c) /I $^{F\downarrow}$**hope** so^{r}./
(d) /O$^{F\downarrow}$**kay**^{r}./
(e) /^{r}O$^{F\downarrow}$**kay**./
(f) /Good$^{F\downarrow}$**bye**^{r}./
(g) /^{r}Good$^{F\downarrow}$**bye**./
(h) /$^{F\downarrow}$**May**be^{r}./
(i) /$^{r\downarrow}$**Here** it $^{F\downarrow}$is./
(j) /$^{r\downarrow}$**There** they $^{F\downarrow}$are./
(k) /Hel$^{f\downarrow}$**lo,** /$^{r\downarrow}$**Sal**ly./
(l) /$^{f\downarrow}$**Hi**, /$^{r\downarrow}$**Tom**./
(m) /$^{r\downarrow}$Not $^{F\downarrow}$**bad**./
(n) /$^{r\downarrow}$Very $^{F\downarrow}$**nice**./

(o) /$^{r|}$That's $^{F|}$**good**./
(p) /$^{r|}$That's $^{F|}$**true**./
(q) /I $^{F|}$**like** it./
(r) /$^{r|}$I $^{F|}$**like** it./

DIALOG THREE

A: /ˈHow ˈlong have you ˈbeen in $^{F|}$**Wa**shington?/
B: /ˌJust aˈbout ˈtwo $^{F|}$**months** ˈnow. / ˈWe ˈcame ˈhere in $^{F|}$**March**./
A: /ˈHave you ˈseen ˈall the $^{R|}$**sights**?/
B: /ˈWell, I've ˈseen a $^{F|}$**lot.** / The $^{r|}$**Ca**pitol, / the $^{r|}$**White** ˈHouse,/
/the ˈWashington $^{r|}$**Mo**nument, / the ˈLincoln Me$^{r|}$**mo**rial . . ./
A: /ˈHave you ˈseen the ˈNational $^{R|}$**Gal**lery?/
B: /Oh $^{F|}$**yes**, / I've $^{F|}$**been** there./
A: /ˈHow aˈbout the $^{F|}$**Zoo**?/
B: /$^{f|}$**No**, / I ˈhaven't ˈbeen $^{F|}$**there**^{r}./

VARIATIONS

(a) /We ˈcame ˈhere in $^{F|}$**March**./
(b) /We ˈcame ˈhere ˈtwo $^{F|}$**months** aˈgo./
(c) /ˈHave you ˈseen ˈall the $^{R|}$**sights**?/
(d) /$^{R|}$**Have** you ˈseen ˈall the ˈsights?/

(The question in (c) is unmarked, neutral; (d), with its focus on the auxiliary verb, suggests a request for clarification of something said previously.)

(e) /I've ˈseen ˈeverything you're sup$^{F|}$**posed** to see^{r}./
(f) /I've ˈseen ˈeverything you're sup$^{F|}$**posed** to^{r}./
(g) /I've ˈbeen to the $^{r|}$**Zoo** . . ./
(h) /ˈHave you ˈbeen to the $^{R|}$**Zoo**?/
(i) /ˈHow aˈbout the $^{F|}$**Zoo**?/
(j) /ˈHave you $^{R|}$**been** ˈthere?/
(k) /ˈHave you ˈbeen $^{R|}$**there**?/
(l) /I ˈhaven't $^{F|}$**been** ˈthere./
(m) /I ˈhaven't ˈbeen $^{F|}$**there**^{r}./

10A FEEDBACK

These are possible answers, though not the only possible ones.

1 a. They're ^{F} leaving.
b. They're ^{R} leaving?
c. They're ^{f} leaving ^{r} . . .

2 a. Are you ^{R} sure?
b. Are you ^{F} sure?
3 a. ^{R} What?
b. ^{F} What?
4 a. When are they ^{F} leaving?
b. When are they ^{R} leaving?
5 a. This is my ^{f} son / ^{F} Henry.
b. This is my ^{F} son / ^{r} Henry.
6 a. Is this your son ^{R} Henry?
b. Is this your ^{R} son / Henry?
7 a. ^{f} Yes / it ^{F} is.
b. ^{R} Yes it is.
8 a. I'll see you to^{F}morrow.
b. (I'll) see you to^{f}morrow^{r}.
9 a. ^{F} Speaking.
b. ^{f} Speaking^{r}.
10 a. Good ^{F} morning / Jack.
b. Good ^{F} morning / ^{r} Jack.
11 a. Roses are ^{r} red / and violets are ^{F} blue.
b. Although some roses are ^{f} red ^{r} / not ^{F} all of them are.
or: Although ^{F} some roses are red ^{r} / not ^{F} all of them are ^{r}.
12 a. Give your ticket to the ^{f} lady / who's sitting by the ^{F} door.
b. Give your ticket to ^{f} Ann ^{r} / who's sitting by the ^{F} door.
13 a. In 'Winter's ^{f} End' / Lisa Lamarr played the leading role ^{F} naturally.
b. In 'Winter's ^{f} End' / Lisa Lamarr played the leading ^{F} role / ^{r} naturally.
14 a. Do you have a pencil or a ^{R} pen?
b. Do you have a ^{R} pencil or a ^{F} pen?
15 a. ^{F} One / ^{F} Two / ^{F} Three / ^{F} Four / ^{F} Five.
b. ^{R} One / ^{R} Two / ^{R} Three / ^{R} Four / ^{R} Five.
c. ^{r} One / ^{r} two / ^{r} three / ^{r} four / ^{r} five.

11

Predicting Word Stress

11.1 Is stress predictable?

In some languages the position of stress in a word is invariable. In Czech and Finnish it is always the first syllable of a word which is most prominent; in Polish the next-to-last syllable is stressed; in French, insofar as there is any stress difference at all, the last syllable is generally the most prominent. In languages like these, where stress is fixed on a particular syllable and therefore predictable, stress cannot differentiate meanings. In contrast, Spanish and Russian have sets of words which differ only in the position of stress. How about English?

English is not like Czech, Finnish, Polish, or French. We have already seen that the stress of a polysyllabic word may be on the first syllable (*'cannibal*), the second (*a'rena*), the third (*after'noon*), or some later syllable. In a general sense stress is variable in English. To be sure, stress is invariable for any specific word. Although there are dialect differences in stress (*garage* is stressed on the second syllable in North America, on the first syllable everywhere else) just as there are dialect differences in vowels (*either*, *half*, *roof*), we are not free to put stress on whatever syllable we want. If a person still learning English as a new language says *'beginner* instead of *be'ginner*, those who already know the language consider it a mispronunciation, even though the meaning is probably clear enough. In English words stress is not fixed – but does that mean that it is not predictable?

On the other hand stress does not play a large role in differentiating words. *Billow* and *below*, *reefer* and *refer* are sometimes cited as pairs of words which differ mostly in position of stress, but there are not many such pairs. There are somewhat more pairs like the noun *'insult* and the verb *in'sult*, noun *'abstract*, verb and adjective *ab'stract*, a type which we examine later, sets of words which are semantically related but grammatically different.

Every English dictionary uses some kind of key to pronunciation. Following the orthographic form of every word that is listed, there is some kind of respelling in the special key to indicate the pronunciation of the word. Such a re-spelling implies that the usual orthography is not sufficiently regular for us to deduce the pronunciation from the ordinary spelling, and of course there is considerable truth in the implication; the irregularities and inconsistencies of English spelling are well known (though sometimes they are exaggerated).

One part of the respelling, for polysyllabic words, is an indication of stress. For every word of more than one syllable the dictionary's respelling indicates which is the stressed syllable; for example *maintain* (mān.tān'). Here again there is an obvious implication: that stress is completely unpredictable, that a reader cannot look at a written word and correctly figure out where the stress is. The implication is not entirely accurate; while it is not possible to predict the stress in all English words, there are many others which follow general principles.

There are general rules which account for the place of stress in numerous words, though not all the words of the language. Many of these rules you know already, though not in a completely conscious way. Words which end in *-tion*, such as *constitution*, *composition*, *interruption*, *proclamation*, *simplification* – literally hundreds of words – are stressed on the vowel before this ending. Similarly, words with a final *-ity* have stress on the vowel before the ending (*asininity*, *humidity*, *mediocrity*, *relativity*, *sentimentality*). These are two small generalizations that can be made about stress placement. There are other, more subtle ones which, by and large, are known to speakers of the language. For example, the following words may be new to you (or half-new), but you can probably stress each one of them correctly:

comatula lobatic metrify polyphase spiriferous

11.2 Stress rules

In the remainder of this chapter we explore the rules – that is, general statements – regarding the place of stress in different groups of words. We will see that there are limits to the rules. Each rule has its particular domain; not everything is predictable.

Stress rules are based on three kinds of information: syntactic, morphological, and phonological.

Syntactic information The place of stress in a word depends partly on what part of speech it is. The noun *'insult* is stressed differently from the verb *in'sult*. Similarly, compare the adjective *con'tent* and the noun *'contents*, the noun *'present* ('gift') and the adjective *'present* ('not absent') with the verb *pre'sent*. The words we examine here are nouns, verbs, and adjectives, and somewhat different rules apply to each of these parts of speech.

Morphological information We have seen that the suffixes +*tion* and +*ity* have a role in the location of stress. Every word has a morphological composition. A word may be SIMPLE, consisting of a single BASE; for example, *arm*, *baby*, *circle*, *fat*, *manage*. Some words, like *armchair*, *babysit*, *ice-cold*, *square dance* are COMPOUNDS, consisting of two bases together (whether our orthographic conventions prefer them written as a single word, or with a hyphen, or with a space between the parts). Finally, some words are COMPLEX, consisting of a PREFIX plus a base (*disarm*, *encircle*, *mismanage*, *renew*) or a base plus a SUFFIX (*babyish*, *fatten*, *happiness*, *management*). A word may contain prefix + base + suffix (*mismanagement*, *unhappiness*), base + base + suffix (*babysitting*, *square dancer*), base + suffix + suffix (*fattening*, *sharpener*), and so forth. The morphological composition has a role in determining stress. We will see that different kinds of suffixes, especially, are important in determining the place of stress.

Phonological information The place of stress in particular words depends in part on the nature of the last two syllables, the ult and the penult, and occasionally on the nature of an earlier syllable. We need to consider whether a syllable has a free vowel or not, and the number of consonants, if any, which close the syllable. Since phonological facts interact with morphological and syntactic facts, we shall see that rules about vowels and consonants are different for nouns, verbs, and adjectives.

To review, a free vowel is one which can occur at the end of a one-syllable word. Free vowels are illustrated in these words:

see, seat	sue, suit	spa, calm
bay, bait	go, goat	law, laud
by, bite	cow, scout	toy, void

Notice that in each of the following words the last syllable, the ult, has a free vowel:

agree remain rely destroy cellophane anecdote

And in each of the next words the next-to-last syllable, the **Penult**, has a free vowel:

arena aroma diploma hiatus horizon

In the next group of words the penult ends with a consonant – the syllable division is between the two consonants:

enigma veranda parental detergent amalgam

But in the following words the penult does not end with a consonant; the single consonant between the last two vowels is ambisyllabic:

abacus cinema generous melody evident.

In the rest of this chapter we will be weaving in and out among the three kinds of phenomena, syntactic, morphological, and phonological.

11.3 Neutral suffixes

It was noted in chapter 5 that when a suffix of Old English origin is added to a word, stress does not change; e.g. *'neighbor*, *'neighborly*, *'neighborliness*, *'neighborhood*. We saw that suffixes of Old English origin (and a few others) are NEUTRAL: they are added to independent words and have no effect on the stress. For example, the words *ab'sorbing*, *'interesting*, *pre'vailing*, and *'terri,fying* have the same stressed syllables as *ab'sorb*, *'interest*, *pre'vail*, and *'terri,fy*, respectively. This *#ing* is a neutral suffix, and so are *#hood*, *#ly*, and *#ness*, illustrated above. (A neutral suffix will be marked with the boundary symbol # before it.) A long list of neutral suffixes (and other kinds of suffixes) can be found in appendix B.

Although most neutral suffixes are of Old English origin, this does not mean that the words to which they are added are necessarily of Old English origin.

11.4 Tonic endings

Nouns which end in *-oon* typically have stress on the ending: *balloon*, *raccoon*, *macaroon*, *saloon*, etc. An ending like this is tonic. Most words that have tonic endings have been borrowed from Modern French, but not all. Some, like *absentee*, have been formed in English with a suffix of French origin. The following are some more examples of words with tonic endings (and more are to be found in appendix B):

debonaire, millionaire
absentee, internee
Congolese, Vietnamese
basinette, kitchenette
antique, technique

11.5 The basic stress rule for verbs

Once we have recognized the neutral suffixes and the tonic endings we are ready for more general statements about stress. Let us consider the following sets of verbs:

1a	2a	3
agree	diagnose	abolish
delay	exercise	consider
exclude	intimidate	develop
cajole	monopolize	imagine
invite	persecute	remember
pronounce	ridicule	solicit

1b	2b
attract	compliment
consist	gallivant
depend	manifest
exempt	
involve	
reverse	

Note that in groups 1a and 1b the last syllable, the **ult**, is stressed; in 2a and 2b the third syllable from the end, the **antepenult**, is stressed; and in group 3 the **penult**, the next-to-last syllable, is the stressed syllable. Why?

The verbs in group 1 have what we may call a stressable ult: either the ult has a free vowel, with or without consonants following (1a), or it ends with at least two consonants (1b). Furthermore, each verb in the group consists of just two syllables. The ult is stressed.

In group 2 also each verb has a strong ult, because of the free vowel (2a) or because of the cluster of consonants at the end (2b). These verbs have three or more syllables. The antepenult is stressed. (In centuries past they were stressed on the ult. Even today, in Scotland and in the Caribbean, one may hear *diagnose* or *intimidate* stressed on the ult.)

Each word in group 3 has an unstressable ult: the ult contains a checked vowel followed by not more than one consonant. The penult is stressed.

This general statement, or rule, for what we have observed for verbs can be put into the form of a decision tree:

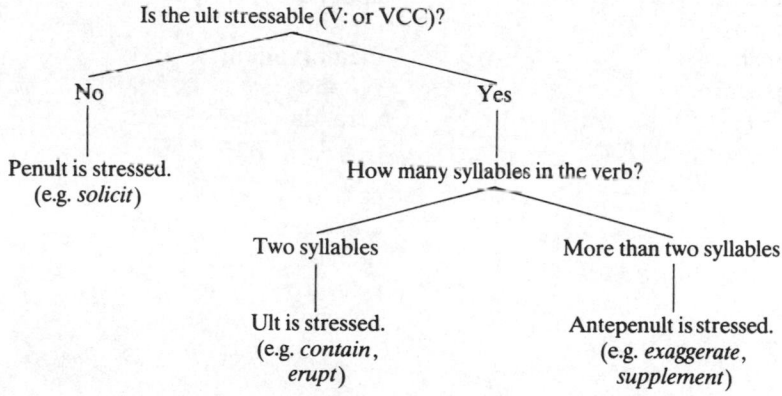

11A EXERCISE

All of the verbs below follow this basic rule. Note which syllable is stressed in each one and mark it 1a, 1b, 2a, 2b, or 3, according to the scheme above. (There aren't many examples of group 2b here because there aren't many such verbs in the language.)

adopt	exonerate	produce
answer	furnish	remark
covet	inhabit	substitute
dehumidify	mechanize	supplement
exhaust	offend	transcribe

11.6 The basic stress rule for nouns

The first question to ask about verbs when determining the position of stress is 'Is the ult stressable or not?' Nouns are different. The first question to ask about nouns is 'How many syllables does the noun have?' The next question is 'Does the ult have a free vowel or not?' It doesn't matter how many consonants occur in final position. Examine these sets of nouns.

1a	2	3a
alcove	appetite	affidavit
membrane	hypotenuse	aroma
statute	institute	horizon
termite	porcupine	hypnosis
textile	vicissitude	papyrus
1b		**3b**
cavern		appendix
focus		intestine
menace		memorandum
premise		synopsis
ticket		veranda
		3c
		camera
		citizen
		deficit
		gelatin
		pelican

Note, first, that each noun of groups 1a and 1b has just two syllables. The penult is stressed whether the ult vowel is free (1a) or not (1b) – but see the note at the end of this chapter. If there are more than two syllables in the noun, it makes a difference whether the ult has a free vowel or not. If the ult vowel is free, as in group 2, the antepenult is stressed. If the ult vowel is not a free vowel, as in group 3, we ask if the penult is stressable. The penult is stressable if it has a free vowel (3a) or ends with a consonant (3b). If the penult is not stressable, the antepenult is stressed (3c).

The basic noun rule can be summarized in this decision tree:

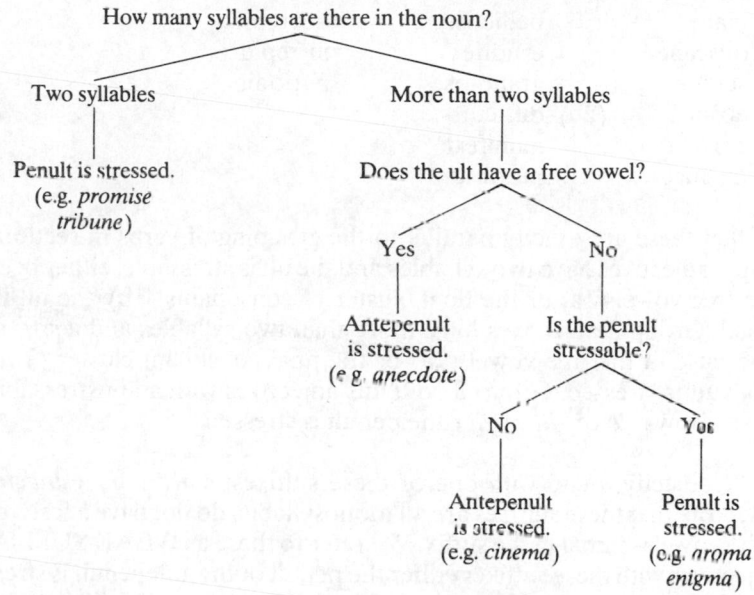

11B EXERCISE

Note the stress in the following nouns and mark each one as 1a, 1b, 2, 3a, 3b, or 3c, according to how it fits the classification above.

javelin	closet	diploma
idea	satellite	veteran
bonanza	opera	platinum
harmonica	hypothesis	neuritis
tabloid	formaldehyde	vestibule

11.7 Rules for adjectives

We do not need a new rule for the stress of adjectives. There are essentially two types of adjectives, so far as the place of stress is concerned: one type follows the stress rule for verbs, the other the stress rule for nouns.

Type I. Observe these sets of adjectives:

(1a)	contrite	(2a)	asinine	(3)	academic
	inane		bellicose		decrepit
	obscene		erudite		intrepid
	serene		grandiose		periodic
(1b)	absurd	(2b)	difficult		
	correct		manifest		
	distinct		moribund		

Note that these are exactly parallel to the grouping of verbs in section 9.6. Group 1 adjectives have two syllables and the ult is stressable, either because of the free vowel (1a) or the final cluster of consonants (1b); the ult is the stressed. Group 2 adjectives have more than two syllables and a stressable ult, because of the free vowel (2a) or the final consonant cluster (2b); the antepenult is stressed. Group 3 contains adjectives with an unstressable ult (almost always *-ic* or *-id* or *-it*); the penult is stressed.

Type II adjectives end with one of these suffixes: *+al*, *+ar*, *+ant/ent*, or *+ous*. Note that these suffixes are all monosyllabic, do not have a free vowel, and the vowel is initial in the suffix. We refer to these as WEAK SUFFIXES. In adjectives with these suffixes either the penult or the antepenult is stressed, depending on the nature of the penult. The following exercise will help you to determine the general rule.

11C EXERCISE

(a) Mark the stress in each of these words:

fatal global polar stellar cogent decent dormant nervous

General statement: If an adjective has a weak suffix preceded by a base of just one syllable, stress is on the _____.

(b) Each of the words below has a base of more than one syllable. Do three things.

1. If the vowel of the penult is a free vowel, put a macron over the vowel letter, e.g. *complācent*;
2. If the vowel of the penult is followed by two consonants (a consonant cluster which cannot occur in word-initial position), draw a line between the two consonant letters, e.g. *abun|dant*;
3. Use the tick to show whether the penult or the antepenult is stressed, e.g. *com'placent*, *re'luctant*, *'adamant*.

ac ci den tal	re luc tant	pe ri phe ral
e ter nal	mag ni fi cent	a na lo gous
vi gi lant	bar ba rous	a bun dant
ma lig nant	ge ne rous	a nec do tal

We note that the penult is stressed if it meets either of these conditions:

(1)

(2)

If the penult meets neither of these conditions, the antepenult is stressed.

Adjectives of this type are just like nouns which have a checked vowel in the ult. In fact, the weak suffix +*ant/ent* appears in nouns as well as adjectives; compare *detergent*, *occupant*, *participant*.

To go a bit farther, we may consider the following noun endings also weak suffixes:

+*a*	mica, aroma, enigma, cinema
+*ance/ence*	hindrance, reluctance, evidence
+*is*	thesis, neurosis, synopsis, emphasis
+*on*	nylon, skeleton
+*um*	fulcrum, platinum
+*us*	circus, hiatus

11D EXERCISE

Consider these words, all of which have a weak suffix:

algebra citrus discipline eloquent integral

These words have weak suffixes; in each word the penult vowel is followed by two consonants (-br-, -tr-, -pl-, -kw-, -qr-), and yet stress is on the antepenult. Are these words exceptions to the rule just formulated?

11.8 Extending the basic stress rules

Consider these verbs and adjectives:

copy envy marry worry easy happy ugly
argue continue issue rescue
borrow follow swallow hollow narrow yellow

The words in the three lines end with vowels that we have written (section 5.7) respectively, as /i/, /u/, and /o/. Are these free vowels? We have seen in section 5.7 that different speakers give different answers to this question. In final position there is no contrast between a free vowel /ii/ and a checked /ɪ/, a free /uu/ and a checked /ʊ/, nor between /ou/ and /o/. For the stress rules these three vowels in final position act like checked vowels, rather than free vowels. The ult is not stressable and therefore stress falls on the penult, just as it is in such verbs and adjectives as *consider*, *deposit*, *comic*, *valid*.

Similarly, in nouns the ult is unstressable if it contains one of these three vowels, as in the following examples:

albino commando macaroni jiujitsu avenue revenue

In the first four of these words the penult is stressable (in the first two words because of the free vowel, in the second two because the penult is a closed syllable) and so receives the stress. If the ult were strong, the antepenult would be stressed. In the last two words neither ult nor penult is stressable; the antepenult is stressed.

Rule: Final /i u o/ count as checked vowels, making the ult unstressable. A word with one of these vowels in final position has stress on the penult or antepenult according to the usual rules.

Next we consider certain vowels which are not final.

11E EXERCISE

(a) Which syllable is stressed in the following words – the ult, penult, or antepenult?

continuous manual casual contiguous

(b) What vowel occurs in the penult?
(c) Is the penult closed with a consonant?
(d) Which syllable is stressed in the following words?

ceremonial	remedial	obedient	radiant
phobia	myopia	calcium	radius

(e) What vowel occurs in the penult?
(f) Is the penult closed or open?

When /i/ and /u/ occur immediately before another vowel, they appear to be free. But as we have seen before (section 5.7), there is no contrast between free /ii/ and checked /ɪ/, nor between free /uu/ and checked /ʊ/, in this position. For stress assignment, /i/ or /u/ in an open penult acts like a checked vowel.

Rule: When /i/ or /u/ occurs in an open penult, the penult is unstressable and stress falls on the antepenult. In this case /i/ must be followed immediately by another vowel; /u/ may be followed by an ambisyllabic consonant.

11F EXERCISE

Here is a list of Type II adjectives, with unstressable ult. Determine for each one whether the penult or the antepenult is stressed, and why.

annual	corporal	feminine
innocuous	internal	luminous
masculine	nocturnal	oriental
ridiculous	significant	similar
superior	tedious	vigilant

11.9 Some variations in stress

Ever since the eleventh century English has been borrowing words from other languages, chiefly French, with stress on the last syllable. Often the stress has been moved forward; *beauty*, *companion*, *element*, and *ticket* are a small sample of the words which were once stressed on the last syllable but no longer are. This process of stress-advancement is still going on.

11G EXERCISE

All of the following words were originally stressed on the ult, and they may still be pronounced that way. But each of them has an alternative pronunciation in which stress falls, instead, on the penult or the antepenult.

(a) Which are possibly stressed on the penult and which on the antepenult?
(b) What determines whether stress advances to the penult or to the antepenult?

chimpanzee	employee	mezzanine
cigarette	lemonade	Portuguese
divorcee	macrame	referee

11H EXERCISE

A number of three-syllable words which end in /iin/, like *magazine*, and *mezzanine*, vary in pronunciation in this way: they may be stressed on the ult or on the antepenult. Examine the next group of words and decide which you stress on the ult, which on the antepenult and which, if any, do you vary?

figurine gabardine gasoline guillotine kerosene
libertine limousine nicotine quarantine submarine
tambourine tangerine trampoline

All of these variable words which may be stressed on the ult or, alternatively, on the penult or antepenult are nouns and of course more than two syllables long. Among two-syllable nouns there is also some variation; *routine*, for example, may be stressed on either syllable. For all such variable nouns our 'rule' is necessarily weak. In fact, our rule is generally weak for two-syllable nouns with a free vowel in the ult. As presented above (section 11.6), the rule says that all two-syllable nouns are stressed on the penult. This is fairly accurate for nouns which do not have a free vowel in the ult, such as *cavern*, *focus*, *ticket*. It is partly accurate for nouns which do have a free vowel in the ult: *alcove*, *statute*, *termite*. However, there are numerous two-syllable nouns with a free vowel in the ult which have final stress: *canoe*, *machine*, *police*. For more examples of all these kinds of nouns see appendix B.

11.10 Mixed endings

Neutral suffixes are mostly of Old English origin. Other suffixes have generally entered English from French, Latin, or Greek, originally as parts of words borrowed from those languages. But often these suffixes have come to have a life of their own in English and are used to form new English words. So it happens that some suffixes behave like strong (stressable) endings in words of foreign origin but act like neutral suffixes in words which have been created in English. Notice the following sets of words:

(a)	(b)
agreement	compliment
encouragement	implement
confinement	document
development	impediment
punishment	monument

In set (a) *-ment* is a neutral suffix. It is added to words which stand alone; stress in each suffixed word is on the same syllable as in the independent word to which the suffix is added. The words in set (b) are regularly stressed, but by a different principle: stress is on the antepenult of each word. In effect, there are two different suffixes, and they should be labeled differently. We might refer to them as $\textit{-ment}_1$ and $\textit{-ment}_2$, but these labels do not tell us what the suffixes have to do with the position of stress. A better device is the notations *#ment* and *+ment*, where '#' indicates that what follows is a neutral suffix and '+' marks a suffix which is not neutral.

The following groups of words illustrate three apparent suffixes which, like *-ment*, turn out to be three pairs of suffixes. In each pair one suffix is neutral and one is not neutral.

(a)	(b)
materialize	apologize
naturalize	antagonize
characterize	mechanize
Americanize	monopolize
popularize	hypothesize

(a)	(b)
federalist	anarchist
industrialist	botanist
modernist	ornithologist
revolutionist	protagonist
violinist	scientist

(a)	(b)
nationalism	ostracism
imperialism	recidivism
parallelism	somnambulism
radicalism	syllogism
secularism	ventriloquism

11.11 Some 'special' endings

Words written with final *-y* are quite numerous. There are two neutral suffixes written with *-ly* (as in *friendly*, and *clearly*), and there are three other neutral suffixes with *-y* (as in *dirty*, *smithy*, and *doggy*). See appendix B for further details. There are some non-neutral suffixes which end in a written *y*. They are illustrated in these words:

delicacy decency geography harmony literary territory

This section deals with stress-placement in such words.

11.11a

Certain nouns have a suffix +*acy*, and certain other nouns have a suffix +*ancy* or +*ency* (just a difference of spelling, so far as stress placement is concerned). These suffixes are like weak suffixes, differing only in having two syllables instead of one. If the syllable before the suffix is stressable or the initial syllable of the word, that syllable is stressed. If the syllable before the suffix is not stressable and not initial, stress is on the second syllable before the suffix. Study these examples:

fallacy	diplomacy	adequacy
legacy		celibacy
piracy		delicacy
privacy		literacy
decency	complacency	competency
frequency	consistency	exigency
pregnancy	dependency	hesitancy
tendency	emergency	presidency

The words in the last columns, on the right, are among the few English words which are stressed on the preantepenult. You have probably noticed that some of these nouns are related to adjectives or other nouns which end in /t/:

piracy - pirate adequacy - adequate
decency - decent hesitancy - hesitant

In chapter 14 we study this relationship further.

11I EXERCISE

What is irregular about the stress of the noun *discrepancy*?

Here is a decision tree for nouns which have the endings *-acy*/*-ancy*/*-ency*:

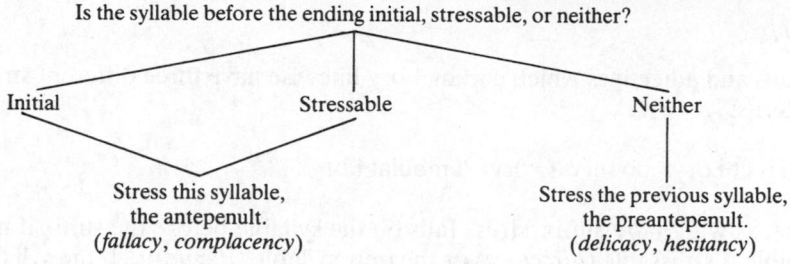

11.11b

Nouns and adjectives which end in +*ary* have three different stress patterns, as in:

compli'ment+ary con'tempor+ary 'veterin+ary

The last of these is uncommon; probably '*disciplinary* is the only other example of a word with two weak syllables between the stressed syllable and the suffix +*ary*. In *contemporary* there is one syllable between the stressed syllable and the suffix; in *complimentary* there is no syllable between.

The stress rule for these words is similar to the rule for weak suffixes. If the syllable before +*ary* is stressable or initial, it is stressed: *compli'mentary*. Otherwise, the preceding syllable is stressed and, in North American English, the first syllable of the suffix +*ary* is strong (and pronounced /eri/): *con'temporary*. In the British Isles and the southern hemisphere the suffix is /əri/ or just /ri/ in both the *complimentary*-type and the *contemporary*-type.

11J EXERCISE

(a) use the tick to mark the stressed syllable in each of these words.

anniversary	elementary	exemplary	arbitrary
adversary	coronary	dictionary	imaginary
commissary	literary	mercenary	monetary
incendiary	proprietary	reactionary	sanguinary
necessary	secretary	visionary	vocabulary
sedentary	sanitary	voluntary	

(b) According to our rule, three of the words are stressed irregularly: *adversary*, *sedentary*, *voluntary*. What is irregular about them?

11.11c

Nouns and adjectives which end in +*ory* likewise have three different stress patterns:

di'rect+ory ob'servat+ory 'ambulat+ory

Here, as with +*ary* suffix, stress falls on the syllable before the suffix if that syllable is stressable (*directory*) or the only syllable (*memory*). If the syllable before the suffix is neither stressable nor word-initial, stress is on the preceding syllable (*observatory*). In a few words there are two weak syllables between the stressed syllable and the suffix (*ambulatory*). When the stressed syllable is right before the suffix (*directory*, *memory*), the penult is weak and the vowel may disappear; when this is not the case, as in *observatory* and *ambulatory*, the first syllable of +*ory* is heavy in North American English; in the British Isles and the southern hemisphere the pronunciation is /əri/ or /ri/.

11K EXERCISE

(a) Decide which of the following words are like *directory* (or *memory*) and which are like *observatory*.
(b) There are three words in the group which are irregularly stressed by our rule. Which are they?

advisory	dormitory	migratory
amatory	explanatory	offertory
armory	illusory	perfunctory
compensatory	inflammatory	repertory
compulsory	interrogatory	inventory
derogatory	mandatory	trajectory

Several words have two possible stressings:

'obligatory, o'bligatory
'laboratory, la'boratory
'preparatory, pre'paratory

Here is a decision tree for the regular words which end in *-ary* or *-ory*. Note that it is identical with the decision tree for words which end in *-acy*, *-ancy/ency*.

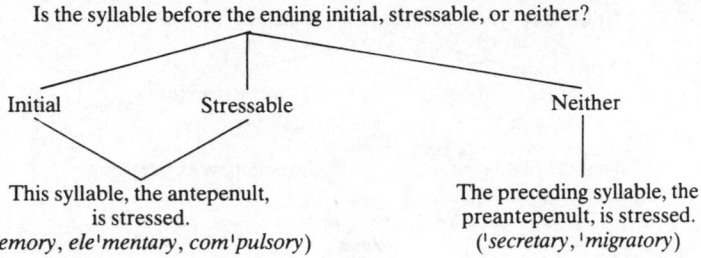

11.11d

There are numerous abstract nouns of Latin and Greek origin which end in +*y* (other than *-ary* and *-ory*). All three-syllable nouns with this suffix are like these examples:

colony energy galaxy harmony lethargy liturgy malady

For words of more than three syllables there are two patterns:

Pattern 1. . . . ˈx x x +*y*

ˈmatriarchy ˈtaxidermy ˈapoplexy
ˈceremony ˈtestimony ˈepilepsy

The penult is strong and the preantepenult is stressed. (There may or may not be syllables before the stressed syllable, as indicated by the three dots.)

Pattern 2. . . . ˈx x +*y*

aˈnatomy biˈology eˈconomy geˈometry phiˈlosophy

(and all the words that end in *-ology*, *-ometry*, *-ography*, *-opathy*). The antepenult is stressed.

11L EXERCISE

(a) In nouns of three syllables with ending -*y* the stressed syllable is always the _____.
(b) In nouns of more than three syllables with ending -*y* the preantepenult is the stressed syllable if _____;
the antepenult is stressed if _____.

Here is a decision tree for this group of nouns:

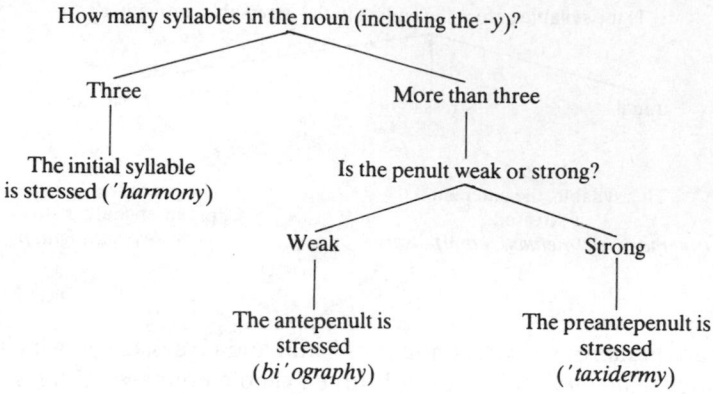

apostrophe catastrophe epitome facsimile

Words like those above, though spelled with a final *-e*, actually belong to the group just studied. If we wrote, for example 'apostrophy', the pronunciation and stress would be no different from what they are.

11.12 Summary

There is a certain degree of regularity in the occurrence of stress in English words. Factors in the determination of stress are syntactic (part of speech), morphological (recognition of different kinds of prefixes, suffixes, and bases), and phonological (free vs checked vowels, open vs closed syllables). First of all, it is necessary to recognize certain **neutral suffixes**, which are never stressed, and **tonic endings**, which are always stressed. Rules for stress assignment do not apply to the second group, and they apply to the first group only after the neutral suffix is removed. Different stress rules have been presented for verbs and for nouns. Adjectives are of two kinds: those which end in *-ic*, *-id*, *-it* follow the verb rule, and those which end in *-al*, *-ar*, *-an*, *-ant/ent*, *-ous* follow the noun rule.

In applying the rules final /i, u, o/ count as checked vowels; so does /i/ in the penult when immediately followed by a vowel; so does /u/ in the penult if immediately followed by no more than one consonant.

In verbs, nouns, and adjectives which consist of three or more syllables and have stressable ults the antepenult is the stressed syllable. Some nouns of this type, however, show variation between stress on the antepenult and stress on the ult. Among two-syllable nouns with a free vowel in the ult some have an initial stressed syllable, some a final stressed syllable, and some vary.

Words with certain endings require more extended discussion. Some endings (*-ment*, *-ize*, *-ism*, *-ist*) may be attached to free bases – independent words – in which case they are neutral suffixes; when these suffixes are attached to bound bases, the words are stressed on the antepenult. Words with the endings *-acy*, *-ancy/ency*, *-ary*, *-ory* are stressed on the syllable preceding the ending if that syllable is initial or stressable, otherwise one syllable earlier. For other abstract nouns with final *-y* the rule is: the antepenult is stressed in a three-syllable word and in a longer word with a weak penult; the preantepenult is stressed in a longer word with strong penult.

11A FEEDBACK

1b	adopt	2a	exonerate	1a	produce
3	answer	3	furnish	1b	remark
3	covet	3	inhabit	2a	substitute
2a	dehumidify	2a	mechanize	2b	supplement
1b	exhaust	1b	offend	1a	transcribe

11B FEEDBACK

3c	javelin	1b	closet	3a	diploma
3a	idea	2	satellite	3c	veteran
3b	bonanza	3c	opera	3c	platinum
3c	harmonica	3c	hypothesis	3a	neuritis
1a	tabloid	2	formaldehyde	2	vestibule

11C FEEDBACK

(a) ˈfatal ˈglobal ˈpolar ˈstellar ˈcogent ˈdecent ˈdormant ˈnervous

General statement: If an adjective has a weak suffix preceded by a base of just one syllable, stress is on the base/initial syllable/penult.

(b)	ac ci ˈden tal	re ˈluc tant	pe ˈri phe ral
	e ˈter nal	mag ˈni fi cent	a ˈna lo gous
	ˈvi gi lant	ˈbar ba rous	a ˈbun dant
	ma ˈlig nant	ˈge ne rous	tre ˈmen dous

The penult is stressable if it meets either of these conditions:

1. it has a free vowel;
2. it ends with a consonant.

11D FEEDBACK

No, because the consonant clusters are the type of clusters which occur word-initially. The first consonant is ambisyllabic; it is not the coda of a syllable.

11E FEEDBACK

(a) the antepenult
(b) /u/
(c) open
(d) the antepenult
(e) /i/
(f) open

11F FEEDBACK

Three of these adjectives have stressed penults:

in ˈternal noc ˈtur nal o ri ˈen tal

Each of the others has an unstressable penult and therefore stress on the antepenult.

11G FEEDBACK

(a) These are likely to be stressed on the penult: chimpanzee, divorcee, employee; the others are more probably stressed on the antepenult.
(b) These three words have stressable penults; the others do not.

11H FEEDBACK

The stressings indicated by one dictionary (*Webster's New World Dictionary*) are these:

In *figurine* and *tambourine* the ult is stressed.

Guillotine, *libertine*, *nicotine*, *quarantine*, and *trampoline* are stressed on the antepenult, the initial syllable.

In *gabardine*, *kerosene*, and *limousine* either the antepenult or the ult may be stressed but initial stress is given first; for *gasoline* and *tangerine* the same two possibilities are indicated, but final stress is listed first.

Submarine is given as having final stress when the word is an adjective but initial stress when it is a noun or a verb.

These are stress possibilities for words in isolation. As we will see later, stress can vary in different sentence positions.

11I FEEDBACK

Stress is on the syllable preceding +*ancy* even though that syllable is light with a lax /ɛ/.

11J FEEDBACK

(a)

anniˈversary	eleˈmentary	exˈemplary	ˈarbitrary
ˈadversary	ˈcoronary	ˈdictionary	iˈmaginary
ˈcommissary	ˈliterary	ˈmercenary	ˈmonetary
inˈcendiary	proˈprietary	reˈactionary	ˈsanguinary
ˈnecessary	ˈsecretary	ˈvisionary	voˈcabulary
ˈsedentary	ˈsanitary	ˈvoluntary	

Among these 23 words only *anniversary*, *elementary*, and *exemplary* have stress on the syllable before +*ary*, and an unstressed suffix. All the others have the more common pattern . . . ˈ x x ary.

(b) In ˈ*adversary*, ˈ*sedentary*, and ˈ*voluntary* the syllable before the suffix is stressable since it ends in a consonant, and yet the preceding syllable is stressed.

11K FEEDBACK

(a) These words have stress on the syllable before +*ory*, like *directory* and *memory*:

advisory, armory, illusory, perfunctory, trajectory

(b) The words *offertory*, *repertory*, and *inventory* should, by the rule, be stressed on the syllable before the suffix, but they are not: ˈoffertory, ˈrepertory, ˈinventory. For the last word there is, in Britain, an alternative pronunciation *inˈventory*.

11L FEEDBACK

(a) In abstract nouns of three syllables with the suffix +*y* the stressed syllable is always the antepenult (the initial syllable).
(b) In nouns of more than three syllables with suffix +*y* the preantepenult is stressed if the penult is strong; the antepenult is stressed if the penult is weak.

12

Prefixes, Compound Words, and Phrases

12.1 Compounds

In the simple word *tennis* the first syllable is the stressed syllable. The simple word *racket* also has an initial stressed syllable. When the two are put together to form a compound, the stress pattern is something like X . x . : the first syllable of *tennis* is stressed but the first syllable of *racket* remains strong. If *tennis racket* is in accent position, the first syllable is the accented syllable, as in:

ˈDo you ˈhave your ˈtennis racket?

Only if *racket* is contrasted with something else can it acquire stress and accent:

ˈtennis ˈ**balls** / and a ˈtennis ˈracket

12A EXERCISE

(a) In the following groups of compound nouns the stress pattern is the same in each group. Indicate the pattern with X for the stressed syllable, x for a strong syllable, and . for a weak syllable, as was done above for *tennis racket*, X . x .

airplane football keyhole Main Street
apple tree basketball movie star waterfall
fire engine grandfather post office wastebasket
filling station physics teacher office worker
department store discussion group collection box
farm equipment tax collector fire department

Some compound nouns have stress on each word of the compound. The second word of the compound is accented if the compound is in accent position.

ˈapple ˈpie ˈkitchen ˈsink ˈLake Louˈise ˈMount ˈEverest

12B EXERCISE

(a) The words in the left-hand column below are compound verbs (sometimes called 'phrasal verbs' or 'two-word verbs'), consisting of a verb plus a particle. The nouns in the right-hand column have a similar composition. How do the verbs, as a group, differ in pronunciation from the nouns, as a group?

to stand up	a look-out
to sit down	a stand-in
to look out	some throw-aways
to go away	a cave-in
to come back	a rip-off
to fall in	a comeback

(b) What is the stress pattern for these adverbial (locative) compounds?

up north	downtown	up front	indoors
down south	backstage	out back	offstage
out west	overhead	underfoot	outside

(c) The following nouns are similar in formation. Do they have the same stress pattern?

an afterthought	backlash	downfall
an inroad	offshoot	upkeep
the overhead	outlook	underwear

Sometimes we have a compound within a compound; for example:

a football team

Football and *team* together make a compound, and *football* is itself a compound of *foot* and *ball*. Note that *foot* is the stressed syllable of the full compound but every originally stressed syllable remains strong. Here are more examples:

the income tax	a goldfish bowl
fingernail polish	pineapple juice

12.2 Compounds and phrases

In general, compound nouns are stressed on the first word of the compound, though, as we will explore later, there are numerous compound nouns with the stress on each compound word. Syntactic groups – phrases – which consist of words of equal semantic weight typically have a stress on each of these words and, as we have seen, the unmarked accent falls on the last word of the group. Syntactic groups include the following:

Noun phrases	a ˈnice ˈday
	some ˈinteresting diˈscussions
Verb phrases	ˈfound a ˈwallet
	ˈworked ˈslowly
Adjective phrases	ˈrather ˈlucky
	ˈstrangely ˈsilent
Co-ordinate phrases	ˈTom, ˈDick, or ˈHarry
	ˈhopped, ˈskipped, and ˈjumped
	ˈtired but ˈhappy
Subject and verb	ˈJean ˈsmiled
	The ˈbus is ˈleaving.

All the major words of a phrase (roughly, the nouns, verbs, adjectives, and adverbs) are stressed, and the last of these major words is a bit more prominent, having the accent. As we know, the accent may be moved to some earlier word for a particular purpose. Examples:

a ˈ**nice** ˈday (emphatically nice)
ˈ**rath**er ˈlucky (not **too** lucky)
ˈ**Jean** ˈsmiled. (not Janet or Jessica or . . .)

Compare these compounds and phrases:

the ˈgreenhouse (a glass structure with artificially controlled heat, for growing plants)
the ˈgreen ˈhouse (the house which is green)
ˈplaying-cards (piece of cardboard, typically 52 to a deck, etc.)
ˈPlaying ˈ**cards** (possible answer to a question 'What are those people doing?')

12C EXERCISE

(a) The following noun compounds and phrases either have stress on the first element (with a strong syllable in the second element), like *'green-house*, or stress on each word, like *'green 'house*. Mark the stresses; assume that there is no accent with special function, that is, the accent will be unmarked and on the last stressed syllable:

a living room	a living wage
a brickyard	a brick house
a darkroom	a dark room
bus-driver	drives a bus

(b) What is the difference between a 'Spanish teacher and a 'Spanish 'teacher?

It has been customary to call such expressions as *armchair*, *Fifth Street*, *information desk*, all with main stress on the first word, NOUN COMPOUNDS and to use the term NOUN PHRASES for expressions with equal stress on the two words, such as *kitchen sink*, *Fifth Avenue*, *Brooklyn Bridge*. This is not a very helpful kind of labeling since there isn't always a clear criterion for deciding what is a compound and what is a phrase, except for knowing what the stress pattern is. We cannot say that compounds have one kind of meaning and phrases have another. In fact, there are dialect differences in stress as in other kinds of pronunciation; *ice cream* and *weekend* are two items which are stressed differently by different speakers of English.

12D EXERCISE

(a) Read the following noun expressions and decide whether the first word is stressed or the two words have equal stress in the pronunciation which is most familiar to you. We will not all agree. Assume that there is no special contrast involved.

It was _____.

the box office	a dividing line
a bay window	no laughing matter
a dollar bill	Swiss cheese
a toy soldier	hay fever
the front door	life insurance

waste paper	yellow fever
a snowman	self-control
a light-year	the ruling class
a fur coat	an X-ray
plate glass	a cure-all
an evening dress	a know-nothing
a fellow citizen	a good-for-nothing
a money order	a white lie

(b) Adjective expressions have similar variation: stress may be on the first word or on both words, and different speakers may not agree. Is it useful to call one kind ADJECTIVE COMPOUNDS and the other ADJECTIVE PHRASES? How do you pronounce the following:

They're _____.

handmade	thoroughbred
home grown	knock-kneed
hard boiled	homesick
middle-aged	trustworthy
old-fashioned	fireproof
broken-hearted	color blind
egg-shaped	dead drunk
bare-headed	worldly wise
near-sighted	blood red
well-mannered	jet black
henpecked	Kelly green
good-looking	air-conditioned
easy-going	tax-free

Adjectives, including compound adjectives like those listed in the previous section, occur in predicative position (e.g., *This egg is hard-boiled*) and in attributive position (e.g. *This is a hard-boiled egg*). In predicative position either the first word is stressed or the two words are equally stressed. The particular stress pattern, initial stress or even stress, is something that is characteristic of each such expression, though, as we have seen, there are dialect differences. In attributive position, however, the following noun is more prominent than either element of the adjective expression because, usually, it has the accent of the tone unit. As a consequence, the pattern which occurs in predicative position may be modified in attributive position. Compare:

1 ˈThis ˈegg is ˈhard-ˈ**boiled**.
  (a) ˈThis is a ˈhard-ˈboiled ˈ**egg**.
  (b) ˈThis is a ˈhard-boiled ˈ**egg**.

2 The ˈbuilding is ˈ**fire**proof.
(a) ˈIt's a ˈfireˈproof ˈ**buil**ding.
(b) ˈIt's a ˈfireproof ˈ**buil**ding

In attributive position the compound adjective may have even stress (1(a), 2(a)) or initial stress (1(b), 2(b)), no matter which pattern it has in predicative position. More examples:

ˈcross-eyed	cross-eyed ˈ**looks**
home ˈgrown	home-grown toˈ**ma**toes
ˈhomesick	homesick ˈ**stu**dents
ˈegg-shaped	an egg-shaped ˈ**jew**el

Adverb (locative) compounds are similar to compound adjectives. Compare the stress pattern of the adverb in predicate position (first column, below), with a pattern of even stress and therefore accent on the second part, with the pattern in attributive position (second and third columns).

It's downˈ**town**	a ˈdown(ˈ)town ˈ**store**	a ˈdown(ˈ)town loˈ**ca**tion
It's outˈ**side**	an ˈout(ˈ)side ˈ**chance**	ˈout(ˈ)side asˈ**sis**tance
They ˈlooked ˌoverˈ**head**	an ˈover(ˈ)head ˈ**fan**	ˈover(ˈ)head proˈ**jec**tors

12.3 Compound verbs

English has several kinds of composite verbs, sometimes called two-word verbs or phrasal verbs. ('Two-word verbs' is not a good name since a three-word sequence like *look out for* behaves much the same as a two-word sequence such as *look for*. 'Phrasal verb' is equally poor since it implies that the verb *look out*, for example, is a phrase whereas the noun *lookout* is a compound.) One kind of compound verb is made up of a verb + a particle; another kind is made up of a verb + a preposition. Particles and prepositions are closed classes of words, few enough in number that they can be listed (which is easier than giving a definition of the classes). Particles are:

away, back, through
down, up
in, out
on, off
over, under

All of the above words except *away* and *back* are also prepositions. Several words, such as *at*, *for*, *of*, *to*, *with*, and *without*, are only prepositions. The difference between particles and prepositions is quite subtle.

A compound verb which is intransitive consists of verb + particle:

stand up start out sit down come back

Some transitive compound verbs consist of verb + particle. If the object of the verb is a noun phrase, it can occur in either of two possible positions. If it is a pronoun, only one position is possible.

look up a word	look a word up	look it up
put on the gloves	put the gloves on	put them on
hand in the paper	hand the paper in	hand it in

Notice how this differs from verb + preposition with an object, noun phrase or pronoun:

look at the pictures	look at them
listen to the record	listen to it
wait for Eddy	wait for him

Compare *look up* as verb + particle with *look up* as verb + preposition:

I looked up the article.	I looked it up.
I looked up the chimney.	I looked up it.

In addition, note that a verb and a preposition may occur side by side without forming a compound verb. *She waited for a friend* has a compound verb; *She waited for an hour* simply has a verb followed by a prepositional phrase indicating time.

A few compound verbs consist of verb + particle + preposition:

put up with this nuisance	put up with it
do away with the old papers	do away with them
look up to his father	look up to him

In a sequence of verb + particle + noun phrase, the noun typically has the accent, and verb and particle may be stressed equally:

She ˈtook ˈback the ˈ**pres**ents.
I ˈcrossed ˈoff your ˈ**name**.
We ˈput aˈway our ˈ**tools**.
ˈDid you ˈturn ˈin your asˈ**sign**ment?

Any construction like this can be converted to an equivalent sequence, verb + noun phrase + particle. In that sequence either the noun or the particle may have the accent, without any appreciable difference of meaning.

She 'took the '**pre**sents 'back.	She 'took the 'presents '**back**.
We 'put our '**tools** a'way.	We 'put our 'tools a'**way**.

If the noun phrase is replaced by a pronoun, the pronoun goes between verb and particle and the particle is accented.

She 'took them '**back.**	I'll 'try it '**on**.
We 'turned it '**in**.	'Did you 'call him '**up**?

Likewise, when verb and particle are at the end of a tone unit, the particle has the accent.

'What did you 'turn '**in**?
'When did they 'pass '**by**?
Is 'this the 'paper you're 'throwing '**out**?
Is 'this the 'sweater she 'tried '**on**?

On the other hand, in a sequence of verb + preposition + noun phrase the preposition is usually unstressed.

'I was 'looking at the '**po**ster.
We 'listened to some '**rec**ords.
He 'asked for a '**raise**.
'Why 'don't you 'laugh at 'my '**jokes**?

If the noun phrase is replaced by a pronoun, the verb is accented and either the preposition or the pronoun is stressed.

'I was '**look**ing 'at them.	'I was '**look**ing at 'them.
'What do you '**think** 'of it?	'What do you '**think** of 'it?

But if the noun phrase is replaced by an indefinite pronoun (*one* or *some*), the pronoun, not the preposition, is stressed.

We '**lis**tened to 'some.
He '**asked** for 'one.

If verb + preposition come last, the verb is accented and the preposition is stressed.

'What did you '**ask** 'for?
'What did they '**listen** 'to?
'What are you '**look**ing 'at?
'What was he '**sit**ting 'on?
Is 'this the 'article the 'doctor re'**ferred** 'to?

12.4 Prefixes

To classify the pieces of a language is not a simple job. We have called words like *down* and *up* particles or prepositions depending upon how they act in compound verbs. Consider the following sentences:

The boat floated down the stream.
The boat floated downstream.

It is usual to say that the first sentence contains a phrase *down the stream*, consisting of a preposition *down* and a noun phrase *the stream*, and that the second sentence has a compound adverb *downstream*. However, the difference is certainly not great. Furthermore, we might equally well say that *downstream* is composed of a prefix *down-* and a base *stream*.

In chapter 11 a distinction was made between neutral suffixes, which are added to independent words (e.g. *arriv # al*, *build # ing*, *procure # ment*), and other suffixes which are attached to bases that typically have no independent existence (e.g. *nomin+al*, *delinqu+ent*, *monu+ment*). Similarly, there are prefixes which can be called neutral and others which are non-neutral. The distinction is seen, for example, in:

re-cover 'to cover again'
recover 'to get over an illness; to regain possession of'

The first, which we represent as *re # cover*, has a neutral prefix; the second, designated *re=cover*, does not. Generally, neutral prefixes are stressed (and sometimes accented) while non-neutral prefixes are not.

Four non-neutral prefixes, *a=*, *be=*, *for=*, *with=*, occur in various types of words – nouns, verbs, adjectives, adverbs – always unstressed.

arise	award	asleep	ahead
behold	belief	beneath	beside
forbear	forget	forgive	forsake
withdraw	withhold	withstand	

In contrast, such neutral prefixes as *after#*, *by#*, *down#*, *fore#*, *in#*, *off#*, *on#*, *out#*, *over#*, *under#*, and *up#* are, as we have seen, typically stressed on the prefix in nouns; verbs with these prefixes have even stress or else stress on the base.

Nouns: afterthought bylaw downfall forearm infield onset outbreak overcoat underbrush upkeep

Verbs: foreclose infringe offload outgrow overcome undergo uphold

There are several noun-verb pairs, written alike, which differ in speech because the nouns are stressed on the prefix, the verbs on the base (or on both):

offset overflow overlap overthrow overlook upset upturn

Compare also these verb-noun pairs:

fore'see	'foresight
out'grow	'outgrowth
over'draw	'overdraft

In a few cases, such as *'bypass*, *'outline*, the verb has been derived from the noun and so is identical in stress. On the other hand, nouns formed from verbs by addition of a neutral suffix, such as *under'standing*, *with'drawal*, have the same stressed syllable as the base verb.

Adverbs with these prefixes have even stress or stress on the second element, the base, as in *down'stairs*, *off'stage*, *over'head*. Since some of these prefixes exist in contrastive pairs, *down* and *up*, *on* and *off*, *in* and *out*, the prefix may become stressed and accented, a form of paradigmatic focus (chapter 9):

'onstage and '**off**stage
'inside or '**out**side

The neutral prefix *mis#* is regular so far as verbs are concerned: *mis'judge*, *mis'lead*, *mispro'nounce*, *mis'spell*, etc. Nouns are less regular: *'misfit* and *'misprint* are stressed on the prefix, but others are stressed on the base, e.g. *mis'deed*, *mis'fortune*; thus there are some verb–noun pairs which are homophonous: *mis'rule*, *mis'trust*.

The prefix *un#* occurs in verbs, nouns, adjectives, and derived adverbs. Some examples:

unbutton undo unfurl unpack unbelief unconcern unrest
untruth uncertain unclean unfair unreal unmercifully
unquestionably unsuitably

In all of these the prefix and base have even stress. However, *un* # , like *mis* # , is often in contrast with zero (the absence of a prefix) and therefore takes on contrastive stress and accent:

ˈdeeds and ˈ**mis**deeds
ˈlocked or ˈ**un**locked

All the prefixes discussed so far are of Germanic (Old English or Scandinavian) origin. In words which have come from Latin, directly or through French, the number of prefixes is larger (about two dozen), the bases to which they are attached are numerous, and of course the number of words formed this way is large. Some prefixes vary in form according to the first phoneme of the base to which they are attached, but the variations are mainly in spelling:

abs=tract ab=solve
ad=apt ac=quire af=fect al=ly an=nex ap=pend as=sume
at=tend
con=cern com=bine co=here col=lect cor=rect
contra=dict
de=tract
dis=tract di=vide dif=fuse
ex=tract e=vict ef=fect
in=tend im=pose il=lude ir=rupt
inter=rupt
intro=duce
ob=struct oc=cur of=fend op=press o=mit
per=fect
post=pone
pro=vide
re=sume
se=lect
super=sede
sub=sume suc=ceed suf=fuse sug=gest sup=press

In all these verbs we can observe a morphological rule for stress: A verb which consists of a prefix plus a one-syllable base is stressed on the base. We can further observe that:

1 Most of the bases are strong syllables, with a free vowel (post=pone, re=sume, suc=ceed) or a cluster of consonants (de=tract, in=tend, sug=gest) so that the base, the ult of the word, is properly stressed by the phonological rule as well as the morphological rule.
2 Some bases are not strong syllables, e.g. o=mit, pro=pel, sup=press; the basic verb rule would put stress on the penult, that is, the prefix; stress follows the morphological rule, not the phonological rule.
3 Some verbs have bisyllabic prefixes, e.g. contra=dict, inter=rupt, super=sede. The basic verb rule would put stress on the antepenult, but they are stressed on the ult because the morphological structure is prefix + one-syllable base. The morphological rule takes precedence.
4 A few verbs contain two prefixes and a base. Stress is on the base:

com=pre=hend cor=re=spond re=pre=sent re=col=lect re=sur=rect

12E EXERCISES

(a) Study the following verbs and determine whether the stress is determined by the morphological rule, or the phonological rule, or both, or neither.

ca'jole com'pel con'sole ex'pect 'govern in'ter per'mit con'cern

(b) The following verbs all have the same base but different prefixes. What irregularities do you find in the stress of these verbs?

con'fer de'fer 'differ in'fer 'offer pre'fer 'proffer re'fer 'suffer trans'fer (or 'transfer)

(c) Here is a list of common bases, all monosyllabic. Using the list of prefixes above, think of at least one verb for each base. (There are no answers in the Feedback. You will probably be able to think of more than one verb containing each of the bases.)

=ceed/cede	=gest	=plete	=solve
=ceive	=gress	=pose	=spect
=cide	=here	=quire	=suade
=clude	=ject	=ride	=sume
=cur	=lect	=rode	=tect
=dict	=lide	=rupt	=tend
=duct	=lude	=scribe	=tract
=fect	=mit	=sede	=trude
=fend	=pand	=sent	=vade
=fess	=pel	=sert	=vene
=fine	=pend	=serve	=vide
=flect	=pete	=sist	=vert

Some verbs with these prefixes have a base which is two syllables long. The second syllable of the base is weak, and stress is on the first syllable of the base, the penult of the word.

con=sider con=tinue de=liver de=termine de=velop ex=hibit
pro=hibit re=member sur=render

Other verbs with prefixes also have suffixes. The suffix determines the position of stress.

com=plic+ate inter=rog+ate in=demn+ity re=cogn+ize

Some adjectives, like verbs, consist of a prefix and one-syllable base of Latin–French origin. The following words are all adjectives, and a few of them are also verbs. Note the stressed base in each one.

ab=surd ad=ept com=plete con=trite cor=rect de=mure
dis=tinct ex=empt in=ane ob=scene oc=cult pre=cise
re=mote suc=cinct

As with verbs, there are adjectives which contain both prefix and suffix, and the latter determines stress, e.g. *im=migr+ant*, *super=lat+ive*.

With some exceptions, then, verbs and adjectives which consist of prefix and one-syllable base are stressed on the base. With adjectives, however, there are more exceptions. Examples: *concave* and *convex* may be stressed on either syllable; *oblong*, *extrovert*, *introvert*, which are nouns as well as adjectives, are stressed on the first syllable.

There are numerous verb–noun pairs of this composition, which are either identical or identical except for stress. Note these three patterns of correspondence:

(a) *de'mand re'lease* – verb and noun both stressed on the base
(b) *'contact 'preview* – verb and noun both stressed on the prefix
(c) verbs *in'sult pro'ject*; nouns *'insult 'project* – verb stressed on the base, noun stressed on the prefix.

Of these three patterns, pattern (b) is the least common. However, there are variations among speakers. The verbs *protest* and *transport*, for example, may be stressed on the ult or, like nouns, on the initial syllable.

12F EXERCISES

(a) The following words are all nouns and verbs, identical at least on paper. Indicate for each whether the noun and the verb follow pattern (a), (b), or (c). We will probably not all agree.

abstract	control	insert	refrain
account	convert	interview	refuse
addict	convict	object	relay
address	converse	overflow	reply
advance	decay	overthrow	report
affix	decrease*	pervert	request
annex	detail	prefix	research
appeal	digest	preview	resort
approach	discard	produce	respect
arrest	discharge	progress	reverse
assent	discount	protest	review
attack	disguise	rebound	revolt
collapse	excerpt	rebuke	subject
combat	exchange	recall	supply
combine	export*	recoil	support
command	express	record	surprise
comment	extract	recount	survey
console	import*	recruit	suspect
contract	incense	refill	transfer
contrast	increase*	reform	transform

* Words like these may require accent on the first syllable for paradigmatic focus. Here we want to observe the neutral occurrence of stress, not the contrastive use.

(b) In the following pairs the verb and noun differ in their final consonants, though the orthography doesn't necessarily show this fact. Do they also differ in stress?

abuse – abuse	descend – descent	pretend – pretense
ascend – ascent	exceed – excess	receive – receipt
believe – belief	excuse – excuse	relieve – relief
conceive – concept	offend – offense	respond – response
deceive – deceit	proceed – proceeds	succeed – success
defend – defense	proceed – process	transcribe – transcript

(c) In the following words each group has the same base, at least from an etymological point of view, but different prefixes. Each group includes nouns and verbs, and there are two adjectives here. Does difference in part of speech correlate with stress differences?

aspect inspect prospect respect
allude interlude prelude
district restrict
bisect dissect insect
distinct instinct
impulse repulse
precinct succinct

12.5 Greek-type compounds

An earlier part of this chapter dealt with compound nouns like *armchair*, *bus-driver*, and *lookout*, nouns clearly made up of smaller, independent words but functioning just like a simple noun such as *chair*, *chauffeur*, or *guard*. There is another type of noun which is made up of two bases (and sometimes a suffix) which are ordinarily not independent words. Some examples: *monograph*, *telegram*, *telephone*, *phonograph*. The elements in these words are largely, but not entirely, of Greek origin, and so have been called 'Greek-type compounds'. The first part typically ends with a vowel, *cata=log*, *tele=phone*, *epi=taph*, *auto=graph*, *poly=gon*, unless the second element begins with a vowel; compare *mono=log* and *mon=arch*, *homo=phone* and *hom=onym*. However, some first elements do not have a vowel at the end, e.g. *syn=drome*, *syn=onym*. If there is such a vowel, we call it the CONNECTING VOWEL. The most common connecting vowel, at least as far as spelling is concerned, is *o*.

We recognize Greek-type compounds through familiarity with the elements that compose them, especially the first element. The following are among the most common first elements. Some of them are illustrated in the words above, and others will be seen in words that appear below.

acro=	ecto=	kilo=	philo=
amphi=	electro=	macro=	phono=
ana=	endo=	mega=	poly=
anti=	epi=	meso=	proto=
apo=	ethno=	meta=	pseudo=
archi=	exo=	micro=	psycho=
auto=	geo=	mono=	stereo=
bathy=	hemi=	neo=	syn=
bio=	hetero=	neuro=	techno=
brachy=	hexa=	ophthalmo=	tele=
cardio=	hippo=	ortho=	theo=
cata=	homo=	osteo=	thermo=
chrono=	hyper=	paleo=	xeno=
deca=	hypo=	para=	xylo=
demo=	ideo=	penta=	zoo=
dia=	iso=	peri=	

If the second element consists of just one syllable, the stress of the word is somewhere in the first element, and the second element has a strong syllable. Study these examples:

archi=tect	dino=saur	dia=log
thermo=stat	pachy=derm	epi=gram
tele=phone	alpha=bet	cata=pult

The first word is *'architect*, and all the other words have the same stress pattern. Main stress does not fall on the corresponding vowel, so it must occur on the only syllable preceding. Note that these words have the same stress pattern as compounds like *motor boat* and *waterfall* – compounds with a two-syllable word followed by a one-syllable word.

Now consider this smaller group of Greek-type compounds. The first element has three syllables and the second element has just one syllable. Again, the stress of the word is in the first element, but where?

electro=lyte	cephalo=pod
kaleido=scope	hetero=dox
opthalmo=scope	biblio=phile

The words on the left have the same stress pattern as *de'partment store* and *col'lection box*. The words on the right have the same pattern as *'platinum mine* or *'radio wave*. Thus the rule for stress in these Greek compounds follows a rule which you already know.

12G EXERCISE

If the second element of the Greek compound has one syllable and the first element has three syllables, main stress is on the penult or the antepenult *of the first element*. What determines whether the stress is on the penult of the first element or the antepenult?

If the second element has more than one syllable, main stress falls on the penult or antepenult *of the whole compound*, according to a rule which is quite familiar to you. Consider these compound words:

bronto=saurus	archi=pelago
dia=betes	biblio=mania
poly=hedron	hippo=potamus
rhodo=dendron	hydro=phobia

Those on the left have a strong penult, which is stressed. Those on the right have a weak penult, so the antepenult is stressed. In both cases the main stress falls in the second element of the compound word. In the words below the penult is weak and so stress is on the antepenult, but the antepenult happens to be the connecting vowel of the compound:

meta=thesis metro=polis thermo=meter

Now consider this set of words:

cata=clysm cate=chism micro=cosm proto=plasm

The stress pattern is, for instance, ˈ*protoplasm* – which is entirely regular if the second element is analyzed as a monosyllable, even though it is pronounced as two syllables. The same is true for the following sets of words, though there seems to be less reason for viewing the second element as a single syllable in any of the words.

agri=culture horti=culture archi=tecture super=structure
melo=drama

Then note the irregular stress in the following words which have appeared rather often in this text:

ˈmonosyllable ˈpolysyllable

Finally, there is a word *intersection* which has two pronunciations – two stress patterns – depending on its meaning. If it is an abstract noun meaning 'the fact of intersecting', as in *the intersection of two lines*, the pattern is *inter'section*. If the word has a more concrete meaning, referring to a place where two streets cross, the usual stress pattern is 'intersection. There is a similar division between *subdi'vision*, the act of subdividing, and *'subdivision*, an area containing houses all built at approximately the same time by the same real estate company.

12.6 A rhythm rule

Up to this point we have been concerned with the position of stress in different kinds of English words. We have also noted the occurrence of a strong syllable *after* the main stress in certain kinds of words:

words with a strong ult, like *interrogate*, *formaldehyde*
compound words, like *blackbird*, *toothpaste*
abstract nouns ending in +*y* with a strong penult, like *apoplexy*, *patriarchy*
in North America, certain words ending in +*ary*, +*ory*, like *ordinary*, *category*.

Long words usually also have a strong syllable *before* the main stress. As we saw in section 5.3, if stress falls on the third (or a later) syllable of the word, one of the pretonic syllables is more prominent than the other(s). An English word does not have two weak syllables in word-initial position.

ban'danna	No'vember	ba'nana	co'median
+ +	+ +	+	+

When there is just one pretonic syllable, that syllable is strong if it ends with a consonant (*ban-dan-na*) or has a free vowel (*No-vem-ber*); otherwise, the syllable is weak (*ba-na-na*, *co-me-di-an*). Thus whether the syllable is strong or weak depends on the nature of its peak or its coda.

Unfortunately, there are exceptions to the rule just elaborated. Here are some of them:

compare concern pertain surpass

When the initial syllable (immediately before the tonic syllable) ends with a nasal or /r/, the syllable is weak and the vowel is /ə/. This may be the case when the initial syllable ends in other consonants, notably /b/ and /d/; compare: *obtain*, *submit*, *advance*, *adventure*.

As we have seen before (chapter 5), there are dialect differences with regard to what vowel is pronounced in an initial pretonic syllable. For example, *direct* may be pronounced with /ai/, making the first syllable strong, or with schwa, creating a weak syllable. Similarly, if *va'cation* has /ei/ in the initial syllable and *pro'motion* has /ou/, these initial syllables are strong; if the words are pronounced with schwa in the first syllable, that syllable is weak.

```
effer'vescent  memo'randum  Japa'nese  invi'tation
+     +        +     +      +     +     +     +
```

When the stressed syllable is preceded by two syllables, the initial syllable is strong. Note that it makes no difference whether that syllable has a free vowel or consonantal coda, it is STRONG BY POSITION. Note also that the second syllable may end with a consonant, as in *effervescent*, and yet that syllable, immediately preceding the stressed syllable, is weak. However, a medial syllable immediately before the stressed syllable is not likely to have a free vowel; note what happens to the second vowel of *invite* when that word becomes part of the bigger word *invitation*; we shall see more about such reduction in section 14.13.

```
halluci'nation  interpre'tation  Mononga'hela
    +     +        +     +          +     +

mulliga'tawny  exemplifi'cation  Senega'lese
 +     +        +     +          +     +
```

When the main-stressed syllable is preceded by three or more syllables, one of the preceding syllables is strong. If the second syllable preceding has a free vowel or a consonant coda, it is naturally strong, as in the words of the first line. If that syllable is not strong by its nature, the third syllable before the stressed syllable is strong by position, as in the second line.

In some instances it seems that the strength of a syllable is determined by analogy rather than by its nature. There is a tendency for a longer word to echo the syllables of the smaller word contained in it. Compare:

```
in'terpret  interpre'tation
   +           +     +

ex'emplify  exemplifi'cation
   +     +     +          +

indi'vidual  individu'ality
+     +      +     +  +

'eligible  eligi'bility
 +         +     +
```

12.7 Summary

Compound words have one of two stress patterns: either the first element of the compound carries the stress, and one syllable of the second element is strong (initial stress), or else the two words of the compound have equal stress (even stress). Compound nouns often, but not always, have initial stress. Compound adverbs are even-stressed. Compound verbs which consist of a verb and a particle have greater stress on the particle, those which consist of verb and preposition have greater stress on the verb. In sequences of preposition and pronoun following a verb, the preposition and the pronoun may both be unstressed or either of them may be stressed.

A **morphological rule** applies to nouns and verbs, and a smaller number of adjectives, which consist of a prefix and a one-syllable base. Verbs and adjectives typically are stressed on the base and nouns on the prefix, but there are numerous exceptions. As noted earlier (11.9), of all categories of words it is hardest to account for stress in two-syllable nouns.

Greek-type compounds consist of a rather limited number of first and second elements which do not occur alone but co-occur in a rather large number of nouns. Typically there is a connecting vowel between the two parts. If the second element of the compound is a single syllable, the word stress occurs in the first element, on the first strong syllable (or only syllable) before the connecting vowel. If the second element has more than one syllable, stress is assigned according to the usual noun rule.

The strength of syllables before the main stress of a word depends partly on the nature of syllables, partly on their number, and partly on analogy. If there is only one syllable preceding, it is strong if it has a free vowel or consonantal coda, otherwise weak. If there are two syllables preceding, the initial syllable is strong **by position**. If there are three or more syllables preceding, either the second syllable preceding is strong by its nature or the third syllable preceding is strong by position. In some instances a long, complex word has a strong syllable where the simple word from which it is derived has stress.

12A FEEDBACK

(a) with one example from each group:

```
'airplane  'apple tree  'fire engine  'filling station
X    x     X   .   x   X  x     .    X .     x   .
de'partment store  'farm equipment 'apple 'pie
 .  X    .    x     X   .  x    .   X  .   X
```

As the examples show, the stressed syllable of a compound noun is usually, but not always, in the *first* word of the compound.

12B FEEDBACK

(a) The verbs have even stress on the two words, e.g. ˈ*stand* ˈ*up*, or just stress on the particle, *stand* ˈ*up*. The nouns have initial stress, e.g. ˈ*look-out*.
(b) Even stress; e.g. ˈ*up* ˈ*north*.
(c) No, there is initial stress; e.g. ˈ*afterthought*. Notice the irregularity of the noun ˈ*after*ˈ*noon*.

12C FEEDBACK

(a)

a ˈliving room	a ˈliving ˈwage
a ˈbrickyard	a ˈbrick ˈhouse
a ˈdarkroom	a ˈdark ˈroom
ˈbus-driver	ˈdrives a ˈbus

(b) A ˈSpanish teacher teaches Spanish. A ˈSpanish ˈteacher is a teacher from Spain.

12D FEEDBACK

(a) Answers will vary. In general it is safe to say that the following have initial stress:

box office	dividing line
snowman	hay fever
light-year	life insurance
evening dress	X-ray
money order	cure-all
	good-for-nothing

This means that half of these items, which were chosen at random, have initial stress and half have even stress. While some specific expressions may be stressed differently by different people, it is likely that such noun expressions have this 50–50 ratio.

(b) With adjective expressions the situation is different. Again, answers will vary, but most of these expressions have even stress in the context indicated. Here are the ones most likely to have initial stress:

egg-shaped	thoroughbred
near-sighted	homesick
henpecked	trustworthy
	fireproof
	air-conditioned

12E FEEDBACK

(a) Morphological rule only: compel, inter, permit. Phonological rule only: cajole. Both: console, concern, expect. Neither: govern.

(b) *Differ*, *offer, proffer*, and *suffer* are irregular, in terms of the morphological construction, in being stressed on the prefix rather than the base. The same is true, of course, for the verb *transfer* if it is stressed on the first syllable.

12F FEEDBACK

(a) These words follow pattern (a), verb and noun both stressed on the base:

account	collapse	rebuke	resort
advance	command	recruit	respect
appeal	control	reform	reverse
approach	decay	refrain	review
arrest	disguise	reply	revolt
assent	exchange	report	supply
attack	express	request	support
			surprise

Only three of these clearly follow pattern (b), verb and noun stressed on the prefix:

comment interview preview

For the remainder, verbs and nouns are stressed differently, following pattern (c), though there is a tendency to stress some verbs on the prefix, like the corresponding nouns, perhaps because the noun is more common than the verb and influences its pronunciation. (On the other hand, the noun and verb may be semantically far apart, as is the case with *console*, *converse*, and *incense*). There is a verb *con'tract* which means 'to become or make smaller', and another verb *'contract*, stressed like the noun, which means 'to make a contract'.

(b) Only four of these verb-noun pairs have different stress:

con'ceive – 'concept pro'ceed – 'process
pro'ceed – 'proceeds tran'scribe – 'transcript

The others are stressed on the ult.
When *offense* means 'something which offends, a transgression', it is stressed on the ult; as a term in sports, contrasting with *defense*, initial stress is common.

(c) The words on the left below have initial stress and those on the right have final stress, whatever the part of speech.

aspect (N) prospect (N, V)	inspect (V) respect (N, V)
interlude (N) prelude (N)	allude (V)
district (N)	restrict (V)
insect (N)	bisect* (V) dissect (V)
instinct (N)	distinct (A)
impulse (N)	repulse (N, V)
precinct (N)	succinct (A)

* *Bisect* is sometimes stressed on the initial syllable; influenced by this verb, the verb *dissect* is sometimes pronounced /dai'sɛkt/ rather than /dɪ'sɛkt/.

12G FEEDBACK

The same rule as for ordinary nouns: if the penult is strong, stress the penult (e'lectro=, ka'leido=); if the penult is weak, stress the antepenult ('cephalo=, 'biblio=).

13

Phonological Processes in Speech

13.1 Different ways of speaking

In chapter 1 we discussed variation in language with respect to differences among users of the language and differences in their uses of it. Probably we notice differences among users more easily than we notice differences in the ways we use our language. People who speak differently attract our attention, but we may fail to recognize how different our own speech is on different occasions. The tempo of our speech and the formality or informality of the occasion have a great effect on what our pronunciation is. In this chapter we first examine the variable pronunciation of certain very common function words which are used frequently and which are pronounced differently in different contexts. We describe these different pronunciations as the results of PHONOLOGICAL PROCESSES which have different effects in different contexts.

13.2 Full forms and reduced forms

Approximately 40 common function words vary in pronunciation according to whether they are stressed or unstressed. For example, consider the pronunciations of the operator, or auxiliary verb, *can* in these sentences:

1 (a) I'**can**'doit.'Who'saysI'**can't**?
  (b) '**Can** I? In'deed I '**can**.
2 (a) '**Who** 'can?
  (b) We '**all** 'can.
3 (a) 'I can '**do** it.
  (b) 'What can we '**do**? (or: '**What** can we 'do?)

In the sentences of group 1 *can* is accented. The word is deliberately accented for emphasis or insistence. In group 2 *can* is stressed but not accented. The emphasis is on the subject – *who*, *we all* – but *can* must be stressed in final position. In the sentences of group 3 *can* is typically unstressed; it occurs between stressed words.

When *can* is stressed, whether accented or not, it is pronounced /kæn/. We call this the FULL FORM of the word. When unstressed, it has a REDUCED FORM which we represent as /kən/, though the actual pronunciation may be [kən] or [kin] or [kn̩] and some other things, depending partly on the context and partly on the speaker. In some positions *can* may be unstressed or stressed; this happens especially in utterance-initial position; for instance:

(ˈ) Can the ˈdoctor ˈsee me ˈ**now**?
(ˈ) Can you ˈ**help** me?
ˈWhat (ˈ) can you ˈtell us aˈbout ˈ**this**?

This function word, then, is accented when the speaker chooses to emphasize it, as in 1 (a), (b), above. It must be stressed, even though not accented, in final position, as in 2 (a), (b); speakers of English do not say *ˈ***Who** */kən/*? * *We* ˈ***all*** */kən/*. It is mostly unstressed (and reduced) when it is adjacent to a stressed word, but in initial position or in a deliberate manner of speaking it may be stressed. Other function words, examined below, are roughly comparable to *can* in the likelihood of stressed or unstressed occurrence and in having a full form and one or more reduced forms.

The word *am* has a full form and two reduced forms:

ˈYes, / I ˈam.	/æm/
ˈWhat am I supˈposed to ˈdo?	/əm/
I'm ˈready.	/m/

The last sentence illustrates a reduced form that is recognized in our written language as a contraction. Contractions are not the only reduced forms in the language.

Which are the function words that undergo reduction? There are six groups of words.

13.2.1 Auxiliaries or operators like CAN and AM

The examples which follow are purposely kept short, and only the accented syllable is indicated – not every possible stressed syllable.

Full forms	*Reduced forms*
CAN	
Yes, I /kæn/.	I /kən/ see it.
COULD	
She /kʊd/ / if she wanted to.	She /kəd/ do it / if she wanted.

WILL	
Yes, we /wɪl/.	What /əl/ we do? He /l/ do it.
WOULD	
He said he /wʊd/.	What /wəd/ anybody do / in that case? He said he /d/ do it.
SHALL	
We /ʃæl/.	What /ʃəl/ we do now?
SHOULD	
You certainly /ʃʊd/	I /ʃəd/ think that's enough.
MUST	
You /mʌst/ do it, / you /mʌst/.	You /məs/ tell us about it / later.
IS	
Yes, it /ɪz/.	Pat /s/ going. Ann /z/ going. Bruce /ɨz/ going.
ARE	
Yes, they /ar/.	What /ər/ you going to do? We /r/ going to be there.
HAVE	
Yes, they /hæv/.	They must /həv/ (or /əv/) eaten it. They must /həv/ (or /əv/ or /ə/) seen it.
HAS	
Yes, he /hæz/.	Pat /s/ gone. Ann /z/ gone. Bruce /ɨz/ gone.
HAD	
Yes, they /hæd/.	What /əd/ they done? They /d/ already finished.
DO	
I /duu/, / too.	When /də/ you leave?
DOES	
Sue /dʌz/, / too.	What /dəz/ that mean?
DID	
Yes, we /dɪd/.	When /dɨd/ (or when /d/) they find out?

There are three other operators, MAY, MIGHT, and OUGHT, which do not have reduced forms.

The reduced forms of auxiliaries IS and HAS are the ones already discussed in chapter 8, along with the regular plural of nouns and some other suffixes. These can be written as contractions after nouns (*Pat's going*, *Ann's gone*), as well as pronouns (*She's going*, *He's gone*). Other auxiliaries which are written as contractions are those which are reduced to a single consonant phoneme, when they occur after pronouns which end with a vowel specificially:

WILL	I'll	he'll	she'll	we'll	you'll	they'll
WOULD	I'd	he'd	she'd	we'd	you'd	they'd
AM	I'm					
ARE				we're	you're	they're
HAVE	I've			we've	you've	they've
HAD	I'd	he'd	she'd	we'd	you'd	they'd

The reduced forms of *had* and *would* are identical but of course are usually identified in context since *would* is followed by the simple form of a verb (*They'd enjoy the play if they had a chance to see it*, *I wish you'd be quiet*) and *had* by the past participle (*They'd wanted to see the play but hadn't been able to*, *I wish you'd been here earlier.*)

Among the sentences above which represent the reduced forms of HAVE are these two:

They must have eaten it. They must have seen it.

In both of these the vowel is reduced to /ə/, and the initial /h/ is lost. The final /v/ may also disappear, a loss more likely to occur before a consonant, as in the second example, than before a vowel.

To summarize, the reduced forms of the operators are derived from the full forms by four processes or rules:

1 In all the reductions the original vowel becomes a central vowel, [ɨ] or [ə], or the sequence of vowel + /n/ becomes a syllabic [n̩]. Using the schwa as a cover symbol for any of these results, our rule is:

$$V \rightarrow ə$$

2 Certain initial consonants, /h/ and /w/, are deleted.

$$C \rightarrow 0 \ / \ \# \ ___$$

3 (a) If there is no initial consonant, or if the initial consonant has been deleted, the vowel may be deleted.

$$V \rightarrow 0 \ / \ \# \ ___$$

3 (b) In *must have*, *could have*, and the like, the final consonant, /v/ is deleted – but this cannot happen if the vowel is deleted; so 3 (a) and 3 (b) are mutually exclusive. The consonant is most likely to be deleted when the following word begins with a consonant.

C /→ 0 / V ___ # (#C)

4 When *is* and *has* have undergone the deletions of (2) and (3a), the remaining consonant adjusts to the final sound of the preceding word:

Pat/s/ but *Ann* /z/.

z → s / [– voice] # ___ #

The other classes of function words, examined below, undergo the same reduction rules. Before leaving operators, however, we need to note some ways in which DO-DOES-DID is special. First, after question words (*what*, *when*, *where*, *how*, etc) the form DOES may be reduced to merely a sibilant consonant, /s/ or /z/, and is thus identical with the reduced form of IS and HAS.

What's that sign mean?	(does)
What's that man doing?	(is)
What's the weather been like lately?	(has)
When's the bus leave?	(does)
How soon's the bus leaving?	(is)
How long's the bus been waiting?	(has)

Next, we should note that when *do*, *does*, or *did* follow *what*, the initial /d/ is frequently deleted in informal speech:

What do you need?	/ˈwɒtəjə ˈ**niid**/
What does it matter?	/ˈwɒtiziɨt ˈ**mætər**/
What did John say?	/ˈwɒtɨd ˈjɒn ˈ**sei**/

13.2.2 Pronouns like HE and YOU

We have already seen that anaphoric words, including pronouns, are typically unstressed but may be accented for special emphasis.

Full Forms	*Reduced Forms*
HE	
She didn't like it / but /**hii**/ did.	Did /ii/ **tell** you?

HIS	
I had **mine** /and Jack had /**hɪz**/.	He had /**ɨz**/ **ten**nis racket with him.
HIM	
You won't catch /**hɪm**/ doing that.	Did you **tell** /ɪm/? (/**ɨm**/)
HER	
The **Browns**? / I know /**hər**/.	Did you **tell** /ər/?
THEM	
They didn't tell **me**. / I told /**ðɛm**/.	Did you **tell** /ðəm/? (/əm/)
YOU	
This is for /**juu**/.	Will /jə/ **tell** them? Will /ju/ **ask** them?
YOUR	
Do **you** / have /**jur**/ keys?	You can leave /jər/ things **here**.
US	
We didn't tell **them**. / They told /**ʌs**/.	They told /əs/ **about** it.

Pronouns SHE, WE, ME, THEY do not have reduced forms. The words I, MY, and OUR sometimes become shortened to /a/, /ma/, and /ar/, respectively, but they do not reduce to /ə/.

13A EXERCISE

For the reduced forms of YOU our illustrations were 'Will /jə/ **tell** them?' and 'Will /ju/ **ask** them?' What determines whether the reduced form is /jə/ or /ju/? (Not all speakers have this difference.)

What do you say? Some speakers consistently use /ɪm/ as the reduced form of HIM and /əm/ as the reduced form of THEM: **Tell** /ɪm/ vs **Tell** /əm/. For other speakers both pronouns have the same reduced form: **Tell** /əm/.

13.2.3 Prepositions like TO

Prepositions are usually followed by a noun, and usually the noun is stressed, the preposition unstressed. A preposition may be accented for contrastive focus, and it is often stressed, but not accented, if it is at the end of a sentence.

Full Forms	*Reduced Forms*
AT	
Not be**fore** noon, / /**æt**/ noon.	They'll be here /ət/ **noon.**

FOR	
What is it /**fɔr**/?	This is /fər/ **you.**
FROM	
Where are you /**frʌm**/? (/**frɒm**/)	I'm /frəm/ Mis**sou**ri.
OF	
Government /**ɒv**/ the people (/**ʌv**/)	a bucket /**əv**/ **ice** a cup /**ə**/ **co**ffee (/**əv**/)
TO	
Talk /**tuu**/ them, not **about** them.	I expect him /**tə**/ **tell** us. I expect him /**tu**/ **ask** us.
WITH	
Who went /**wɪθ**/ them? (/**wɪð**/)	She came /**wɨθ**/ a **friend.** (/**wɨð**/)

The prepositions BY, DOWN, IN, OFF, ON, OUT, THROUGH, UP do not have reduced forms, nor do two-syllable prepositions like ABOUT and BESIDE.

13B EXERCISES

(a) When is the unstressed form of TO most likely to be /tuu/ and when is it /tə/?
(b) When is the unstressed form of OF most likely to keep the /v/, and when is the /v/ more likely to be deleted?
(c) Why do some children – and maybe some adults – write *would of gone*, *might of taken*, etc. for *would have gone*, *might have taken?*

13.2.4 Determiners like SOME

Pronounced in isolation or with emphasis the words A, AN, THE, and SOME are, respectively, /ei/, /æn/, /ðii/, and /sʌm/. When they occur before a noun, they are usually unstressed and their respective pronunciations are:
/ə/; /ən/; /ðə/ before a consonant and /ðii/ before a vowel; /səm/. The determiner THIS, before a noun or not, is likely to be stressed and therefore unreduced (ˈThis maˈchine is ˈ**bro**ken), but in frequently used phrases like *this afternoon*, *this evening* the word is destressed and reduced to /**ðɨs**/. Other determiners such as THESE, THAT, THOSE, EACH, NO, ALL, BOTH are stressed and not reduced.

13.2.5 Conjunctions like AND

Six more function words, typically unstressed, can be classified as conjunctions.

Full Forms	*Reduced Forms*
AND	
Jack /**ænd**/ Jill –/ **both** of them.	Jack /ən/ **Jill**
OR	
Jack /**ɔr**/ Jill –/ **ei**ther of them.	Jack /ər/ Jill
AS	
/**æz**/ I was **say**ing . . .	It's /əz/ sharp /əz/ a **tack**.
BUT	
Is he clever? / Anything /**bʌt**/.	He's good /bət/ not **cle**ver.
THAN	
What is it **worse** /ðæn/?	It's sharper /ðən/ a **tack**.
THAT	
I didn't hear **when** the accident happened/, only /**ðæt**/ it happened.	I'm glad /ðət/ you're **here**.

13.2.6 Miscellaneous

There are two more words which are typically, but not always, unstressed. They don't fit into any of the above classifications. One is the word THERE when it functions as a sort of pronoun (not when it means 'in that place'). Stressed, /ðɛr/; unstressed /ðər/:

/ðər/'s a ˈlot of ˈwork to be ˈ**done**, / ˈ**isn**'t ˈ/ðɛr/?

The other word is NOT, which is different from other function words in the way that its reduced form is related to the full form. The vowel is deleted, and the initial /n/ becomes syllabic. The reduced form occurs after the auxiliaries or operators. The combinations of auxiliary + reduced form of NOT are the so-called contractions written with *-n't*. Here is the full list:

AM	—	CAN	can't
IS	isn't	COULD	couldn't
ARE	aren't		
		WILL	won't
WAS	wasn't	WOULD	wouldn't

WERE	weren't		
		SHALL	shan't
HAS	hasn't	SHOULD	shouldn't
HAVE	haven't		
HAD	hadn't	MAY	—
		MIGHT	mightn't
DOES	doesn't		
DO	don't	MUST	mustn't
DID	didn't		
		OUGHT	oughtn't
		NEED	needn't
		DARE	daren't

The negative contraction adds /nt/ to the auxiliary, and is therefore a two-syllable word, except in the following cases:

Can't is formed by dropping the final /n/ of the auxiliary and *shan't* drops a final /l/, so that the /n/ of NOT does not become syllabic.

Don't and *won't* are completely irregular.

Aren't and *weren't* are bisyllabic, with syllabic [n̩], in the New York City area, but elsewhere are one-syllable words.

One more negative contraction must be mentioned: AIN'T. This form is in use throughout the English-speaking world though it is everywhere considered non-standard. It originated as a contraction of AM NOT but may also have been influenced by one pronunciation of AREN'T and perhaps HAVEN'T, through another form *hain't*.

Chart 13.1 summarizes the kinds of reduction that the other function words undergo. As the chart indicates, and as suggested above, the reductions are essentially four different rules which apply to the full forms, one after another:

1 The full vowel of the function word is reduced to /ə/. This applies to almost every one of the words in question.

2 An initial consonant is deleted. Obviously this does not apply to every initial consonant. It can apply to every initial /h/. It applies to the initial /w/ of WILL and WOULD, but not of WAS, WERE or WITH. It applies to the initial /ð/ of THEM and THAN but of no other word. (Historically speaking, the reduced form *'em* /əm/ for THEM does not come from THEM but from an Old English pronoun *hem*, which otherwise does not survive in Modern English. The pronouns THEY, THEIR, THEM were brought to Britain, and to the English language, by Scandinavian invaders.)

3 (a) The vowel is deleted. This applies only to operators (not to the preposition OF, for instance) which either had no initial consonant or have deleted the initial consonant by rule 2.

3 (b) A final consonant is deleted. This applies to auxiliaries which end with two consonants, MUST and AND. It also applies to HAVE and OF, which lose their final /v/.

By rules 1, 2, and 3 (a) the word HAVE becomes just /v/. By rules 1, 2 and 3 (b) the same word becomes just /ə/. If both 3 (a) and 3 (b) could apply, there would be nothing left of HAVE, but both cannot apply. They are mutually exclusive and that is why they are numbered 3 (a) and 3 (b).

4 Consonants which come together as a result of rules 1 to 3 undergo assimilation. By this rule the /z/ of HAS and IS becomes /s/ after voiceless consonants. This change is obligatory. If previous rules have deleted everything except the sibilant consonant, the sibilant consonant must be voiceless after a voiceless consonant.

Rule 4 also changes the /n/ of CAN to /m/ before a labial consonant (*can pass*, *can be* (*seen*)) and to /ŋ/ before a dorsal consonant (*can keep*, *can give*), but this change is optional.

	æm	*iz*	*ar*	*wʌz*	*wɜr*	*hæv*	*hæz*	*hæd*	*duu*	*dʌz*	*did*
1	əm	iz	ər	wəz	wər	həv	həz	həd	də	dəz	did
2						əv	əz	əd			
3 (a)	m	z	r			v	z	d			
3 (b)											
4		s					s				

	kæn	*kʊd*	*wɪl*	*wʊd*	*ʃæl*	*ʃʊd*	*mʌst*
1	kən	kəd	wil	wəd	ʃəl	ʃəd	məst
2			il	əd			
3 (a)			l	d			
3 (b)							məs

	juu	*jur*	*hii*	*hɜz*	*hɪm*	*hɜr*	*ɪt*	*ʌs*	*ðɛm*
1	jə	jər		hiz	him	hər	it	əs	ðəm
2			ii	iz	im	ər			əm

	æt	*fɔr*	*frʌm/frɒm*	*ʌv/ɒv*	*tuu*	*wʒθ/wɪð*
1	ət	fər	frəm	əv	tə	wiθ/wið
2						
3 (a)						
3 (b)						

	ænd	*ɔr*	*æz*	*bʌt*	*ðæt*	*ðan*
1	ənd	ər	əz	bət	ðət	ðæn
2						ən
3 (a)						
3 (b)	ən					

	ei	*æn*	*ðii*	*sʌm*	*ðɛr*
1	ə	ən	ðə	səm	ðər

Chart 13.1

13C EXERCISES

The words *to*, *too*, and *two* are said to be homophones, but it would be more accurate to say that they are potential homophones. They are identical in pronunciation when they are stressed, but, as we have seen, the first has a reduced form which the other two do not have. Comment on the following sets of words.

(a) the auxiliary verb *have* (*has*, *had*); the transitive verb *have*; and the catenative verb *have* (*to*).

They have bought a new **car**.
They have a new **car**.
They have to buy a new **car**.

Apart from stress, what pronunciation differences are there in the following?

I have **two.**	I **have** to.
She has **two**.	She **has** to.

(b) The next group of sentences illustrates three words: the number *one* (different from *two*, *three*, *four*, etc.); the noun phrase substitute *one* (plural *some*); and the noun substitute *one* (plural *ones*). Which of them is unstressed and reduced?

I have one ticket / – just **one**.
I wanted to buy a paper / and I **bought** one.
(I wanted to buy some papers / and I **bought** some.)
The committee scrapped **that** plan / and initiated a **new** one.
(The committee scrapped **those** plans / and considered some **new** ones.)

(c) The sentences below have a word *some* in unstressed position and a word *some* in stressed – accented – position. Is it the same word? In which function does *some* seem to be the plural of the indefinite article *a*, *an*?

Some people were **wai**ting. How **ma**ny?
Some people / were **wai**ting. / Others / had **left**.

(d) Are the demonstrative word *that* and the conjunction or relative pronoun *that* homophones?

Do you need that **file**?
Did you say that you **need** it?
Is this the file that you **need**?

13.3 More about phonological processes

In describing the variant forms of function words it was convenient to refer to *full forms* and *reduced forms* and to describe the reduced forms as derived from the full forms through the application of certain rules, which are called phonological processes. The words which undergo these processes do not lose their meanings nor change their meanings; all that changes is the pronunciation of the forms. It is important to recognize that the changes are not random or irregular. Particular vowels and consonants undergo particular changes in certain environments. That is why the changes can be stated as rules.

The same kinds of processes – in fact, the same processes – apply to other language forms in different styles of speech, especially the more rapid tempos and the more informal styles. We give some illustrations of all the processes already introduced: Vowel Reduction, Vowel Loss, Consonant Loss, Assimilation.

Vowel reduction happens frequently to checked vowels in unstressed syllables, especially, it seems, if followed by a single consonant in that syllable. The verb in each of the following sentences has a lax vowel followed by a single consonant. Each verb is unstressed and just before a word with greater stress. Vowel reduction is likely, as shown.

ˈYou sit /sɨt/ ˈover ˈ**here**.
ˈHe'll come /kɨm/ ˈright ˈ**back**.
ˈDon't get /gɨt/ ˈ**an**gry.

Reduction like this does not occur with a verb that has a free vowel or a vowel followed by two consonants.

ˈYou stand ˈover ˈ**here**.
ˈHe'll go ˈright ˈ**back**.
ˈDon't stay ˈ**an**gry.

Vowel reduction, then, is a process which affects checked vowels in weak syllables, without the 'protection' of consonants. However, the word *just*, in spite of the two final consonants, is typically pronounced /jɨst/ in unstressed position:

just now just a minute

A special form of vowel reduction is that in which the high-front vowel /ii/ is changed to the glide /j/. This can happen whenever the unstressed high vowels are immediately followed by another vowel. The word *alien*, in a larger context, may be pronounced in three syllables, /ˈeiliɨn/, or in two syllables, /ˈeiljɨn/. The word *alienate* may similarly be four syllables or just three. Here is a list of common words with possible variation between /ii/ and /j/. Which words have the vowel in your usual pronunciation? Which have the glide? Which vary?

ammonia	champion
anemia	colonial
bacteria	furious
barrier	helium
cafeteria	lenient

There is a similar alternation of high-back /uu/ and the corresponding glide /w/, as in *usual(ly)*, /ˈjuuʒuəl(i)/ or /ˈjuuʒwəl(i)/; similarly with *casual(ly)*, *mutual(ly)* and the like.

Vowel loss is another familiar process of rapid, casual speech. A word-initial unstressed vowel may be deleted, especially after a word-final vowel, as in:

Go (a)way. I (e)xpect so.

A schwa may be deleted in an initial unstressed syllable if the consonants on each side 'fit together'; thus

police → /pliis/
balloon → /bluun/

Especially common is the loss of a vowel in a medial posttonic syllable, as in the following:

especially /ɨˈspɛʃɨli/ → /ɨˈspɛʃli/
family /ˈfæmɨli/ → /ˈfæmli/
history /ˈhɪstəri/ → /ˈhɪstri/
national /ˈnæʃɨnɨl/ → /ˈnæʃnɨl/

13D EXERCISE

The following words all have a medial posttonic syllable. In some of the words the vowel of this posttonic syllable is deleted in casual speech. In the kind of speech you are most familiar with, which words are most likely to have the vowel deleted? (We may not all agree.) Can you suggest what factors are favorable to deletion?

agony aspirin bachelor buffalo camera cantaloupe capital cardinal carefully Catholic chocolate civilized diamond elementary factory ivory liberal mackerel memory monopoly mystery opera operate original salary separate (adj.) separate (verb) temperature

This process of medial vowel loss is a kind of change going on in the English of today. It is not a new phenomenon, however. If we compare *captain* and *chimney*, for instance, with the French words *capitaine* and *cheminée*, from which the English words were derived, we see that loss of the vowel in a medial posttonic syllable is nothing new. Five centuries ago *capitain* and *chiminey* were three-syllable English words; now *captain* and *chimney* have two syllables each. We do not know the exact details of this historical change, but we can be sure about what did *not* happen. It was not the case that at one period everybody said *capitain* and *chiminey* and then suddenly everybody changed to *captain* and *chimney*. When change occurs, there is variation among speakers. Something like the following is a more likely kind of historical scenario:

Stage 1: All speakers of English say *capitain* (and *chiminey*) with three syllables.
Stage 2: Some speakers always say *capitain* while others vary between *capitain* and *captain*.
Stage 3: Some always say *capitain*, some vary between the two pronunciations, and others always say *captain*.

As time goes by, however many stages there may be, the number of those who have the three-syllable pronunciation decreases and the number of those who have a two-syllable pronunciation increases, until finally all speakers know only the form *captain*.

We observe a similar situation today. Some people always say *capital* and *salary*, with three syllables, /ˈkæpitəl, ˈsæləri/; others vary between these pronunciations and the two-syllable /ˈkæptəl, ˈsælri/; and others always have the two-syllable forms. The actual situation is more complex than the hypothetical one traced for *captain* because it involves a large number of words, which may be treated differently by different parts of the English-speaking population.

Consonant loss is likewise a familiar process. Like vowel loss, it is characterized by variation among different speakers and in different situations. We have already dealt (in chapter 7) with the simplification of consonant clusters as in *asks*, *risked*, *sixths*, and the like. Similar simplification, through loss of a consonant, occurs in words and phrases like these:

Ar(c)tic	san(d)wich
frien(d)ly	su(g)gest
Secon(d) Street	the firs(t) day

Since /d/ and /t/ are among the most frequently occurring consonants, it is not surprising that they are frequent in clusters and thus frequently subject to deletion. Here again we find variation among different speakers and in different situations. Consider these sets of phrases, all with a word-final /t/, which may be deleted.

(a) next time, the first day, last December
(b) last May, most people, the best night
(c) next winter, the best one, last week
(d) next afternoon, last October, the best idea
(e) the most, the best, the last

The five groups are meant to represent, roughly, a range of probability for the deletion of the consonant /t/ (which is preceded here by /s/ and perhaps another consonant). The /t/ is most likely to be dropped before a following /d/ or /t/, as in group (a); somewhat less likely before other consonantal segments – group (b); still less likely before the glide /w/ – group (c); rather unlikely before a following vowel – group (d); and quite unlikely in final position – group (e).

Looking at the matter in a slightly different way, we may say – and again with the intention of making only rough descriptions – that the greatest number of people (perhaps all speakers of English) delete /t/ in phrases like those of group (a), and the smallest number consistently delete the consonant in contexts such as those of group (e). Yet it is worth noting that some people – those most likely to be considered socially deprived – have no /t/ in any of the five contexts illustrated.

The last phonological process to be considered is assimilation, the change in which one consonant is replaced by another segment which is more similar to some neighboring segment. We are already familiar with some examples of assimilation. The regular plural suffix appears as /z/ in *beds* but as /s/ in *bets*. The regular past tense suffix is /d/ in *lived* but /t/ in *sniffed*. These are examples of assimilation in voicing; after a voiceless consonant /z/ is replaced by /s/ and /d/ becomes /t/. In these cases it is the second consonant which takes on the feature, [+ voice] or [− voice], of the preceding consonant. The technical term for this is PROGRESSIVE ASSIMILATION.

The opposite is REGRESSIVE ASSIMILATION, in which one segment becomes more like the following segment. We have already seen examples of this in the forms *have to*, /hæftu/, and *has to*, /hæstu/. Here /v/ and /z/ change to the corresponding voiceless consonants before the following /t/.

Assimilation may be a change in the articulator and/or place of articulation. In phrases like *can pay*, *can buy* the tongue-tip /n/ is likely to be replaced by a labial /m/. Similarly, before dorsal consonants /k/ and /g/, as in *can come*, *can go*, the consonant /n/ may change to /ŋ/. This assimilatory change of /n/ to /m/ or /ŋ/ occurs whether *can* is stressed or not, though to be sure it is more likely when the word is unstressed. Similar changes may occur with the /n/ of *in* and *on* and perhaps other words: *in back*, *in part* with /m/, *in cash*, *on guard* with /ŋ/. Note that final /m/ and /ŋ/ do not become assimilated to a following consonant as final /n/ does.

Another assimilation in articulator and place of articulation is seen in the following:

is she	does she	was she	has she
/ʒʃ/	/ʒʃ/	/ʒʃ/	/ʒʃ/

The apical fricative /z/ is replaced by the frontal /ʒ/ before another frontal consonant /ʃ/. We see a similar assimilation in compounds *horseshoe* and *spaceship*, which are more likely to be /ˈhɔrʃʃuu/, ˈspeiʃʃɪp/ than /ˈhɔrs ʃuu, ˈspeis ʃɪp/. In this case there is complete assimilation – /s/ becomes identical with the following consonant – whereas in all the previous examples the assimilation is only partial; one segment takes on some feature or features of the neighboring segment – voicedness, labial articulation, etc. – but does not acquire all its features.

A special form of assimilation goes by the name of PALATALIZATION. When a tongue-tip consonant, /t d s z/ occurs at the end of a word and the next word has an initial /j/, the tongue-tip consonants may change to the corresponding tongue-front consonants, becoming, respectively, /č ǰ ʃ ʒ/. Often the /j/ is deleted when the change occurs.

won't you	/wount juu/	or	/wounčuu/
did you	/dɪd juu/	or	/dɪǰuu/
unless you . . .	/ʌnlɛs juu/	or	/ʌnlɛʃuu/
as you . . .	/æz juu/	or	/æʒuu/

Palatalization is an optional process across word-boundaries, as in the above examples. It may or may not occur. Furthermore, it does not occur, even optionally, with every word-final /t d s z/ followed by a word-initial /j/. Palatalization is usual in frequent word-groups like these:

not yet	/. . . č . . ./
next year	/. . . č . . ./
would you	/. . . ǰ . . ./

this year	/...ʃ.../
as yet	/...ʒ.../

However, it is not usual – or at least less usual – in *that year*, *wide yard*, *this yacht*, or (he) *loves yoga*. This phonological process seems to be limited to frequently used word combinations.

13E EXERCISE

Casual speech forms often show the effects of several phonological processes. The forms below are transcribed two ways, one to indicate the most careful pronunciation and one to suggest the most casual; there may exist one or more in-between pronunciations. Examine each casual form and say what process(es) account for the difference from the precise form.

pumpkin	/ˈpʌmpkin/	/ˈpʌŋkin/
probably	/ˈprɒbəbli/	/ˈprɒbli/
supposed to	/səˈpouzd tuu/	/ˈspoustə/
don't know	/dount ˈnou/	/doˈnou/

13.4 Summary

Some of the variation that exists in language is due to differences in the situations and purposes of its use and to the fact that commonly used words are likely to be pronounced differently depending on their positions within utterances. The most commonly used words in English are the so-called function words. About 40 of these, all of them monosyllabic and most of them lax-voweled, show variations that may be regarded as the result of phonological processes, changes which operate on the full forms of these words to produce reduced forms. The processes include **vowel reduction**, **vowel loss**, **consonant loss**, and **assimilation**.

The same processes, especially vowel reduction and consonant assimilation, apply sporadically to other language forms. In assimilation one phoneme is replaced by another phoneme which shares certain features of a neighboring phoneme; the most common kinds of assimilation are in voice and in place of articulation. Assimilation is said to be **progressive** when one phoneme is replaced by another under the influence of a preceding phoneme; assimilation is **regressive** when the influencing phoneme follows. Assimilation may be mutual: two phonemes in sequence are replaced by a single phoneme which has some features of each phoneme replaced. The most obvious example of mutual assimilation in English is **palatalization**, in which one of the tongue-tip obstruents /t d s z/ at the end of a word 'merges' with initial /j/ of the next word, resulting in a tongue-front obstruent /č ǰ ʃ ʒ/, respectively.

Phonological processes which occur in speech are **optional**.

13A FEEDBACK

The reduced form is likely to be /juu/ before a vowel and /jə/ before a consonant.

13B FEEDBACK

(a) the /tuu/ is more likely before a word which starts with a vowel, /tə/ before a word which begins with a consonant.
(b) The /v/ is more likely to be kept before a word beginning with a vowel and lost before one which begins with a consonant.
(c) OF and HAVE can have the same reduced forms, /ə/ or /əv/, and as a consequence the two words are easily confused in writing, just as other homonyms are easily confused.

13C FEEDBACK

(a) The auxiliary *have* may be reduced (contracted): *They've bought a new car*.

The 'catenative' verb *have*, the verb that occurs before *to*, becomes partly assimilated to the /t/ of *to*. Auxiliary *have* and transitive *have* do not become assimilated. Therefore:

I ˈhave ˈ**two**. = /ai ˈhæv ˈ**tuu**/ I ˈ**have** ˈto. = /ai ˈ**hæf**ˈtuu/
She ˈhas ˈ**two**. = /ʃii ˈhæz ˈ**tuu**/ She ˈ**has** ˈto. = /ˈʃii ˈ**hæs**ˈtuu/

(b) The number *one* and the noun phrase substitute *one* are always stressed, whether accented or not. They are pronounced /wʌn/ or /wɒn/ depending on dialect.

I ˈhave ˈ/wʌn/ ˈ**ticket**/ – ˈjust ˈ/**wʌn**/. (/wɒn/)
I ˈwanted to ˈbuy a ˈ**pa**per / and I ˈ**bought** ˈ/wʌn/. (/wɒn/)

The noun substitute *one*(*s*) is unstressed, /wən(z)/, if it comes right after the accented word.

The com'mittee i'nitiated a '**new** /wən/.
The com'mittee con'sidered some /səm/ '**new** /wənz/.

However, if the accented word follows, *one(s)* is stressed and pronounced /wʌn/, /wʌnz/.

'Did you 'see the 'film at the '**Ti**voli / or the '/wʌn/ at the '**Ro**ma?
'These re'ports aren't '**rea**dy. / The '/wʌnz/ on the '**desk** 'are.

(c) Just as *a* or *an* is used before a singular countable noun (*a pear*, *an apple*), the unstressed *some*, /səm/, occurs before plural countable nouns (*some pears*, *some apples*) and singular uncountable nouns (*some glue*, *some soup*) with the same general meaning, 'indefiniteness'. With stress, *some*, /sʌm/, still has the meaning of indefiniteness but the stress brings it into contrast with *all* and with *no* or *none*. The sentence '*Some 'people were '**wai**ting* says, in effect, 'It is not true that all people were waiting, and it is not true that no people were waiting.'

When *some* is used as an anaphoric pronoun, a substitute for an indefinite noun phrase, plural or accountable, it is stressed.

'Would you 'like some '**Thanks,** /I '**have** 'some.
'These 'men are 'looking for '**jobs.**
'**Some** of them / have been 'out of 'work for '**months**.

(d) Demonstrative *that* is stressed, /ðæt/, as are *this*, *these*, and *those*. The conjunction and relative pronoun *that* is unstressed, /ðət/, and it may be deleted.

Do you 'need 'that /ðæt/ '**file**?
Is 'this the 'file (that /ðət/) you '**need**?
Did you 'say (that /ðət/) you '**need** it?

13D FEEDBACK

There seem to be three factors involved. First, the vowel is more likely to be deleted in words which form a common part of one's vocabulary than in words which are rather rare. Since some words may be common for some speakers but not so common for other speakers, there are differences in the scope of deletion. Probably *aspirin*, *chocolate*, and *memory* are common in the usage of all adults, whereas *agony*, *ivory*, and *mackerel* may not be frequently used words. Consequently, the first three are more likely to be pronounced as two-syllable words than the last three.

Second, the following syllable must be a weak syllable. The words *cantaloupe* and *civilized* have free vowels in the ult and therefore do not show deletion of the medial vowel. Similarly, there is no vowel loss in *operate* though there is in *opera*; the verb *separate* does not show vowel deletion, but the adjective *separate* does.

Third, an unstressed vowel is more likely to be dropped if the consonants on each side 'fit' well together. Notice that in most cases of vowel loss the following consonant is /l/ or /r/.

13E FEEDBACK

Pumpkin: /ˈpʌmpkin/ to /ˈpʌŋkin/ shows deletion of /p/ between two consonants and assimilation in which /m/ becomes /ŋ/ before /k/.

Probably: /ˈprɒbəbli/ to /ˈprɒbli/ shows deletion of a medial posttonic vowel and loss of /b/ – or reduction of /bb/ to /b/.

Supposed to: /səˈpouzd tuu/ to /ˈspoustə/ shows vowel loss in the initial syllable; loss of /d/ before /t/; voice assimilation in which /z/ becomes /s/ before /t/; and of course the vowel reduction of /tuu/ to /tə/.

Don't know: /dount ˈnou/ to /doˈnou/ illustrates loss of /t/ and reduction of /nn/ to /n/.

14

Phonological Processes and the Lexicon

14.1 Words and morphemes that change

Chapter 8 dealt with processes that affect some morphemes because of phonotactic conditions: the insertion of a vowel within a morpheme-final cluster like that of //dɪzæstr//, the deletion of a consonant from a morpheme-final cluster like that of //dæmn//, and the voice assimilation in suffixed items like //kæt#z// and //lʊk#d//. These can be called phonotactic processes.

In chapter 13 we described phonological processes which operate in the speech that all of us produce day by day. The phonological processes explain some of the variations that exist in different ways of speaking, how full forms like *have* /hæv/ and *for* /fɔr/ are reduced to /v/ and /fər/. For brevity we call these speech processes.

There are other morpheme alternations which cannot be attributed to phonotactic conditions nor to style of speaking; for instance:

noun *thief* /θiif/, plural *thieve#s* /θiivz/; verb *thieve* /θiiv/; noun *thef+t* /θɛft/
adjective *wide* /waid/, noun *wid+th* /wɪdθ/ (or /wɪtθ/)
noun *atom* /ˈætəm/, adjective *atom+ic* /əˈtɒmik/
noun *circle* /ˈsɜrkəl/, adjective *circul+ar* /ˈsɜrkjulər/

As these examples show, there may be an alternation of vowels or consonants, or of stress, or the insertion (or deletion) of a vowel or consonant. More than one of these may occur in a morpheme. In fact, alternation of stress, as in *atom*, *atomic*, almost always involves vowel alternation as well.

Variations like these are due, not to phonological processes of the present time, but to processes that operated in the past (though two of the processes are similar to processes operating today). Such variant forms are the topic of this chapter.

There are two kinds of alternation, PHONOLOGICALLY CONDITIONED ALTERNATIONS and MORPHOLOGICALLY CONDI-

TIONED ALTERNATIONS. An alternation is phonologically conditioned if a given phoneme (or sequence of phonemes) alternates with another phoneme (or sequence) under phonological conditions – the alternation depends on the kind of consonant or vowel which precedes or follows, or on occurrence in a stressed syllable or an unstressed one. Phonotactic processes and speech processes are phonologically conditioned, and so are some lexical processes. An alternation is morphologically conditioned if a given phoneme (or sequence) alternates with another phoneme (or sequence) under morphological conditions – the alternation depends on a specific suffix or group of suffixes which follow. In some cases the 'suffix' is really an abstract element which makes a grammatical change: it converts a singular noun to a plural, or a present tense verb to the past tense, or a noun to a verb, and the alternation is the only evidence for the abstract 'suffix'. These statements will become clear if we examine some data.

give – gif+t twelve – twelf+th

In these two pairs the alternation of /v/ and /f/ is phonologically conditioned. The /v/ is basic and it changes to its voiceless counterpart /f/ before voiceless consonants /t/ and /θ/.

mischief – mischiev+ous belief – believe
wife – wife+'s – wive+s

Here we see an alternation of the same two consonants, /f/ and /v/, but under quite different conditions. The /f/ of *mischief* is basic; it is replaced by /v/ before the suffix *+ous*, but there is no phonological reason for the change. With the next pair, *belief* and *believe*, there is no obvious reason for saying that the noun is derived from the verb or the verb from the noun. Because of other such pairs to be examined later we prefer to derive the verb from the noun; we say that *belief*, occurring in the environment ___ + {Verb}, results in, or becomes, *believe*. With regard to the last set we say that *wife* occurs as an independent word, of course, and also in the environment ___ + (Possessive) and the environment ___ + (Plural). The morphemes (Possessive) and (Plural) have the same allomorphs /s, z, iz/ (chapter 8), so the alternation of *wife* before the plural suffix cannot be a phonological matter. The plural and the possessive singular of *wife* would be identical if *wife* were a regular noun, but it is not. The morpheme *wife* has the alternant *wive-* before (Plural) and *wife* before (Possessive). The choice of /z/ for (Plural) and of /s/ for (Possessive) is phonologically regular; it is the choice of *wife* or *wive-* that has no phonological basis. The lexical processes that we will examine in this chapter are partly a matter of phonological conditioning but more largely of morphological conditioning.

English has numerous sets of related words which show interchanges of vowels, alternations that reflect sound changes that occurred in the history (and pre-history) of the language. The set of vowels in *sing-sang-sung*, for instance, has come down from Proto-Indo-European, the distant ancestor of English spoken perhaps in the third millennium BC, perhaps in the area between the Black and the Caspian Seas. The vowel sets seen in *food* and *feed*, *goose* and *geese*, *man* and *men*, and other pairs reflect a number of phonetic changes that began in Proto-Germanic, a closer ancestor of Modern English, probably spoken in what is now Germany, Holland, and Denmark in the first centuries of the Christian era. The vowel sets which we are going to examine later in this chapter reflect relationships that existed, and changes that occurred, in Middle English, centering around the fourteen and fifteenth centuries.

14.2 Underlying forms and lexical processes

When we describe speech processes, it seems obvious that we should begin with the isolated, careful pronunciations as the forms to which the processes apply and derive the casual, contextual pronunciations as the result of these processes. We derive the /v/ of *I've* from the full form /hæv/, *have*. The rules of derivation seem 'natural' with respect to present-day English: in this case, loss of a weak consonant and loss of a vowel (following vowel reduction). Similarly, we have recognized the naturalness of phonotactic processes, such as the insertion of a vowel between sibilants in *horses*, for instance, and the loss of /n/ in *damn*. We consider //hɔrs#z// and //dæmn// the basic, or underlying, forms from which the pronunciations, the surface forms, are derived.

When we turn to lexical processes, however, it is not so obvious which is the base form and which is the derived form or forms. Among the three allomorphs /θiif θiiv θɛf/, for instance, which one is the source from which the other two are derived? And what are the rules for derivation? The basic form should be the one from which the others can be derived by rules that seem natural. A little thought will convince us that, in this case, there are no rules which are wholly natural. To be sure, it is natural that /f/, and not /v/, occurs before a voiceless consonant (*theft*) but when we see that both /f/ and /v/ occur in word-finally (*thief*, *thieve*), there is no reason for calling one of these basic and the other derived. Similarly, although we should expect a checked vowel like /ɛ/ rather than a free vowel like /ii/ before a consonant cluster, as in *theft*, there is nothing in the pronunciation which explains why it is these particular vowels that alternate – even though the alternation of these two vowels is fairly frequent in the vocabulary.

In short, the alternations cannot be wholly explained within the framework of present-day English phonology, and there is no basis for choosing one allomorph as basic, or underlying. The underlying form is necessarily something abstract. We can represent the morpheme this way: //, {f,v}//. The symbols in curly brackets, { }, indicate a choice that must be r and the rules which apply to the underlying form tell us which choice to m in what circumstances. In this case there is choice between a free vowel an checked vowel and between a voiceless consonant and a voiced one. We w see other instances of alternations with the {ii, ɛ} pair and alternations with the {f,v} pair and, more important, other free vowel/checked vowel pairs and other voiceless consonant/voiced consonant pairs. Recognizing *kinds* of alternation, or choice, allows us to make the rules for derivation as general as possible.

By the same token, we want to give general names to rules. The choice {ii, ɛ} is one pair affected by a rule called VOWEL SHIFT; the choice {f,v} is one pair affected by a rule called VOICING. Instead of the very specific notation //θ{ii, ɛ} {f,v}// we can represent the same morpheme this way:

//θiif// [V. shift] [voicing].

These are equivalent notations, so long as one knows what the terms mean, of course. When we introduce alternations and rules, we will want a more specific listing. As we move on, we will prefer a more general sort of notation. The morpheme which occurs in *wide*, *wid-th* can be represented specifically as //w{ai,ɪ}d// and more generally as //waid// [V. shift].

14.3 Checked vowel reduction

We have observed sets of words like the following in which stress occurs on different syllables of related words:

ˈatom aˈtomic ˈcontinent contiˈnental ˈgenerous geneˈrosity
ˈmelody meˈlodic ˈorigin oˈriginal origiˈnality
ˈtempest temˈpestuous

We can also observe a common alternation: a checked vowel in an open stressed syllable is 'reduced' to /ə/ in an unstressed syllable, such as the first syllable of *atomic*, the second syllable of *melody*; the same reduction occurs when the vowel is followed by a single consonant or *-nt* or *-st* in word-final position, as in *atom*, *continent*, *original*, *tempest*. The reduced vowel may be schwa or barred ɪ, depending on context and dialect. As before, we use schwa as a cover symbol. We show these alternations as derivations:

	//#ætɒm#	#ætɒm+ɪk#//
s	ˈ	ˈ
reduction	ə	ə ɨ
urface	/ˈætəm	əˈtɒmɨk/
	//#kɒntɪnɛnt#	#kɒntɪnɛnt+æl#//
Stress	ˈ	ˈ
V. reduction	ɨ ə	ɨ ə
Surface	/kɒntɨnənt	kɒntɨˈnɛntəl/
	//#ǰɛnər+ɒs#	#jɛnər+ɒs+ɪti#//
Stress	ˈ	ˈ
V. reduction	ə	ɨ
Surface	/ˈǰɛnərəs	ǰɛnəˈrɒsɨti/
	//#mɛlɒd+i#	#mɛlɒd+ɪk#//
Stress	ˈ	ˈ
V. reduction	ə	ə ɨ
Surface	/ˈmɛlədi	məˈlɒdɨk/
	/#ɔrɪǰɪn#	#ɔrɪjɪn+æl# #ɔrɪǰɪn+æl+ɪti#//
Stress	ˈ	ˈ ˈ
V. reduction	ɨ ɨ	ə ɨ ə ə ɨ ɨ
Surface	/ˈɔrɨǰɨn	əˈrɪǰɨnəl ərɪjīˈnælɨti/
	//#tɛmpɛst#	#tɛmpɛst+ju+ɒs#//
Stress	ˈ	ˈ
V. reduction	ə	ə
Surface	/ˈtɛmpəst	tɛmˈpɛsčuəs/

The appearance of /č/ in the surface form of *tempestuous* is the result of Palatalization, a process which is examined below.

14.4 Palatalization

In chapter 13 we considered a phonological process which might apply to certain speech forms or might not, producing these variants:

won't you	/ˈwountjuu/	or	/ˈwounčuu/
did you	/ˈdɪdjuu/	or	/ˈdɪǰuu/

miss you	/ˈmisjuu/	or	/ˈmɪʃuu/
as you	/æzjuu/	or	/æʒuu/

The process of PALATALIZATION replaces a tongue-tip obstruent, //t d s z// plus //j// with the corresponding tongue-front consonant, /č ǰ ʃ ʒ/ (which are called palatal consonants by some linguists). Palatalization is optional as a speech process; that is why we can say /wountjuu/ or /wounčuu/. As a vocabulary process it is obligatory, not optional. Notice these pairs of words:

architect	architecture	proceed	procedure
/t/	/č/	/d/	/ǰ/
press	pressure	compose	composure
/s/	/ʃ/	/z/	/ʒ/

The suffix added is the same one which is added to *fail* to make *failure* (/feil, feiljər/), but here the /j/ of the suffix produces a change in the final consonant of the base word. The four apical consonants are replaced by the corresponding laminal consonants before /j/ and a vowel. We see the same change for /s/ and /z/ when /i/ plus a vowel follows:

face - facial confuse - confusion

The palatalization rule is:

$$\begin{bmatrix} t \\ d \\ s \\ z \end{bmatrix} \rightarrow \begin{bmatrix} č \\ ǰ \\ ʃ \\ ʒ \end{bmatrix} / ___ \begin{Bmatrix} j \\ i \end{Bmatrix} [+\text{syl}]$$

(Two pairs of square brackets in a rule, with an equal number of items in each pair of brackets, is an abbreviation for that number of changes; here the rule says that *t* becomes *č*, *d* becomes *ǰ*, and so on.) After palatalization takes place, the /j/ or /i/ which caused the palatalization is deleted if the following vowel is unstressed. We shall call this the I-drop rule or the J-drop rule.

$$\begin{Bmatrix} i \\ j \end{Bmatrix} \rightarrow 0 / \begin{Bmatrix} \text{Palatal} \\ \text{consonant} \end{Bmatrix} ___ \begin{Bmatrix} \text{Unstressed} \\ \text{vowel} \end{Bmatrix}$$

Here are two of the derivations:

	//#arkɪtɛkt#	#arkɪtɛkt+jur#//
Stress	ˈ	ˈ
Palatalization	—	č
J-drop		0
Vowel reduction	ɨ	ɨ ə
Surface	/ˈarkɨtɛkt	ˈarkɨtɛkčər/

	//#feis#	#feis+i+æl#//
Stress	ˈ	ˈ
Palatalization	—	
I-drop		0
Vowel reduction		ə
Surface	/feis	ˈfeiʃəl/

14A EXERCISES

(a) Each of the words below ends with /t/ or has /t/ before a suffix. By adding a suffix or changing the suffix you can form a related word which has /č/ instead of /t/.

depart legislator moist sculptor spirit

(b) For each of these words which contains /d/ you can find a related word which has /ǰ/ instead.

fraud grade grand proceed residue

(c) For each of these words with /s/ give a related word with /ʃ/.

admissible coerce grace fallacy ferocity sacrifice

(d) For each of these words with /z/ find a related word with /ʒ/.

compose disclose expose infuse pleasant revise

(e) We need to look more closely at the I-drop rule. Each word below has /ʃ/, resulting from the palatalization of //s// before /i/ and another vowel. In the words on the left the /i/ which caused palatalization has been deleted. In the words on the right the /i/ has not been deleted. Why is this? (Notice that the words may be spelled with *c* or with *t*, but the spelling has nothing to do with it.)

official	officiate
judicial	judiciary
partial	partiality
confidential	confidentiality

14.5 Alternation with zero

14.5a

Consider this group of base words, which end the same way:

angle circle fable miracle table vehicle

At least one of the following suffixes can be added to each of the base words: +*ar*, +*ate*, +*ous*. Then we have, in orthographic form, *angular*, *circular*, *circulate*, *fabulous*, etc. The phonemic forms of the first pair are /ˈæŋgəl/ and /ˈæŋgjulər/. The /ə/ of *angle* – and *circle*, *fable*, etc – is the same as that of *fiddle*, *juggle*, etc. It is inserted by a phonotactic rule. But the /ju/ of *angular*, *circulate*, etc. is different. It is part of the underlying form, alternating with zero. We can represent the underlying form of *angle*, *angul-* this way: //æŋg{ju,0}l// or this way: //æŋg(ju)l//. Since the latter is slightly simpler, we shall use this form from now on. Material in parentheses alternates with zero; the material is present in one allomorph and absent in another. The words listed above have these underlying forms:

//sɛrk(ju)l, f{ei,æ}b(ju)l, miræk(ju)l, t{ei,æ}b(ju)l, viihɪk(ju)l//

The rule which applies is:

Choose /ju/ when a non-neutral suffix follows; otherwise choose zero.

And here is a sample pair of derivations:

Underlying	//#sɜrk(ju)l#	#sɜrk(ju)l+ær#//
Stress	ˈ	ˈ
ju-rule	0	
V. reduction		ə
Surface	/ˈsɜrkəl	ˈsɜrkjulər/

14.5b

The adjectives *long*, *strong*, *young* end with /ŋ/. The corresponding comparative forms, *longer*, *stronger*, *younger*, and superlative forms, *longest*, *strongest*, *youngest*, have /g/ before the suffixes, /ər/ and /ɨst/. The underlying forms for the adjectives, then, are //#lɒng# #strɒng# #jʌng#// and there are two rules:

an assimilation rule $n \rightarrow ŋ / ____ g$
a deletion rule $g \rightarrow 0 / ŋ ____ \#$

Sample derivations would look like these:

Underlying	//#lɒng#	#lɒng+er#//
Stress	ˈ	ˈ
N assimilation	ŋ	ŋ
G deletion	0	—
Surface	/lɒŋ	/lɒŋgər/

Generative phonologists consider that there is no underlying phoneme //ŋ//. There is a surface phoneme /ŋ/, of course, but as we have seen (chapter 7), it is restricted in its occurrence. It never occurs initially, and it is rare in intervocalic position. Its principal occurrences are in final position and before /k/ and /g/. Furthermore, there is no such final cluster as /ŋg/ – at least, not in the speech of most people. Thus, from the viewpoint of most generative phonologists, the underlying forms of such words as *sing*, *sink*, *anger*, and *anchor* contain //n// (or just a feature [+ nasal]). It is predictable that a nasal consonant in these positions must be /ŋ/, and that no /g/ will be pronounced in final position after a nasal consonant. What is predictable is stated as a rule. The underlying form gives the information about a linguistic form which is not predictable.

From this point of view the assimilation rule should be much more general:

$$[+\text{ nasal}] \rightarrow \begin{cases} m / ____ & \text{labial C} \\ n / ____ & \text{apical C} \\ ŋ / ____ & \text{dorsal C} \end{cases}$$

14.5c

Consider the words *normal*, *senatorial*, *intellectual*. They contain the base words *norm*, *senator*, and *intellect*, respectively. At first glance it might seem that they contain suffixes *-al*, *-ial*, *-ual*, respectively. But are there actually three different suffixes? In each case the suffix has the same function, m an adjective from a noun. In this respect they are alike. Is there a free choi adding *-al*, *-ial*, or *-ual* to a particular base? Obviously not. No one c choose to say **normial* or **normual*. Nor is the choice of *-al*, *-ial*, or *-ua* dependent on some phonological feature of the base word. Thus the presence of *i* or *u* or neither of them is part of the underlying form of the base word. The underlying forms are:

//nɔrm// //sɛnətɔr(i)// //ɪntəlɛkt(ju)//

We call the //i// of //sɛnətɔr(i)// and the //ju// of //ɪntəlɛkt(ju)// AUGMENTS. //sɛnətɔri// and //ɪntəlɛktju// are the AUGMENTED FORMS of //sɛnətɔr// and //ɪntəlɛkt//, respectively. //nɔrm// has no augmented form. If there is an augment, it is deleted when no suffix follows.

augment → 0 / ____ #

14B EXERCISE

All the words below occur with such suffixes as *-al*, *-ous*, *-ic* (//+æl//, //+ɒs//, //+ɪk//, respectively) but always in an augmented form. Give the augment for each word, using ordinary spelling – *i* for *senator*(*i*), *u* for *intellect*(*u*), for example.

act	aroma	contempt
habit	symptom	commerce
sense	sympath + y	event
sex	apolog + y	attitude
tempest	part	longitude
finance	manager	spasm
race	professor	drama
dogma	dictator	opera

14.6 Spirantization

Certain morphemes have an alternation of /t/ and /s/ or, as we shall put it, an underlying //{t,s}//; a rule that is called Spirantization tells when to choose each of these alternants. More simply, it tells when to choose one of these, and the other occurs under other conditions.

ıder these pairs of words:

ntimate intimacy analytic analysis part partial

Let us say that the underlying forms are these:

//#intima{t,s}# #intima{t,s}+i#//
//#anali{t,s}+ik #anali{t,s}+is#//
//#par{t,s}(i)# #par{t,s}(i)+al#//

A tentative statement of the spirantization rule, which we will want to modify later, is this:

In the choice {t,s} choose /s/ before the noun suffixes +i# and +is# and before the augment (i) followed by a vowel; elsewhere choose /t/.

This can also be expressed as a formula:

$$\{t,s\} \rightarrow \begin{cases} (1) & /s/ \ / \ \underline{\quad} \begin{cases} +i\# & (a) \\ +is & (b) \\ +i+[+syl] & (c) \end{cases} \\ (2) & /t/ \end{cases}$$

For *partial* the palatalization rule applies after the spirantization rule and is responsible for the /ʃ/ in that word.

Underlying	//#ɪntɪmə{t,s}+i#//	//#ænælɪ{t,s}ɪs//
Stress	ˈ	ˈ
Spirantization	s	s
V. reduction		ə ɨ ɨ
Surface	/ˈɪntɨməsi	əˈnælɨsɨs/

Underlying	//#par{t,s}(i)+æl//
Stress	ˈ
Spirantization	s
Palatalization	ʃ
V. reduction	ə
Surface	/ˈparʃəl/

Rather than the notation {t,s} we can indicate morphemes affected by spirantization this way:

//ɪntɪmət//[Spir.] //ænælɪt//[Spir.] //part(i)//[Spir.]

14C EXERCISES

(a) Each of the following words has one of the suffixes mentioned in the spirantization rule, with an /s/ immediately preceding. For each word you should be able to think of a related word which has no suffix or a different suffix and has /t/ rather than /s/. For example, the first word below, *confederacy*, should remind you of *confederate*.

confederacy	complacency	ecstasy	catharsis
delicacy	frequency	geodesy	diuresis
democracy	hesitancy	galaxy	hypnosis
diplomacy	infancy	heresy	narcosis
hypocrisy	presidency	idiocy	neurosis
literacy	vacancy	lunacy	synopsis
piracy			synthesis
prophecy			
secrecy			

(b) If we have /t/ before +*ic* in *analytic*, *ecstatic* and the like, how do we account for the fact that *basic* has /s/?

14.7 Velar softening

The words *medical* and *medicine* show an alternation of /k/ and /s/. The words *analogous* and *analogy* show an alternation of /g/ and /ǰ/. Further investigation shows us that these alternations are frequent in words of Latin and Greek origin. In fact, our orthography uses the letter *c* for both /k/ and /s/ and the letter *g* for both /g/ and /ǰ/. The underlying forms of these and similar morphemes contain an alternating pair {k,s} and {g,ǰ}
//#mɛdɪ{k,s}+æl#, #mɛdɪ{k,s}+in#; #ænælɒ{g,ǰ}+vs#, #ænælɒ{g,ǰ}+i#//

The choice to be made in {k,s} and {g,j} is slightly more complex than the choice for {t,s}. The rule will be given after you do the next exercise.

14D EXERCISES

(a) The following words all contain /k/ at or near the end. For each word think of a related word which has /s/ instead.

critical electric italic(s) reciprocal romantic

(b) The following words contain /g/ at or near the end. For each word think of a related word which has /ǰ/.

demagog fragment legal pedagog regal rigor

(c) Do the words *signi-fic-ant* and *magni-fic-ent* have the same suffix?

Rule: From the underlying pair {k,s} choose /k/ and from the pair {g,j} choose /g/ before # and before the adjective suffix +*ous* //ɒs//, the abstract noun suffix +*or* //ɔr//, and the suffix +*ant* //ænt//; choose /s/ and /ǰ/ before this group of suffixes: +*y*, +*ize*, +*ism*, +*ist*, +*ity*, +*ine*, +*ic*, +*id*, +*ent*, +*ile*, and the augment +*i*+.

Examples of all of these follow:

/k/ or /g/ — electric# pedagog# clinic+al reg+al analog+ous rig+or
/s/ or /ǰ/ — pedagog+y critic+ize romantic+ism apolog+ist
electric+ity medic+ine rig+id reg+ent frag+ile
music+i+an litig+i+ous Patric+i+a

The simpler notations are, for example:

//mɛdɪk// [Vel. soft.] //ænælɒg// [Vel. soft.]

and here are sample derivations:

	//#mɛdɪk+æl#	#mɛdɪk+ɪn#	#ænælɒg+ɒs#	#ænælɒg+i#//
Stress	ˈ	ˈ	ˈ	ˈ
Velar soft.	—	s	—	ǰ
V. reduction	ɨ ə	ɨ ɨ	ə ə ə	ə ə
Surface	/ˈmɛdɨkəl	ˈmɛdɨsɨn	əˈnæləgəs	əˈnæləǰi/

14.8 The sequence of rules

The word *commerce* ends with /s/. The word *commercial* contains /ʃ/, formed by palatalization of //s// before (i) and a vowel: //kɒmɜrs(i)æl//. The following words are like *commercial*. Each one is formed with an ending *iVC*, *i* followed by a vowel, followed by a consonant, added to a word that ends with /s/.

confession gracious malicious palatial spacious

Here is a pair of sample derivations:

	//#mælɪs#//	//#mælɪs(i)ɑs#//
Stress	ˈ	ˈ
Palatalization	—	ʃ
I-drop		0
V. reduction	ˌ ɨ	ə ə
	/ˈmælɨs	məˈlɪʃəs/

14E EXERCISES

(a) The next group of words also contains /ʃ/, and each word has an ending *iVC* added to a base word. However, in each of these cases the base word ends with /t/, not /s/.

action	assertion	exemption	inertia	partial	vibration
act	assert	exempt	inert	part	vibrate

Each of these base morphemes has the choice pair {t,s} and there is an augment (ɪ). What seems to be a change from /t/ to /ʃ/ is the result of two rules. What are they?

(b) The next words also contain /ʃ/, and each word also has an ending of the form *iVC* added to a simpler base word. What is the final consonant of the base word? What rules account for the change of this consonant to /ʃ/?

electrician	logician	mathematician	magician	musician
electric	logic	mathematic	magic	music

The spirantization rule, as it was presented in section 14.6, was called a tentative statement. The rule indicated that underlying //t// becomes /s/ before the suffix //+i// as in *intimacy*, //+ɪs// as in *hypnosis*, and before the sequence //i V// as in *partial*. In words like *partial* and *direction* (compared with *part* and *direct*) we see the result of both spirantization and palatalization, namely /ʃ/. But *digestion* and *exhaustion* have /č/, not /ʃ/, and so do *bestial*, *Christian* and other words in which underlying //t// is preceded by //s//. Compare these derivations for *direct*, *direction*, *digest*, and *digestion*.

	//#dɪrɛkt#	#dɪrɛkt+ion#	#dɪǰɛst#	#dɪǰɛst+ion#//
Stress	ˈ	ˈ	ˈ	ˈ
Spirantiz.	—	s	—	—
Palataliz.		ʃ		č
I-drop		0		0
V. reduction	ɨ	ɨ ɨ	ɨ	ɨ ɨ
Surface	/dɨˈrɛkt	dɨˈrɛkʃɨn	dɨˈǰɛst	dɨˈǰɛsčɨn/

The //t// of *direction* changes to /s/ (spirantization), and this /s/ changes to /ʃ/ (palatalization). The //t// of *digestion* does not undergo spirantization because it is preceded by //s//, so that palatalization affects the original //t//, changing it to /č/.

14.9 Change in voicing

The voiceless obstruents, especially /f, θ, s/ alternate with the corresponding voiced obstruents under certain conditions. For example, we have noted these alternations which are phonologically conditioned:

give - gif+t twelve - twelf+th

and these alternations which are morphologically conditioned:

mischief - mischiev+ous belief - believe wife - wife'+s - wive+s

The morphological rules for the alternation {f,v} are:

$$\text{choose } v / \left\{ \begin{array}{l} ____ \text{ +ous} \\ ____ \text{ \{Verb\}} \\ ____ \text{ \# (Plural)} \end{array} \right\}$$

The underlying forms must contain the choice {f,v}. Other words like *cuff* and *hive* form their plurals, *cuffs* and *hives*, respectively, in the regular way.

14F EXERCISES

(a) Each word below has either /f/ or /v/ in the surface form. For each word there is another form of the same word or a related word in which /f/ is replaced by /v/ or /v/ is replaced by /f/. Can you think of the word(s)? (There may be other changes, chiefly involving vowels, in some of the words.)

calf	leaf	wharf	proof	five
half	life	knife	relief	sieve
dwarf	loaf	wolf	strife	bereave
elf	scarf	shelf	grief	cleave

(b) Which of these alternations are morphologically conditioned?

(c) All of the following words end with voiceless /θ/. For each one there may be some related word with /ð/. Can you think of it? There are also vowel alternations in some words.

bath	cloth	mouth	south	worth
breath	loath	north	teeth	wreath

(d) There is similar alternation of /s/ and /z/. For example, corresponding to the noun *glass* there is a verb to *glaze*.

(i) What is the verb corresponding to the noun *grass*? What is the verb corresponding to the noun *advice*?

(ii) The written words *use*, *abuse*, *excuse* and *house* are pronounced differently depending on whether they are nouns or verbs. How do they differ?

(iii) Are the noun *grease* and the verb *to grease* pronounced the same, or not? Does *greasy* have /s/ or /z/?

(iv) Is the plural of *house* pronounced /ˈhawsiz/ or /ˈhawziz/?

(v) The following verbs consist of prefix and base. Examine the pronunciation of the bases.

con=serve	re=serve	per=sist	re=sist
con=sume	pre=sume	in=sert	de=sert

There is a rule which determines whether the base is pronounced with initial /s/ or /z/. What is the rule?

(vi) In *example*, *executive*, *exert*, *exist*, *exonerate* the letter *x* represents /gz/. In *sex*, *taxi*, *execute*, *lexicon*, *taxidermy* the same letter stands for /ks/. Again, there is a rule that determines whether /gz/ or /ks/ occurs. What is the rule?

(e) The noun *absorption* is formed from the verb *absorb*. The two words should have the same underlying form, except for the ending -//tion// in the noun. Is the alternation phonologically or morphologically conditioned?

(f) The words *segment*, *section*, and *sector* have the same base with different suffixes. What would you propose as the underlying form of this base?

The words *fragment*, *fraction*, and *fracture* have the same base and different suffixes. What would you propose as the underlying form of the base?

14.10 The vowel shift rule

Prefixes and suffixes have an obvious function in the derivation of complex words from simpler words. *Befriend* and *enrich* have partly the meanings of *friend* and *rich*, respectively; *growth* and *amusement* have the meanings of *grow* and *amuse*, respectively, plus something else. Suffixes are also used for inflection, as in the plural form *horses* and the past tense form *waited*. Derivation and inflection are also accomplished by inner changes, changes in the vowels and consonants of the base words. The words *lose* and *loss* are related to each other in the same way that *grow* and *growth* are related; *full* and *fill* are related in about the same way as *deep* and *deepen* or *rich* and *enrich*. Just as the past tense of *walk* is formed by suffixation (*walked*), the past tense of *run* is made by change of vowel (*ran*). Similarly, vowel change is the mechanism for the formation of plural *mice* and *geese* from singular *mouse* and *goose*, respectively, a function that is more frequently accomplished by suffixation. In the above examples of vowel change, the replacement of one vowel by another performs some kind of function. Sometimes, however, vowel change accompanies suffixation, as in *deep/depth*, *wise/wisdom*, *lose/lost*, or change of suffix, as in *ferocious/ferocity*.

Consider the vowels alternating in these pairs of words:

1 wise, wisdom	4 profound, profundity
2 extreme, extremity	5 goose, gosling
3 volcano, volcanic	6 provoke, provocative

In each pair of words there is an alternation of two stressed vowels, one free and the other checked. The two vowels in each set are quite far apart in Modern English, but our school tradition refers to the two vowels in set 1 as 'long I' and 'short I'; the ones in set 2 as 'long E' and 'short E'; those in set 3 as 'long and short A', respectively; and those of set 6 as, respectively, 'long and short O'. Our school tradition has no name for the pairs illustrated in sets 4 and 5; that is partly due to the fact that these alternations are not as common as the other four.

The vowels of each set are quite far apart in the pronunciation of our day, but in the early fourteenth century they were undoubtedly much closer. In each pair the two vowels were phonetically identical except that one was long (and/or tense) and the other was short (and/or checked). Then all the long vowels changed (the so-called Great Vowel Shift). Some of the short vowels changed a little, and others not at all. The consequence of these changes is that what were originally similar vowels in related words have become far apart, as the six pairs of examples above illustrate.

To explain the relationships that exist in Modern English we use underlying forms which contain a choice pair of vowels, one free and one checked. The underlying forms for the six sets of words above are:

1 //#w{ai, ɪ}z (+dɨm)#//
2 //#ɛkstr{ii, ɛ}m (+iti)#//
3 //#vɒlk{ei, æ}n(o/+ik)#//
4 //#prɒf{au, ʌ}nd (+iti)#//
5 //#g{uu, ɒ}s(+ling)#//
6 //#prɒv{ou, ɒ}k(+æt+iv)#//

To simplify and generalize, we list such morphemes with the free vowel indicated and the following notation, '[V shift]':

//waiz/ [V shift]
//ɛkstriim// [V shift]
//vɒlkein-// [V shift]
//prɒfaund//$_n$V shift]
//guus// [V shift]
//prɒvouk// [V shift]

Thus the morpheme which appears in *wise* and *wisdom* has the underlying form //w{ai, ɪ}z//. In the surface forms the free vowel appears in the unsuffixed word (*wise*) and the checked vowel in the suffixed word (*wisdom*). The other five pairs of words also have a single morpheme with alternating free and checked vowels. In these pairs also the free vowel occurs, generally, in the word without a suffix and the checked vowel in a suffixed word. However, the conditions for choice of the free or the checked vowel are somewhat more complicated than this.

The checked vowel is the one which is chosen when two or more consonants follow (unless the two consonants are *nd*, *ld*, or *st*); when two or more syllables follow in the same word; and when certain suffixes follow – namely, the *-ic* of *volcanic*, the *-id* of *valid*, and the *-ish* of *demolish*. Only the first of these is important here.

We can re-state the preceding paragraph in a formula:

$$\text{Vowel} \rightarrow \text{checked} \quad \underline{\quad / \quad} \begin{cases} C_2 \\ C\,V\,C\,V \ldots \# \\ + \text{ɪk, ɪd, ɪʃ\#} \end{cases}$$

This rule affects the second word in each of the six sets above.

	//#ɛkstriim#	#ɛkstriim+iti#//
Stress	ˈ	ˈ
V. shift	ii	ɛ
V. reduction		ɨ
Surface	/ɛkˈstriim	ɛkˈstrɛmɨti/

	//#vɒlkeino#	#vɒlkein+ɪk#//
Stress	ˈ	ˈ
V. shift	ei	æ
Surface	/vɒlˈkeino	vɒlˈkænɪk/

Here are derivations to illustrate sets 4, 5, and 6:

	//#prɒfaund#	#prɒfaund+ɪti#//
Stress	ˈ	ˈ
V. shift	au	ʌ
V. reduction	ə	ə ɨ
Surface	/prəˈfaund	prəˈfʌndɨti/

	//#guus#	#guus+lɪng#//
Stress		ˈ
V. shift	uu	ɒ
Voice assimilation		z
NG rule		ŋ
Surface	/guus	ˈgɒzlɪŋ/

	//#prɒ=vouk#	#prɒ=vouk(æt)+ɪv#//
Stress	ˈ	ˈ
V. shift	ou	ɒ
V. reduction	ɵ	ɵ ə ɨ
Surface	/prɵˈvouk	prɵˈvɒkətɨv/

(The augment (æt) seen in *provocative* is discussed in section 14.12, More about augments.)

14G EXERCISE

Here are more words with checked vowels in six sets. Each word has a suffix. Remove the suffix and identify the word with the corresponding free vowel.

(i) width fifty typical derivative divinity sublimity Biblical wilderness precision Palestinian Cypriot (For this last word add a new suffix.)
(ii) kept obscenity supremacy competitive adrenalin intervention shepherd
(iii) sanity chastity explanatory urbanity profanity Spanish inflammatory
(iv) abundant southern pronunciation
(v) fodder lost
(vi) phonic composite jocular nostril diagnostic microscopic

14.11 Free and checked vowels

The use of underlying forms helps us to see the systematic relationships which exist between the allomorphs of certain morphemes, as in *compose* and *composite*, *volcano* and *volcanic*. But the facts that we have observed do more than tell us about specific morphemes; they point to some general facts about the language. Free and checked vowels are in contrast in some environments, for example, before a single final consonant, as in *pane* and *pan*. But in certain other environments only free vowels occur or only checked vowels; there is no contrast.

We have seen that a checked vowel occurs in a syllable that is closed by a consonant.

c*a*ndy	r*a*pture
det*e*ctive	Nov*e*mber
mal*i*gnant	rel*i*nquish
d*o*ctrine	*o*ption
ind*u*lgent	rel*u*ctant

Usually when the antepenult of a word is stressed, its vowel is a checked vowel, but this does not apply to *u*.

*a*necdote	c*a*lendar
d*e*mocrat	*e*bony
curr*i*culum	m*i*nimum
d*o*cument	m*o*nitor

but: f*u*neral l*u*dicrous

A vowel is typically checked if it occurs before the suffixes +*ic*, +*id*, and the verbal suffix +*ish* (as in *vanish*; not the adjective suffix, as in *Danish*). But note that the vowel *u* is not checked before the first two of these suffixes.

mech*a*nic	voc*a*lic	pl*a*cid	v*a*lid	b*a*nish	est*a*blish
epid*e*mic	proph*e*tic	f*e*tid	intr*e*pid	bl*e*mish	repl*e*nish
terr*i*fic	cr*i*tic	fr*i*gid	ins*i*pid	dim*i*nish	f*i*nish
econ*o*mic	l*o*gic	s*o*lid	st*o*lid	ast*o*nish	dem*o*lish
				p*u*blish	p*u*nish

but: c*u*bic m*u*sic l*u*cid p*u*trid

On the other hand, a free vowel occurs in an open syllable.

ch*a*os	l*a*ity
n*e*on	p*e*ony
l*i*on	sc*i*ence
p*o*et	b*o*a
cr*u*el	fl*u*id

In the environment ____ C_1^1 (r) i V . . . that is, before one consonant (plus, possibly, /r/), then /i/ and another vowel only the free vowels /ei ii ou/ occur, and not /æ ɛ ɒ/.

r*a*dium p*a*triot aud*a*cious n*a*tion
amn*e*sia comp*l*etion d*e*vious m*e*dium
atr*o*cious j*o*vial p*o*dium n*o*tion

But in this position checked /ɪ/ occurs and not free /ai/.

amb*i*tion civ*i*lian nutr*i*tious Virg*i*nia

(Note that palatalization may occur if the consonant is /s/.)

The rule for free vowel choice can be stated in this formula:

$$\text{Vowel} \rightarrow \text{Free} \;/\; \begin{cases} \underline{\quad}\ \text{Vowel} \\ \begin{bmatrix} \overline{\quad} \\ \text{non-low} \end{bmatrix} \# \\ \begin{bmatrix} \overline{\quad} \\ \text{non-high} \end{bmatrix} C_1^1\ (\text{r})\ \text{i Vowel} \end{cases}$$

This rule applies after the stress rules; this means that stress rules apply as if the final vowel of *macaroni*, *continue*, *volcano*, etc. were a checked vowel.

14H EXERCISE

A large number of (originally) related words follow, showing the opposition of free vowel and checked vowel. You should have no trouble in accounting for the environment of the checked vowel. (There is no feedback. In the unlikely case that you can't explain why a particular word has a checked vowel, review the preceding section.)

depraved, depravity	creed, credulous
fable, fabulous	female, feminine
grain, granary	femur, femoral
inane, inanity	gene, generate

Kate, Katherine
labor, elaborate
opaque, opacity
page, paginate
sacred, sacrament
  Bible, Biblical
  crime, criminal
  file, filament
  imbibe, bibulous
  mine, mineral
  rabbi, rabbinical
  reside, residual
  sine, sinuous
  title, titular
  tyrant, tyranny
bereave, bereft
clean, cleanse
heal, health
redeem, redemption
  grave, gravid
  pale, pallid
  prevail, valid
  rabies, rabid
arthritis, arthritic
cycle, cyclic
lyre, lyric
parasite, parasitic
satire, satiric
  bile, bilious
  collide, collision
  expedite, expeditious
  Palestine, Palestinian
  reconcile, reconciliation
  reptile, reptilian
  suffice, sufficient
helix, helical
hero, heroine
legal, legislate
repeat, repetitive
species, specimen
  code, codify
  globe, globular
  local, locative
  mediocre, mediocrity
  mode, modify
  omen, ominous
  onus, onerous
  opus, opera
  provoke, provocative
  sole, solitude
defile, filth
drive, drift
scribe, script
thrive, thrift
  athlete, athletic
  exegesis, exegetic
  kinesis, kinetic
  meter, metric
colon, colic
embryo, embryonic
episode, episodic
neurosis, neurotic

There exist a number of pairs of words with the same vowel contrasts which cannot be explained within the rules given. Examples:

cave, cavern
face, facet
glaze, glass
Jane, Janet
shade, shadow
feet, fetters
heath, heather
mead, meadow
please, pleasant
sheep, shepherd

vale, valley	zeal, zealous
dine, dinner	close, closet
final, finish	coal, collier
dike, ditch	hole, hollow
pike, pickerel	know, knowledge
whine, whinny	throat, throttle

The relationships seen in these word-pairs are the result of the same historical processes as those previously considered, but the original conditioning factors have been lost: *shadow* and *southern* once had an extra syllable at the end; *valley*, *dinner*, *closet* were originally stressed on the ult, for which reason the vowel of the initial syllable was short; *ditch* and *shepherd* have short vowels because the vowels were once followed by two consonants. It is interesting to note that some of these pairs are still semantically related but others, like *feet* and *fetters*, *mead* and *meadow*, now have no common meaning. Other historically related pairs with no present semantic kinship can be cited. Who now would see what *bonfires* have to do with *bones*, or *shackles* with *shaking*, or *spaniels* with *Spain*?

14.12 More about augments

Consider these sets of words:

admire - admiration	imagine - imaginative
define - definition	describe - descriptive
convene - convention	exclaim - exclamatory
inscribe - inscription	expose - expository

Again there is a problem of deciding how much belongs to the base and how much is a suffix. The words in the right-hand columns are apparently formed by adding suffixes *-tion*, *-tive*, *-tory* to the verbs in the left-hand columns, but there seems to be something else in between.

It is simplest to recognize special augments which are added to many Latin-derived verbs when any of the suffixes +*ion*, +*ive*, +*ory* (or +*or* as in *compositor*) follows. The augment is (æt), (ɪt), or just (t) depending on the base, and in all of them the //t// is subject to spirantization, with /s/ becoming /ʃ/ before *-ion*. The augment is part of the underlying form. It is not predictable and thus cannot be stated as a rule. It is part of the knowledge of any person who uses such words as *invite*, *invitation*; *expose*, *expository*; *describe*, *descriptive*, and the like. The augmented underlying forms of the bases in the words above are:

//ædm{ai, ɪ}r(æt)// //ɪmæǰɪn(æt)//
//=f{ai, ɪ}n(it)// //=kl{ei, æ}m(æt)//
//=v{ii, ɛ}n(t)// //=p{ou, ɒ}z(ɪt)//
//=skr{ai, ɪ}b(t)//

Many augmented forms are irregular. Some examples:

resolve, resolution	//=sɒlv(AUG)// = /səluut/
inquire, inquisitive	//=kwair(AUG)// = /kwɪzɪt/
introduce, introductory	//=d(j)uus(AUG)// = /dʌkt/
retain, retentive	//=tein(AUG)//=/tɛnt/

A number of bases which end in //t// or //d// have an augmented form in which that final consonant is replaced by /s/. Some examples:

include, inclusive	//=kluud(AUG)// = /kluus/
divide, division	//=v{ai, ɪ}d(AUG)// = /vɪz/
respond, responsive	//=spɒnd(AUG)// = /spɒns/
permit, permission	//=mɪt(AUG)// = /mɪs/

14I EXERCISE

Here is an opportunity for you to prove that you know the augmented underlying forms for certain words which are similar to the ones discussed above. You probably have not thought about these words in terms of underlying forms and augments, but these terms simply refer to concepts which are our way of accounting for the knowledge that you have. If you add +*ion* to *propel*, the result is *propulsion*. Let's state it simply, this way:

propel +ion = propulsion

What are the results of these additions?

intrude + ion	=	submit +ive	=
revolve +ion	=	compel +ory	=
offend +ive	=	inform +ion	=
evoke +ive	=	suspend +ion	=
define +ive	=	comprehend +ive	=
inflame +ory	=	preserve +ion	=

14.13 Applications

Consider the following pairs of words:

1	2
Canada	Canadian
comedy	comedian
felony	felonious
melody	melodious
remedy	remedial

Each pair of words must have the same underlying form, except for the ending. The same set of rules should apply to all the words in column 1, and another set of rules should apply to all the words in column 2.

All words in column 1 have the canonical form CVCəCV; all words in column 2 have the canonical form CəCV:CiVC. The first vowel in all the underlying forms must be a checked vowel; it remains a checked vowel when stressed, as in column 1, and it becomes a schwa when unstressed, as in column 2. The second vowel must also be a checked vowel in the underlying form; otherwise the stress would not be on the antepenult in the words of column 1. How then do we account for the free vowel in the surface forms of the words in column 2? We observe that there is an environment for free vowel choice, ____ CiV. So the derivation for the first pair of words is like this:

Underlying	//#kænædæ#	#kænæd +i+ æ n#//
Stress	ˈ	ˈ
Free vowel rule		ei
V. reduction	ə ə	ə ə
Surface	/ˈkænədə	kəˈneidiən/

Write out the derivations for the other four pairs of words.

Study the derivations for the words *rite* /rait/ and *ritual* /rɪčuəl/.

Underlying	//#rait(ju)#	#rait(ju)+æl#//
Augment choice	0	ju
Stress	ˈ	ˈ
V. choice	ai	ɪ
Palatalization		č
J-drop		0
V. reduction		ə
Surface	/ˈrait	ˈrɪčuəl/

Using the above as models, determine what should be the derivations for the following:

vice /vais/	vicious /vɪʃəs/
habit /hæbɨt/	habitual /həbɪčuəl/

14.14 Summary

Just as phonemes, the units of sound, have variant pronunciations called allophones, so many of the meaningful units of the language, the morphemes, have variant forms called **allomorphs**. In this chapter we have taken the point of view that each variable morpheme has a single abstract form, the **underlying representation** or **underlying form**, and the allomorphs are different surface forms which are derived from the underlying form by application of certain **rules**, or **processes**.

A few rules are quite special, but we have not investigated any of them in this chapter. The classic example of a special rule in English is the formation of the past tense of the verb *go*: *go* + Past = *went*. No other verb – in fact, nothing else in English – is like this. We come to a better understanding of the language by considering the most common rules that govern alternations.

Some alternations are **phonologically conditioned**. In this chapter we have dealt with three of these, all of which resemble processes discussed in previous chapters. Obstruents are affected by **voice assimilation**, so that they agree in voice with a following obstruent. Checked vowels in unstressed open syllables or final syllables undergo **vowel reduction**. And the tongue-tip consonants /t d s z/ are affected by **palatalization** when they are followed by /j/ plus a vowel or, in the case of the fricatives, by /i/ and a vowel.

If the allomorphs of a morpheme are **morphologically conditioned**, the choice of one or another depends on the morphemes that occur next, including **abstract morphemes** such as **past tense** or **verb**. An alternation, such as that between /f/ and /v/ may be phonologically conditioned in some environments and morphologically conditioned in others.

When allomorphs are at least partly morphologically conditioned, we have followed the procedure of showing the alternating phonemes as a choice pair in the underlying form, with symbols in curly brackets; thus, {f,v}, {ii,ɛ}, and others. The rules which affect specific choice pairs are called by traditional names. **Spirantization** is the rule which applies to the pair {t,s}. The rule of **velar softening** applies to two pairs, {k,s} and {g,j}. The **voicing** rule affects {f,v}, {θ,ð}, and {s,z}. The **vowel shift** rule operates on six pairs of free and checked vowels, {ii,ɛ}, {ei,æ}, {ai,ɪ}, {ou,ɒ}, {uu,ɒ}, and {au,ʌ}, of which the first four are frequent in alternation, the last two uncommon.

The vowel shift rule and vowel reduction rule should help us to understand an important characteristic of English orthography. Our spelling patterns are often a kind of underlying form. Consider such word sets as these:

define, definitive, definition
compete, competitive, competition
provoke, provocative, provocation

The spelling *defin-* does not represent one single pronunciation, but three of them, and the same is true of *compet-* and *provok/provoc-*. The variation, however, is not irregular. Those who speak, read, and write English have become accustomed to the fact that one vowel letter has different values in different places. In a way they have acquired the rules which are described in this chapter.

Another kind of allomorphic variation is alternation of a phoneme with zero. Certain of these phonemes are called augments. Before the adjective suffixes *+al*, *+an*, *+ous* the augments (i) and (u) – /ju/ – are common. Verbs of Latin origin often have (a{t,s}), (i{t,s}), ({t,s}), or a similar augment before suffixes *+ion*, *+or*, *+ory*, *+ive*.

14A FEEDBACK

(a) departure legislature moisture sculpture spiritual
(b) fraudulent gradual grandeur procedure residual
(c) admission coercion gracious fallacious ferocious sacrificial
(Notice the vowel alternation in *fero / ou / cious* and *fero / ɒ / city* and the vowel alternation in *sacrifi / ai / ce* and *sacrifi / ɪ / ial*.)
(d) composure disclosure exposure infusion pleasure revision
(e) The rule says that /i/ is deleted before a checked unstressed vowel; this applies to *official*, *judicial*, *partial*, *confidential*. On the other hand, in *officiate* and *judiciary* the /i/ is right before a vowel in a strong syllable, and in *partiality* and *confidentiality* the /i/ is before a stressed vowel, so it is not deleted.

14B FEEDBACK

act(u)	aroma(t)	contempt(u)
habit(u)	symptom(at)	commerc(i)
sens(u)	sympath(et)	event(u)
sex(u)	apolog(et)	attitud(in)
tempest(u)	part(i)	longitud(in)
financ(i)	manager(i)	spasm(od)
rac(i)	professor(i)	drama(t)
dogma(t)	dictator(i)	opera(t)

14C FEEDBACK

(a)

confederate	complacent	ecstatic	cathartic
delicate	frequent	geodetic	diuretic
democrat(ic)	hesitant	galactic	hypnotic
diplomat(ic)	infant	heretic	narcotic
hypocrite	president	idiot(ic)	neurotic
literate	vacant	lunatic	synoptic
pirate			synthetic
prophet(ic)			
secret			

As these examples show, from the underlying //{t,s}// we choose /t/ in final position and before the suffix +*ic*.

Note the alternation of vowels in *diure/ii/sis*, *diure/ɛ/tic* and in *hypno/ou/sis*, *hypno/ɒ/tic*; *narco/ou/sis*, *narco/ɒ/tic*. These alternations are treated in the vowel shift rules, section 14.10.

(b) The answer is that the underlying form of *base*, *bas+ic* does not contain {t,s} but simply //s//. The underlying form is the same as the surface form.

14D FEEDBACK

(a) criticize, criticism electricity italicize reciprocity romanticism

(b) demagogic fragile legislate legitimate pedagogy regent rigid

(c) The unstressed suffixes *-ant* and *-ent* have the same pronunciation, /ənt/. The element before these suffixes, written *-fic-*, has two pronunciations, /fɨk/ in *significant* and /fɨs/ in *magnificent*. But as we have seen, vowel reduction changes various different vowels – underlying vowels – to /ə/, and velar softening is able to explain why *-fic-* may be /fɨk/ or /fɨs/.

Underlying	//#sɪgnɪ+fɪ{k,s}+ænt#	#mægnɪ+fɪ{k,s}+ɛnt#//
Stress	ˈ	ˈ
Velar soft.	k	s
V. reduction	ɨ ə	i — ə
Surface	/sɪgˈnɪfɨkənt	mægˈnɪfɨsənt/

14E FEEDBACK

(a) First, //t// → /s/ through spirantization; then /s/ → /ʃ/ through palatalization. Here is a sample derivation:

	//#ak{t,s}#	#ak{t,s}+ion#//
Stress		ˈ
Spirantization	t	s
Palatalization		ʃ
I-drop		0
V. reduction		ɨ
Surface	/ækt	ˈækʃɨn/

(b) The final consonant is /k/: electric, logic, mathematic, magic, music. Velar softening yields /s/ from the underlying {k,s}, and then /s/ becomes /ʃ/ through palatalization. A pair of sample derivations:

	//#ɛlɛktr+ɪk#	#ɛlɛktr+ɪk+i+an#//
Stress	ˈ	ˈ
Velar softening	— k	— s
Palatalization		ʃ
I-drop		0
V. reduction	ə ɨ	ə ə
Surface	/əˈlɛktrɨk	əlɛkˈtrɪʃən/

14F FEEDBACK

(a) calf: pl. calves, verb calve
half: pl. halves, verb halve
dwarf: pl. dwarves (also dwarfs)
elf: pl. elves
wharf: pl. wharves (also wharfs)
knife: pl. knives
wolf: pl. wolves
shelf: verb shelve
five: fifth, fifteen, fifty
sieve: sift
bereave: bereft
cleave: cleft
leaf: pl. leaves
life: pl. lives, verb live
loaf: pl. loaves
scarf: pl. scarves (also scarfs)
proof: verb prove
relief: verb relieve
strife: verb strive
grief: verb grieve

(b) The last group (*five*, *sieve*, *bereave*, *cleave*) are the only ones in which the alternation of /v/ and /f/ is phonologically conditioned. The vowel alternations are also phonologically conditioned, as we shall see.

(c)

bath: verb bathe	cloth: verb clothe	mouth: verb mouth
breath: verb breathe	loath: verb loathe	north: northern
south: southern	worth: worthy	
teeth: verb teethe	wreath: verb wreathe	

All these alternations are morphologically conditioned, but it must be recognized that /ð/ is much more frequent than /θ/; hence *southern*, *northern*, *worthy*.

(d) (i) graze; advise

(ii) The nouns *use*, *abuse*, *excuse*, and *house* all end with /s/. The corresponding verbs end with /z/.

(iii) That depends on dialect. Generally in Scotland and in the greater part of the US and Canada the noun and verb are identical, /griis/, and the adjective is /ˈgriisi/. In much of Britain and the southern US the noun and the verb are different, the noun having /s/ and the verb /z/, and the adjective is /ˈgriizi/. However, the pronunciations with /s/ in verb and adjective seem to be spreading on both sides of the Atlantic.

(iv) For most speakers of English the plural of *house* is /ˈhauzɨz/. In some areas the form is /ˈhausɨz/.

(v) In words of this type there is an initial /s/ in the base if the prefix ends with a consonant. If the prefix ends with a vowel, the base has initial /z/.

(vi) Compare *eˈxecutive* and ˈ*execute*. /gz/ occurs before a stressed vowel, /ks/ after the stressed vowel.

Incidentally, the words *exile* and *exit* are pronounced with either /gz/ or /ks/. Several centuries ago the verbs *exile* and *exit* were pronounced with /gz/, the corresponding nouns with /ks/.

(e) A phonological change

(f) To judge from these words alone, we might with equal reason choose either of two approaches. (1) We might say the underlying forms are //seg// and //frag// and there is a rule which changes //g// to /k/ before a following voiceless consonant (as in +tion, +tor, +ture). Or (2) we might say that the underlying forms are //sɛk// and //fræk// and there is a rule which changes //k// to /g/ before a following voiced consonant (such as +ment). If we look beyond these examples, we find that voiceless consonants do occur before /m/ (as in *appointment*) and other voiced consonants, but voiced consonants do not ordinarily occur before voiceless ones. These considerations make the first of our two approaches seem preferable to the other.

14G FEEDBACK

(i) wide five type derive divine sublime Bible wild precise Palestine Cyprus
(ii) keep obscene supreme compete adrenal intervene sheep
(iii) sane chaste explain urbane profane Spain inflame
(iv) abound south pronounce
(v) food lose
(vi) phone compose joke nose diagnose microscope

Notice the words *wild*, *chaste*, *abound*, *pronounce*. Before final consonant clusters /ld, st, nd, ns/ a free vowel may occur, but not before other consonant clusters.

14I FEEDBACK

intrusion	submissive
revolution	compulsory
offensive	information
evocative	suspension
definitive	comprehensive
inflammatory	preservation

Appendix I

Some Different Analyses of English Vowels

I.1 Why are there different analyses?

If one compares the analyses of English consonants that have been made by various phoneticians and phonologists, one finds that these analyses differ only in details. There are a few differences in the ways of symbolizing: the IPA symbols /j/, /ʃ/, and /ʒ/ which are used in this book and many others for, respectively, the initial consonant of *yet*, the initial consonant of *shoe*, and the medial consonant of *azure* are replaced by some linguists, with /y/, /š/, and /ž/, respectively. This is a mere difference of symbols. The initial consonants of *chin* and *gin* are represented in some analyses as /tʃ/ and /dʒ/, respectively, rather than /č/ and /ǰ/, which we have used. This is a bit more than a difference of symbolization; it raises a question as to whether the first elements of *chin* and *gin*, for instance, function each as a single consonant or as a sequence of two consonants. In addition to differences in symbols, there are sometimes differences in the way certain consonants are classified: is /h/, for example, considered a fricative or a glide – or something else? Is /r/ a liquid or a frictionless continuant or a glide (semiconsonant)? Despite these differences, there are great similarities in the total treatment of consonants – the inventory, the classification, and the symbols used.

It is not so with vowels. There are quite different systems used for transcribing English vowel-units, and anyone who reads extensively in English phonology is bound to come in contact with more than one widely used system. One reason for differences is in the matter treated – the dialect or dialects which the analyst deals with. As indicated in chapter 4, different dialects have somewhat different inventories of vowel contrasts. Another difference in analysis is a reflection of the fact that language has redundancy: the vowels of *sheep* and *ship*, for instance, differ in several possible ways: in quality (higher versus somewhat lower), in duration (longer versus shorter), in complexity (diphthongal versus monophthongal), and in tenseness (tense versus lax) – though the last of these is not, in itself, an audible difference. One analysis may consider the difference of quality the distinctive difference and the other differences merely concomitant, non-distinctive. In another analysis the complexity may be viewed as the essential distinction; in still another, length or tenseness. A third cause of differences in the vowel systems of different linguists has to do with the purpose of what is presented: a theoretical statement is concerned with neatness of presentation, economy of statement, whereas a description which is intended for pedagogical application is likely to lean in the opposite direction, emphasizing what seems important for learning accurate pronunciation, not just making essential differences. Finally, it has to be said that linguists, like all of us, live at a particular time in history and so may or may not be influenced by some other description. As we will see, some analyses are to some extent re-analyses of previous work.

I.2 Daniel Jones

Daniel Jones had a long and productive career. He taught at the University of London from before the First World War until the mid-1950s, and he published numerous works about phonetics in general and English pronunciation in particular, most notably his *English Pronouncing Dictionary*, and *An Outline of English Phonetics*, both of which have gone through many editions. In a field that has never been crowded he thus exercised a great influence on a lot of people concerned with learning, teaching and/or describing English.

The form of English which Jones described he called Received Pronunciation ('received' in the sense of 'universally accepted'). This is the speech of the educated English middle class, sometimes also called 'BBC English', since it is the pronunciation used by newsreaders and announcers on the British Broadcasting Corporation in national and overseas services. The variety which has been taught overseas by members of the British Council, it is the only dialect which continental Europeans and non-native speakers in the Commonwealth have thought worth learning – and some native speakers of other English dialects have made efforts to acquire this more fashionable 'accent'.

As a member of the International Phonetic Association (IPA) Jones used the symbols devised by that organization, the International Phonetic Alphabet (also IPA). To describe the quality of English vowels Jones used the IPA device of Cardinal Vowels. Cardinal vowels and English vowels are shown in the chart below, with the usual arrangement from high (top) to low (bottom) and from front (left) to back (right). Explanations follow.

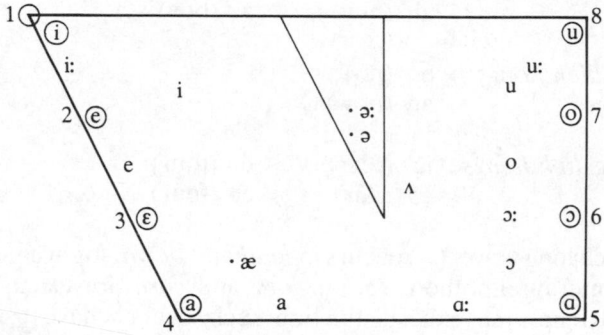

The cardinal vowels are reference points in phonological space (the inside of a speaker's mouth). If, while stretching the lips, you raise the front of the tongue as high as it can go without producing friction when air is expelled, you articulate cardinal vowel 1. If you lower the front of the tongue to its lowest position while still keeping the lips rounded, you can articulate cardinal vowel 4. Arbitrarily dividing into three parts the line that goes from cardinal vowel 1 to cardinal vowel 4 gives the positions of cardinal vowels 2 and 3. Similarly, raising the back of the tongue as high as it can go without producing friction and simultaneously rounding the lips will give the posture for articulation of cardinal vowel 8. When the tongue-back is in its lowest possible position, with lips still rounded, cardinal vowel 5 is articulated. An arbitrary division into three parts of the line between cardinal vowels 5 and 8 locates vowels 6 and 7. These are reference points, as indicated on the outer edges of the chart. In the interior are dots and accompanying symbols for English simple vowels and the more prominent elements of English diphthongs (one vowel, *e*, coincides with cardinal vowel 3). The quality of these vocalic elements is thus shown by their location with reference to cardinal vowels.

The chart shows 14 such vocalic elements, most occurring as separate vowels, some only as parts of diphthongs. Altogether Jones recognized 22 vowel-units in RP (and a couple of others that we can ignore, which are mere variants), classified as follows:

6 short vowels	i (pit)	u (put)
	e (pet)	ʌ (putt)
	æ (pat)	ɔ (pot)
5 long vowels	iː (beat)	uː (boot)
	əː (Bert)	
	ɑː (Bart)	ɔː (bought)

3 fronting diphthongs	ei (bay)	
	ai (buy)	ɔi (boy)
2 backing diphthongs	ou (no)	
	au (now)	
4 centering diphthongs	iə (fear)	uə (tour)
	ɛə (fair)	ɔə (four)

(The low-back long vowel (ɔ:) occurs in *laud* and *dawn*, for instance, and the low-back centering diphthong (ɔə) in *lord* and *corn*, for example. Not all speakers of RP now make this distinction; such speakers have (ɔ:) in all such words, or vary between the two vowel-units.)

These 22 units occur in stressed and unstressed syllables, according to Jones. One more vowel, symbolized with the schwa (ə), occurs only in unstressed syllables. Three degrees of stress are noted in the *Pronouncing Dictionary*, symbolized, as we have done, with a superior tick (ˈ) for the main stress, an inferior tick (ˌ) for a subordinate stress, and no mark for an unstressed syllable; thus: *book-learning,* ˈbukˌlə:niŋ. Jones recognizes some compounds as 'double-stressed'; for example, ˈ*ice* ˈ*cold*. The syllable *cold* in this example would most likely carry a change of pitch – a tone – if the compound is pronounced in isolation or if it occurs at the end of an utterance (*This water is ice-cold*) and thus be more prominent, perceptually, than the syllable *ice*. Jones thus recognizes four degrees of prominence while distinguishing stress and accent, to use the terms which we have used in this book.

The *Pronouncing Dictionary* has one more symbol, an asterisk (*) which appears, for example, at the end of the transcription given for *car* (kɑ:*), *war* (wɔ:* or wɔə*), and *dinner* (ˈdinə*). The asterisk stands for a 'linking R', which was discussed in chapter 4.

I.3 Two adaptations of Jones's system

In representing English vowels Jones used symbols fairly much as they were used by the IPA, to indicate phonetic values, areas of articulation in the oral cavity. Since English has a rather large number of vowel units and they are well differentiated from one another in their articulation, it is possible to use a rather large number of symbols to represent them – and Jones did just that. However, a greater concern for the *system* of vowels, the relationships between vowels, would lead one to ask how different the symbols need to be and how many different symbols are needed.

Consider the low unrounded vowels, for instance. Jones has the symbol (æ) for the low-front vowel of *bat*; (a) for the more retracted low vowel which occurs only as part of diphthongs, (ai) in *bite* and (au) in *bout*; and (ɑ), always long, that is, always accompanied by the colon, for the low-back vowel of *car* and the like. The three different symbols provide phonetic accuracy, but phonologically they are in complementary distribution: one occurs alone, one only with *i* or *u*, and one only with *:*. If length, symbolized by the colon, is assumed to be a distinctive feature, separating *beat* and *bit* (*i:* and *i*, respectively), *shooed* and *should* (*u:* and *u*, respectively), and *caught* and *cot* (ɔ*:* and ɔ, respectively), even though the members of each pair also differ in quality, a structural analysis would suggest that length is also the distinctive difference between *cat* and *cart* in this form of English, so that one symbol alone would do for the vowel of *cat*, the same symbol with the colon would represent the vowel of *cart*, and the same symbol could be combined with *i* and *u* to represent the units of *kite* and *cow*, respectively. And, indeed, Jones himself pointed out the possibility of this more systematic sort of analysis.

A greatly simplified, and more systematic, analysis is embodied in the set of symbols which follow. This transcription was used, for instance, in the third, completely revised edition of *A Grammar of Spoken English*, originally written by Harold Palmer and first published in 1924. The first edition and the second (1939, by Palmer and F. G. Blatchford) used the Daniel Jones analysis; the third (1976) edition, revised and rewritten by Roger Kingdon, 'uses fewer unfamiliar symbols and thus makes it easier for the uninitiated to read the examples'.

Short vowels	i	(pit)	u	(put)	
	e	(pet)	ʌ	(putt)	
	a	(pat)	o	(pot)	
Long vowels	i:	(beat)	u:	(boot)	
	ə:	(Bert)			
	a:	(Bart)			o: (bought)
Fronting diphthongs	ei	(bay)			
	ai	(buy)	oi	(boi)	
Backing diphthongs			ou	(no)	
			au	(now)	
Centering diphthongs	iə	(fear)	uə	(tour)	
	eə	(fair)	oə	(four)	

The transcription above emphasizes economy of symbols and systematic relationship of vocalic elements. Quite a different approach is that of A. C. Gimson, *An Introduction to the Pronunciation of English* (3rd edition, 1980), which recognizes the same number of vowel-units with one exception (it ignores the contrast illustrated in *saw* and *sore*, which for an increasing number of RP speakers are homophonous). Though the inventory of vowel-units recognized is practically identical, the inventory of symbols to represent them is much larger, since the aim is to indicate, indeed to emphasize, phonetic differences. The purpose is to make more obvious what different articulations are used by speakers of this form of English.

Short vowels		ɪ	pit		ʊ	put
		e	pet		ʌ	putt
		æ	pat		ɒ	pot
Long vowels		i	beat		u	boot
				ɜ Bert		
				ɑ Bart	ɔ	bought
Fronting diphthongs	eɪ		bay			
				aɪ buy	ɔɪ	boy
Backing diphthongs				əʊ no		
				aʊ now		
Centering diphthongs	ɪə		fear		ʊə	tour
	εə		fair			

It might be said that a transcription like this one is superior for pedagogical purposes, since its great variety of symbols emphasizes phonetic facts. By representing the vowel of *beat* as /i/ and that of *bit* as /ɪ/ this transcription emphasizes that the two vowel-units differ in length and in quality. For a structurally oriented phonologist, on the other hand, only one of these features can be distinctive, and the other is then redundant. It is interesting that both the Kingdon system, above, and the Gimson analysis are said to offer advantages to the novice.

I.4 Kenyon and Knott

John S. Kenyon and Thomas A. Knott attempted to do for American English what Daniel Jones had done for one form of British English in his *English Pronouncing Dictionary*. The result was *A Pronouncing Dictionary of American English*, published in 1953 though most of the work had been completed some time before. Like the *EPD*, Kenyon and Knott's dictionary gives accepted pronunciations (but no definitions, synonyms, etymologies, or the like) for a large number of words. It differs from the Jones dictionary in its attempt to include a variety of regional pronunciations. Kenyon and Knott assumed that the English spoken in the United States shows three general dialect areas, which they labeled 'Eastern' (E), 'Southern' (S), and – for want of a better term – 'Northern' (N). The first term, Eastern, applies to eastern New England and the New York city metropolitan area; Southern includes 'Virginia, North Carolina, South Carolina, Tennessee, Florida, Georgia, Alabama, Mississippi, Arkansas, Louisiana, Texas, and parts of Maryland,

West Virginia, Kentucky, and Oklahoma'. 'The North includes the rest of the US' – a dialect region that has been called 'General American' by others. Subsequent research by dialect geographers has shown that this tripartite division, whatever the labels used, is not sufficiently accurate as a description of US dialects. However, the purpose here is not to explain dialects but to introduce one widely used transcription system.

At any rate, where variant pronunciations are given in the Dictionary for specific words, one variant is often labeled 'E' or perhaps 'S' or both. Any pronunciation given with no such label is 'Northern' or in use in all three of the hypothetical regions. Kenyon and Knott did not include the 'centering diphthongs' of Jones's *fear*, *fair*, *tour*, *four* in their inventory of vowel-units since they treat such items as having vowel plus consonant /r/ – though Eastern and Southern dialects do have centering offglides just like RP. This exclusion reduces their repertory of vowel symbols, but, on the other hand, the coverage of dialects introduces a need for some extra symbols, so the inventory of vocalic symbols is about the same.

i beat						u	boot
ɪ pit						ʊ	put
e bay	ɝ	Bert		manner	ɚ	o	no
	ɜ	Bert**		manna	ə		
ɛ pet		ʌ putt					
æ pat							
	a*		ɑ Bart			ɔ	bought
						ɑ#ɒ	pot***
aɪ buy		aʊ now		ɔɪ boy		ɪʊ	few****

* *a* = vowel of Bostonian *Harvard yard* or 'Southern' *buy* (with no fronting offglide).

** *ɜ* = the vowel in an 'R-less' dialect, without tongue retraction.

*** The two symbols represent low-back vowels, respectively unrounded and rounded; the two phones occur in American dialects but are nowhere in contrast. Indeed, as noted in chapter 4, the vowel in *pot*-words is either identical with that of *bought*-words or *Bart*-words for most North Americans. For the New York City area, where *bought*, *pot*, and *Bart* are in contrast, the chart is not valid, since *pot* is low-central and *Bart* is farther back.

**** *ɪʊ* = a falling diphthong in which the first part is high-front unrounded and the offglide is high-back rounded.

It is interesting to note that, with the exception of *aɪ*, *aʊ*, *ɔɪ*, and the marginal *ɪʊ*, Kenyon and Knott represent each vowel-unit with a single symbol. This analysis thus implicitly rejects the notion that English vowels are distinctively different in length, or tenseness, or in complexity (except for the diphthongs noted). What distinguishes them from one another is essentially the difference of quality, the shape of the oral chamber determined by the position of the tongue in the mouth.

I.5 Variations of the Kenyon–Knott system

The kind of vowel analysis used by Kenyon and Knott has been widely accepted by American linguists but generally modified. The idea of representing vowel-units as single items, each with a single symbol (except those in *buy*, *boy*, *now*) is accepted, but a simpler system can be obtained by avoiding dialect variations. Here, for example, is the way American English vowel units are represented in Victoria Fromkin and Robert Rodman, *An Introduction to Language* (3rd edition, 1982):

i	beat			u	boot
ɪ	pit			ʊ	put
e	bay	ə	*a*bove	o	no
ɛ	pet	ʌ	ab*o*ve		
æ	pat		a pot	ɔ	bought
	ay buy		aw/æw now	ɔy	boy

With modification of one or more symbols this sort of system can be found in many works on North American English.

I.6 The Trager–Smith 'overall analysis'

In 1942 Bernard Bloch and George L. Trager produced an analysis of English vowels which might be considered a structuralist reworking of the Daniel Jones system. The Jones analysis recognized five kinds of vowel-units: a number of short vowels (V), some long vowels (V:), fronting diphthongs (Vi), backing diphthongs (Vu), and centering diphthongs (Və). The symbols which Bloch and Trager used for individual vowels were quite different from those used by Jones, but the essential difference in their analysis is that they reduced Jones's five types of vowel-units to four types:

6 short, or simple vowels (V)
5 or 6 fronting diphthongs (Vj, where 'j' is equivalent to Jones's 'i' as the second part of a diphthong)
a smaller number of backing diphthongs (Vw, where 'w' = Jones's 'u')
up to 6 other vowel-units, or 'vocalic nuclei' (Vh, where 'h' represents length) (thus equivalent to Jones's V:) or a centering offglide (thus equivalent to Jones's Və), depending on the vowel with which it occurs.

Bloch and Trager thus proposed that vowel length and centering offglide are not in contrast, but instead are in complementary distribution: length is a feature of some vowel-units, and movement of the tongue to mid-central position is a feature of other vowel-units – or perhaps with some vowel-units the two features vary freely.

It is useful to understand the nature of the Bloch–Trager analysis, but it is not worthwhile to describe the details of their use of symbols, because their analysis was superseded nine years later. In 1951 Trager, with Henry Lee Smith, Jr, presented an augmented version of the 1942 version. In the Trager–Smith system there are – potentially – 36 vowel-units ('vocalic nuclei') in English as a whole: nine simple vowels (V), nine nuclei characterized by movement of the tongue-front upward (Vy), nine characterized by movement of the tongue-back upward (Vw), and nine nuclei in which there is contrastive length or else a movement of the tongue to mid-center position (Vh). To be sure, no single dialect of English has all 36 vowel-units in contrast, but if one takes into account all the contrasts which exist in any dialect, the total, it is claimed, will be 36. This is an 'overall' analysis of the English phoneme system.

Fundamental to the 'overall' approach is a firm belief that a language has a structure, which usually means that its elements are symmetrically arranged, that a contrast which exists in one area is paralleled by a corresponding contrast in another area. If English uses three degrees of tongue height (as in *pit*, *pet*, *pat*) and three degrees of tongue-advancement (as in *cat*, *cot*, *caught* or *cat*, *cart*, *cot*, depending on dialect), it would seem to follow that speakers of English have available the possibility of nine distinct areas for discriminating vowels. Similarly, if there are short vowels, fronting diphthongs, backing diphthongs, and other units which are either long or centering, then supposedly all the potential contrasts of such a system are exploited by some speakers of the language.

The four groups of vocalic nuclei are symbolized as follows. Descriptions of their occurrences are given below.

i	ɨ	u	iy	ɨy	uy	iw	ɨw	uw	ih	ɨh	uh
e	ə	o	ey	əy	oy	ew	əw	ow	eh	əh	oh
æ	a	ɔ	æy	ay	ɔy	æw	aw	ɔw	æh	ah	ɔh

The three lines, in each square are, from top to bottom, HIGH, MID, and LOW. The three columns are, from left to right, FRONT, CENTRAL, and BACK.

Simple vowels Five of the simple nuclei are easily identified by all dialects: the front vowels, /i, e, æ/, are those of *pit*, *pet*, *pat*; high-back /u/ is the vowel of *put*, and the schwa, /ə/, is the vowel of *putt* and of both the stressed and the unstressed vowel of *above*.

The low-back /ɔ/ is the vowel of Standard British *pot*, *bomb*, *bother*, *stock* (contrasting with *bought*, *stalk* which have /ɔh/ and *balm*, *father*, which have /ah/). The low-central /a/ is what most North Americans have in the *pot*-words; for those who have the same vowel in all these words – *pot*, *bomb*, *bother*, *stock*, *bought*, *stalk*, *balm*, *father* – /a/ is the appropriate symbol, so long as we are dealing with this form of English alone.

High-central /ɨ/ appears sporadically in the speech of people in many parts of the English-speaking world, for example, in the first syllable of *children* (/čɨldrɨn/ alternating with /čildrɨn/ and /čuldrɨn/ for many people). In various parts of the United States this vowel can be heard in the stressed syllable of *sister*, *miracle*, *window*, for instance. In unstressed syllables /ɨ/ is the vowel of *roses*, as distinct from the /ə/ of *Rosa's*. In South Africa the original high-front vowel has 'split', remaining high-front /i/ in the environment of frontal and dorsal consonants (e.g. *king*, *ship*, *chin*) and becoming high-central /ɨ/ in other environments (e.g. *build*, *tip*, *miss*). In New Zealand the high-central /ɨ/ is the norm for all environments.

Mid-back /o/ is used by many in the fast pronunciation of *going to*, generally written '*gonna*', /ˈgonə/, which does not have the longer, gliding /ow/ of *bone* and *bonus*. (For some speakers *gonna* has /ə/ in the first syllable, like *gunner*.) There are small, dwindling groups of people in the north of England and in New England and upstate New York who preserve an old distinction: *whole* and *rode* have a short vowel /o/ while *hole* and *road* have a longer /ow/.

Vowels with /h/ Low-back /ɔh/ and low-central /ah/ have already been shown in contrast, in some dialects, with the simple /ɔ/ and /a/, respectively, but there is no need for all four in all dialects. An approximate description for several dialects would be like this:

	stock bomb	stalk bought	stork corn	stark barn	father balm
RP	ɔ	ɔh	ɔh	ah	ah
E. New England	ɔh	ɔh	ɔh(r)	ah(r)	ah
NYC	a	ɔh	ɔh(r)	ah(r)	ah
General American	a	ɔh	ɔhr	ar	a

Similarly, /əh/ represents the vowel-unit in *turn*, *burst*, etc, in a R-less dialect, as opposed to the simple vowel /ə/ of *ton*, *bust*, and the like. In three nuclei, then, /ah, ɔh, əh/, the *h* represents length. In the same way, those who have a longer low-front vowel in *can* (tin container), *halve*, *bad*, as opposed to the shorter low-front vowel of *can* (be able), *have*, *pat*, the two contrasting nuclei are /æh/ and /æ/.

In other units with /h/ – /ih, eh, uh, oh/ – the /h/ represents the centering offglide of an R-less dialect, as in *we're*, *wear*, *tour*, *wore*, respectively. The last of these, mid-back /oh/, occurs in *wore* and *hoarse*, contrasting in some dialects with the low-back /ɔh/ of *war* and *horse*. Here is a problem: in some

Southern American dialects, as among older or more conservative speakers of RP, *horse*, *lord*, *corn* have a low-back vowel with centering offglide [ɔə] and *law*, *laud*, *dawn*, for example, have low-back vowel which is merely long [ɔ:]. Daniel Jones, as we have seen, distinguished these as /ɔə/ and /ɔ:/. Trager and Smith have only /ɔh/ for the two sets of words, since they maintained that length and centering offglide are never in contrast, but many disagree. While one's first impression of the T–S system is that it is too big, there are those who have criticized it as being too small.

It is hard to find justification for including the high-central /ɨh/ in the system of vowel contrasts. Trager and Smith stated that this can occur in the second syllable of 'Yes sir', but no other examples have been offered.

Vowels with /y/ High-front /iy/ occurs in *beat* and the like, mid-front /ey/ in *bait*, for example, and low-central /ay/ in *bite* – for many speakers. High-central /ɨy/ is merely a dialect variant of /iy/. In some dialects *buoy*, *ruin*, and (chop) *suey* are pronounced as single syllables with a high-back diphthong /uy/.

In parts of the southern USA *pass*, *mash*, *bag*, *candy* (the sets of words varying from region to region) have a low-front vowel with fronting offglide, represented by /æy/, as distinct from a simple vowel in, for example, *pat*, *passage*, *candid*, represented by /æ/. In a different dialect, Cockney, the same /æy/ occurs, but in a different set of words; here it is heard in words in which RP has /ey/: *make*, *bait*, Eliza Doolittle's *lady*, and the like.

The mid-central fronting diphthong /əy/ also occurs in different dialects with different correspondences. In various parts of Canada and the US the vowel-unit of *knife*, *white*, *like*, etc. (with a voiceless consonant following) is just this (whereas *lie*, *wide*, *rise*, without a voiceless consonant following have a low-central starting point, hence are represented as /ay/). In a single dialect these two are, of course, in complementary distribution, not in contrast, but to outsiders they sound different, so the overall analysis includes both. The nucleus /əy/ also occurs in New York City, New Orleans, and parts of the Carolinas, but in a different set of lexical items – words such as *first*, *bird*, *church*, that is, where other dialects have /əh(r)/ followed by an apical or frontal consonant. Historically, a postvocalic /r/ became a front glide in this position in dialects which took root in these areas.

In a more limited geographic area the same change of postvocalic /r/ to /y/ is found after other vowels. If *porch* and *scorch* have the vowels of *hoarse* and *horse*, as they do for speakers who make this distinction, and if, as in the south-eastern part of the US, the original /r/ is now a front glide, the contrast of /oy/ and /ɔy/ is established. To be sure, most dialects of English have no such contrast.

Vowels with /w/ The contrastive existence of nine units with a high-back offglide is rather hard to establish. All speakers of English have three units, illustrated in *lewd*, *load*, *loud*, which essentially have upward movement of the tongue-back; of course, the higher the starting point of the vowel-unit, the shorter is the movement of the tongue. The first of these, *lewd*, has a high-back starting point, hence the nucleus is represented as /uw/. The second, *load*, can, according to dialect, be designated /ow/ or /əw/ or even /ew/. The third, *loud*, may be /aw/ or /æw/. Furthermore, those who have /ʌy/ instead of /ay/ before voiceless consonants, as in *nice night*, have /ʌw/ instead of /aw/ before voiceless consonants, as in *out of the house*. Thus /əw/ occurs in some dialects in *goat*-words and in other dialects in *gout*-words. The justification for so many *w*-diphthongs seems to lie in the existence of dialect variants and the various ways they correspond to units of other dialects.

To deal with the remaining nuclei with backing offglide, consider a pair like *food* and *feud*. For most speakers these are, in Trager–Smith notation, /fuwd/ and /fyuwd/, respectively. An older pronunciation of the second word – and of course items like *few*, *new*, *beauty* – has a falling diphthong, represented in this system as /iw/ or even /ɨw/.

In some southern and midland dialects of the United States the nucleus in words like *law*, *dawn*, *caught*, rather than being long or center-gliding, has an upward glide of the tongue-back, hence /ɔw/ in this system.

Though the full Trager–Smith system of vowel notation is not used by many descriptivists today, adaptations are much in evidence. Especially the device of distinguishing between simple vowels, represented with single letters, and compound vowels, represented with a closing *y*, *w*, or, less commonly, *h* – is widespread.

Appendix II

A List of Word-Endings and their Effects on Stress

II.1 Neutral suffixes

A neutral suffix has no effect on stress. It is added to a word which has independent status, and the stress in the suffixed word is on the same syllable as in the word to which the suffix is added, e.g. *pro'pose*, *pro'posal*. However, there are sometimes changes in the vowels or consonants of the base word, as shown below.

#*al*$_1$ (makes abstract nouns from verbs) (dis)approval, arrival, burial, denial, dismissal, proposal, rehearsal . . .

#*dom* (rare: makes abstract nouns from adjectives and nouns) freedom, martyrdom, officialdom . . . Note the vowel change in *wisdom*.

#*ed* (forms participles of verbs, many of which are used as adjectives; forms adjectives from nouns; frequent in compound adjectives) bearded, candied, interested, (un)prejudiced, privileged, salaried, absent-minded, three-legged . . .

#*en*$_1$ (forms verbs from nouns and adjectives) broaden, cheapen, heighten, lengthen, sharpen, strengthen, threaten . . .

#*en*$_2$ (forms adjectives from nouns of material) earthen, golden, wooden, woolen . . .

#*en*$_3$ (makes participles from certain verbs, used as adjectives) drunken, forsaken, mistaken, swollen, (un)written . . .

#*er* (nouns of agent or instrument from certain verbs; nouns meaning 'inhabitant' from some nouns and adjectives; frequent in noun compounds) announcer, carrier, divider, islander, laborer, Londoner, southerner, bus-driver, dish-washer, two-wheeler . . .

#*ess* (forms feminine nouns from other nouns) actress, laundress, sorceress, waitress . . .

#*ful*$_1$ (makes nouns of measurement from other nouns; the suffix is a strong syllable with /ʊ/) 'armful, 'handful, 'houseful, 'mouthful . . .

#*ful*$_2$ (makes adjectives from nouns and verbs; a weak suffix with /ə/) cheerful, graceful, joyful, mournful, resentful, tactful . . .

#*hood* (makes abstract nouns from nouns and adjectives) childhood, falsehood, likelihood, motherhood, neighborhood . . .

#*ing* (a versatile and frequent suffix, forms adjectives and nouns, including compounds, from various sources) absorbing, (un)compromising, gathering, intoxicating, opening . . .

#*ish*$_1$ (forms adjectives from various sources) devilish, feverish, ticklish, yellowish, old-maidish, five-o'clockish . . .

#*less* (makes adjectives, mostly from nouns) bottomless, humorless, penniless, regardless, relentless . . .

#*ling* (rare; makes nouns from nouns and verbs) changeling, fledgeling, hireling, underling . . .

#*ly*$_1$ (makes adjectives, mostly from nouns) cowardly, friendly, neighborly, slovenly, westerly . . .

#*ly*$_2$ (makes adverbs from adjectives) completely, joyfully, similarly, thoroughly, tremendously . . . Note that *daily*, *weekly*, *monthly*, *yearly* are both adjective and adverb.

#*ness* (makes abstract nouns from adjectives) consciousness, exactness, heartiness, preparedness, thoroughness . . .

#*ship* (makes abstract nouns from adjectives and nouns) censorship, partnership, scholarship . . .

#*some* (makes adjectives from various sources) burdensome, cumbersome, quarrelsome, venturesome . . .

#*wise* (makes adverbs from various sources) (counter)clockwise, crosswise, lengthwise . . .

#*th*$_1$ (rare; makes abstract nouns from adjectives and one verb; note vowel change in most words) breadth, depth, growth, length, width, strength . . .

#*th*$_2$ ≈ *eth* (forms ordinal numbers) seventh, tenth, twentieth. (Note vowel and consonant change in *fifth*.)

#*y*$_1$ (makes adjectives, mostly from nouns) feathery, hungry, silky, (un)wieldy . . . Note vowel deletion in *angry*, *hungry*.

#*y*$_2$ (rare; forms nouns, mostly from other nouns) ministry, smithy . . .

#*y*$_3$ (alternating in spelling with *ie*, forms diminutives) cookie, dolly, kitty, mommy . . .

(Note that when *-ly* is added to adjectives of more than one syllable which end in /l/, such as *careful*, *partial*, only one /l/ is pronounced. There may be two /l/'s pronounced in such words as *coolly*, *fully*, *solely*, *wholly*.

The words *able*, *gentle*, *humble*, *noble*, *simple* have two syllables each. When the adverbial suffix #*ly*$_2$ is added to one of them, it still has two syllables and one /l/.

When #*ly*$_2$ is added to words which end in #*ed* or #*ness*, such as *alleged*, *confused*, *marked*, there is a vowel insertion before /d/:

/əˈlɛǰɨdli ð kənˈfjuuzɨdlið ˈmarkɨdnis/.)

II.2 Tonic endings

A tonic ending is always stressed (chapter 11). As was also indicated in that chapter, there has been a tendency in the history of the English language for stress to move forward, mostly from the ult to the antepenult. Numerous words which originally had tonic endings are now stressed on the antepenult. We find the same tendency at work today, so that some of the words listed below may be stressed – sometimes and by some people – on the antepenult instead of the ult.

+*aire* (in nouns and adjectives) debonaire, doctrinaire, concessionaire, millionaire, questionnaire
+*ee* (pronounced /ii/; productive now in formation of new nouns) absentee, endorsee, internee, licensee, nominee, refugee
-*e*(*e*), -*et* (pronounced /ei/; in various words) ballet, bouquet, café, crochet, matinée, negligée, valet [In British English these have stress on the initial syllable.]
+*eer*, +*ier* (nouns which indicate persons) auctioneer, conventioneer, engineer, mountaineer; bombardier, grenadier
+*esce* (in a small group of verbs) acquiesce, coalesce, convalesce, effervesce, rejuvenesce [Perhaps the verb *reminisce* might be included here.]
+*ese* (nouns and adjectives of nationality) Burmese, Congolese, Japanese, Senegalese, Sudanese, Vietnamese
+*esque* (in certain adjectives) grotesque, picturesque, Romanesque
+*ette* (in nouns, originally with a meaning of diminutive) basinette, brunette, kitchenette, marionette
-*eur*, -*euse* (in nouns denoting people) chauffeur, connoisseur, masseuse, raconteur, chanteuse
-*ique* (in a few nouns and adjectives) antique, critique, oblique, physique, technique, unique
-*oon* (in nouns) baboon, balloon, cartoon, cocoon, harpoon, lagoon

II.3 Strong endings

What we call a strong ending here is a single syllable with a free vowel. Some of the endings listed here might qualify as suffixes, at least in some of the words in which they occur, in which case they might be so designated with a + preceding, but they are all marked here with a hyphen. If a word with a strong ending has three or more syllables, the main stress is on the antepenult. Two-syllable verbs and adjectives have stress on the ult, while two-syllable nouns have stress on the penult.

Here are nine typical strong endings, with examples in this order: (a) words of three or more syllables; (b) two-syllable verbs and adjectives; (c) two-syllable nouns.

-*ane* (a) cellophane, hurricane; (b) germane, inane, mundane; (c) membrane, methane, propane
-*ene* (a) acetylene, ethylene, kerosene; (b) obscene, serene; (c) benzene, hygiene, phosgene
-*ide* (a) cyanide, sulfanilamide; (b) provide, divide; (c) bromide, chloride, oxide
-*ine* (a) alkaline, aquiline, asinine, concubine, porcupine; (b) divine; (c) carbine, quinine, strychnine, turbine

The adjective *alpine* is exceptionally stressed on the initial syllable; such words as *bovine*, *canine*, *equine*, *feline*, which function as nouns and adjectives, are stressed like nouns.

-*ite* (a) anthracite, appetite, dynamite, erudite, extradite, parasite, satellite; (b) contrite, ignite, polite, unite; (c) calcite, graphite, lignite, quartzite, termite

Exceptions: The nouns *stalactite* and *stalagmite* may be stressed on the penult or on the antepenult; the same is true for the adjective *recondite*.

Note the adjective ˈ*finite*. In 3-syllable adjectives like *definite*, *infinite* the ult is not strong.

-*oid* (a) adenoid, alkaloid, asteroid, anthropoid, trapezoid; (b) — ; (c) deltoid, mastoid, rhomboid, typhoid, spheroid
-*ose* (a) bellicose, comatose, grandiose, diagnose, varicose; (b) jocose, morose; (c) dextrose, glucose, lactose, sucrose
-*ule* (a) miniscule, molecule, ridicule, vestibule; (b) — ; (c) capsule, globule, module, ovule, schedule
-*ute* (a) constitute, destitute, dissolute, institute, persecute; (b) acute, astute, dilute, pollute, salute; (c) statute, tribute

Exceptions: The verbs *atˈtribute* and *conˈtribute* are stressed on the penult. The adjectives *absolute* and *resolute* vary; stress may be on the antepenult or on the ult.

In addition to these nine endings there are other, less well defined words with a free vowel in the ult. Here are some random examples:

(a) anecdote, exercise, formaldehyde, hypotenuse
(b) amuse, anoint, cajole, extreme, obey, supreme, sublime
(c) alcove, athlete

II.4 Weak endings

In almost all cases these 'endings' can be called suffixes. Each is a single syllable with a checked vowel and occurs in nouns and adjectives. Stress is on the penult if the penult is heavy or the first syllable of the word, and otherwise on the antepenult. Ten of these suffixes are listed below (we call +*ant* and +*ent* one suffix and +*ance* and +*ence* one suffix).

+*a* (in numerous nouns) delta, lava, mimosa, placenta; opera, taffeta

+al_2 (in adjectives) fatal, tribal, anecdotal, eternal, oriental, universal; criminal, general, radical

+*ar* (a variant of +*al* occurring after bases which have an /l/) lunar, polar, stellar; perpendicular, similar, triangular

+*ant*/+*ent* (adjectives and some nouns) dormant, prudent, silent, vacant, adherent, defiant, resistant; evident, permanent, vigilant

+*ance*/+*ence* (nouns, many of them corresponding to adjectives with +*ant*/*ent*) balance, hindrance, prudence, sentence, contrivance, interference; extravagance, reverence

+*is* (in abstract nouns of Greek origin) crisis, thesis, catharsis, hypnosis, synopsis; emphasis, genesis, metropolis

+*on* (in certain nouns of Greek origin or made up by modern scientists from Greek and other elements). This is actually two different suffixes, one pronounced /ən/, the other /ɒn/, with variation among speakers as to the pronunciation in specific words. In general, these are pronounced with /ən/:

colon, mammon, cotyledon, horizon, rhododendron; phenomenon, skeleton

The following are pronounced with /ɒn/:

neutron, nylon, proton, electron; automaton, cyclotron, silicon

+*ous* (an adjective suffix) callous, pompous, desirous, disastrous, stupendous; onerous, magnanimous, preposterous
In *hazardous* the suffix is neutral, added to a free word *hazard*.

+*um* (in nouns of Latin origin) album, fulcrum, quorum, decorum, memorandum; curriculum, platinum

+*us* (in nouns of Latin origin, or where a Latin ending has replaced an original Greek ending) circus, focus, alumnus, papyrus; abacus, phosphorus

In addition, there are endings which cannot properly be called suffixes. Three groups can be recognized:

-an, *-en*, *-ine* pronounced /in/ or /ɨn/
-ace, *-ice*, *-ise* pronounced /is/ or /ɨs/
-it, *-ite* pronounced /it/ or /ɨt/

Examples with initial syllable or strong penult preceding:

menace, premise, promise; affidavit, intestine

Examples with weak penult preceding:

cardigan, citizen, deficit, gelatin, javelin, nitrogen,
oxygen, pelican, precipice, puritan, specimen, veteran

The penult is strong if it ends in a consonant, as in *agenda*, *alumnus*, *amalgam*, or has a free vowel. Of course the spelling of the word indicates that there are two consonants, and so we know by looking that the penult is heavy and is stressed. On the other hand, our spelling does not indicate whether the penult vowel is free, and therefore stressed, or checked, and therefore not stressed. Compare these two groups of words:

(a) angina, arena, aroma, diploma, emphysema, empyema, glaucoma, idea, Korea, mimosa, sonata
(b) camera, cholera, cinema, cupola, formula, malaria, nebula, opera, spatula, tempera, uvula

It would be good if our orthography indicated when a vowel letter stands for a 'long' or 'free' vowel and when it stands for a 'short' or 'checked' vowel. As we saw in chapter 14, there are some clues derived from redundancy; only free vowels occur in certain positions and only checked vowels in certain other positions. However, in an open penult either a free or a checked vowel may occur, as in the examples above, and our spelling does not indicate the difference. Note that the letter *e* is especially ambiguous, as the following two sets of words show:

idea, panacea	cornea, nausea
museum	cameo, stereo, nucleus
emphysema, empyema	cinema, enema
European	Caesarean

It may be helpful to look at some more words which have a weak penult. Note that the vowel letter is *e*, *i*, *o*, or *u* but seldom *a*.

-e- ˈcerebral, ˈcompetent, ˈcovetous, ˈfederal, ˈintegral, iˈtinerant, ˈliberal, peˈripheral, pheˈnomenal, ˈtolerant
-i- abˈdominal, ˈabstinence, ˈdecimal, ˈdominant, ˈeminent, exˈorbitant, inˈheritance, inˈtelligent, ˈlubricant, ˈmadrigal, ˈmedical, ˈmilitant, ˈnegligent, parˈticipant, ˈpestilence, ˈprincipal, pyˈramidal, ˈradical
-o- diˈagonal, ˈeloquence, ˈignorant, ˈresonance
-u- ˈambulance, ˈcasual, ˈcenˈtrifugal, conˈstituent, haˈbitual, ˈopulent, ˈpetulant, ˈrapturous, ˈstimulant, ˈturbulence, ˈvirtuous

II.5 Post-tonic suffixes

It is helpful to recognize certain suffixes, few in number but frequent in occurrence, which always follow the stressed syllable of the word in which they occur. Three of them are one syllable long: +*ic*, +*id*, +*ish*$_2$; others are two syllables long with a weak penult: +*ify*, +*itude*, +*ity*; and one of them, +*ion*, may be considered two syllables in the underlying form with loss of the first vowel through palatalization.

+*ic* (forming adjectives, some of which are also nouns) academic, automatic, barbaric, dynamic, economic, periodic . . .
Exceptions: ˈ*Arabic*, ˈ*catholic*, ˈ*lunatic*, ˈ*politic*; also compare the nouns *aˈrithmetic*, ˈ*heretic*, ˈ*rhetoric* with the adjectives *arithˈmetic*, *heˈretic*(*al*), *rheˈtoric*(*al*)
+*ics* (in nouns which designate fields of study) acoustics, ballistics, calisthenics, economics, semantics . . .
Exception: ˈ*politics*
+*id* (in certain adjectives, some of which are also nouns) acid, arid, candid, insipid, intrepid, lucid, timid, vivid . . .
Note: Compare the noun ˈ*invalid* and the adjective *inˈvalid*.
+*ify*/*efy* (in a large group of verbs) amplify, diversify, exemplify, identify, liquefy, personify . . .
+*ion* (in thousands of abstract nouns) adoption, communion, intention, opinion, solution, simplification, volition . . .
+*ish*$_2$ (in a small number of verbs) abolish, astonish, demolish, diminish, extinguish, relinquish, replenish, vanish . . .
Exception: *imˈpoverish*
+*itude* (in certain abstract nouns) altitude, exactitude, fortitude, longitude, solicitude, vicissitude . . .
+*ity*/*ety* (in a large number of abstract nouns) absurdity, complexity, continuity, humidity, notoriety, society . . .

(There is often more than one way of classifying and labeling. Instead of calling +*ify*/*efy* and +*itude* posttonic suffixes, we could just as well say that +*fy* and +*tude* are strong endings. The effect would be the same.)

II.6 Some special suffixes

There are some suffixes of high frequency which cannot be categorized in any simple way. They are treated in this section.

#able, *+able* This adjective suffix is neutral in many words: acceptable, breakable, (in)excusable, foreseeable, impressionable, regrettable.

In all formations like these *#able* is added to an existing independent word. When not added to an independent word, it is like a weak suffix. Stress is on the preceding syllable if that syllable is strong or initial.

delectable; affable capable durable liable

If the preceding syllable is weak and not initial, stress is on the next syllable to the left:

abominable amiable charitable (in)habitable memorable
navigable reputable (in)separable venerable

The next group of words vary. They may be stressed on the first syllable or the second syllable of the base word.

(in)applicable despicable (in)hospitable

In some other words the suffix may act as a neutral suffix or as a weak suffix:

(in)com'par#able	(in)'compar+able
pre'fer#able	'prefer+able
re'pair#able	(ir)'repar+able
(ir)re'voke#able	(ir)'revoc+able

Notice that the word *admirable* is not what it would seem. It is not **ad'mir#able* but instead it has a weak suffix: *'admir+able*.

+ible is best considered a weak syllable. In a few cases it is added to an independent word (for example, *convertible*, *repressible*), but mostly it appears in words where the base is not an independent word. Then stress is on the preceding syllable if that syllable is strong or word-initial:

edible (in)defensible

If the preceding syllable is weak and not initial, stress is one syllable to the left:

(in)eligible negligible

#*age*, +*age* Although spelling does not differentiate, there are two different noun endings. One is a neutral suffix pronounced /-ɪǰ/:

acreage bondage mileage percentage . . .

The other ending, pronounced /-aʒ/ or /aǰ/, is a tonic ending in two-syllable nouns:

barrage corsage massage . . .

and a strong ending in words of three syllables:

camouflage fuselage sabotage

The word *espionage* shows a regular, though uncommon, phenomenon: if the antepenultimate vowel is itself followed immediately by a vowel, stress is on the preantepenult.

+*ate*, is a frequent suffix in verbs, where it is pronounced /eit/, in adjectives, where it is pronounced /ət/, and in nouns, where the pronunciation is usually /ət/.

In *create* and *equate* the stress is on the ult. In other two-syllable verbs, like those below, stress may be on the first or the second syllable.

collate cremate dictate migrate narrate vibrate . . .

(Of course, this does not apply to verbs like *debate* and *inflate*, where -*ate* is part of the base, not a suffix. Verbs of more than two syllables which have this ending (there are more than 1000 of them) are stressed on the antepenult:

ˈdesignate ˈelevate ˈhibernate inˈterrogate perˈpetuate . . .

There are a handful of exceptions.

Stress on the preantepenult:

deˈteriorate ˈoxygenate ˈperegrinate

Stress on the penult or antepenult:

eructate impregnate infiltrate remonstrate

Nouns and adjectives of more than two syllables are likewise stressed on the antepenult. The following are exceptionally stressed on the penult:

ap'pellate a'postate in'carnate in'sensate in'testate

+*ive* This frequent adjective suffix appears in words with four different stress patterns. Except for the word *conducive* it is always preceded by *t* or *s*. These are the four patterns:

(1) 'x + ive

(2) x 'x + ive

(3) (x) 'x {a, e, i, u} t + ive

(4) . . . 'x x-at- + ive

The first pattern is, of course, what occurs when the suffix is preceded by a single syllable:

'active 'captive 'cursive 'massive 'missive . . .

Pattern (2) is usual when the suffix is preceded by a prefix and a one-syllable base:

col'lective de'cisive ex'pansive of'fensive per'missive . . .

Pattern (3) occurs when *at*, *et*, *it*, or *ut* follows a single syllable:

'additive 'lucrative 'negative 'relative
'positive 'sedative 'talkative 'tentative . . .

It is also the pattern when there is a prefix and a one-syllable base before *at*, *it*, or *ut*:

ac'cusative con'servative con'secutive di'minutive e'vocative
in'formative pro'hibitive . . .

Pattern (4) is found when *at* follows a base of more than one syllable. There are two sub-patterns. In one of them the syllable with *a* is weak and the ult is strong:

ˈgenerative iˈnitiative ˈnominative ˈoperative

In the other sub-pattern the syllable with *a* is strong and the ult is weak:

ˈimitative ˈlegislative ˈmeditative

This sub-pattern is restricted to North America, *imitative* and the like being identical in stress with *generative* in Britain and in the southern hemisphere. Even in North America a number of words vary between the two sub-patterns:

adˈministrative comˈmunicative ˈdecorative
iˈmaginative reˈmunerative

Finally, note the variation between pattern (3) *conˈtemplative* and pattern (4) *ˈcontemplative* and between *exˈpletive* (British English) and *ˈexpletive* (American English).

+*or* This is actually three different endings. One, which is spelled *-our* in British English, occurs in a number of abstract nouns, always with stress on the preceding syllable:

ardor behavior candor color demeanor favor fervor . . .

A second ending, more properly described as *-ior*, is found in words derived from Latin comparative adjectives. Stress is on the syllable preceding the suffix:

anterior exterior inferior interior junior senior superior

The third *or* ending is always preceded by *t* or *s*. Nouns with this ending designate actors or instruments. There are several stress patterns.

ˈx-or when a single syllable precedes:

actor censor doctor

x ˈx -or when there is a prefix and a one-syllable base:

aggressor collector conductor detector inventor incisor . . .

(x) ˈx it-or, *(x) ˈx ut-or* when the *-or* is preceded by *it* or *ut*:

auditor contributor editor exhibitor executor monitor solicitor . . .

Notice that in a number of these nouns *or* is like a neutral suffix added to an existing verb (contribute, edit, exhibit).

When a noun ends in *-ator*, the *or* is almost always a neutral suffix added to a verb that ends in *+ate*. Therefore the penult is strong and the stress is on the preantepenult of the word:

ˈagitator ˈelevator ˈillustrator ˈpercolator . . .

Note, in contrast, the noun *conˈspirator* from the verb *conˈspire*.

As noted above, two-syllable verbs like *dictate*, *narrate*, *spectate*, *translate* are commonly stressed on the second syllable in British English but the first syllable in American English. This means that the corresponding nouns, *dictator*, *narrator*, *spectator*, *translator*, and so on are stressed on the second syllable in British but the first syllable in American English.

+ure This ending also occurs after *t* or *s*. There are several patterns, very similar to the pattern for *+ive* and *+or*.

ˈx-ure This is the pattern for words of two syllables:

capture censure lecture pressure sculpture . . .

x ˈx-ure The pattern of prefix plus one-syllable base:

composure departure erasure exposure indenture . . .

ˈx-at-ure, *ˈx-it-ure* The first syllable is not a prefix:

armature curvature furniture ligature signature . . .

xˈx-it-ure The first syllable is a prefix:

expenditure investiture . . .

ˈx x ature Only six words; in four of them the penult is weak:

caricature literature miniature temperature;

in one word the penult is strong:

legislature

and one varies:

ˈnomenclature (American English, with strong penult),
noˈmenclature (British English, with weak penult).

Notes

Notes for Chapter 1

The distinction between users and uses of a language seems to have been first drawn by Halliday, McIntosh, and Strevens 1964.

Standard histories of the English language in Britain include Jespersen 1909–49 and Pyles 1971. At the present time there is no comprehensive study of what may be called World English; the closest approximations are anthologies such as Bailey and Görlach 1982 and Kachru 1982, which include sketches of the status of the language in countries where it has official, commercial, and/or educational use but it is not the native language of the general population, as well as descriptions of the English of the British Isles, Canada, the United States, the Caribbean, Australia, New Zealand, and South Africa. The pronunciation of English in native-speaker areas is the subject of Wells 1982.

The role of gestures, stance, and appearance in communication ('body language') has been the topic of various popular works and some serious studies; an example of the latter is Knapp 1972. The nature of non-verbal, vocal elements in communication (paralanguage) was explored in Trager 1949 and, more ambitiously, in Crystal and Quirk 1964.

For further description of dialect differences, regional and social, registers, and ways of studying them see Fasold 1984, Trudgill 1984.

Hockett 1958 is a good introduction to the study of linguistics in a structuralist approach. Lyons 1968 has a more general approach. Makkai 1972 is an annotated anthology of articles showing the development of phonological theory in various schools. Sommerstein 1977 is a good survey of phonology. The seminal work in English phonology in a generative framework is Chomsky and Halle 1968.

The terminology of linguistics, like that of any discipline, can be bewildering to the beginner. A good dictionary of terms is Crystal 1985.

The definition of *discourse* given on p. 6 is from Halliday and Hasan 1976: 3.

On children's acquisition of the suffixes which indicate plural number see Berko 1958.

The terms 'Standard British English' and 'Received Pronunciation' are not exactly identical. Dictionary-makers and grammarians of the eighteenth and later centuries, such as Johnson 1755, Lowth 1762, are responsible for the establishment of a standard, which, by and large, has been accepted as the 'correct' form of written English in Britain and, with various modifications, throughout the English-speaking world. 'Received Pronunciation' refers to the way of speaking of the educated upper middle class in Britain. The term, and the description of this speech, came into existence in the early years of the present century with the development of a science of phonetics.

Notes for Chapter 2

The study of sound is well-established. For a more technical approach, see Lieberman 1977. For further discussion of speech production Pike 1943 and O'Connor 1973 can be recommended.

The features introduced here, and in chapter 3, are taken from Chomsky and Halle 1968.

Jakobson 1941 is a pioneering work, still valuable, in explaining how infants acquire the sound system of the language of the community into which they are born. Lenneberg 1967 is likewise a pioneer statement that language acquisition is biologically determined to a large extent, something that a child does at the appropriate stage of maturation, much as it learns to sit up, to crawl, to walk, etc. when it is ready to do so. Clark and Clark 1977 and Dale 1976 contain good accounts of the language acquisition process.

Notes for Chapter 3

Features used here are, with one exception, those which were introduced in Chomsky and Halle 1968 and which are widely accepted. The exception is the feature [sibilant], which ought to be justified on both phonetic and phonological grounds. The phonetic realizations of the phonemes /s z ʃ ʒ č ǰ/ are all articulated with a groove along the centerline of the tongue, a tongue shape not used for any other articulation in English. Phonologically these consonants form a natural class: regular nouns ending with these consonants form the plural number, for example, in the same way and differently from other nouns – see chapter 8.

Notes for Chapter 4

The three kinds of difference in phonological systems of the dialects of a single language – inventory, incidence, and phonetic realization – were first sketched by Troubetzkoy (1939).

The use of key words to designate the vowels of English derives from Wells 1982. Wells should also be consulted for more detailed descriptions than are given here, in section 4.4, of the actual phonetic realizations of vowel phonemes in the different varieties of English.

Notes for Chapter 5

The literature dealing with the syllable in (English) phonology is extensive but was produced within a relatively short period of time. The following are cited: Bailey 1968,

1978, 1980; Bell & Hooper 1978a, 1978b; Fallows 1981; Hoard 1971; Malmberg 1955; O'Connor & Trim 1953; Pulgram 1970; Rudes 1977; Vennemann 1972.

Notes for Chapter 6

Reference to other writings does not seem necessary here because readers may well feel that this chapter provides more information than they wanted to have. These works have been especially helpful in detailing allophonic variation: Jones 1976; Kurath 1967; Hubbell 1950.

On a nasalized vowel as the representation of vowel plus nasal consonant, see Malécot 1960.

Notes for Chapter 7

Gimson 1980 contains a similar account of the clusters of consonants which occur in word-initial, -medial, and -final positions. A rather different approach is that of Trnka 1935, which examines the sequences that exist for each phoneme in combination with every other phoneme that may follow it or precede it.

Notes for Chapter 8

Descriptions of English pronunciation which avoided the recognition of the syllable as a unit of phonology, such as Trager and Smith 1951 and Hockett 1958, attempted to account for such differences as *night rate* and *nitrate* as a difference in translation between phonemes. Thus *night rate* was said to have open transition (or 'plus juncture') between /t/ and /r/ while *nitrate* has closed transition (or lack of 'plus juncture') between the two phonemes.

Notes for Chapter 9

The terms *tone unit*, *tonality*, *tone*, and *tonicity*, as used here were introduced by Halliday 1967 and 1970, as well as the concept of marked and unmarked focus. Halliday uses the term *tonic syllable* for what is here called the accented syllable. Certain scholars, notably Brown, Currie, and Kenworthy 1980, Currie 1980 and 1981, have questioned the assumption that a tone unit contains only one accented syllable. Currie, on the basis of empirical studies with a number of subjects, claims that subjects do agree in identifying the accented word but only when it is marked – is not at the end of a tone unit. Here highest pitch, maximum change of pitch, and greatest intensity co-occur on the accented syllable. But when the accented syllable occurs in the last lexical item of the tone unit – supposedly unmarked focus – there is likely to be more than one syllable with maximum prominence.

The use of the terms *paradigmatic* and *syntagmatic* to describe purposes of marked accent first appeared in Kreidler 1984. What is here called 'paradigmatic' is called 'contrastive' by some authors, e.g. Bolinger 1961a and Bing 1983. My reason for preferring 'paradigmatic' can best be explained through examples like the following:

Did ˈJohn ˈleave at ˈ**noon**?
I ˈdon't ˈknow ˈ**when** he ˈleft.

Does ˈ**Mary** ˈknow about ˈthis?
ˈ**E**verybody's been ˈtold.

When is not in contrast with *at noon*, nor *everybody* with *Mary*. The two words have special functions with regard to their syntacto-semantic classes, the first as interrogative-relative, the second to express totality.

The examples 'I thought it would **rain** today' and 'I **thought** it would rain today' are taken from Crystal 1969: 265.

The description of de-accenting and its role in discourse cohesion owes much to Halliday and Hasan 1976 and to Ladd 1980. These are highly recommended to the reader, as is Couper-Kuhlen 1986 for a general survey of prosodic elements in English. Coulthard 1977 contains a chapter which deals with the uses of prosody in discourse structure.

In any discourse what is 'old (or given) information' versus 'new information' is indicated by syntactic and lexical devices as well as prosodic ones. The topic is treated from various points of view by Allerton 1978; Chafe 1976; Daneš 1960; Gunter 1974.

Notes for Chapter 10

Descriptions of English intonation contours differ considerably from one another in mode of description and in details of what is described, and yet there is a commonality in what is described. The following must be cited: Bing 1980; Bolinger 1983, 1986; Brown, Currie, and Kenworthy 1980; Couper-Kuhlen 1986; Crystal 1969; Glenn 1976; Halliday 1967; Kingdon 1958b; Ladd 1980; Leben 1976; Lehiste 1970; O'Connor and Arnold 1973; Pierrehumbert 1987; Pike 1945.

For the work of the 'Dutch School' see Willems 1982 and the bibliography cited there.

On the perception and acquisition of tone see Gandour 1978 and Li and Thompson 1978.

Notes for Chapters 11 and 12

The fact that stress is regular in certain groups of English words was stated as early as Walker 1791. The 'rules' presented here are essentially those of Chomsky and Halle 1968, a work which led to further explorations of stress placement, as in the following: Fudge 1984; Goyvaerts and Pullum 1975; Halle and Keyser 1971; Halle 1973; Halle and Vergnaud 1987; Poldauf 1984; Ross 1972; Schane 1975, 1979, 1981. Earlier discussions of stress are: Arnold 1957; Newman 1946. Pedagogical treatments of stress placement are: Dickerson 1975; Guierre 1984.

A different way of accounting for stress is that of Liberman and Prince 1977.

The perception of stress is sometimes explained as the motor theory of speech perception. See Lane 1965 for discussion.

Notes for Chapter 13

The description of colloquial speech processes presented here is intentionally quite conservative. The difference between formal speech and what occurs in casual exchanges can be quite great. For a description of very casual speech see Lee and Howard 1974. Foreign learners of English are not easily persuaded that the language has variety of this sort, and some native speakers are inclined to doubt the validity, or even the existence, of casual speech forms. Palmer and Blandford 1976, originally appearing in the 1920s, is as good a statement of these occurrences as any.

Notes for Chapter 14

The rules presented are essentially derived from Chomsky and Halle 1968. The examples of vowel alternation in section 14.11 are drawn largely from Lightner 1972. On the relationship between spelling and pronunciation see Dickerson 1978; Friederich 1967; Venezky 1970; Wijk 1966.

The terms *palatalization* and *velar softening* are intended to be merely labels. To call the consonants /t d s z/ 'dentals' and /č ǰ ʃ ʒ/ 'palatals' is traditional but not realistic inasmuch as both series are articulated on the alveolar ridge, the former with the tongue-tip, the latter with the tongue-front. The term 'velar softening' derives from the habit of referring to /s/ and /j/ as the 'soft' values of the letters C and G, respectively, and /k/ and /g/ as their respective 'hard' values.

Bibliography

Allerton, D. J. 1978. The notion of 'givenness' and its relation to presupposition and to theme. *Lingua*, 34:1–29.

Anderson, J. M. and Jones, C. 1974. Three theses concerning phonological representations. *Journal of Linguistics*, 10:1–26.

Anderson, Stephen R. 1974. *The Organization of Phonology*. New York: Seminar Press.

Arnold, G. F. 1957. Stress in English words. *Lingua*, 6:221–67.

Bailey, Charles-James N. 1968. Dialectal differences in the syllabication of non-nasal sonorants in American English. *General Linguistics*, 8:79–91.

— 1973. *Variation and Linguistic Theory*. Arlington, VA: Center for Applied Linguistics.

— 1978. *Gradience in English Syllabication and a Revised Concept of Unmarked Syllabization*. Bloomington, IN: Indiana University Linguistics Club.

— 1980. Evidence for variable syllable boundaries in English. In Waugh, L. R. and Schooneveld, C. H. (eds). *The Melody of Language*. Baltimore: University Park Press, 25–39.

Bailey, Richard W. and Görlach, Manfred (eds) 1982. *English as a World Language*. Ann Arbor: University of Michigan Press.

Bailey, Richard W. and Robinson, Jay L. (eds) 1973. *Varieties of Present-Day English*. New York: Macmillan.

Bell, Alan and Hooper, Joan Bybee (eds) 1978a. *Syllables and Segments*. Amsterdam: North Holland.

— 1978b. Issues and evidence in syllabic phonology. In: Bell and Hooper 1978a: 3–22.

Berger, Marshall D. 1968. Accent, pattern, and dialect in North American English. *Word*, 24:55–61.

Berko, Jean. 1958. The child's learning of English morphology. *Word*, 14:150–77.

Bing, Janet M. 1980. *Aspects of English Prosody*. Bloomington, IN: Indiana University Linguistics Club.

— 1983. Contrastive stress, contrastive intonation and contrastive meaning. *Journal of Semantics*, 2:141–56.

Bloch, Bernard and Trager, George L. 1942. *Outline of Linguistic Analysis*. Baltimore: Waverly Press.

Bloomfield, Leonard. 1933. *Language*. New York: Holt.

— 1935. The stressed vowels of American English. *Language*, 11:97–116.

Bolinger, Dwight L. 1958. A theory of word accent in English. *Word*, 14:109–48.
— 1961a. Contrastive accent and contrastive stress. *Language*, 37:83–96.
— 1961b. *Generality, Gradience and the All-or-none*. The Hague: Mouton.
— 1983. Where does intonation begin? *Journal of Semantics*, 2:101–20.
— 1986. *Intonation and its Parts: Melody in Spoken English*. Stanford, CA: Stanford University Press.
Brazil, David, Coulthard, Malcolm, and Johns, Catherine. 1980. *Discourse, Intonation and Language Teaching*. London: Longman.
Bronstein, A. J. 1960. *The Pronunciation of American English*. Englewood Cliffs, NJ: Prentice-Hall.
Brown, Gillian, Currie, Karen L., and Kenworthy, Joanne. 1980. *Questions of Intonation*. Baltimore: University Park Press.
Bruck, A., Fox, R. A., and LaGaly, M. W. 1974. *Papers from the Parasession on Natural Phonology, April 18, 1974*. Chicago: Chicago Linguistic Society.
Chafe, Wallace L. 1976. Givenness, contrastiveness, definiteness, subjects, topics and points of view. In Li, Charles N. (ed.). *Subject and Topic*. New York: Academic Press, 25–55.
Chomsky, Noam. 1971. Deep structure, surface structure, and semantic interpretation. In Steinberg, D. D., and Jakobovits, L. A. (eds). *Semantics*. Cambridge: Cambridge University Press, 183–216.
Chomsky, Noam, and Halle, Morris. 1968. *The Sound Pattern of English*. New York: Harper and Row.
Clark, Herbert H. and Clark, Eve V. 1977. *Psychology and Language: An Introduction to Psycholinguistics*. New York: Harcourt Brace Jovanovich.
Clements, George N. and Keyser, Samuel Jay. 1983. *CV Phonology: A Generative Theory of the Syllable*. Cambridge, MA: MIT Press.
Coulthard, Malcolm. 1977. *An Introduction to Discourse Analysis*. London: Longmans.
Couper-Kuhlen, Elizabeth. 1986. *An Introduction to English Prosody*. London: Edward Arnold.
Crystal, David A. 1969. *Prosodic Systems and Intonation in English*. Cambridge: Cambridge University Press.
— 1985. *A Dictionary of Linguistics and Phonetics*. Oxford: Blackwell.
Crystal, David and Quirk, Randolph. 1964. *Systems of Prosodic and Paralinguistic Features in English*. The Hague: Mouton.
Currie, Karen L. 1980. An initial 'search for tonics'. *Language and Speech*, 23:329–46.
— 1981. Further experiments in the 'search for tonics'. *Language and Speech*, 24:1–28.
Dale, P. S. 1976. *Language Development*, 2nd edn. New York: Holt, Rinehart and Winston.
Daneš, Frantisek. 1960. Sentence intonation from a functional point of view. *Word*, 16:34–54.
Delattre, Pierre. 1963. Comparing the prosodic features of English, German, Spanish, and French. *International Review of Applied Linguistics*, 1:193–210.
Denes, Peter and Pinson, E. N. 1968. *The Speech Chain*. New York: Harper and Row.
Dickerson, Wayne. 1975. Predicting word stress: Generative rules in an ESL context. *TESL Studies*, 1:38–52.

— 1978. English orthography: A guide to word stress and vowel quality. *International Review of Applied Linguistics*, 16:

Dillard, Joey L. 1972. *Black English: Its History and Usage in the United States*. New York: Random House.

Fallows, Deborah. 1981. Experimental evidence for English syllabilification and syllable structure. *Journal of Linguistics*, 17:309–17.

Fasold, Ralph W. 1984. *The Sociolinguistics of Society*. Oxford: Blackwell.

Francis, W. Nelson. 1958. *The Structure of American English*. New York: Ronald Press.

Friederich, Wolf. 1967. *Englische Aussprachelehre*. Munich: Max Huebner Verlag.

Fries, Charles C. 1964. On the intonation of 'yes-no' questions in English. In Abercrombie, D. D. et al. (eds). *In Honour of Daniel Jones*. London: Longmans, 242–54.

Fromkin, Victoria A. (ed.). 1978. *Tone: A Linguistic Survey*. New York: Academic Press.

— and Rodman, Robert. 1983. *An Introduction to Language*. New York: CBS Publishing, Holt, Rinehart and Winston.

Fudge, Erik. 1975. English word stress: an examination of some basic assumptions. In Goyvaerts & Pullum 1975: 277–323.

— 1984. *English Word Stress*. London: Edward Arnold.

Gandour, Jackson T. 1978. The perception of tone. In Fromkin 1978: 41–76.

Gimson, A. C. 1980. *An Introduction to the Pronunciation of English*, 3rd edn. London: Edward Arnold/New York: St. Martin's Press.

Glenn, Marilyn. 1976. *Pragmatic Functions of Intonation*. PhD Dissertation, Georgetown University.

Goyvaerts, D. L. and Pullum, G. K. (eds). 1975. *Essays on the Sound Pattern of English*. Ghent: Story-Scientia.

Guierre, Lionel. 1984. *Drills in English Stress Patterns*. Paris: Armand Colin – Longman.

Gunter, Richard. 1974. *Sentences in Dialog*. Charleston, SC: Hornbeam Press.

Halle, Morris. 1973. Stress rules in English: A new version. *Linguistic Inquiry*, 4: 451–64.

Halle, Morris and Clements, George N. 1982. *Problem Book in Phonology: A Workbook for Introductory Courses in Linguistics and in Modern Phonology*. Cambridge, MA: MIT Press.

Halle, Morris and Keyser, Samuel Jay. 1971. *English Stress: Its Form, its Growth, and its Role in Verse*. New York: Harper and Row.

Halle, Morris and Mohanan, K. P. 1985. Segmental phonology of modern English. *Linguistic Inquiry*, 16: 57–116.

Halle, Morris and Vergnaud, Roger. 1987. *An Essay on Stress*. Cambridge, MA: MIT Press.

Halliday, M. A. K. 1961. Categories of the theory of grammar. *Word*, 17:241–92.

— 1967. *Intonation and Grammar in British English*. The Hague: Mouton.

— 1970. *A Course in Spoken English: Intonation*. London: Oxford University Press.

Halliday, M. A. K. and Hasan, Ruqaiya. 1976. *Cohesion in English*. London: Longmans.

Halliday, M. A. K., McIntosh, Angus, and Strevens, Peter. 1964. *The Linguistics Sciences and Language Teaching*. London: Longmans.

Hoard, J. E. 1971. Aspiration, tenseness, and syllabification in English. *Language*, 47:133–40.

Hockett, Charles F. 1955. *Manual of Phonology* (= International Journal of American Linguistics, Memoir 11).

— 1958. *A Course in Modern Linguistics*. New York: Macmillan.

Hooper, Joan. 1972. The syllable in phonological theory. *Language*, 48: 525–40.

Hubbell, Allen F. 1950. *The Pronunciation of English in New York City: Consonants and Vowels*. New York: Kings Crown Press.

Hyman, Larry. 1975. *Phonology: Theory and Analysis*. New York: Holt, Rinehart and Winston.

Jakobson, Roman. 1941. *Kindersprache, Aphasie und allgemeine Lautgesetze*. Uppsala: Universitetsarskrift 9. tr. Allan R. Keiler. *Child Language, Aphasia, and Phonological Universals*. The Hague: Mouton, 1968.

Jespersen, Jens Otto Harry. 1909–49. *A Modern English Grammar on Historical Principles*. Copenhaven: Ejnar Munksgaard.

Johnson, Samuel. 1755. *Dictionary of the English Language*. London: W. Strahan. Reprinted, New York: Arons Press, 1979.

Jones, Daniel. 1967. *Everyman's Pronouncing Dictionary, Containing over 58,000 Words in International Phonetic Transcription*, 13th edn, edited by A. C. Gimson. London: Dent.

— 1976. *An Outline of English Phonetics*, 9th edn. Cambridge: Cambridge University Press.

Kachru, Braj B. (ed.) 1982. *The Other Tongue: English across Cultures*. Champaign/Urbana: University of Illinois Press.

Kahn, Daniel. 1976. *Syllable-based Generalizations in English Phonology*. Bloomington, IN: Indiana University Linguistics Club.

Kenstowicz, M. and Kisseberth, C. 1979. *Generative Phonology: Description and Theory*. New York: Academic Press.

Kenyon, John S. 1958. *American Pronunciation*, 10th edn. Ann Arbor: George Wahr.

Kenyon, John S. and Knott, Thomas A. 1953. *A Pronouncing Dictionary of American English*. Springfield, MA: Merriam.

Kingdon, Roger, 1958a. *The Groundwork of English Stress*. London: Longman.

— 1958b. *The Groundwork of English Intonation*. London: Longman.

Knapp, Mark L. 1972. *Nonverbal Communication in Human Interaction*. New York: Holt, Rinehart and Winston.

Kreidler, Charles W. 1972a. English orthography: A generative approach. In Alatis, James E. (ed.). *Studies in Honor of Albert H. Marckwardt*. Washington: Teachers of English to Speakers of Other Languages, 81–91.

— 1972b. Teaching English spelling and pronunciation. *TESOL Quarterly*, 5:3–12.

— 1984. The uses of accent in English sentences. *SECOL Review*, 8:9–27.

Kurath, Hans. 1967. *A Phonology and Prosody of Modern English*. Ann Arbor: University of Michigan Press.

Kurath, Hans and McDavid, Raven I., Jr. 1961. *The Pronunciation of English in the Atlantic States*. Ann Arbor: University of Michigan Press.

Labov, William, 1966. *The Social Stratification of English in New York City*. Washington: Center for Applied Linguistics.

Ladd, D. Robert. 1980. *The Structure of Intonational Meaning*. Bloomington: Indiana University Press.

Ladefoged, Peter. 1962. *Elements of Acoustic Phonetics*. Chicago: University of Chicago Press.

— 1982. *A Course in Phonetics* 2nd edn. New York: Harcourt, Brace, Jovanovich.

Lane, Harlan L. 1965. The motor theory of speech perception: A critical review. *Psychological Review*, 72:275–309.

Lass, Roger. 1984. *Phonology: An Introduction to Basic Concepts*. Cambridge: Cambridge University Press.

Leben, William R. 1976. The tones in English intonation. *Linguistic Analysis*, 2:69–107.

Lee, Gregory and Howard, Irwin. 1974. Another mouthful of divinity fudge. In Bruck et al. 1974: 220–32.

Lehiste, Ilse. 1970. *Suprasegmentals*. Cambridge, MA: MIT Press.

Lenneberg, E. 1967. *Biological Foundations of Language*. New York: Wiley.

Li, Charles, N. and Thompson, Sandra A. 1978. The acquisition of tone. In Fromkin 1978: 271–84.

Liberman, Mark and Prince, Alan. 1977. On stress and linguistic rhythm. *Linguistic Inquiry*, 8:249–336.

Lieberman, Philip. 1977. *Speech Physiology and Acoustic Phonetics*. New York: Macmillan.

Lightner, T. M. 1972. *Problems in the Theory of Phonology, vol. 1*. Edmonton: Linguistic Research, Inc.

Lowth, Robert. 1762. *A Short Introduction to English Grammar*. London: A. Miller and R. and J. Dodsby. Facsimile reprint: Menston: Scolar Press, 1967.

Lyons, John. 1968. *Introduction to Theoretical Linguistics*. Cambridge: Cambridge University Press.

Makkai, Valerie Becker (ed.). 1972. *Phonological Theory: Evolution and Current Practice*. New York: Holt, Rinehart and Winston.

Malécot, André. 1960. Vowel nasality as a distinctive feature in American English. *Language*, 36:222–9.

Malmberg, Bertil. 1955. The phonetic basis for syllable division. In Lehiste, Ilse (ed.). *Readings in Acoustic Phonetics*. Cambridge, MA: MIT Press.

Newman, Stanley, S. 1946. On the stress system of English. *Word*, 2:171–87.

O'Connor, J. D. 1973. *Phonetics*. Harmondsworth: Penguin.

O'Connor, J. D. and Arnold, G. F. 1973. *Intonation of Colloquial English: A Practical Handbook* 2nd edn. London: Longman.

O'Connor, J. D. and Trim, J. L. M. 1953. Vowel, consonant, and syllable: A phonological definition. *Word*, 9:103–22.

Palmer, Harold and Blandford, F. G. 1976. *A Grammar of Spoken English*, 3rd edn. revised and rewritten by Roger Kingdon. Cambridge: Cambridge University Press.

Pierrehumbert, Janet Breckenridge. 1987. *The Phonology and Phonetics of English Intonation*. Bloomington, IN: Indiana University Linguistics Club.

Pike, Kenneth, L. 1943. *Phonetics: A Critical Analysis of Phonetic Theory and a Technique for Transcribing*. Ann Arbor: University of Michigan Press.

— 1945. *The Intonation of American English*. Ann Arbor: University of Michigan Press.

Poldauf, Ivan. 1984. *English Word Stress: A Theory of Word Stress in English*. Oxford: Pergamon.

Pulgram, Ernst. 1970. *Syllable, Word, Nexus, Cursus*. The Hague: Mouton.

Pyles, Thomas. 1971. *The Origins and Development of the English Language*, 2nd edn. New York: Harcourt Brace Jovanovich.

Quirk, Randolph, Greenbaum, Sidney, Leech, Geoffrey and Svartvik, Ian. 1972. *A Grammar of Contemporary English*. London: Longman.

Ross, John Robert. 1972. A reanalysis of English word stress. In Brame, M. K. (ed.). *Contributions to Generative Phonology*. Austin: University of Texas Press.

Rudes, Blair A. 1977. *Another Look at Syllable Structure*. Bloomington, IN: Indiana University Linguistics Club.

Sag, Ivan A. and Liberman, Mark. 1975. The intonational disambiguation of indirect speech acts. *Chicago Linguistic Society*, 11: 487–97.

Schane, Sanford A. 1975. Noncyclic English word stress. In Goyvaerts & Pullum, 1975: 249–59.

—— 1979. The rhythmic nature of English word accentuation. *Language*, 55:559–602.

—— 1981. Rhythm, accent, and stress in English words. *Linguistic Inquiry*, 10.

Sherman, Donald. 1975. Noun-verb stress alternation: An example of the lexical diffusion of sound change in English. *Linguistics*, 159:43–71.

Sloat, Clarence, Taylor, Sharon H. and Hoard, James E. 1978. *Introduction to Phonology*. Englewood Cliffs, NJ: Prentice-Hall.

Sloat, Clarence and Taylor, Sharon. 1983. *The Structure of English Words*, 3rd edn. Eugene, OR: Pacific Language Associates.

Sommerstein, Alan. 1977. *Modern Phonology*. London: Edward Arnold.

Stampe, David. 1969. The acquisition of phonetic representation. *Chicago Linguistic Society*, 5:443–54.

—— 1972. *A Dissertation on Natural Phonology*. PhD Dissertation, University of Chicago.

Thompson, Henry S. 1981. *Stress and Salience in English: Theory and Practice*. Palo Alto, CA: Xerox.

Trager, George L. 1949. *The Field of Linguistics*. Baltimore: Battenburg Press.

Trager, George L. and Smith, Henry Lee, Jr. 1951. *Outline of English Structure*. (= *Studies in Linguistics*, Occasional Papers 3).

Traugott, Elizabeth Closs. 1972. *A History of English Syntax*. New York: Holt, Rinehart and Winston.

Trnka, Bohumil. 1935. *A Phonological Analysis of Present-day Standard English*. Prague: Charles University. Revised edition 1966, Tokyo: Hokeiou Publishing Co. and 1968, University of Alabama Press.

Troubetzkoy, N. S. 1931. Phonologie et géographie linguistique. *Travaux du Cercle Linguistique de Prague*, 4:228–34.

—— 1939. *Grundzüge der Phonologie*. (= Travaux du Cercle Linguistique de Prague VII). tr. J. Cantineau. *Principes de Phonologie*. Paris: C. Klincksieck. 1949. tr. Christiane A. M. Baltaxe. *Principles of Phonology*. Berkeley/Los Angeles: University of California Press. 1982.

Trudgill, Peter. 1974. *Sociolinguistics: An Introduction to Language and Society*. Harmondsworth: Penguin.

Vanderslice, Ralph and Ladefoged, Peter. 1972. Binary suprasegmental features and transformational word-accentuation rules. *Language*, 48:819–38.

Venezky, Richard L. 1970. *The Structure of English Orthography*. The Hague: Mouton.

Vennemann, Theo. 1972. On the theory of syllabic phonology. *Linguistische Berichte*, 18:1–18.

—— 1975. Word and syllable in natural generative grammar. In Bruck et al., 1975: 346–74.

Walker, John. 1791. *A Critical Pronouncing Dictionary*. London: Robinson. Facsimile reprint. Menston: Scolar Press 1968.

Wells, J. C. 1982. *Accents of English*. 3 vols. Cambridge: Cambridge University Press.

Wijk, Axel. 1966. *Rules of Pronunciation for the English Language*. London: Oxford University Press.

Willems, Nico. 1982. *English Intonation from a Dutch Point of View*. Dordrecht: Foris Publications.

Williams, Juanita and Burke, V. M. (eds). 1971. *A Various Language: Perspectives on American Dialects*. New York: Holt, Rinehart and Winston.

Wolfram, Walt and Johnson, Robert. 1982. *Phonological Analysis: Focus on American English*. Washington: Center for Applied Linguistics.

Zwicky, Arnold. 1970. Auxiliary reduction in English. *Linguistic Inquiry*, 1:323–36.

Index

This index lists all technical terms and names mentioned in the book, with the number of the chapter(s) or section(s) in which the term or name is introduced and/or discussed. A number in boldface indicates that the term is (part of) the title of the chapter or section. Since some terms – e.g. *vowel*, *syllable*, *stress* – appear on almost every page, it would be counter-productive to cite every occurrence, but the index does contain a citation for the discussion of every term.

abstract environment 14.1
abstract noun suffix -/θ/ 8.1
abstract nouns 11.11
abstract suffix 14.1
accent 5.1
accent on operators 9.10
adjective 5.6
adjective stress rules 11.7
adverbial (locative) compounds 12.1
affirmative 9.10
affix 1.2
affricate 3.4
air stream 2.9
allomorph 8.1
allophone 1.2, 6
alveolar 3.1
alveolar ridge 3.1, 6.1, 6.2
ambisyllabic 5.4, 6.7, 7.5, 11.2
amplitude 2.3
analogy in syllable weight 12.6
analyses of vowels 4.1, **I**
anaphoric words 9.7
Angles, Saxons, and Jutes 1.1
antepenult 5.6, 11.2
[anterior] 3.7
aperiodic 2.2
apex 3.3
apical 3.3, 6.1
apicoalveolar 3.3, 6.1
apicodental 3.3, 6.1
articulation 2.6
articulator 3.1
articulatory feature 1.2, 2.9, 3
arytenoid cartilages 2.7
aspirated 5.3
aspirated release 6.5, 8.3
aspirated stop 5.1
assimilation 6.1, 13.3
assimilation, mutual 6.2
assimilation rule 14.9
atonic syllable 5.3, 6.7
attributive position 12.2
augment 14.5, 14.12
augment deletion 14.5
augmented form 14.5
Australia 4.3
auxiliary verbs 9.10, 13.2

babbling 2.9
base (morpheme) 1.2
basic stress rules 11.5–8
bilabial 3.2, 6.1
binary features 3, 4.7
bisyllabic prefix 12.4
blade of tongue 3.4
borrowed words 7.7

Britain 1.1
British and American stress patterns 5.6
British Broadcasting Corporation 1.1

Canada 1.1, 6.7
canonical form 5.2
Caxton, William 1.1
Celtic languages 1.1
change in voicing 14.9
checked vowels 4.3, 7.9, 9, 14.2
clear /l/ 6.1
coarticulated 6.1
Cockney 4.3
coda of syllable 5.1
complex words 11.2
compound adjectives 12.2
compound nouns 12.2
compound tunes 10.6
compound verbs 12.1, 12.3
compound within a compound 12.2
compound words 5.6, 11.2, 12.2, 12.3, 12.5
conjunctions 13.2
consequences of phonotactics 8
consonants 3
consonant cluster 5.3–4, 7.1–7
consonant cluster simplification 13.3
consonant loss 13.2–3
[consonantal] 2.9, 3.1
constraints 5.2, 7
[continuant] 2.9, 3
contour approach to intonation 10.1
contracted form of auxiliary *has* 8.1
contracted form of *is* 8.1
contractions 13.2
contrast and variation 7.3
contrastive focus 9.4
Cornwall 1.1
[coronal] 3.7
cycle 2.2

dark /l/ 6.1
de-accenting 9.7, 9.8–9
decision tree 11.5–7, 11.11
deletion rule 14
dental 3.7
derivation of surface forms 8.1, 14
determiners 13.2
dialects, geographic or regional 1.1
dialects, social, 1.1
dictionary 11.1
diphthong 4.4
discourse 1.2
discourse, role of prosody in 9.1
distinctive feature 1.2
distinctive function for stress 11.1
dorsal 3.5, 6.1
dorsopalatal 6.1
dorsovelar 6.1
dorsum 3.5
duration 2.5

either 9.6
ending *-acy* 11.11
ending *-ancy/ency* 11.11
ending *-ary* 11.11
ending *-ory* 11.11
ending *-y* 11.11
energy 2.2
environment 6
epenthesis 7.8
esophagus 2.7
excursus 10.1

falling tunes 10.3
fall-rise 10.4
feature, articulatory 2.9
final 6.5
final syllable 5.3
flap 6.7
focus 9.1
formula 6
free vowels 4.3, 7.9
free vowel/checked vowel pairs 14.10
free vowel rule 14.11
French 1.1
frequency 2.2
fricative 2.9, 3
fricative /r/ 6.2, 8.3
Fromkin and Rodman I.5
frontoalveolar 6.1
full compound 5.6
full forms 8.1, 13.2
full vowel 5.3, 5.6
function words 13.2

functional load 7.10
fuzziness of syllable boundary 5.1

G-deletion 14.5
General American **I**.4
generative grammar 1.3
generative phonology 1.3
Gimson, A. C. **I**.3
glide 2.9, 4.8
glottal stop 6.7
glottalized consonants 6.5
glottis 2.7
grammatical morphemes 8.1, 8.7
grammatical suffixes 8.1
Great Vowel Shift 14.10
Greek origin, words of 7.1
Greek-type compounds 12.5

has 8.1
hearing 2.1
Hertz 2.3
high tag 10.5
hold 6
homonyms 1.2
homophones 1.2, 13.2
homorganic 5.8, 7.4
homorganic sequence 6.1

I-drop rule 14.4
Industrial Revolution 1.1
initial 6.5
initial consonant deletion 13.1
initial syllable 5.3, 6
initiation 2.6
initiator 2.2
insertion of consonant 7.8
intensity 2.6, 5.1
intention of speaker 9.1
intervocalic 6.5, 6.7
intervocalic consonant 5.1
intervocalic /t/ 6.7
intonation 9.1, 10
intonation and perception 10.1
intrusive R 4.3
Ireland 1.1
Irish English 4.3
Irish Gaelic 1.1
is 8.1

/j/ 7.2
J-drop rule 14.4
James I 1.1
Jamestown 1.1
Jones, Daniel **I**.2
ju-deletion 14.5

Kenyon and Knott **I**.4
key to pronunciation 11.1
Kingdon, Roger **I**.3
knowledge, general or rule-governed 1.3
knowledge, specific 1.3

labial 2.9, 3.7, 6.1
labiodental 3.2, 6.1
laminal 3.9
laminoalveolar 6.1
larynx 2.6
[lateral] 3.8
lateral release 6.5
length 5.1, 6.6
length, sonorant 8.3
levels approach to intonation 10.1
lexical anaphora 9.8
lexical contrast 9.10
lexical morphemes 8.7
lexical process 14.1
lexicon 1.3
line of declination 10.1
Linking R 4.3, **I**.2
lip consonants 3.2
lip shape 6.3
liquid 2.9, 3.8
listing intonation 10.6
London 1.1
long fall 10.3
long rise 10.4
loudness 2.3
low rising tag 10.6
low tag 10.6
lower lip 3.1, 3.2
lungs 2.6

marked accent 9.4, 9.5
medial syllable 5.3
medium 2.2
meridian of Greenwich 3.7
minimal pair 1.3

miscellaneous reducible words 13.2
mixed endings 11.10
mobile stress 5.5
modality contrast 9.10
monophthong 4.4
monosyllabic word 5.2
morpheme 1.2, 5.2, 8.1
morpheme division 8.3
morpheme variation 8.2
morphological information 11.2
morphologically conditioned alternations 8.2
morphologically conditioned processes 14.1
morphology 1.3
mouth 2.6
multiple variation 6.7

n-deletion rule 8.2
[nasal] 2.9, 3
nasal assimilation 14.5
nasal cavity 2.6, 6.4
nasal release 6.5
nasality 6.4, 8.3
nasalized tap 6.7
negative 9.10
negative contractions 13.2
neutral prefix 12.4
neutral suffixes 8.2, 11.3, **II**.1
neutralization 4.5, 5.7
New Zealand 1.1, 4.3
Newfoundland 1.1
non-neutral suffix 8.2
non-rhotic dialect 4.3
North America 1.1, 4.3
North of England 4.3
not 13.2
noun 5.6
noun compounds 12.2
noun phrases 12.2
noun stress rule 11.6

obstruent 2.8, 3
omission of consonant 7.8
onset of segment 6.4
onset of syllable 5.1
operators 9.10, 13.2
optional contraction 8.1
oral cavity 2.6, 3
order of rules 8.1, 14.8
ordinal number suffix /θ/ 8.1
orthography 11.1
overall analysis **I**.6

palatal 3.7
palatal or prevelar 6.1
palatalization 13.3, 14.4
palate 2.8, 3.7
paradigmatic focus 9.4
particle 12.3
past tense suffix 8.1
peak of syllable 2.9, 5.1
penult 11.2
perception 10.1
period 2.3
periodic 2.3
pharynx 2.8
phonation 2.6
phoneme 1.2, 6
phonetic chart 4.4
phonetics 1.1
phonological analysis 1.3
phonological information 11.2
phonological processes 13
phonologically conditioned processes 14.1
phonology 1.2
phonotactics 5.2, 7
pitch 2.3, 2.7, 10.1
place of articulation 3.7, 6.1
plosive 2, 3
plural 14.1
plural suffix 8.1
Plymouth 1.1
point of articulation 3.7, 6.1
polarity contrast 9.10
polysyllabic words 5.3, 11
position of accent 9.1
position of occurrence 6
position of stress 11
possessive 14.1
possessive suffix 8.1
post-alveolar 6.2
posttonic 5.3
preantepenult 11.1

predicative position 12.2
prefixes 1.1, 12.4
prepositions 12.3, 13.2
pretonic 5.3
primary stress 5.3
probability of consonant deletion 13.3
progressive assimilation 13.3
pronouns 13.2
Proto-Germanic 14.1
Proto-Indo-European 14.1

quality 2.4, 4.4
quaternary stress 5.3

r-coloring 4.4, 5.8
R vowels 4.3
Received Pronunciation (RP) 1.1, 4.3
receiver 2.2
reduced forms 13.2
reduced vowel 5.3
reduction of contrast in unstressed syllables 5.7
redundancy 2.11
redundant feature 1.2
registers 1.1
regressive assimilation 13.3
relative prominence of syllables 5.3
release 6.5
resonance 2.4
resonance chamber 2.4
rhotic dialect 4.3
rhythm 11
rhythm rule 12.6
rhythmic adjustment 12.2
rule in generative phonology 1.3
rule, optional 1.3
rule, variable 1.3
rules for derivation 8.1

scale of sonority 7.1
schwa insertion rule 8.1, 14.5
Scotland 1.1
Scots Gaelic 1.1
Scottish English 1.1, 4.3
secondary stress 5.3
segment 1.22
segmental phonology 9.1
sequence of rules 14.8
short fall 10.2
short rise 10.3
[sibilant] 3.3, 3.4
simple contour 10.2–4
sonorant 2.7, 2.8, 3, 6.6
South Africa 1.1, 4.3
special endings 11.11
speech and language 1.2
spirantization 14.6
staccato adjustment 12.2
stream of speech 6
stress 5.1, 11, 12
  primary 5.3
  quaternary 5.3
  secondary 5.3
  tertiary 5.3
  weak 5.3
stress advancement 12.2
stress rules 11.5–11
stress timing 5.1, 9.3
strong endings **II.3**
strong syllables 5.3, 9
strong ult 11.2
structural linguistics 1.3
structure of syllable 5.2
suffix 1.2, 5.6, B.1, B.5, B.6
suffix *-ism* 11.10
suffix *-ist* 11.10
suffix *-ize* 11.10
suffix *-ment* 11.10
suffixes 1.2, 5.6
superior tick 5.3
suprasegmental phonology 9.1
surface forms 8.1–2, 14
surface phoneme 14
[syllabic] 2.9
syllabic consonants 5.8
syllabic /n/ 5.8
syllable 1.2, 2.9, 5
  final 5.3
  initial 5.3
  medial 5.3
  posttonic 5.3
  pretonic 5.3
  strong 5.3
  tonic 5.3
  weak 5.3

syllable division 5.4
syllable prominence 5.1
syllable structure 5.1, 5.2
syllable timing 5.2, 9.3
syntactic information 11.2
syntagmatic focus 9.5
syntax 1.3

tag 10.5
tag question 10.5
tag vocative 10.5
tap 6.7
teeth 3.3
tenseness, vowel 4.4
tertiary stress 5.3
there 13
third person singular present 8.1
thyroid cartilage 2.7
tonality 9.1
tone 2.7
tone of voice 10.1
tone unit 1.2, 9.1
tongue-back 3.5
tongue-front 3.4
tongue shape 3.1
tongue-tip 3.3
tonic endings 11.4
tonic syllable 5.3
tonicity 9.1
too 9.6
trachea 2.6
transitional consonant 7.7
triphthong 4.4
type I adjective 11.7
type II adjective 11.7

ult 11.2
underlying form 7, 14.2
underlying phoneme 14
unmarked accent 9.4
upper lip 3.1
users of language 1.1
uses of language 1.1
utterance 1.2

variable symbol 5.7
variant 6
variation 6
variation, language 1.1
variation in friction 6.2
variation in length 6.6
variation in lip-shape 6.3
variation in nasality 6.4
variations in stress 11.9
velar 3.5
velar softening 14.7
velic 2.8, 6.5
velum 2.8, 3.5
verb 5.6
verb + particle 12.3
verb + particle + preposition 12.3
verb + preposition 12.3
verb stress rule 11.5
vibration 2.2
vocal cords 2.7, 3
vocal tract 2.8, 3
[voice] 3
voice assimilation rule 8.1
voice onset time 3.1
voiced 2.7, 3
voiced obstruent 6.5
voiceless 2.7, 3
voiceless onset 6.5
voiceless release 6.5
voicing 3
voicing rule 14.2
vowel 2.9, 4
vowel complexity 4.4
vowel features 4.4, 4.7
vowel insertion rule 8.1
vowel inventories 4.2, 4.3
vowel length 4.4, 6.6
vowel loss 13.2–3
vowel occurrence, limits on 7.8
vowel quality 4.4
vowel reduction 13.2–3, 14.3
vowel shift rule 14.7
vowels, incidence of 4.2, 4.5
vowels, phonetic realization 4.2

Wales 1.1
weak endings **II**.4
weak stress 5.3
weak suffixes 11.6–7
weak syllables 5.3, 11.2

weak ult 11.2
Welsh English 1.1
Welsh language 1.1
Wh questions 10.2–3
word 5
word-final 6.5
word-initial 6.5
word-medial 6.5

yes-no question 10.3

zero coda 5.1
zero onset 5.1